Incredible Wild Edibles

---

36 plants that can change your life

SAMUEL THAYER

Forager's Harvest

FORAGER'S HARVEST PRESS
BRUCE, WI

Publisher's Cataloging-in-Publication data
Thayer, Samuel James, author.
Incredible wild edibles : 36 plants that can change your life / Samuel Thayer.

Includes bibliographical references and index.
Bruce, WI : Foragers Harvest, 2017.

ISBN 978-0-9766266-2-6 | LCCN 2017945534

LCSH Wild plants, Edible—United States. | Plants, Useful—United States. | Medicinal plants—United States. | Cooking (Wild foods) | BISAC NATURE / Plants / General | COOKING / General

LCC QK98.4 .T53 2017 | DDC 581.6/32—dc23

Book and cover design by Fiona Raven
Photographs and artwork by Samuel Thayer, except as otherwise credited in captions.

First Printing July 2017, 16,000 copies
Printed in China

Published by Forager's Harvest
709 West Arthur Avenue
Bruce, Wisconsin, 54819
www.foragersharvest.com

Forager's Harvest

To my son,

Hoping we have many years
to dig tinpsila and watch bison together.

Acknowledgments

The plants have the answers; they give them generously to those who ask, just as they give their bodies to those who hunger. I live in the shadow of those gifts, and sleep in the light of them. To say that I am grateful is an understatement. Before me came generation upon generation of keen foragers—farmers, peasants, healers, laborers, hunters, gatherers, children, mothers, grandmothers—into the Paleolithic and deep beyond. The hard but joyful work of these countless hungry innovators built the traditions that form the foundation of my craft. I thank them for making my life possible.

Many people have enriched the content of these pages in more specific ways. Fiona Raven, Johanna Rosenbohm, Erica M. Davis, Ellen Zachos, and Mike Krebill were instrumental in the production of this book. I need to thank my North Carolina friends for inviting, hosting, feeding, and teaching me: Sarah Haggerty, Kim Calhoun, Doug and Todd Elliott, Yanna Fishman, Emanual May, Bill Faust, Alan Muskat, and more. I owe the deepest gratitude to Jerome and Theresa High Horse of Wanblee, South Dakota; we came to them as strangers and left as friends. And to Bob and Mary Grime-Epps, who sent me to Pine Ridge. I thank Linda Black Elk for deepening my understanding of tinpsila. Kelly Kindscher put poppy mallow in my head, while Jesse Bennett and Jaye Maxfield told me about a 700-mile shortcut to find it.

This book benefited greatly from the help of librarians in general, and Kathryn Maloney in particular. I owe thanks to more than I will recall, or have space to recount, but here are some: Adam Haritan, for guiding me through the perilous streets of Pittsburgh. François Medion, for the steamed and buttered campanule, and for his magnificent Duluth Grill gardens. Josh Morey, for showing me shagbark all those years ago. Mark Pollock, for challenging me. Boyce Wofford, for his insights into commercial pokeweed canning. Casey Dahl, for finding the oil press. Briana Wiles, for teaching me about western sweet cicely and hops. Little John, for the persimmon wine. Dan Nelson, for guiding me in maple endeavors. To Abe Lloyd, who always helps; Roger Reynolds, who always supports; and Edelene Wood, who always encourages. And of course, my wife and three children, who share my meals but not my shortcomings.

Fortunately, many people are leading others to the sacred food. I would like to express my appreciation for the other professionals who believe in foraging, including (but absolutely not limited to): John Kallas, Nancy Turner, François Couplan, Kat Anderson, Tom Elpel, Leda Meredith, Mark Vorderbruggen, Stephen Barstow, Arthur Haines, Steve Brill, Lisa Rose, Linda Conroy, Hank Shaw, Karen Monger, Rachel Mifsud, Jim McDonald, Sergei Boutenko, and Bob's chicken.

If I have forgotten anyone, please don't be jealous of Bob's chicken.

Contents

Plant Accounts (continued)

Introduction

The Earth's wish is to be clothed in rambunctious greenery, from the crumbling pavement of Pittsburgh to the shaggy slopes of the Olympic Peninsula. To know that greenery as a friend makes either place look more like home. This is a book about 36 plants that have enriched my life: plants that I wake up dreaming about, that I crave at the breakfast table, that refresh and energize me. They are the characters that fulfill my fantasies of self-sufficiency, and enliven my heart countless times when I glimpse their familiar forms glowing with an unbreakable promise.

But can they really change your life? Oh, yes. I have witnessed their power. When the ugly, garbage-strewn thicket along the expressway's off-ramp transforms into a secret orchard of perfect fruit, the unnamed angst of modern life is supplanted by the comfort of ancient wisdom. In bits and pieces, fits and starts, your heart awakes to a different reality, a better world. You will close your eyes to a different daydream, step with a quiet confidence, rest in a deeper sleep, crave a secret flavor. Prayers of supplication give way to thanksgiving, as you learn to read the untranslated Book of Life. And as you walk those green pages, you eventually come to understand: This is a good place, and you belong here. Partake of this joy, and hold it sacred.

I wrote this book to introduce you to some fantastic food plants, but it is designed to give you more than just a picture and a name. It answers the questions you have about a new plant before you eat it: Where do I find it? What, exactly, does it look like? Is there anything I'm likely to confuse it with? When do I pick it? What part do I use? How do I know it's at the right stage to collect? How can I be certain that I'm collecting it responsibly and sustainably? How does it taste? How has it been used traditionally? What shall I do with it?

There are hundreds of wild edibles in North America; this book covers just a few dozen of the best ones. And this is not a comprehensive field guide. Instead, it is limited to 36 excellent plants with which I have a significant amount of experience. In selecting these plants, I have tried to include something for everyone. There are leafy greens, stalks and shoots, root vegetables, berries, fruits, nuts, and seasonings. There are plants of backyards and sidewalk cracks, plants of farm woodlots and gardens, plants of the wilderness, of the prairie, of the mountains, of meadows and marshes, of ditches and dumps. There are plants of the East, West, North, and South. My criteria was this: They have to be exciting, fascinating, superb—incredible, in my estimation.

I have written two books previously about edible wild plants: *The Forager's Harvest* and *Nature's Garden*. The present volume is the third title in my foraging series, and follows a similar format and vision. Each plant or group of plants is covered in a chapter of varying length, split into sections discussing its identification, habitat, harvest, and preparation. There is no overlap in the plants covered by the three volumes.

WHY FORAGE?

Because it contains all the good things in life, seamlessly folded into a single activity.

In 2014, our family of four spent five pleasant Sundays in the beautiful summer air, watching ground squirrels and grouse, playing catch, hiding from each other, swimming, and crawling around the heath picking blueberries—not because we had to, but because we love to. The take-home was 83 gallons of "superfood"—all the frozen blueberries we wanted for the next 18 months, 30 pounds of fruit leather, 3 dozen blueberry pies, and 5 gallons of blueberry juice for the days we really wanted to feel extravagant—all of which would have cost us about $9,000.

Only a forager gets to eat like that. Only a forager will ever get to suck the pulp of a perfectly tree-ripened wild persimmon or pawpaw, or will be so lucky as to have an opinion about which is better: a thimbleberry or cloudberry. Only a forager's spring salad mix includes stitchwort, shepherd's purse, miner's lettuce, sassafras leaf, or sheep sorrel. You can't buy calamus lemonade or caraway greens in even the most hip market, but you can effortlessly garner them yourself, sometimes from the same ditch. Foraging makes the world richer, fuller, funner. It will change your life, for good.

This is a very good reason to gather wild food.

FORAGING SAFELY

Despite the common yet unfounded fears of non-foragers, gathering and eating wild plants is one of the safest hobbies you can engage in. Although a few adults per decade will die from ingesting random, unidentified wild plants, I am not aware of even one documented case in the last 50 years in which an adult forager making a legitimate attempt to identify a plant mistakenly ate a poisonous plant and died from the error. (If you hear of one, please let me know.) People with a modicum of common sense can keep out of trouble with foraging by following the basic safety rules:

1. **Identify plants with absolute certainty before eating them.** In the wise words of Sergei Boutenko's rap song, *"Don't eat something if you don't know what it is."* "Absolute certainty" means there is no guessing, hoping, or presuming. You can't just look at a picture or two; you need to carefully read the description and match all the characteristics to the plant in the field. If you don't know if you are certain, then you are not.

2. **Confirm which part of the plant is edible, and how it is prepared.** Some plants have certain parts that are edible, while other parts are toxic. An example is mayapple: the ripe fruit is delicious, but the leaves, roots, and stems are dangerous. Some plants, such as pokeweed, need to be prepared in specific ways to be safe. Pay attention to all such details as you read about a plant. On countless occasions, I have had plant walk or class participants intentionally disregard my instructions to not eat something raw. At least twice this has resulted in vomiting. I did not observe these symptoms myself—they were sheepishly recounted to me after the fact. Which means I have no idea how many times this has happened. Don't be that fool.

3. **Collect from a chemically safe environment.** Lead has settled heavily in the soil near all major roadways that were present before 1975. Insecticides and pesticides are also a serious concern. Herbicides are the greatest chemical threat today (see "The Roundup Revolution," page 32). Do not collect in or near conventional orchards, crop fields, or golf courses unless you understand the spraying regimen and make an informed choice. When collecting aquatic plants, assess the pollution status of the waterway in which the plants are growing. In general, use your common sense.

4. **Eat a small portion the first time you try a new food in case you have an adverse reaction.** Allergies and intolerances are unlikely to show up the first time you eat a new food, but it is possible. And occasionally, a plant that is generally edible will cause gastric discomfort or diarrhea in sensitive individuals.

5. **Do not eat what disagrees with you or is distasteful.** This rule is not a substitute for identification, nor is it foolproof, but it helps keep you safe in the unlikely scenario that you misidentify a plant. If you mistake dogbane for

Common dogbane (left) and common milkweed (right) shoots appear very similar. They both have milky sap and are often mistaken for one another. To tell them apart, you'll need to read descriptions and look carefully. (These species are covered in *The Forager's Harvest*.) If you accidentally start eating a dogbane shoot (and this happens to many people every year), it will be very bitter. That's your mouth's way of telling you to spit it out. Listen to your mouth, or your stomach will have something to say about it later.

milkweed, it will be extremely bitter—spit it out and save yourself a bellyache. This rule also helps protect you from eating a poisonous plant misidentified or supplied by another party, from eating an edible plant improperly prepared, or in a situation where you have received false or incomplete information from the literature. Finally, this rule helps prevent you from overindulging on a seasoning like horseradish or garlic just because it is listed as "edible." However, this rule is *not* a way to test unknown plants for edibility! I don't believe in that.

HOW TO POSITIVELY IDENTIFY A NEW PLANT

A forager must be impeccable with identification. But don't let that discourage you—with careful attention to detail, you can confidently identify a wild plant. Positive identification consists of four steps. **Do not eat something unless you have gone through the whole process.**

1. **Tentative identification.** This is when you think you know what a plant is. Perhaps you saw a picture in a book that looks like the plant in front of you. Perhaps you just have a strong hunch. Perhaps your friend Masquimpson told you what it is, and you aren't ready to trust your life to his plant skills. For the sake of foraging, even identifying the plant with a dichotomous key should

be considered tentative. (Keys often rely on single characteristics, and single characteristics can vary, or can be misinterpreted.)

Foolish people sometimes stop with the tentative identification; this is how misidentifications happen. Don't be lazy. You must proceed through all four steps before eating a new plant.

2. Reference comparison. Use reputable identification resources, preferably several of them. Compare every available part of the plant to the images in your references, to be sure they match. Then, carefully read the verbal descriptions and observe your plant to make sure the details match. No matter how much it looks like the pictures, *do not skip the reading part*! Text often gets you to observe features that are not evident in photographs. Text can also explain which features are variable, which are consistent, and which are diagnostic. The telltale features may not be the things you notice first.

During the reference comparison, keep in mind that some characteristics are more consistent than others. Form, proportion, and arrangement are generally more important than size, color, or number. Beware of relying on descriptors that can easily be misinterpreted, such as "large," "sharp," or "rough." Never identify a plant by a single characteristic—always look at all the available features. Any single characteristic may vary in an occasional individual, or be misinterpreted by you, or be misrepresented or incorrect in the text. When you encounter unfamiliar vocabulary, look up the meaning in the glossary—don't guess at the meaning or skip over that feature.

Finally, but most importantly, don't "make it fit." Do not mentally force your plant to fit the description of the plant you hope you have found. Your plant should fit the description easily and reasonably, without any lenient comparisons or stretched definitions. People have an amazing ability to see what they want to see. Don't fool yourself.

3. Specimen search. Once you have positively identified your plant, go find more of them. Finding more specimens forces you to repeatedly confirm your identification and helps you understand the plant's range of variability. If the plant has multiple forms (such as those with a basal rosette stage and a flowering stage), find both stages of growth. Look for the plant until you are never confused about its identity. The specimen search builds your "search image," a subconscious process by which you recognize plants (or any other category of objects). Your search image is important because it incorporates features, such as texture and leaf angle, that often cannot be seen in photographs or adequately described in text. Only when you are thoroughly familiar with a plant this way are you ready to consider eating it. It may take you a few minutes or a few years, depending on the plant in question and how easily you can find it.

4. Assessing confidence. Before you eat any wild plant, you need to be completely certain that you have identified it correctly. Not pretty sure—absolutely positive. There should be no doubt, no hesitation—just the unwavering confidence that comes from thorough and diligent effort at steps 2 and 3 above. If your confidence falls short of this standard, you are not ready to eat the plant. Go back to steps 2 and 3.

USING AND UNDERSTANDING PLANT NAMES

There is no organization assigning plant names, common or scientific. Some species have multiple common names, and many common names are used for multiple plants. A great deal of misinformation is spread by authors who mix up the attributes of different species that go by the same common name. With the plants in this book, I try to use the common names that are in widest circulation, unless these are confusing or misleading—in which case I choose a name that I think best facilitates learning. I prefer names that are short and unique, if they are available. I try to avoid names that are derogatory, convoluted, misleading, or derived from people's names.

To reduce confusion, taxonomists created a naming system in the 18th century using Latinized binomials, which today we usually call "scientific names." These names are the same for botanists everywhere in the world. Scientific names consist of two parts, the first word indicating the genus (a group of closely related organisms), the second word indicating the species. The genus name is capitalized, while the species name is not. Scientific names are set in italics.

Due to disagreements and reorganizations in plant classification, scientific names can also be confusing. (For example, there are three different scientific names used for Japanese knotweed.) There are many reasons for these differences. Some taxonomists lump multiple species or genera together, while others split a single genus or species apart. As we learn more about evolutionary relationships through genetics, we discover that some species belong in groups different from those to which they were originally assigned. With surprising frequency, one taxonomist names a "new" plant without realizing that it has already been discovered and named.

Further complicating things, most plants don't actually have a common name. Since the typical reader is uncomfortable with Latin names, field guide authors feel compelled to create a common name to keep them happy. These "contrived names," such as "three-nerved Joe Pye weed," are highly variable from book to book and are not in common use by anybody.

There are certain groups of similar plants for which the same common name is used. For example, "common chickweed" is applied to three species: *Stellaria media*, *S. neglecta*, and *S. pallida*. When writing about such groups, many authors use one scientific name to represent the entire group (in this case, *S. media*), which creates the mistaken impression that there is just one species.

Similar situations exist with "lamb's quarters" (simplified to *Chenopodium album*), "smartweed" (simplified to *Persicaria maculosa*), "curly dock" (*Rumex crispus*), and many other groups. I call these names, applied to a group as if its members were a single species, "flagship names."

Throughout the book I will try to be clear about which species I am referring to, and use the actual scientific name. I will lump together groups under one common name, but not under one Latin species name. I will express uncertainty when appropriate rather than use a flagship name so that I can pretend to know the exact species.

We give names a lot of power over our perception. Many people use the name of a plant as an important clue to its identification. We need to let go of this dysfunctional habit; it tricks us into false conclusions and creates misidentifications. I have heard it said many times that wood nettle can be told from stinging nettle because it doesn't sting—but actually, wood nettle has larger and more formidable stingers, and more of them. Other people who get stung by wood nettle are positive that it is "stinging nettle." Because it stings, duh. These simplistic thought processes account for many falsehoods in the literature.

Name-based assumptions are not confined to amateurs; they result in real scientific consequences. Name confusion has made the native red mulberry *Morus rubra* unknown to most conservationists in the northern part of its range (see page 234). Because of name confusion, government agencies in several of the most scientifically advanced countries in the world are convinced that one of the world's most commonly eaten vegetables (the *Solanum nigrum* complex) is deadly.

Tether your identification to the scientific name, not the common one. Read the description and match the identifying features; don't assume *anything* based upon the name. Bladder campion may not be the only campion with a bladder. Curly dock may not be the only dock with curly leaves. Mayflower may not be the only flower that blooms in May. Maybe mayapples may not ripen in May. Mountain ash is not an ash, and it often grows in big, flat swamps. A maple with black bark is probably not a black maple. And a gyroscope may not be an instrument for inspecting gyros.

This is a white mulberry, *Morus alba*. Don't let the name fool you. I didn't make up these ridiculous names, and neither did you, but we have to deal with them.

WHERE TO FORAGE: LEGALITY AND PRACTICALITY

Vegetation will appear wherever there is sunlight, moisture, and a trace of soil. Some of that vegetation will be food. The first rule here, in all circumstances, is *be reasonable and considerate.*

Urban life is full of public spaces where you can lean over and grab a handful of shepherd's purse or field garlic with hardly a glance cast in your direction. Nobody will miss that handful of weeds—except you, if you don't take it. What law regulates the weeds growing in the lawn at the library, or the samaras hanging from the Siberian elm along your alley? Who knows? Who cares? Just be reasonable and considerate.

Most of the vegetation in urban green spaces is non-native and considered invasive. Eat these invasives if you want. Anyone who tells you not to is either ignorant, or is on a power trip. Maybe both. Be prepared for these abundant people. If you don't want to deal with them, look over your shoulder. If you forage openly, it *will* attract attention, especially in busy urban areas. I have literally had crowds gather to watch. Regardless of the legality or propriety, some dim-witted defender of normality will be inclined to whip out his cell phone and dial the authorities in these situations. If you get questioned by law enforcement, be honest and friendly, and mention any ethnic connection the food has—this helps normalize and explain what they see as unusual behavior. In urban green spaces, there may be a few native plants left. Use careful judgment about collecting them. But you should become a vigilante ecologist—protect them and care for them. It is very unlikely that anybody in the park department is doing that.

In rural areas, foraging most often takes place along the sides of small country lanes—but this is a gray area in terms of legality. Who owns the elderberries on the shoulder of a road? In most places, this is considered a public right-of-way. But does that right-of-way extend to the picking of vegetation? Depends on who you ask. Most people won't care. Some will. The easiest way to be sure is to drop in and ask. If you want to go beyond the roadside, this is the only way. Mention a specific, well-known edible you saw from the road. Bring children. After collecting, stop in to say thank you. Compliment the landowner's house, property, truck, and pond. Show your appreciation. These visits can create meaningful relationships, which are much cheaper (and can be more valuable) than buying land.

Many public lands allow limited foraging. Find the rules that apply to the land of your choosing and abide by them. Ask wardens or managers about common invasive edibles, like garlic mustard or dandelion; they are likely to grant permission, and even encourage you to harvest. The wildest areas receive the least harvest pressure and are usually the least regulated.

Even when you are gathering legally, you may run into conflict. I have had unpleasant experiences with belligerent landowners who hate wild rice harvesters. On one memorable occasion while gathering lotus nuts, a game warden detained and harassed me for an hour, despite the unavoidable fact, which I kept bringing up, that what I was doing was explicitly legal. As we talked, I built a fire, roasted a few lotus heads, and gave him a sample. Suddenly, he understood, and quit pestering me.

Not everyone is ready for foraging. Be responsible, be reasonable, be considerate, and be ready for them.

EQUIPMENT FOR FORAGING

I am an equipment minimalist. I am likely to forget anything besides my clothing (and often forget parts of that). Foraging requires no cash outlay, but there are a few basic items that can make it easier. Certain plants have specialized tools associated with them, which will be discussed in those particular accounts.

Bags: I have clean bags for greens, shoots, or mushrooms; and dirty bags for roots. Nuts might go into either kind, depending on whether they come from the tree or the ground. I usually carry a bag of bags: a large cloth bag containing a few folded cloth bags and a few clean plastic bags. For transporting or storing nuts, I like to use gunnysacks.

Buckets, tubs, bowls, and blickeys: For gathering nuts, I like a squat tub; when this is full, I dump the nuts into a gunnysack. (Collecting directly into the sack will slow you down considerably.) For berry picking, I like a blickey—a one-gallon container strapped around my waist (you have to make these yourself). When this is full, I dump it into an absolutely awesome food-grade 3.5-gallon tub. For berries that are low to the ground, I pick directly into a container that I scoot around as I go. For greens that will be used immediately, I use a large bowl. For root vegetables, I like a 5-gallon bucket: Fill the bottom half with roots, then cover them with leaves for short-term storage (up to 2 weeks), or sand for longer storage.

Scissors: These can be very helpful with certain greens, especially those that are small and grow in dense patches or on very loose soil. This is almost a necessity for people with no fingernails. I love scissors for chickweed and dandelion, and they make it easier to avoid being stung by nettles.

Fingernail: Speaking of which, when I say "no fingernail," I really mean "one that does not project beyond the fleshy digit." My thumbnail is my most important non-vascular foraging appendage. I monitor its status almost as often as Millennials check Facebook. The effortless combination of pinch-slice-bend will pluck off almost any tender green or stem—even an inch-thick poke shoot. Although occasionally it gets damaged, my thumbnail repairs itself, and I never forget to bring it along.

Shovel: For root vegetables, you probably need one. It could be a big one, as I suggest for burdock or parsnip, or a mini dandelion shovel, a sturdy digging stick, a well-made garden trowel, or a hori-hori knife. There is always this to balance: the larger shovel works better, but is a burden to carry around.

Fruit strainer: Many wild fruits have seeds, skins, stems, or cores that you will want to separate from their pulp before making finished products like jam, fruit leather, or pie. You can use a bowl colander and your hand, a cone colander with a wooden pestle, a Foley-style food mill, or a Victorio-type strainer.

Straining bag: A cotton cloth works fairly well for juicing many fruits or making nut milks, but something sold as a nutmilk bag or a jelly bag will usually work better and last longer.

GUIDELINES FOR SUSTAINABLE GATHERING

Foraging is a well-tested, ancient, low-impact, and sustainable use of natural resources. Don't let the ignorant anti-foragers convince you otherwise. If practiced irresponsibly or selfishly, foraging has the potential to negatively impact local plant populations. Responsible wild food gatherers exercise careful judgment and moderation in their harvest, because they care about the plants they collect and the habitats they are part of. Gatherers should treat the landscape like a sacred garden that is a privilege to harvest from, seeking to leave it in better condition than they found it. Following are a few basic rules to follow when foraging:

1. **Know what plants are protected in your area, and leave them alone.** Additionally, don't assume this means that every plant that isn't protected is fair game. Your government cannot be trusted to reliably identify the plants that need protection; there are always some species that should be listed as endangered or threatened but are not.

2. **Harvest plants only where they are thriving.**

3. **Never take more than the remaining population can easily replace.** Although you might hear a rule of thumb regarding this, such as "take one of every three," there is no simple and foolproof guideline. You must make a judgment call based on your understanding of the plant's reproduction strategy, its place in the landscape, and likely harvest pressure.

4. **Collect in the way that is least harmful to the plant and its environment.** For example, if you want some wild leek flavor in a salad, just pluck one leaf per plant instead of digging up whole bulbs. For any plant, distribute your collecting throughout a colony—don't just take everything from one side because that's easier.

5. **Observe the area you collect from to monitor changes, and alter your practices when necessary.**

6. Care for the land beyond your foraging. Pick up trash, pull some invasive shrubs, thin saplings to create diversity to compensate for past abuse, plant a native herb that has been eliminated by cattle.

7. Give thanks. Gratitude makes you think good thoughts, and good thoughts translate to good actions.

The stewardship outlined by these rules can be implemented only by understanding the life history and ecology of the plant in question. That's why these topics are explored in some detail in each of the plant accounts later in the book. The considerations for conservation are very different for different groups of plants, and also depend upon the part of the plant to be harvested. Some plants are easily overharvested, while the populations of others are nearly impossible to put a dent in. Here is a general overview of these considerations:

Weedy annuals are heavy seed producers whose populations are limited primarily by the availability of disturbed soil. Your harvest of seeds or greens will have little to no impact on their populations, but you want to leave a portion of them to go to seed.

Biennials are also heavy seed producers whose populations can expand very fast when soil is disturbed. When digging roots from these species, take no more than a third of the plants present; your excavations will make ideal germination sites. Most biennials will actually do better when the colony is partially

Gathering a plant does not have to harm its population. When I transplanted this highbush cranberry to the brushy edge of my yard, I noticed a few sprigs of mint scattered among the canary grass, sedges, and goldenrod. We pick the mint regularly, but three years later it is about 200 times as common as it was when we first started collecting it. That's because we weed out a little grass every time we grab some mint.

harvested each year than when it is left undisturbed. Shoots and leaves can also be collected—this will not kill the plant, but will either delay its flowering by a season or cause it to be smaller and less fruitful. Again, let more than half the plants go to seed unmolested.

Perennials with single, edible storage organs can be highly susceptible to overharvest. Some of them take many years to mature. These underground storage organs should be gathered at low rates—generally less than 10% per year. They should be dug only where they are overcrowded, or by people actively involved in the management of the population.

Perennials with edible shoots or greens can usually withstand substantial harvest of about a third of the leaves or shoots once per season. If they have a single shoot, you should not collect in the same area more than once per year, and even then, collect from less than a third of the plants.

Weedy, colonial perennials such as milkweed, nettle, and goldenrod can generally sustain heavier harvest a few times per season, especially if they are growing in full sun.

Fruits, berries, and nuts are gifts from the plant in exchange for seed dissemination; you are not hurting the plant by collecting them. Like all plants, these produce far more seeds than can possibly have a chance to grow—but be sure to leave some for the wildlife. By pooping indoors, you're not really holding up your end of the dissemination deal, so be fair and plant a few if you get the chance.

Invasive plants are non-native species that thrive in our landscapes and crowd out native plants. They could belong to any of the categories listed above. Feel free to eat them to your heart's content. In fact, you may want to pull them out even when you don't intend to eat them.

Gathering Thoughts

(Some Essays on Wild Food)

FORAGING AGAINST THE INVASION

Non-native plants have reached our shores, and some of them outcompete native species and are spreading rapidly across our landscape. These "invasive plants" have appeared first and spread most rapidly in degraded landscapes, but the hope that they will not expand beyond these areas is wishful thinking. Some have already penetrated deep into wild places. The boreal forest and tundra will probably be the communities least affected by imported plants, because the Bering Land Bridge has allowed for repeated colonization by the Old World species adapted to these conditions. But most other habitats will be greatly affected. Through competition, non-native plants will reduce the populations of native species. If we want to conserve native plant communities, we will have to prevent the exotic species from taking over. Not because the exotic plants are evil, but because we have decided that we want the native ones to thrive.

Controlling invasive plants will require the perpetual input of a great deal of labor and resources. As a society we have already made it clear that we intend to do nothing about this problem. We want to control invasives the easy way, with herbicides—and this, by itself, never works. Herbicides create an ecological void, which will be quickly recolonized by invasive plants. The current environmental paradigm cannot justify the expense of effective control measures to an ecologically apathetic public, except for here and there as an academic exercise. Although ecologists speak of invasives as one of the greatest threats to the environment, they know that there will be no effective, large-scale government program to control them. We don't even have the will to do this in our most heavily visited and highly managed parks and preserves. In a few centuries our idea of wilderness will be turned on its head. Remote lands will be hopelessly infested with exotic species, and native plant communities will persist in populated areas, at the will of human caretakers.

Not only has our collective reaction to invasive plants been insufficient, it's been unrealistic, overly emotional, largely random, and mostly cosmetic. Plants that colonize roadsides, backyards, and agricultural land are often prioritized in invasive control programs simply because they are highly visible, while widespread and serious invaders of natural habitats are often completely ignored. We seem to find comfort in transferring the blame for ecological degradation from humans to other organisms, so rather than actually eliminate the problem in our parks and preserves, we put up posters, hold meetings, and whine a lot—watching passively until the problem grows beyond controllability. This bizarre response by authorities helps feed the contrarian opinion that sees invasive plants as no problem at all—even, as some claim, an ecological blessing.

We should not delude ourselves toward either extreme. Invasive plants are not swallowing ecosystems as corn and soybeans have, but they do pose real and serious dangers to native communities. Foragers should be careful not to spread these plants, and we should eat them freely—but our responsibility goes further than that. Gatherers should participate in the deliberate control

On the left is a plant of purple prairie clover *Dalea purpurea*, an astoundingly beautiful native species that I collect for tea and flavoring. On the right is spotted knapweed *Centaurea stoebe*, a fiercely invasive plant that likes exactly the same habitat as prairie clover, and has crowded it out of thousands of acres and caused dramatic decreases in population. Few people care, or notice, this happening. I notice, because I'm a forager. Every time I select a few sprigs of prairie clover, I spend a few minutes pulling out spotted knapweed. There's no other way we will keep these sand prairies. If millions of people collected prairie clover, it would not be decimated; it would be abundant and thriving.

of invasives. We don't need to think of this as a war against evil plants; it is just tending the garden. Our role here is vitally important—the responsibility, in the long run, will fall to us alone.

Who will provide the perpetual labor to maintain native plant communities? Who will have the plant knowledge and ecological understanding to devise management strategies tailored to each piece of ground? Who notices a buckthorn seedling at 4 inches tall and pulls it out right then, rather than waiting 40 years until there is a half-acre thicket requiring drastic measures to control? Who will have the personal, moral, emotional, and economic incentive to be responsible for the work getting done, on even a small tract of Earth? Let's be realistic: foragers who draw sustenance from the land, or nobody.

In central Kentucky, not far south of I-64, you'll find Fort Boonesborough State Park, a forager's paradise replete with black walnuts, hickories, persimmons, pawpaws, mulberries, black raspberries, black cherries, pokeweed, and dozens of other edibles. Here you can hike the Pioneer Forge Trail along a small stream through a forest touted for its native wildflowers. The woods are magnificent on a spring morning, lush with an unusual diversity of native plants, full of the calls of redstarts hunting gnats in the low branches. But something is wrong. Invasive honeysuckle claws in from all sides; leafing out early, it shades out the ground cover that is adapted to American trees, slowly killing it off. It displaces the redbud, red mulberry, spicebush, and pawpaw that belong here. Garlic mustard and field garlic creep among the rich ground cover, slowly taking over. Whatever native plants survive the competition are unlikely to escape the chemical warfare waged by these plants. The time is short for this ancient garden of native edibles. In fact, half the area is already choked away under honeysuckle. Does anybody care? Will the Kentucky Department of Parks save this precious floral gem? It seems doubtful; action is already 35 years overdue. Few people use this low-priority feature of the park—it doesn't bring much revenue.

Here is a place that desperately needs foragers, a garden begging to be tended. A plant community that would gladly give a fistful of violet leaves to anyone who would pull a patch of garlic mustard. If these spicebushes could scream, they'd offer twigs to anyone who'd cut out a honeysuckle. The redbuds would dangle their flowers and second the request. The *Allium canadense* would meekly implore, "Leave me alone and take out this field garlic," and foragers would comply. The honewort, wood nettle, aniseroot, American chervil, wild lettuce, waterleaf—all of these would bless the bodies of the caring foragers who trod this rich, sacred soil and stooped to tend the garden. Not because garlic mustard is evil, but because spring beauty is good.

Conventional wisdom says that foraging would destroy native plant communities. But conventional wisdom is naive. Gatherers will gather to save these plants, or nobody will do it.

THE CHICKEN FEATHERS GUY

Once upon a time, a goodhearted, intelligent, health-conscious young man deeply concerned about sustainability got four hens and a rooster so he could raise his own eggs. He let two of his hens raise broods, so he could butcher some birds for meat. In July, when the pullets were ready, he assembled all the tools for the somber deed. Now, this fellow was an odd sort of hybrid between bleeding-heart liberal and bloodthirsty redneck, so when he chopped the first chicken's head, dipped the bird in the scalding pot, and began plucking it, a wave of grief swept over him, because . . . the feathers were going to waste.

"Aren't there uses for feathers?" he thought. "Sure. I could stuff pillows. Maybe even coats, or comforters. I could dye them and tie flies. . . . Ooooh, feather dusters!" A smile spread across his bearded countenance. "Maybe I should start a business. *Fluffy Flock Featherworks.*"

He got a big bin, but after plucking a few birds he realized that he'd have to dry out all those soaked feathers. So he got another bin and plucked the rest without scalding. This had its own problems: the dry feathers either stuck to his bloody fingers, or they blew away in the breeze. Plucking this way also ripped up the skins and took so long that he couldn't get all the birds done before he had to leave by bicycle for his grant-funded job painting murals on abandoned buildings. He tried to stuff the unfinished birds in his fridge, but they wouldn't all fit, so he ran to the gas station for a bag of ice, filled his cooler, and still had two extra chickens, which he set on the lid before dashing off to work.

The fact that he arrived for work 27 minutes late was much less distressing than the scene awaiting him when he returned home. The two chickens on the cooler lid had already begun to smell bad and had attracted a swarm of flies, which had placed eggs all over the exposed parts. More importantly, chicken blood had oozed into his vegan girlfriend's homemade tahini. After copious apologies, he stayed up until 3:12 AM to finish the butchering job. Two packages, labeled "questionable," ended up getting thrown out later.

But he got those feathers.

The wet ones were a pain to dry, and lost their fluff. The dry ones were filthy, so he had to wash them anyway. He sorted the feathers by size and type, which took all his spare time for a week. He made a chicken "down" pillow, which was poky, smelled bad, and never got used. It attracted carpet beetles, whose larvae ate the bits of skin attached to the base of feathers, then rolled out into the pockets of inattentive guests who cuddle up with a stinky pillow while watching *Harold and Maude*, or some other terrible movie.

The Chicken Feathers Guy eventually came up with a solution to all this: He got rid of his chickens. The fresh eggs were nice, but he just didn't have time to deal with all the feathers.

He's recovered from the ordeal and is doing just fine these days. I know, because he comes to my plant classes—occasionally even dressed as a woman. He's the one who keeps the peelings from the burdock and parsnip roots so he can take them home for "hash browns." He kindly asks for the waste that comes out of the end of the fruit strainer when we make gooseberry puree. He picks fiddleheads that are way too old, and defiantly says they are just fine that way. He doesn't mind the chaff on goosefoot seeds, and he *loves* the taste of acorn grubs. He actually gets angry at me when I toss the squeezed-out contents from my nutmilk bag.

I sympathize with the desire to be resourceful—that's part of the appeal of foraging. But this thrifty instinct can be carried too far. Plants have indigestible parts. You are not a ruminant. You don't have to eat everything that is theoretically ingestible. Plant foods are meant to be selected carefully, then sorted, separated, juiced, peeled, shelled, or winnowed as appropriate. Let compost be compost.

If you really have a use for something, use it. Experiment to your heart's content. But don't let the Chicken Feathers Guy smother the true aboriginal inside you. If you let him, he'll turn foraging from a hobby into a chore, transforming meals from indulgent dining to a reluctant obligation. That's not why we're into this.

NUTS, BERRIES, AND BOTANICAL LINGO

The word "prerogative" was esoteric and rarely used before Bobby Brown's 1988 hit song "My Prerogative." Then it suddenly jumped into every teenager's lexicon—but with a new pronunciation, and subtly changed meaning. The word "decadent," another victim of pop culture, has been more drastically reinvented in the last twenty years. Cinnamon was "cinnamom" a few generations ago, and cardamom appears headed down the same path. Like it or not, this is how language works: A mistake or odd use that proliferates through peer emulation eventually becomes defensible through majority rule, after which it morphs into consensus and becomes correct. Dictionaries eventually reflect these changes because dictionaries are not law; they describe how words are used and spelled. *Our use rules the dictionary*—knot the other way around.

Botanical language, despite the officious façade of technicality, works in the same haphazard way, only more so. Nobody is given the prerogative to define botanical terms, so their use is erratic and inconsistent. For example, most botanists define *tuber* as an enlargement of an underground stem. But some also include an enlargement of the root. The first group disagrees with this broader definition and call these latter thingamabobs "tuberous roots" or "tuberous enlargements." Some claim that a tuber must be underground, while others discuss aerial tubers.

With wapato (*Sagittaria latifolia*) the water gets very muddy. In the botanical literature I have seen this vegetable called a tuber, a corm, and a turion. I can see the argument for tuber: It *is* an enlargement formed at the end of a stem. But when the new stem starts growing, and the old stem is dead and detached, the wapato sure looks like a corm. But familiar corms like jack-in-the-pulpit live for multiple years; a wapato only lives a few months, then withers away. Enter the term "turion." Definitions of this word are harder to find, but Kaul et. al. (2011) use: "A compact, overwintering shoot tip with congested leaves." That description almost fits wapato, too.

The purpose of language is to communicate, and the purpose of technical language is to communicate precisely, without repeating long, cumbersome descriptive clauses. Unfortunately, many specialists forget the purpose of language, and delight in using "imbricate" where "overlapping" would suffice. They also derive evident pleasure in correcting lesser folks for technical wrongness—like calling one of those little hard things that grows into a new plant a "seed" when it is actually a seed with a thin layer of material around it (a "pericarp," no less) that makes it, technically, an "achene."

The thing is, plants don't care about our categories and have no inclination to fit into them. Quibbling over uncertain definitions and imaginary categories is pointless. The objective is to describe the plant part and its life cycle in a way that your audience can understand. You can do that equally well calling a wapato a tuber, turion, or corm. Multiple ways of describing things can be "technically correct."

Most of us already recognize the technicality police as insecure, but it is comforting to realize how often they are just plain wrong. Yes, the cousin who tells you every summer that a tomato "is a fruit, not a vegetable," is mistaken—it is a fruit *and* a vegetable. And like that nameless relative, the botanical technicality police deeply suffer the confusion of false dichotomies. (Probably from all those keys.) It is perfectly acceptable to call an achene with a tight-fitting exterior a seed. The presence of a little packaging around the seed does not change the fact that it is a seed. Do you cease to be a person when you put your clothes on?

It gets worse, though. Some bygone botanist once decided to use "nut" and "berry" as technical terms—applying stricter definitions to these words than they are associated with in common language. According to the specialized botanical definitions, neither a walnut nor a hickory nut is a "nut"; and blackberries, raspberries, mulberries, and strawberries are not "berries." Distinct technical words were adopted for most fruit forms—achene, schizocarp, loment, drupe, samara, pome, syncarp—so it is hard to imagine why taxonomists settled for "nut" and "berry" over similarly unambiguous terms. Since everybody already knew the definitions of "nut" and "berry," the subsequent botanists who felt compelled to correct them sounded petty, inane, and condescending. Some of them don't want to.

These strictified definitions typically arise from the misguided use of "true" as a modifier. "True berry" is introduced as a technical term with a specialized use, while "berry" remains the same regular old word we have used for a millennium. Inevitably, some people misunderstand the composite nature of these terms, and think that "true" nullifies the original and broader definition of the word. (Other common examples of this phenomenon are "true bug," "true hibernation," and "true grain.")

The purpose of technical language is to eliminate ambiguity, not to create it. However it happened, accepting "nut" and "berry" as technical terms shows an egregious lack of forethought. Taxonomists not only disrespect the "lay" public by attempting to redefine common words, they misconstrue their own authority. Botanists need technical jargon to facilitate the accurate description of plants and their parts, but nothing about this need grants us the authority to discard the meanings of everyday words for everyone else. Yet it is common for plant scientists to "correct" non-botanists for their supposedly mistaken usage of such words. These corrections are without merit, because technical language is carried in a framework of common English, which includes the words "nut" and "berry" in their well-established meanings.

The resolution of this conundrum will not come through thirteen more decades of smug pontification by the botanical elite until the weary public finally succumbs to this silly demand. A reasonable and long-overdue solution is for botanists to correct their own mistake, and stop pretending that "nut" and "berry" are technical words. The strict definitions that botanists want to use can easily be attached to novel terms. Make up a damn word, and stop bugging people for speaking English. *We control the dictionary.* So never hang your head when corrected for calling a walnut a nut—*please* keep doing it.

IN DEFENSE OF THE GREEN MEAL

Greens are packed with nutrition. Besides being loaded with essential vitamins and minerals, they contain a plethora of phytochemicals that provide varying health benefits. Greens are high in fiber and low in calories, so they promote healthy gut biomes and reduce stress on the pancreas and its delicately important Islets of Langerhans. It should be no surprise that the famous Mediterranean diet is characterized by huge quantities of greens. Eating more greens is good for you.

But we hardly ever eat them. A meal based on greens is almost unheard-of in the modern American kitchen. Greens are a side dish—*occasionally*—but never the main course. A host of reasons have conspired to reduce our consumption of leafy vegetables.

Food used to be expensive; now it is cheap. The drastic lessening of the cost of food over the last few centuries has had an almost unfathomably profound effect on our behavior, thought, eating patterns, and health. Whereas it now takes an average American worker about 6 minutes of wages to pay for a dozen eggs, in 1900 the same food required 34 minutes of pay.[1] Imagine paying $16.83 for a dozen eggs—and consider that prices in 1900 were already dramatically lower than a century before that.

In a landscape of small traditional farms, incidental greens grow themselves without any input of human labor and with no land allocated to their production. When food was expensive, the economizing offered by such a resource was too great to pass up. Today, when food is incredibly cheap, the meager savings offered by free greens is a pittance easily ignored by the overfed masses. A hundred years ago, most North Americans lived in the countryside, and long-distance transportation of fresh fruits and vegetables to these areas was not feasible. Thus, there was an intense craving for fresh greens in spring. Today, most of our population lives in cities and has access to oranges and broccoli all winter, so the springtime craving for greens is subdued. Furthermore, what were free foods to our forebears are now some of the most expensive calories in the grocery store. And, since most greens do not keep well, our stores offer just a few boring choices, and these are often wilted or rotting. It makes sense to eat heartily of greens when they are available in an array of superb, fresh forms, for free; but every one of these advantages has disappeared.

There are psycho-social reasons for avoiding greens as well. Many people associate them with a backward past of rural poverty—things that were eaten only begrudgingly, out of hard necessity. Our instinctive tendency to avoid indigestible fiber and seek the most calorie-dense foods when possible also inclines us away from greens. Throw on top of this the unfounded villainization of fat as a source of calories over the last 70 years, which made frying—a basic traditional method of preparing greens—off-limits to educated, health-conscious consumers.

---

1   The cheapening of commodities over time is a well-established trend, but it is so important to my argument here—and people are so often ignorant or incredulous of it—that I want to show you how I came up with this figure. For comparison, I tried to match a continuously existing profession that earns average wages with a location and commodity that seemed comparable over time. After some thinking and searching, I chose house painting, St. Louis, and eggs. According to the US Department of Labor (1934) the average house painter in St. Louis made 37.5¢ per hour in 1900, and according to reference.com (accessed January 12, 2017), the price of a dozen eggs at that time was 21¢ per dozen (not specific to St. Louis). In 2016, union painter's wages in St. Louis averaged $30.59 per hour, or $45.69 with benefits (T. Bryant 2016). According to expatistan.com (accessed January 15, 2017), an average of 19 price points for a dozen eggs in St. Louis is $2.97—which is expensive compared to most metro areas.

As greens transformed from cheap seasonal sustenance to expensive dietary supplements, the definition of the word "salad" shifted from "a mess of cooked greens" to "a mess of raw greens." People used to cook greens because they actually *needed* to digest them. They even used to eat the fat on animals. Today, the food economy has turned on its head—we now seek to *reduce* the digestibility, and the calorie content, of our food. Modern cooks and food writers smugly mock our thinner, hungrier, harder-working ancestors, poking fun at them for "overcooking" their vegetables, as if they did this out of culinary ignorance. But we are culturally ignorant of the benefits of poverty, hard labor, and daily hunger—and the joke is on us. The punch line is diabetes, and it's not very funny.

In sum, greens are expensive, boring, of poor quality, not well liked, and hard to digest. Fried wild greens fix all that.

A meal—a prepared combination of foods that sates us for an extended period of time—must provide, at the bare minimum, *some protein* and *enough calories*. Calories come in only three basic forms: protein, carbohydrate, and fat. Protein deficiency will kill you, but consuming exclusively protein will kill you faster. Therefore, a meal must combine protein with at least one of the other sources of calories. If it isn't carbohydrate, it must be fat; usually and preferably, it's both. Analysis of traditional eating patterns, and my relatives at Thanksgiving, confirms this preference. A satisfying meal also requires high digestibility and calorie density, because you need to fit enough food in your stomach to meet your caloric needs. Strong phytochemicals (chemicals from plants) is the final (and rarely acknowledged) requirement of a satisfying meal.

You can see these components in the anatomy of any common or traditional meal. Take pizza: There is protein in the crust (about 11%), the cheese (about 25%), and the meat topping (if there is one). The crust provides carbohydrates. Most of the calories in the cheese (about 70%) are fat. Some phytochemicals may come from vegetable toppings, but they are always supplied in the sauce. You can see all the same components in a burrito, a gyro, a hamburger, a pasty, lasagna. Complete a salad with croutons, meat or cheese, and dressing. A hot dog needs a bun, and relish or mustard. To cod, add breading, then deep fry, add tartar sauce and coleslaw. How about bacon, eggs, and toast? Good start, but you need phytochemicals: coffee, orange juice, jam. Your cravings unconsciously feed this formula. The proof is printed on every menu of every restaurant on Earth. You cannot escape it.

Greens obviously have loads of phytochemicals. Most of the calories in leaves are in the form of protein, but there is also some carbohydrate embedded in the fiber matrix. Thus, if you want to make a meal of greens, you add fat. If you want to have a more complete protein, use a variety of greens, each of which is rich in different amino acids. Cooking helps break down the fiber, making the protein and the coveted mineral nutrients of greens more accessible to your body. Fat helps transfer more intense heat to the greens, breaking them down better, and desiccating them, so they take up less space. It also helps your body absorb and utilize certain micronutrients. The oil coats your tongue; this, along with the reduced moisture in the greens, buffers your experience of the water-soluble bitter compounds in many greens. The combination of smaller size, higher digestibility, and toned-down flavor allows you to eat far more greens cooked with fat than you would ever eat raw. Green meals = better health. Don't fear that oil; welcome it.

I wish I had figured this out a long time ago. My mother believed in a diet of mostly refined carbohydrates and milk. I grew up eying all fat with suspicion; butter was disgusting, bacon drippings were liquid heart attack, and lard was unthinkable. We were the brainwashed victims of the pseudoscientific and oversimplified advice of the world's most advanced medical professionals (eat carbs!) and the misguided "food pyramid." I bet you fell for that, too. An outside observer might think that these ideas were part of a national diabetes causation program, but I'm optimistic enough to believe that it was just overwrought conclusions from limited data that was perpetuated by timid groupthink, sending millions of us to premature death. Even long after I had abandoned the silly idea that fat was unhealthy, I mostly avoided putting fat with greens just out of habit.

And then I started spending time in the South, where the tradition of eating greens fried in pork fat remains strong—particularly pokeweed, creasy greens (wintercress), and cut-leaf coneflower. Such dishes were served to me on several

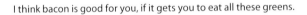

I think bacon is good for you, if it gets you to eat all these greens.

occasions, and eventually I began preparing and serving them to myself. I've undergone a revolution in my thinking, one which has changed my life, and my nutrition, for the better. I no longer find the thought of fried greens even slightly objectionable. In fact, I think this dish is the easiest and most effective way to use foraged plants to improve your nutrition. Fried greens is a common dish for healthy peasants all over the world—one that overfed but undernourished Americans would be well served to adopt.

There are some other good ways to increase your consumption of greens, all of which also rely on increasing digestibility and balancing calorie sources. In many poor areas of the world, where diets are chronically low in protein, people traditionally eat greens boiled for very long times until they are broken down into a sort of green pudding. This increases the portion of the protein available to the body. Americans, being almost never deficient in protein, rarely find this appealing, but it's not bad.

Another great way to increase your consumption of greens is the smoothie. (Thanks again, Sergei Boutenko.) The smoothie is not an ancient tradition. It relies on a blender to break the leaves into a gazillion tiny pieces—way more than your mouth would ever do—so that your body can easily access all their marvelous constituents. And, unlike the other methods, this one is raw, so certain components that are not heat-stable remain intact. For a green smoothie, use tender young leaves of mild-tasting species—some good choices are miner's lettuce, *Lactuca canadensis*, quickweed, chickweed, nettles, creeping bellflower. Mix your smoothie in a base of milk, your preferred milk substitute, or plain water. Add some fresh fruit or juice. You can make an incredible variety of combinations of this convenient and healthy snack.

I was introduced to another good green main course by Alan Muskat of Asheville, North Carolina, and now we make it at home on a regular basis. Take a mixture of tender greens and chop them really, really fine. Sprinkle in seasonings (we use salt, cumin, and paprika), then mix in just enough egg to coat the surface of the leaves, and press them together into patties and fry them. Served on wholesome bread with a slice of cheese, this is surprisingly filling and satisfying.

The fashionable new gig with greens is to make chips. This practice is not exclusive to kale; any large, thick leaves (still meristematic) will work. Coat your chosen greens with a mixture of oil and seasonings and bake them until they are crisp. This practice is, in many ways, homologous to frying greens. The leaves dry out, so strong flavors are experienced less. Lipid calories are added, to make it more satisfying. And the crisp leaves crumble in the mouth, fragmenting easily into tiny pieces that increase the surface area upon which your digestive system can act.

The point is this: Eat more greens, have more fun, save money, and be healthy.

THE ROUNDUP REVOLUTION

We have lived through a revolution in land use as great as the invention of irrigation, the plow, or the internal combustion engine. Just now. You and I. Did you notice? Trust me, farmers did. So did everyone else whose job involves managing vegetation. The killing of plants, which was done mechanically for millennia, is now done with chemicals—mostly glyphosate, which has now become the most-used agricultural chemical of all time (Main 2016).

Only fifteen years ago I mentioned to one of my weekend classes my distress over noticing some farmers spraying herbicide to kill off hay before turning the field over to corn. (It used to be, they'd plow and harrow repeatedly to kill the hay crop.) One woman in the class, who grew up on a dairy farm, was furious at me for claiming such nonsense—no farmer would do a thing like that, she said. Today, this has become the standard practice. And it's not just hayfields.

No more weed-whacking along the electric fence—it's Roundup to the rescue. No more trimming around the mailbox, just bring out the backpack sprayer. Say goodbye to those weeds around the silo—the ones that were hard to cut because of all the clutter. They weren't really hurting anything, and they fed the pheasants, and they sheltered a brood of bunnies . . . but it's just so darn easy to knock them down with a little toxic mist.

Herbicide saves time. It's not only easy, it's fun. Kind of like a video game. Makes you feel powerful. I watched the local power company's trigger-happy crew kill wild plums and elderberries with a flick of the wrist, spraying beyond

This hayfield was sprayed a week ago in preparation for plowing and planting—contrasting with the normal vegetation in the foreground and background. For the first few days, the sprayed vegetation looked normal, too.

their right-of-way, even though these shrubs could never grow tall enough to interfere with the lines. Railroads spray from the sides of special railcars, right into the rivers, streams, and marshes they cross.

I have a power line along the front of my property, and beneath it are beautiful thickets of elderberries, red raspberries, blackberries, and wild plums. I have received repeated assurances from the power company that my property is on the "do not spray" map. One summer, I went to pick elderberries with my children. The berries seemed to fall off the bushes just a little too easily, so I suggested that we not eat them; we put them in the fridge and waited three days. During that time, everything growing under our power line wilted and turned black. This is the herbicide foe we face as foragers.

Obviously, watch out for wilted plants. Never collect from roadsides or weedy areas unless you know the spray schedule (or are certain there isn't one). Avoid chain-link fences, especially in front of nice buildings. Look for unkempt spaces that nobody has a reason to care about. Unfortunately, there is no easy answer for how to avoid eating sprayed vegetation. Just pay attention. But there is something that worries me even more: The ecological devastation caused by overuse of herbicide is quietly growing to immense proportions, and as a society we have not yet reacted; we have been too busy staring at our smartphones to notice.

Along the railroad beside my childhood home, we had dozens of active woodchuck dens within a half mile of the house. Back then, the tracks were mowed twice a summer, and along them grew a rich variety of perennial herbs and shrubs, teeming with cottontails. Today, with herbicides replacing mowing, there are no woodchuck dens along the railroad, and cottontails are sparse. The only vegetation left is weedy annuals. This same scene is playing out in millions of locations across the country.

We don't often think of roadsides as important habitats, but in many regions they are the last refuges of native plant communities. It is common on the Great Plains to drive through miles of crop fields or range land where the only vestiges of real prairies are narrow strips between the road shoulders and the barbed wire. It is only here that the prairie clover, eryngo, compass plant, bush morning glory, and prairie camas bloom. I have seen similar situations in California. Some native plants can survive or even thrive under occasional mowing, but when the road department unceremoniously switches to spraying herbicide, it means the end of all these magnificent flowers, some of them a century old, within a few growing seasons. It's like cutting an old-growth forest, without the fanfare. We have all heard of the precipitous decline of the monarch butterfly—but hundreds of other species are being equally decimated by the same hands. Massive declines of numerous native plants have already occurred. The crisis is summed up well in *The Flora of Nebraska* (Kaul et al. 2011, 10–11):

> The decline of Nebraska's remaining post-sodbusting native flora was
> accelerated in the second half of the 20th Century by widespread use
> of herbicides to control weeds. . . . Extensive and nonselective spray-
> ing of herbicides on rights-of-way of roads, railroads, and public and
> private utilities has killed much of the native flora. . . . We have seen
> robust stands of native plants in state, county, and municipal parks
> and preserves and along roads and railways assailed with mowers,
> saws, and herbicides. . . . With the decline of native vegetation, the
> native fauna has also decreased dramatically.

Of course, this phenomenon is not confined to Nebraska. Every year, I see
herbicide in more places where I did not expect it. This summer it was in the
pine barrens of northern Wisconsin, where thousands of acres were sprayed
after logging to prevent the regrowth of undesirable species that might compete
with the jack pines desired for paper pulp—"worthless" stuff like blueberries,
dewberries, New Jersey tea, wood lily, blazing star, prairie clover, prairie onion,
bearberry, bur oak, northern pin oak, sandcherry, chokecherry, pincherry,
black cherry, strawberry, and hazelnut. Camping this fall in the Ozark National
Forest in Arkansas, I came across an entire hilltop of regenerating pine, about

I think you can tell which part of this barrens has been sprayed—destroying Nature for a very
small increase in pulpwood sales 50 years from now. If there were more foragers, this would not
be legal on public lands, or tax-subsidized private timberlands (as in this instance).

In St. Francis National Forest in Arkansas, the understory here was obliterated by chemicals after a shelterwood cutting to increase the regeneration of desirable timber species. So much for "multi-use."

5 acres, doused with herbicide to protect the view at a historical site. In certain national forests, herbicides are even being sprayed after shelterwood cuts, to kill off all the native vegetation that might compete with the seedlings of desirable timber species.

If you know of a picturesque tree in a farm fencerow, take a photo now to show your grandchildren. The spray drift from regular herbicide application will not kill every tree outright the first year, but the added stress will increase mortality rates, and soon enough, old fencerow trees will be a thing of the past. We have begun an arms race: The more we use these chemicals, the more resistant the weeds will become. The more resistant they become, the more we will have to use these chemicals—and we'll have to find new and more deadly ones. And the stupidest thing about overusing herbicides is that applying them to perennial communities *guarantees* the proliferation of annual weeds—the very thing the herbicides were designed to get rid of.

Society is not going to stop its use of herbicides, but we are still figuring out the social norms and regulations surrounding this new technology. You need to be a part of that process. Let your municipality and power company know how you feel. Mention something to the town board or the road department. Report spray violations. Give your neighbor a friendly frown if necessary. And those national forests—they are yours. Complain, loudly and clearly and politely. Write a letter to the local paper—most people don't know this is happening. Talk to legislators about reasonable limits to the use of herbicides (Ontario, for example, recently banned the use of glyphosate for cosmetic purposes).

And of course, vote through your food choices.

DOES FORAGING DESTROY NATURE?

Although there is virtually no documentation of ecological harm inflicted through the gathering of wild plants for food, a few environmentalists perceive foraging as a threat to Nature. This misinformed attitude is aptly displayed in an article by Lisa Novick from the *Huffington Post* (May 31, 2016), "Forage in the Garden, Not in What's Left of the Wild." In her diatribe against gathering, Novick claims, "If even a tiny percentage of our population goes into the wild, in search of native ingredients for our latest recipe, we will devastate what's left of the natural environment." She soon repeats that "if even an infinitesimal percentage" of the population goes foraging, "it will be carnage."

Far more people than that are already foraging, and they have been doing it since time immemorial—yet Novick provides no example of this carnage and devastation. That's because it isn't real.

There is actually a strong relationship between foraging and careful stewardship of native plant communities. Perhaps Novick should visit an Indian reservation in the Dakotas, where she might note that the only native prairies left are on tribally owned lands where wild plants have been harvested for generations—and the devastation she speaks of can be seen on the inholdings of white farmers who have never tasted a prairie turnip, a ground plum, or a cup of leadplant tea.

Novick presents Nature as a frail, inept virgin, begging not to be defiled by lustful, omnipotent conquerors. In this belief system, Nature is useless. Beauty is its only purpose: a benchmark by which we can measure our own power and restraint. Nature is unproductive and incompetent—only Man is creator. This philosophy, which I have come to call "Nature schizophrenia,[2]" posits that there are only two ways of relating to Nature: destroying it and replacing it for economic gain, or leaving it untouched. These approaches may seem like polar opposites, but in fact they are the right and left hands of alienation, working together toward annihilation. As long as we believe that Nature can be only a virgin or a whore, marriage will elude us.

In the real world, foraging does not play out anything like Novick imagines. Nature is not a fancy wine glass perched on a flimsy railing, in peril of shattering

---

2   This idea was originally shared by ethnoecologist M. Kat Anderson.

at the next graceless bump; it is the tenacious, unconquerable force that reclaims Detroit and Chernobyl in defiant greenery. Foragers are not a mindless plague of starving locusts; we are a loose affiliation of Nature's missionaries, sparsely scattered among an ecologically oblivious nation. Foragers do not converge upon and greedily decimate the few remaining nature preserves; we volunteer at those preserves and support the conservation organizations that run them. We judiciously gather our fare in such a way that our work can scarcely be noticed. We are not auk-egg hunters, seeking the last of imperiled rarities to satisfy pointless desires; we provide for our most basic needs, conscientiously and thoughtfully, from Nature's surplus. We eat the weeds that respectable society scorns, and the invasive plants that ecologists abhor. Foragers are not the destroyers of Nature; we are its staunchest protectors. Unlike Novick, I can show examples to support that claim.

There are thousands of people in the upper Great Lakes region who harvest wild rice for food—and many of them do so commercially. I have never gathered any wild plant for which there is even a remotely comparable level of human harvest competition. This, then, should be the perfect test case for the utter devastation that Novick predicts. But after many hundreds of years of this supposedly rapacious abuse, the rice beds remain. There is no indication that the traditional harvest has caused any decline, anywhere, ever. The rice beds are still teeming habitat for waterfowl, fish, frogs, turtles, herons, otters, muskrats.

But there is more to the story: Many lakeshore homeowners and fishermen passionately hate wild rice. Risking fines, they spitefully pull it out from their shorelines. Decades ago, waterfront property owners successfully conspired to eliminate this plant from many of our lakes—and the government agencies given the responsibility to protect our natural resources looked the other way. It was wild rice harvesters, largely Anishinaabe, who organized to stop this ecocide, and who got laws passed or enforced to protect the plant. It is because of the harvesters that today we have research, management programs, and reintroduction efforts—all aimed at combating the real threats to wild rice: pollution, runoff, development, invasive species, and people who want weed-free lakes. The rice beds today remain *because of* all these harvesters, not in spite of them. The fishermen and wardens know this—which is exactly why some of them still single us out for harassment.

What happens when there are no gatherers to protect a plant? We have an excellent comparable case: American lotus. This native plant (the harvest, use, and ecology of which is covered in detail in my book *Nature's Garden*) is despised as strongly as wild rice, and for all the same reasons. I once enjoyed three days on the Mississippi River with a lifelong conservationist who had spent his entire career working there. Much to my shock, he said to me, "I love everything about this river except one thing." He then pointed to a lotus pad and said, "I absolutely hate that [expletive] plant." Nothing I said could convince him of its virtues.

The wealthy landowners on Swartswood Lake in New Jersey feel the same way about lotus. Although the plant is classified as an endangered species in New Jersey, the lake association organized and petitioned the New Jersey Department of Environmental Protection, asking that the plant be removed from the endangered species list so that they can eliminate 95% of the annoying weed from the lake. The organization's complaint: lotus interferes with recreation (SLWA 2010). The result? The New Jersey DE"P" agreed to eliminate 50% of this endangered species, for the sake of more convenient boating and swimming. (Although I could do jail time if they caught me harmlessly eating a nut.) The plant occupied a whopping 3.8% of the lake, which is apparently way too much if it is near a millionaire's dock. Where were the conservationists? The media? The *law*? If this can be done, the Endangered Species Act is a joke. The state forester championed the lotus massacre (Avery 2012). The local media was wholeheartedly against the lotus. One reporter (ibid.) called the plant "A

Spring Lake near Savannah, Illinois, has about 2,000 acres of lotus (better then 90% coverage), teeming with egrets, herons, frogs, waterfowl, muskrats, otters, shellfish, and turtles. Despite this native plant being an endangered species in New Jersey, the state's Department of Environmental Protection determined that 3.8% coverage of lotus on Swartswood Lake was "too much." The state agreed to use heavy machinery to eliminate 50% of it, for the purpose of improving recreational opportunities for wealthy lakefront property owners.

silent, ever-expanding menace . . . [that] threatened the delicate balance of the lake's ecology—and the fun as well." But he didn't mention any actual ecological harm that "the insidious offender" caused.

One man, Randy Sprague, spearheaded the lotus-killing efforts. For years, he spewed ignorant anti-lotus nonsense to all who would listen—and they did. Sprague claimed that the plant wasn't native, despite records that it grew in the lake in the 1800s. He acted as if 20 acres is an unusually large lotus colony (it's not), and as if the plant's spread in the lake was abnormal, unnatural, and unprecedented (it wasn't). He claimed that the lotus was causing ecological harm (it wasn't, and apparently nobody asked him to elaborate). For his campaign to decimate one of the few populations of a rare native plant in New Jersey, he was given an Outstanding Citizen Award by the local community and publicly lauded as a hero. Ironically, just recently, the *actually* non-native, *actually* invasive water chestnut *Trapa natans* was found on the lake. It will probably spread much more rapidly with the lotus removed.

This is what happens when there are no gatherers. This is why we need more people harvesting native plants, not fewer. I only know of the plight of lotus on Swartswood Lake because a local forager wrote to me in dismay, asking for help defending the plant from those who wanted it destroyed. She cited the many birds, reptiles, fish, and amphibians that relied on the lotus for habitat. Such foragers are the very people who Novick claims are doing something that is "comparable to eating shark-fin soup or hunting elephants . . . or condors."

Laurie Reid (2005) studied the impact of two different gathering methods employed by traditional Native sweetgrass harvesters, comparing these to control plots where the plants were not harvested. Her study was designed to show which of the two methods was least destructive. Instead, it showed that both kinds of harvested plot thrived and expanded, while sweetgrass clumps in the unharvested control plots struggled and shrunk (Kimmerer 2012). This counterintuitive result shocked those ecologists, who, like Novick, had smugly oversimplified their understanding of Nature to fit a preconceived dogma about the human role in it.

I am a strong supporter of preservationist strategies that are ecologically necessary for the protection of imperiled species and ecosystems. But such preserves are temporary, stopgap measures—buying us time to find ways to permanently and positively alter our relationship with the land. The Nature schizophrenics don't want these relationships at all; they believe that Nature has one "correct" state of being that is both static and identifiable, and excludes humans. The maintenance and pursuit of that correct state equates to ecological morality; anything short of it is defiled and thus worthless. The conundrum is that maintaining this human-free state requires human intervention. And we can't find a natural community that qualifies; our most cherished wilderness areas have been subject to extensive human manipulation. This dichotomy between pure and fallen spaces is fictitious.

Only 12% of North America is cleared for agriculture or otherwise developed, and a much smaller fraction is meaningfully preserved. The gray area in between comprises most of a continent: woodlots, deserts, brushland, range land, marshes, swamps, meadows, and public and industrial forests. These areas are already managed by humans with resource-extraction strategies, such as timber production and grazing, that alter their ecology in ways far exceeding any potential impact of foraging. Why make a blanket declaration condemning the simplest and most benign form of human participation in the ecology of these landscapes?

Ironically, Novick's alternative to the "rapaciousness" of foraging is that "we should landscape with the native plants that we crave, creating more habitat, supporting biodiversity. . . . In our agricultural areas, we should convert some of the non-native monocultures to various native species that yield the desired seasonal ingredients and support healthy, functioning food webs and ecosystems. In Southern California, for example, there could be orchards of elderberry, toyon, and catalina cherry interspersed with white sage, buckwheat, and manzanita. In fact, every part of the United States could celebrate its authentic natural character by cultivating native plants for their culinary ingredients." This would create, in her mind, "some of the greenest jobs imaginable."

Novick's argument displays perfectly the irrational hypocrisy of the Nature schizophrenics. She touts human-constructed imitations of natural communities as vibrant habitats for wildlife that produce a sustainable surplus for human consumption—yet she furiously denies that the same could be true of *actual* natural communities. It is the ugly dogma of conquest: Nature is useless, but humans can replace it with something productive.

Nevertheless, I think her idea is brilliant. It reminds me of the wetter portions of my orchard, which I have converted from crop fields and pasture to a mixture of native edible shrubs: elderberry, nannyberry, wild plum, chokecherry, highbush cranberry, and aronia. Between these shrubs I have planted and encouraged native, perennial, edible herbs: pokeweed, angelica, cow parsnip, giant St. John'swort, cut-leaf coneflower, jerusalem artichoke, cup plant, common milkweed, stinging nettle, wood nettle, hops, two native mints, and ostrich fern. Despite her claim that I am "irresponsible" and doing something "tantamount to ecocide" when I pick these things where they occur naturally at the edge of my woods, she and I have a lot of common ground, and have come to many of the same conclusions.

Novick needs to recognize that foragers are her allies. We've been putting her vision into life for years already. In fact, foraging people all over the world have spent thousands of years working out strategies for complex, productive, and sustainable management of native plant communities. Foragers are the *only* people doing this. We are the customers who will buy the produce of this kind of endeavor. And we are the only ones preserving, maintaining, and developing the knowledge and skills that make something like this possible.

The inconsistency of Novick's position—and her use of caricature, hyperbole, imaginary problems, just-so statements, and made-up facts—suggests that her real desire may not be conservation of Nature, but control of people. Humans are foraging animals who exhibit group territoriality. When we see a stranger taking something from our territory, we experience a powerful jealous reaction. Most seasoned foragers have encountered this attitude, usually justified by irrational and baseless concerns like Novick's. Such possessiveness should not masquerade as ecological righteousness.

Novick's premise that *nobody* should do something unless *everybody* can do it is devoid of common sense—and isn't followed in any arena of life. The same simplistic, knee-jerk arguments used against foraging have long ago been rejected when it comes to wildlife and hunting. Waterfowl hunters have done more to help ducks than any other segment of society. In my region, the only voice speaking up to protect the pine barrens—a unique and ecologically important part of our natural heritage—is the Sharp-Tailed Grouse Society. The hunters that compose this organization donate their time and hard-earned money to preserve and manage the habitat of a bird of which, if they are lucky, they will eat one per year. Hundreds of species of plants and animals benefit as a result. These hunters make this disproportionate sacrifice because of the deep personal relationships they have forged with this bird and the landscape it calls home.

We only protect what we love, and we only love what provides for us. While many outdoor pastimes promote appreciation of Nature, hunting and gathering have a unique and irreplaceable role in conservation. These ancient occupations lead us to a visceral and deeply emotional recognition of interdependence that cannot be preached or explained into existence. Foragers are conscientious, knowledgeable, thoughtful, and deeply concerned about the species that we gather and the habitats they are part of. Our impact on the landscape is something we evaluate constantly. We abandon the dogmatic belief that all human impact is destructive—the forlorn religion of a rootless people. We are gatherers. We are the caretakers. Someday, we pray, the self-exiled majority will join us on this path, and the world will prosper.

Foraging Calendar

Timing is vital with foraging; the season for a food is often fleeting. Below you will find the major wild food products discussed in this book arranged into a chart showing when they are available for harvest. I have used seasons rather than calendar dates so that readers are not distracted by numbers that do not pertain to their particular locality. The sequence is most accurate from 40–50° north latitude and away from the West Coast. Areas with milder winters often have plants growing throughout the cool months that would be gathered in spring in cold climates, which causes some of the sequences to break down. Also, plants in arid regions often respond more to moisture than to temperature. Elevation, proximity to water, and slope exposure all have a great impact on the timing (phenology) of seasonal events. Taking notes on local plant phenology is a great way to keep yourself attuned to Nature. Feel free to copy this chart and alter it in any way to fit your specific climate.

	Late Winter	Early Spring	Mid Spring	Late Spring	Early Summer	Mid Summer	Late Summer	Early Fall	Late Fall	Early Winter
Black mustard greens					▓	▓				
Black mustard seeds							▓	▓		
Bladder campion greens			░	▓						
Blackberry and dewberry							▓			
Bramble shoots				░ ▓						
Red raspberry					░	▓				
Black raspberry						▓				
Thimbleberry						░				
Wineberry							▓			
Salmonberry					▓					
Plumboy, Nagoonberry						▓				
Cloudberry							▓			
Calamus base		░	▓	▓						
Calamus spike					▓					

▓ = Peak of Season   ░ = Coming into/out of Season

This calendar may be photocopied and altered for private use.

	Late Winter	Early Spring	Mid Spring	Late Spring	Early Summer	Mid Summer	Late Summer	Early Fall	Late Fall	Early Winter
Caraway greens and stalks		░	■	■	░					
Caraway root	■	░						░	■	■
Caraway seed						■	░			
Chickweed	░	■	■	░				░	■	■
Chufa	■	░						░	■	■
Creeping bellflower greens		░	■	■						
Creeping bellflower roots	■	■	░					░	■	■
Fennel shoots and greens		░	■	■	░					
Fennel seeds						░	■	■	░	
Field garlic greens	■	■							░	■
Native wild garlic greens		░	■	■	░					
Field and wild garlic bulbs	░	■	■	■	░			░	■	■
Gooseberry					■	░				
Hickory nuts (incl. pecan)								░	■	■
Hops shoot			■	░						
Japanese knotweed shoot			■							
Kentucky coffeetree seed	■	■	░					░	■	■
Maple sap	■	░								
Miner's lettuce	░	■	■							
Mulberry fruit					■	░				
Mulberry greens			░	■	░					
Pawpaw								■		
Persimmon								░	■	░
Poke greens and shoots			░	■	░					
Prairie turnip										
Purple poppy mallow roots	■	░						░	■	■
Purslane					░	■	░			

■ = Peak of Season   ░ = Coming into/out of Season

This calendar may be photocopied and altered for private use.

	Late Winter	Early Spring	Mid Spring	Late Spring	Early Summer	Mid Summer	Late Summer	Early Fall	Late Fall	Early Winter
Quickweed				░	█	░				
Rose petals				░	█	░				
Rose hips								░	█	█
Sassafras root	█	█	█	█	█	█	█	█	█	█
Sassafras greens			░	░						
Shepherd's purse greens		░							░	░
Sochan greens		░		░			█	█	█	░
Sochan shoots				█	░					
Strawberry spinach greens				░	░		█			
Strawberry spinach fruit						░	█	░		
Sweetroot roots	█		░						█	█
Sweetroot shoot			░	█	░					
Sweetroot leaves			░	█	░			░		
Violet greens			█	░	░					
Violet flowers			█	░						
Watercress	░	░	░	░	░			░	░	░
Water parsnip root	░							░	█	█
Water parsnip greens			░	░	█	░				
Wild radish greens		░	░	░	░	░			░	
Wild radish pods				░	█	█	░	░	░	
Wintercress	░	█	░						░	░

█ = Peak of Season   ░ = Coming into/out of Season

This calendar may be photocopied and altered for private use.

Black Mustard

Brassica nigra

As a teenager I lived near an urban forager's paradise: a complex of overgrown vacant lots, rubble dumps from razed buildings, boxelder and Siberian elm groves, and neglected urban meadows—the whole thing intersected by unnamed streams channelized into arrow-straight ditches. Huge clumps of black mustard grew in this nameless urban wildland, including one that covered

A linear roadside colony of black mustard in peak bloom, midsummer, standing 6–7 feet tall.

about three acres and was so thick that it was nearly impossible to traverse. If you wrestled your way through it in early autumn, the mustard seeds would shatter out of the pods and rain down on your head, collecting in your hood, pockets, and shoes.

It was from one of these clumps that I collected my first mustard greens, and gathered my first cup of the spicy seeds to try my hand at making my favorite condiment. Decades later, despite all the development that has swallowed my old foraging haunts, that patch of black mustard still stands there, welcoming me home when I return to visit my family.

DESCRIPTION

Black mustard is hard to overlook. It is a massive plant—the tallest and largest of our wild mustards—and it often grows in dense, nearly pure colonies. Mature plants range from 4–9 feet tall (1.6–2.5 m), and they may grow as much as an inch thick (2.5 cm) at the base. Although the stalk sports numerous spreading branches, these are absent near the base, and the aspect of the whole plant is usually much taller than wide. Stems are smooth and roundish, solid, with faint ridges running down from each petiole; they are coated with a light bloom and often have purple areas. The lower part of the stem has some large, stiff, needle-like hairs, but these become less prevalent as you go up the stem, and in the top part are absent, or nearly so.

Black mustard is an annual that has a basal rosette for only a short period after germination. The stalk sheds its lower leaves as it grows. The leaves are largest in the bottom third of the plant, growing up to a foot (30 cm) long and nearly as wide. These larger leaves typically have 2–4 small lobes near the base that may be completely divided from the rest of the blade. The large terminal segment encompasses most of the leaf's surface area. It is coarsely and irregularly toothed, often with some shallow lobes—3 of which tend to be more prominent. The leaves have scattered hairs on the lower surface, smaller than those at the stem base. Farther up the stem, the leaves become smaller and are unlobed. All the leaves are borne on short petioles.

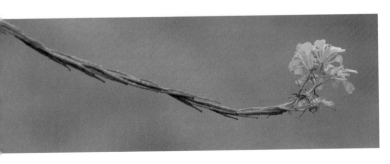

The long, sinuous inflorescence of black mustard, with open flowers only at the tip, and thin, overlapping pods appressed to the rachis.

The upper third of the black mustard plant is lanky, sparse, and almost leafless. The uppermost leaves are a good distinguishing feature; they are long and very narrow, entire, and droop on short, thin, limp petioles. The numerous fruiting branches in the top are thin and flimsy-looking, often drooping at the tips and curving this way and that like my hair does most days. The flowers and fruits, like those of other mustards, are borne in racemes. These may be up to 20 inches (50 cm) long, but only 4–12 flowers at the tip are blooming at any one time. The little, 4-petaled yellow flowers are about a quarter inch (6 mm) across and bloom in mid summer. They ripen into very thin pods just under an inch long with a beak-like tip, roughly rounded with 4 ridges in cross section. The pods are numerous and overlapping, nearly appressed to the stem. The seeds inside are spherical and brownish to nearly black, similar to commercial mustard seeds.

HABITAT

Black mustard, an introduced weed, is widespread but also picky. It can survive almost anywhere but thrives only in areas with hot, moist growing seasons and especially rich soils. It benefits from slopes since they result in soil disturbance after heavy rains. Accordingly, it reaches its apogee in hilly areas of the lower Midwest, the Northeast, and parts of California and Oregon. It also thrives in vacant urban lots, especially around piles of yard waste or other composting organic debris, and often pops up in areas of building or road construction. Once

Black mustard *Brassica nigra*. Blue = area of greatest abundance. Lighter blue = present, but variably common.

established, black mustard colonies are more tenacious than most other annuals. It grows taller than most competitors and thick enough to shade them out, and reseeds heavily. It is also allelopathic, releasing chemicals that inhibit the growth of many other species (Turk and Tawaha 2003; Al-Sherif et al. 2013). In the richest soils it is sometimes able to persist or even dominate along fencerows and roadsides even where it has to compete with tough perennials.

HARVEST AND PREPARATION

Black mustard is a hot-weather plant; don't look for it until summer is well under way. But when those first hot days of early summer send a few dark mulberries to the sidewalk, these spicy greens are ready for picking. Once it warms up, they grow fast—and fast means tender. Gather tender leaves from

Above left The uppermost leaves of black mustard, associated with the inflorescence branches, are entire, drooping, and nearly linear. **Above right** The seeds of black mustard along with the dry pod halves they were just winnowed from. These seeds are easy to collect, easy to separate, and make an excellent condiment. The inside of the seed is dull yellowish. **Opposite** A young black mustard plant in early summer. The top half of this plant's stem, and all the leaves attached to it, are tender. Few other greens have this much bulk.

young plants up to about three feet tall, along with any portion of the stem that remains tender. Later in summer, when the plants are much taller, there will still be some tender leaves near the growing tip (and even when they are in full bloom, you can often find a few late starters mixed among the mature plants, still sporting nice greens).

Black mustard greens range from mildly pungent to extremely hot; the closer one gets to the flowering parts, the hotter they become. The most potent part is the incipient branches of the flowering top, when the plants are 3–6 feet (1–2 m) tall. This is the spiciest green of any mustard I have tried. The lower leaves are not nearly as strong. And the hotness diminishes greatly with cooking. You can use black mustard greens just as you would use those of cultivated mustard. The youngest ones are good chopped and mixed in salads, if used sparingly. The stalks and leaves can also be steamed or boiled as a potherb. But their best use, in my opinion, is as fried greens. If there is a particularly large portion of tender stem, these are great used as a sort of slightly spicy broccoli in soups, rice dishes, or stir-fries, or served as a stand-alone vegetable. Since black mustard is so prolific, you may have the opportunity to store some greens for out-of-season use. You can blanch and freeze them, or pressure-can them, and I suspect that the leaves or chopped stems would make a great addition to kimchi.

Black mustard is one of the species whose seeds are used commercially as a seasoning and to make the familiar mustard condiment (others are *Brassica juncea* and *Sinapsis alba*). The seeds are fun and easy to collect: Take a wash-tub into a mustard patch in early fall, along with a stick to beat the dry, brown tops, and you will have little trouble getting enough of them to make your own mustard, or to grind and use alone as a seasoning. If the pods are ripe but not quite dry, you can cut the tops and bundle them to dry for a few days, then beat the seeds out later. Or you can stuff the racemes loosely into a bucket so that they can dry out there, and the ripe seeds of any shattering pods will drop to the bottom. If kept safe and dry, mustard seeds will stay good for years, to be used at your convenience.

Making mustard spread is quite simple—I'll just provide a basic overview, and you can come up with an infinite variety of recipes. Grind some mustard seed. Mix in vinegar and another liquid, like beer, water, or wine. OK, now you have mustard. It will be super hot, but if you let it sit in the fridge for three weeks, the spiciness will diminish to a bearable level. You can also mellow the heat using some combination of (1) diluting it with a thick material (applesauce works well); (2) adding a sweetener, like honey; or (3) cooking it. I also recommend adding salt, and maybe some black pepper. Keep experimenting until you find a sauce that you like. Next, invite your foraging friends over, grill some brats or chicken breasts, and impress them with your homemade wild mustard.

The next time you spy a formidable grove of thick weeds with yellow flowers and tangled, wiry tops so tall they almost scare you, check to see if they are black mustard. Someday, perhaps, they will welcome you home, too.

Bladder Campion

Silene vulgaris (Silene cucubalus), **and** *Silene csereii*

Acool, dewy dawn in early summer, and the frantic sunrise singing of robins and chestnut-sided warblers calls me out to meet the morning. I take a groggy walk before I have to report to my job as a cook in a little café. East I go, past the ball field, across the creek, around the big bend that follows the bay on Lake Nebagamon, to a narrow dirt road, along which lies a sandy hillside meadow that I like to visit. Here I turn a few logs, looking for a prairie skink or a smooth green snake; I pick a few strawberries, sniff a handful of sweet fern, keeping my eye out all the while for a clump of delicate, blue-green sprigs. There at my feet, I find a marvelous few flowers at the tip of an elegant

Bladder campion *Silene vulgaris* in bloom.

little plant. Alas, I am too late. I make a mental note for next year, and vow to be here two weeks earlier. This, I have learned, is the fate of the forager who procrastinates.

DESCRIPTION

Bladder campion is a perennial growing from a tough but thin root. Larger plants will produce several stems, which reach 2–3 feet (60–90 cm) long and are typically leaning or weakly upright, sometimes toppled over by the time of flowering. Tender shoots are weakly erect. The stems are rounded with a small hollow in the center, smooth and nearly hairless, rarely more than an eighth inch (3 mm) thick, and bulging at the nodes; they have little taper.

To eat these greens, you'll have to identify the plant early, without the conspicuous and distinctive flowers. You can mark the spot in the summer when it is easy to identify, and then return the following spring to find the new shoots.

Young bladder campion looks something like a glaucous chickweed with clumped stems. Bladder campion starts out with a few pairs of leaves packed close to the bottom of the stem. These basal leaves are longer than typical stem leaves, 2–3 inches (5–8 cm), and have long-tapered, narrow bases that someone might call a short petiole. By the time of flowering, bladder campion's basal leaves will usually have withered and turned brown.

The stem leaves are in widely spaced pairs. They are ovate to lanceolate on the lower stem but become narrowly long-lanceolate toward the flowers. The leaves are sessile and usually clasping, with the tips often down-curved. They often squeak when rubbed together. The blades are entire and hairless on both sides, but they do have fine hairs on the margins. The midvein is conspicuously light, but the secondary veins are scarcely

The other bladder campion, *Silene cserii*, about to bloom. Note the thicker, larger leaves and less inflated bladder.

The flowers of white campion *Silene alba*—the plant often wrongly called bladder campion. Notice how the bladder has ridges, and all vegetative parts are densely hairy.

evident; close examination reveals that they are faintly raised on the upper surface. (This is a good identifying feature, as most plants have depressed veins on the upper surface.) The leaves and stems are smooth and coated with a light bloom, giving the whole plant a bluish-gray cast.

Bladder campion's stems may fork near the base; then they remain unbranched until near the tip, where they make a broad, 2-way fork 2–3 times. At the first fork the stems are a few inches long, but the subsequent forks get shorter, and the flowers are held closely together in small groups. Each flower has an inflated, balloon-like calyx of fused sepals at its base, light glaucous-green, hairless and nearly smooth (but veiny), elliptic, and about a half inch (13 mm) long. At the tip of this calyx, 5 white petals spread about an inch (2.5 cm) wide, each petal much broader at the tip and lobed nearly to its base, giving the appearance of 10 petals at the first glance. The calyx dries into a smooth, light-brown capsule that holds the mature seeds until they rattle out.

Silene vulgaris can be found listed with a small multitude of scientific names in the botanical literature, which should be considered when you are looking it up in other sources. Both *S. vulgaris* and *S. csereii* are usually called "bladder campion," but some call the latter species "smooth campion" or "Balkan catchfly." These two plants are similar enough that *S. csereii*, although widespread and common, is often overlooked, and is rarely mentioned in field guides. It differs from the regular bladder campion in having thicker, broader, more succulent leaves, and in that the stem is always totally hairless (the common species occasionally has sparse hair near the stem base). The bladder-like calyx of *S. csereii* is less inflated and lacks the raised veins on the surface. Although this species is perhaps the better of the two for eating, the average person does not differentiate them. The species' habitats overlap, and they can be used similarly for food, so in this account I am treating them collectively as "bladder campion."

People occasionally confuse bouncing bet *Saponaria officinalis* with bladder campion. Bouncing bet is much larger and has straight, erect stems without basal leaves. The secondary veins are depressed above and protruding below. The leaves of bouncing bet are not glaucous like that of bladder campion, and are bitter enough that you'd almost certainly spit them out.

White campion: Bladder campion has a common weedy relative, the white campion, that also goes by way too many Latin names, most often *Lychnis alba* or *Silene alba*. White campion is very easy to tell from bladder campion: All parts are densely hairy, almost velvety. However, it is often mistakenly called bladder campion because it also has a bladder-like inflated calyx.

White campion is edible. It is occasionally gathered and eaten by North American foragers who mistake it for bladder campion. However, white campion isn't half as good as bladder campion, and would never warrant a chapter in this book. While white campion is occasionally mentioned as a traditional green in Europe (Pieroni 1999; Paoletti et al. 1995), bladder campion is mentioned with such frequency that it is clearly favored.

HABITAT

Bladder campion is an introduced weed that is of little concern as an invasive. It's been here a long time, and rarely shows up in natural habitats; when it does it isn't dominant. Under the right conditions, in response to human disturbance, it can be abundant. It likes dry, well-drained soil in full sun, and is most common in rocky or sandy regions. It grows where the soil is poor to moderately rich. While bladder campion benefits from disturbance, it is not one of the first plants to colonize broken ground. But being perennial, it can persist for many years once it becomes established.

Composite range of *Silene csereii* and *Silene vulgaris.*

Bladder campion is most common on roadsides and along railroads. Look for it also along trails, in vacant lots, dry open woods, abandoned fields, meadows, gravel pits, backyards, construction sites, steep river banks, and the upper reaches of beaches. It is not commonly found in pastures because livestock will readily eat it, although you may see it around an old piece of farm equipment or other object that obstructs the beasts from getting to it. Because bladder campion is short and sprawling, it can't compete well with tall plants on rich soil; look for it where vegetation is short and sparse.

White campion is more common generally. It is found in the same places as bladder campion, often beside it, but also thrives in richer and moister soil.

It can grow taller to compete with robust perennial herbs, and is a common weed of barnyards, meadows, and hayfields.

HARVEST AND PREPARATION

The shoots with young leaves are gathered in spring. I prefer to pick them at four to nine inches in length. If they are in the shade and really lanky, the terminal eight inches might still be tender on an eighteen-inch stalk. When the flower buds are formed but not yet open, you can still get a tender few inches at the tip of the stem, but it will be more bitter than the younger growth, and should be boiled to alleviate this.

Several authors suggest getting them when they're really, really short— two inches or less. I suppose something terrible might happen when they cross that monumental threshold and broach *three inches*. (Read with sarcasm, then insert evil laugh.) There is a pattern of paranoia here. I find it frustrating to read ridiculously short sizes at which we are supposed to harvest wild shoot vegetables—one finds this repeatedly, with almost every species. This is unrealistic and dishonest: Nobody actually gathers campion shoots when they are two inches long. The two-inch stems are usually growing sideways along the ground and have not even entered the shoot phase—they're poor in quality, and usually dirty. These authors need to understand that many beginning foragers are apprehensive and take these claims at face value. I trust you to use your own judgment about the flavor and texture of your food. And if you make bad salads from overgrown greens and disappoint your guests, I trust that you will not sue me.

The young greens can be eaten raw, but do have a slight bitter aftertaste. They are fine in salad, but I don't like them as the base of it. Blanching the greens by covering with mulch in the spring has been suggested to reduce the

If you are going to eat white campion, this is the best stage. But the real bladder campion is much better.

bitterness, and I'm pretty sure it would work, but since the plant doesn't grow on my property, I've never had the chance to try this. As a boiled or steamed potherb, bladder campion greens become very mild, and are in fact one of my favorites. Their texture is superb, and they are great in any of the simple or complicated ways that potherbs are prepared.

In 1783, the English economic botanist Charles Bryant wrote of the bladder campion, "Our kitchen-gardens scarcely furnish a better flavoured sallad than the young, tender shoots of this plant, when boiled." (Note that in those days, "sallad" did not mean raw greens.) Bladder campion is one of the most popular foraged greens in southern Europe. In one study on the wild plants eaten in rural Spain, bladder campion was the second most popular of 123 species mentioned by the informants (Tardio et al. 2005). In another study (Rivera et al. 2007), it was the most frequently reported plant eaten out of the 154 wild species gathered. Yet today, bladder campion seems only slightly known among American foragers, despite being widespread and quite common. Could it be that the confusion between this species and its less toothsome relative has damaged the bladder campion's reputation? Or is it that, in two hours, nobody can manage to collect enough one-inch shoots for a serving? Hopefully my discussion here will help remedy this.

Once you start eating bladder campion, the young growth won't be so hard to spot; the blue-green of the smooth, rubbery leaves will stand out on the weedy road banks where before it might have hidden from you. It will stop looking like an anonymous weed, and take on the much more interesting and friendly hue of a vegetable.

Opposite A clump of bladder campion shoots, over a foot tall. The top 6 inches or so of these (two or three pairs of leaves) are nice and tender. You can also get them when they are much smaller.

Bramble Berries

(Blackberry, Dewberry, Red Raspberry, Black Raspberry, Thimbleberry, Wineberry, Salmonberry, Plumboy, Cloudberry)

Genus *Rubus*

ramble berries are the most popular wild foods on our continent. Along with blueberries and wild strawberries, these are the only wild berries one can collect and still be considered totally normal. In fact, in their desire to remain normal, normal people don't even consider these berries wild. When I am speaking to an audience of the general public—a crowd that does not consist of self-described foragers—I often begin with this question: "Who here has collected and eaten wild food?" Perhaps eight or twelve out of a hundred hands will go up. Then I ask a much more specific question, such as "Who here has collected and eaten wild blackberries?" Eighty more hands will shoot up. Impossible, but fascinating.

The normal-people berries all have a few things in common. They are native to Eurasia as well as North America, so using them is a nearly universal tradition

Cloudberry is a very good reason to walk in a spruce swamp.

in the Northern Hemisphere. They are abundant and easy to recognize. All were domesticated recently, so their cultivated forms are scarcely different from the wild plants. And because they were domesticated only recently, they could only be obtained from wild plants until a few generations ago. They all are eaten raw without any preparation, and have no large seeds that need to be removed. And perhaps most of all, they are incomparably delicious—good enough to make people overlook our most pervasive food prejudice.

DESCRIPTION

In this section, what I am calling brambles are members of the genus *Rubus*, which includes all of the blackberry and raspberry-like fruits that grow on canes or creeping stems. Brambles are so commonplace and familiar that it is easy to forget the physical uniqueness that defines them. This genus is enormous, containing well over a hundred species in North America. Every one of them produces an edible berry, nearly all of which are superbly flavored. This genus can be recognized by the form of its berry, technically an aggregate of drupes. Each berry is actually a cluster of several small, single-seeded fruits pressed together at their sides and borne on a fleshy receptacle. In some species, such as blackberries and dewberries, the fruitlets remain attached to the receptacle, which is picked as part of the berry. In other species, such as salmonberries, thimbleberries, and raspberries, the fruitlets detach from the receptacle but remain loosely bonded to each other, coming collectively off the plant as one thimble-shaped structure.

Most brambles have a compound leaf with 3 or 5 leaflets, occasionally more. A few have simple leaves that are palmately lobed. Most species are armed with some sort of prickle, spine, or thorn—but some are totally unarmed. Brambles are members of the rose family, all having 5 petals, numerous stamens, and numerous pistils attached to a receptacle. In most species the petals are white, but a few are rose to purple.

Our best known brambles have a growth pattern putting them somewhere between a shrub and an herb. They are perennials growing from a tough rhizome, with multiple stems. The individual stems live for two years. In the first year they grow quickly to their full height but do not flower, hardening and becoming semi-woody by autumn. In their second-year these stems grow short branches that bear flowers and fruit, after which they die. A plant normally has both one and two year old stems each summer. A few members of the genus differ from this pattern, however, in having no woody tissues above ground, or no woody tissues at all. Salmonberries, on the other hand, have fully woody canes that persist for several years.

For more specific descriptions, see the accounts below.

Blackberry (many species)

Blackberries are sun-loving brambles characteristic of disturbed areas in temperate forests. They
are absent from the far north and high elevations, but are abundant in most of the Eastern
Woodlands and Pacific Northwest. Blackberries
have palmately compound leaves, usually with
5–7 leaflets, each on its own stalk. This is an
incredibly diverse group, with dozens of species
separated by subtle characteristics. Blackberries have the most formidable prickles of all the

Composite range of blackberries,
dewberries, and bristleberries.

brambles, and grow on robust canes that may reach ten feet or more in length.
The berries are borne in loose panicles, in ideal cases with a couple dozen berries
each; each berry is at the end of its own long stem. The berry is usually longer
than wide, ripens to dark purple-black, and retains its receptacle inside when
picked. Since the flowering is almost simultaneous within the panicle, the berries ripen almost uniformly and are thus easy to pick in quantity.

One of our many excellent species of blackberry. Note the palmately compound leaves and long-
stemmed berries in racemes.

Blackberries in bloom.

Blackberries ripen in mid to late summer. It's pretty easy to average two gallons per hour in a good patch. Blackberry seeds are larger than those of our other brambles, and some people are adamant that they be removed, especially if the berries are being used in any cooked desert. You can do this with a simple fruit strainer or colander. When we get a bumper crop of blackberries, we strain them and then freeze the puree in quart jars, which we thaw out occasionally in the winter and drink as a sort of premade blackberry smoothie. I greatly prefer this over canned juice.

Dewberry and Bristleberry (many species)

Dewberries and bristleberries are much like blackberries, but rather than growing on erect or arching canes, they grow on creeping, runner-like stems or low, spreading, nearly prostrate canes. There are numerous species. Dewberries and bristleberries tend to be smaller than blackberries, less elongated, and produced more sparsely. A few species ripen to red rather than black. In flavor, these average at least as good as blackberries—and some species are outrageously delicious. Dewberries and bristleberries grow in many habitats where blackberries do not, such as swamps, bogs, pine barrens, and sandy prairies.

Ripe dewberries growing in pine barrens.

Red Raspberry

The red raspberry *R. idaeus* is the most prolific bramble in North America. It is a northern forest species whose range extends much further south in the mountains, both in the East and the West. Over many thousands of square miles red raspberry is ubiquitous in every clearcut, forest edge, or young woods. It thrives in well-drained, sandy, or rocky uplands as well as in wet ground in shrub swamps and along the margins of lakes, rivers, and swamps. To find a good patch, just walk any logging road in mid summer. Red raspberries thrive on or around the rotting remnants of old piles of woody material.

Red raspberry *Rubus idaeus*. In the southern parts of the range, occurrence is sporadic, mostly at high elevations or in cool ravines.

Having stiff hairs rather than the broad-based prickles of blackberries, red raspberry thickets are quite innocuous to clamber through. The leaves have three or more commonly five leaflets—in the latter case they are pinnately compound.

Ripe red raspberries. This is the most abundant and widespread species of *Rubus* in North America.

Leaflets are ovate and irregularly toothed, and occasionally lobed. The familiar berries, ripening to light red and easily falling from the receptacle when ripe, are more labor-intensive to collect than blackberries or black caps, but their incredible flavor makes them well worth it. Because they flower and ripen over a long period, the crop is more consistent than that of many other wild fruits.

Black Raspberry (Black Cap)

There are two nearly identical species that go by these names: *R. occidentalis* of the East and *R. leucodermis* of the West. Black raspberry has broad-based, stout prickles like those of blackberry, but they are not as large and dangerous. The canes characteristically arch over and root at the tips where they touch the ground, forming a hoop perfectly designed to trip a berry picker and spill her bucket. The leaves are compound with three leaflets, which are silvery-white on the underside. The stem is generally smooth between the prickles, with a purplish color and a heavy coating of bloom. The berries are borne in tight clusters and ripen in early summer, a month or more before blackberries. They turn dark purple-black at maturity, easily fall off their receptacle, and are usually coated with a heavy bloom.

The ranges of the very similar eastern (*R. occidentalis*) and western (*R. leucodermis*) black raspberries do not overlap.

Over the heavily populated eastern United States, this is the most popular wild berry. Millions of people head to parks, backyards, fencelines, and rural roadsides every June or July to fill pails with this beloved fruit. Black caps are mild in flavor, less tart than a blackberry, and less sour than a red raspberry—and in many people's estimation, have a perfect balance of flavor.

Black caps *R. occidentalis* in fruit. This is probably our most commonly collected bramble fruit.

Above top A typical colony of black raspberry, the drooping, vine-like tips with leaves of descending size are evident. **Above bottom** The surface of black raspberries is densely coated in white bloom.

Thimbleberry

Thimbleberry *Rubus parviflorus* has no armor, and its leaves are not compound—they are palmate, like a big fuzzy maple leaf, and aromatic. Thimbleberry likes cool summers, such as one finds in the Pacific Northwest, in the Rockies, and around the northern Great Lakes. (A very similar relative, the purple-flowered raspberry *R. odoratus*, is found in much of the East.) Thimbleberry thrives in sparse woodlands and at forest edges, and almost always grows where the ground is sloped—especially a small but steep slope, such as a road bank. The berry is broad and shallow, composed of very small fruitlets, and

Thimbleberry *Rubus parviflora* = blue. Purple-flowered raspberry *R. odoratus* = red. (There is a small area of range overlap in Michigan and Ontario.)

is easily pulled off the receptacle. It ripens to red in late summer. Although the berries are larger than most other brambles, they are produced rather sparsely and are thus hard to get in quantity.

There seems to be two highly diverging schools of opinion about thimbleberry. One says that the fruit is dry, seedy, and insipid. The other regards thimbleberry as having the strongest and most delicious flavor of any berry whatsoever. I'm in this latter camp.

Thimbleberries are called "salmonberries" in some regions, especially in the southern Rockies, where *R. deliciosus* is found—because that species is also called thimbleberry. If you've been confused by this, you aren't the first.

Above right Purple-flowered raspberry looks amost exactly like thimbleberry, except for the flower color. **Below** Thimbleberry *R. parviflorus* in fruit—see how just one ripens at a time.

Wineberry

Wineberry *R. phoenicolasius* is an introduced bramble that has become very common over much of the East, especially the mid-Atlantic states, where it is a popular berry. The fruit ripens in mid summer, peaking after the black caps but before the blackberries. Ripe berries are bright orange-red and covered with erect, sticky hairs, as are the twigs and petioles. Wineberries detach

Wineberry *Rubus phoenicolasius*

from the receptacle when ripe. The canes are large and have a long, even arch that often brings their tips back to the ground. The stems are covered with prickles that are more formidable than those of red raspberry, but not as fearsome as those of blackberry. The leaves have three leaflets, much like those of red raspberry.

Wineberries, a bit under-ripe because someone got there before we did.

Salmonberry

Salmonberry *R. spectabilis* is a true woody perennial, having foregone the two-year life cycle of other brambles. It stands erect and may reach fifteen or more feet in height. The leaves have three leaflets, ovate and double-toothed, the side leaflets usually with small lobes. The flowers are reddish. This shrub is confined to the coastal rain forests of the Pacific Northwest, where it is often a dominant component of the understory, especially at forest edges.

Salmonberries separate from the receptacle, and are larger than any of our other thimble-like bramble fruits, which makes them fun to collect (although they are typically scattered about and not easy to get by the gallon). The berries

Left Ripe fruit of salmonberry *R. spectabilis*. **Right** Most brambles have white flowers, but not salmonberry *R. spectabilis*. (Photos by T. Abe Lloyd)

ripen to yellowish, orange, or red in early summer. The flavor is very mild compared to any other North American bramble. While I think they make a good snack fresh from the bush, the flavor is so weak that they make a poor option for jam, jelly, juice, pie, or cobbler—unless mixed with another, more strongly flavored berry.

Salmonberry *Rubus spectabilis*

Plumboy and Nagoonberry

Plumboy and nagoonberry are two very similar species that are unarmed, herbaceous, and form colonies by runners. The runners root at the nodes and then form small plants that flower and fruit the following year. Each plant only produces a few flowers or berries. These species are regarded very highly by most who know them—they have a unique, candy-like flavor that is hard to describe, but it gives me a sensation deep in my sinus when I eat them.

The dwarf raspberry or plumboy *R. pubescens*. Candy in the aspens.

The arctic raspberry or nagoonberry—a delicacy of the Far North.

Nagoonberry (*R. acaulis* or *R. arcticus*), also called arctic raspberry or arctic plumboy, is primarily a species of bogs and tundra, and it is more famous, probably because it tends to fruit more heavily in its open habitat than the plumboy *R. pubescens* of boreal forests. At the southern end of their range, these berries ripen in early summer; but in the Far North, like almost everything else, they ripen in August or September.

Range of plumboy or dwarf raspberry *Rubus pubescens* and arctic raspberry or nagoonberry *Rubus arcticus/acaulis*. The light blue area to the south has *R. pubescens* only; the extreme north has *R. acaulis* only, but in most areas the ranges overlap, and the species frequently hybridize.

Bakeapple (Cloudberry)

Bakeapple or cloudberry, *R. chamaemorus*, is another herbaceous, unarmed northern species, famous in the area where it grows. It is a plant of open bogs and tundra, rising less than a foot high, with a palmately lobed and deeply ruffled or cupped leaf. Each plant usually produces a single flower per year, and thus

Bakeapple or cloudberry *R. chamaemorus* with ripe fruit.

a single berry at most. The fruitlets are larger than any others in the genus, but there are relatively few of them—only 3–14 per berry. Also unusual, the fruit lightens rather than darkens as it gets ripe—they are orange-red at first, but turn yellowish as they soften.

The cloudberry is a unique tasting bramble berry; some people love it, while others find it a bit odd. I think it is delicious. It reminds me of a bletted cranberry—one that has stayed on the vine all winter, frozen and softened but not spoiled. (Another similar tasting fruit is the Pacific crabapple *Malus fusca* after it has softened in late autumn.) The name "bakeapple" is a corruption of the French *baie qu'appelle*, which means "whatcha-callit berry." In Alaska these are sometimes also called salmonberries.

Cloudberry or bakeapple *Rubus chamaemorus*.

Goldenseal fruit. **Not edible**. This is about the only inedible thing I can imagine being confused with a bramble fruit, and it's a stretch.

STORING AND USING BRAMBLE BERRIES

The best thing to do with brambles is gorge while you're out picking, in constant awe that something so delicious could possibly exist. Only with that accomplished do I consider making stuff out of them. Most kinds are great for jam: Red raspberry, black raspberry, and thimbleberry are some of my favorites. If you've never made jam before, these are great fruits to start with. Brambles make great pie—for this I think black raspberry is the best, but all sorts are good.

If you want to try a unique, delicious, and not-super-sweet dessert from bramble berries that your mom doesn't know about, try a fruit gel thickened with acorn starch. (You can make your own acorn starch, or buy it at most Asian grocers, imported from Korea). First, take three cups of mashed berries and sweeten to taste (I use a half cup of maple syrup). Heat this mixture, whisk in ¾ cup of acorn starch, and stir vigorously until it reaches a rolling boil, then pour it into a casserole pan. Let it cool for an hour or so, then place it in the fridge. When it sets up fully, cut it into bars and serve: super-simple, quick, totally wild, totally awesome, arguably healthy, *even vegan* Jell-O-like stuff. You will make it a second time.

I love to make fruit leather, but none of the brambles are good for this by themselves, as they do not have sufficient fiber in their juicy pulp. If you dry them you get a sticky, gooey film with scattered seedy chunks. However, if you have some apple puree sitting in the pantry, you can mix it with any bramble berry about half and half, and it will add enough body to make a good fruit leather. All of the brambles store well frozen, tasting almost as good when thawed as they were the moment you picked them. When we're camping during berry season and don't have access to a freezer for a few days, we sometimes can blackberries or black caps in a water bath canner over the campfire. It is important to act quickly after picking these berries, for they spoil with remarkable haste—sometimes being ruined by the morning after picking.

It seems almost impossible that anyone needs my help deciding how to use bramble berries, so replete is our literature and media with recipes for them. So I'm going to stop right here and let you explore the endless culinary possibilities of *Rubus* berries on your own.

Tea and Shoots: A tea is traditionally made from the young leaves of raspberries and blackberries. This mildly astringent drink is generally taken as a medicinal, most often as an

Raspberry gel, thickened with acorn starch. A delicious, all-wild dessert that kids love.

Above top Peeled salmonberry shoot. Bramble shoots are one of my favorite late spring snacks—especially salmonberries and black and red raspberries. **Above left** Red raspberry shoots, a bit too old to peel easily. This is a good age to gather the leaves for tea. Note that at their base, *Rubus pubescens* is about to bloom. **Above right** Thimbleberry shoot, half limp and still tender. I peeled this one and loved it.

astringent for diarrhea, but some people like it well enough to drink it purely for pleasure. You can find this tea for sale in many health-food stores. Like many teas, it is often bruised and allowed to ferment before drying, but you can use it fresh.

A less well-known product of bramble berries is the peeled shoots. These can be gathered from any of the species with larger canes, most notably black raspberry, salmonberry, red raspberry, and thimbleberry—and I prefer them in that order. (The shoots of blackberry are rather astringent and hard to peel, but I do nibble them occasionally as well.) You must get the shoot when it is tender and bends easily (the tough skin will usually prevent it from snapping off, though). The flesh inside should be greenish throughout—if it has developed any white or pith in the center, it is too far gone. After breaking the shoots, I grab the bark from the base and peel it off in strips before eating the tender center. The flavor is sweet and mild, reminding me a little of sumac shoots. I have always eaten these raw.

I have spent much of my life with scratched-up thighs. That's a small price to pay for the best berries on Earth.

Black caps. Solstice ambrosia.

Calamus (Sweet Flag)

Acorus americanus, A. calamus

One summer day when I was a young boy, I crashed through some thick flags along a lakeshore in pursuit of a frog, and an unforgettable scent broke into the humid summer air. I was mesmerized, stupefied, as I leaned into the tall leaves to inhale their luscious fragrance. Calamus has been captivating humans with olfactory delight, just like this, from time immemorial. It is among the most popular aromatic herbs of the temperate world, probably exceeded in this respect only by mint. Calamus is mentioned multiple times in the Old Testament, indicating that even then it was an herb of commerce. It was among the plants found in Tutankhamen's tomb (Bown 1988). Today, calamus is found across the Northern Hemisphere, but this was not always so. It is native to North America and eastern Asia, but was brought to Russia by the Tartars at least as early as the 13th century (Buell 1935), and was being cultivated in Austria by the 16th century (Grieve 1971). It quickly became so popular in Europe that it was introduced into every country and was widely adopted into local traditions. The rhizomes and leaves found a dazzling variety of applications. Besides the two most common names listed at the chapter head, this plant has earned a

A colony of American calamus in a shallow river edge, early summer.

huge array of names just in the English language: sweet rush, sweet cane, myrtle sedge, pine root, gladdon, and calomel are just a few of them. An entire book of this size could be written on the traditional uses of calamus.

Overshadowed by this plant's rich history as an aromatic and medicinal herb is the fact that it is also a first-rate food plant, producing two completely different delectable vegetables. We'll get to that.

DESCRIPTION

Calamus is a flag—an underused term referring to wetland plants with long, flat, sword-like basal leaves. Other flags include cattail, iris, and bur reed. Scent alone is sufficient to distinguish sweet flag from any of these. However, the plant is also easy to learn by sight.

Sweet flag is a perennial spreading by rhizome, but it rarely fills entire marshes as cattails and bulrushes tend to do. More commonly, calamus forms a narrow band along the shoreline, or grows in erratic clumps interspersed with other flags. Every few inches the branching rhizome produces a distinctive cluster of erect leaves. The clusters are flattened, with sharp edges, and each leaf, rather than being folded, has a slot in one margin, into which an adjacent leaf fits. Only irises have leaves with similarly split margins and bundles constructed this way, but iris leaves are proportionately broader, less erect, and lack a central ridge. The interior of iris leaf clusters is whitish to yellow at the base, while this part of calamus has pink or purple highlights. Sweet flag leaves are somewhat shorter and narrower than cattails, rarely more than 4½ feet (1.5 m) tall or an inch (2.5 cm) wide, and they have a yellowish-green hue. The leaf margins are

American calamus around a pond. Rather than forming large marshes, calamus is normally a narrow band around a water body, as seen here; at full height it is shorter than the reed canary grass and sedges behind it.

flat and sharp, with the middle being slightly inflated and spongy, with a ridge running the entire length.

Among the more robust leaf clusters there is usually a flowering stem, which, if present, is utterly distinctive. This is actually a leaf and stem grown together as one, and the top is exactly like a typical leaf. But the lower portion has one side narrow and sharp (like a leaf) while the other side is thicker, with two sharp edges and a U-shaped channel between them. At the top of this channel is a densely packed phallic spike 2–4 inches (5–10 cm) long, held in an ascending to vertical position. The flowers and buds borne on this spike are exceedingly small; the plant is so distinct that there is no need to examine their minutiae for identifying purposes.

The rhizome of calamus is stout but erratically constricted, varying from 0.5–1.1 inches (13–28 mm) across. It runs horizontally and branches occasionally, bearing numerous leaf scars. The surface of the rhizome is pink to purple on new growth, usually becoming white on the older parts. (This rhizome, in common parlance, is most often called the root.) The rhizome bears numerous small fibrous roots on the lower half, all along its length, and all of these roots are oriented downward.

Taxonomists have been troubled by calamus—it was formerly classed with the arums, but is now placed in its own family. Interestingly, it is now believed to be the oldest living member of the monocot lineage (Duvall et al. 1993).

HABITAT

The habitat of sweet flag is generally listed as marshes, wetlands, or lakeshores, but its habitat preferences are much more specific than that. It likes drainage water, and is found less frequently in springwater. It is found primarily in river systems, where it seems to benefit from the fluctuating water level. Less commonly, it is found in isolated wetlands without flowing water. Being shorter than cattails, bulrushes, and wild rice, it is unable to compete with them, so it is rarely found where the muck or silt is deep and rich. Sweet flag is most characteristic of shores and marshes with a thin layer of muck over a bed of mineral soil such as sand, gravel, or clay. The two best locations to find it are manmade flowages and reservoirs in regions of poor soil (in these young bodies of water the muck has

Native range of *Acorus americanus* is blue. The area inhabited exclusively by introduced *A. calamus* is red. (*A. calamus* has also been introduced in parts of the mapped range of *A. americanus,* especially in the more heavily populated eastern half. There are scattered introduced populations outside the mapped range.)

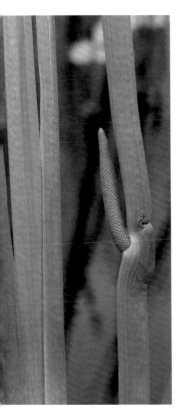

Above left American calamus showing the distinctive stem and spike. This spike is small and immature, but still unmistakable. Above right American calamus shoots in spring, at the ideal time to get the tender interior. Below American calamus rhizome and attached leaf clusters, freshly pulled from the sand in late spring.

had relatively little time to accumulate), and near the mouths where rivers and streams enter larger water bodies. It can be abundant in brackish estuaries. Small, shallow bays along rivers and streams are also good places to look, as here the muck gets periodically washed away. It is usually found where rivers or streams enter the Great Lakes. Isolated populations are found erratically on wet ground all around North America, largely due to people propagating the plant for their own use.

The range of native calamus corresponds largely to glaciated regions with poor soil. The numerous young lakes of the Canadian Shield are much to its liking, and it is common in the Great Lakes region. Introduced populations have been established well outside the native range, and their occurrence sometimes defies these habitat expectations.

HARVEST AND PREPARATION

The **rhizome** of this plant is by far its best known and most sought-after part. Calamus has been among the world's most widely used and highly esteemed articles of herbal medicine—rivaled by ginseng in legend, but not in application. Like ginseng, it was widely considered an aphrodisiac, but its uses extended well beyond the relational problems of old guys. The Tartars used it to make drinking water safe. It was widely used as an antiseptic, an antifungal, and an insecticide (particularly against lice and fleas), and to kill intestinal worms. It has been used to induce abortion, to aid in milk flow after childbirth, to reduce menstrual pain, and as a contraceptive. I have not had a chance to try all of these things. One of the most widely reported uses is to relieve flatulence. I should try some of these things. It is esteemed in its power to soothe the upset tummy. Also, as a laxative. Some use it as a pain reliever. Or for heartburn. Toothache. Calamus root was widely used to treat cholera. It has been employed by those tending the ill to prevent the transfer of contagious disease. (For an overview of medicinal and cosmetic uses for calamus root, see Motley 1994.)

Native Americans have long held sweet flag in high regard, taking it for specific ailments and also using it as a general tonic. A piece of rhizome is chewed to allay fatigue in many cultures. Strath (1903) reported that in 1892, among the Cree north of Winnipeg, "large bundles of this plant can be seen hanging in every tepee or wigwam, tent or house." He related that hunters and travelers carried a piece of calamus root so that "when feeling exhausted by hunger and fatigue, a small piece slowly chewed will restore the flagging energies in a most wonderful manner." Even today the dried rhizomes are an item of trade and commerce among Native Americans. For a few years I collected a supply of the rhizomes for a Lakota elder and healer. These were administered, in combination with other plants (the identity of which I was never told), to diabetics.

Most names for this plant in Native American languages associate it with muskrats, apparently in reference to that animal's fondness for eating it. Both Anishinaabe and Lakota whom I know call it "muskrat root" in English. The Anishinaabe word, variously spelled, is *wikay*; it is also commonly used by whites in the Great Lakes Region. Those who first try the stuff are often floored by the intensity of flavor packed into a little piece of calamus rhizome—it is every bit as potent as ginger or horseradish, but not suggestive of either.

I keep only a few medicinal herbs on hand, and calamus root is one of them. I find it very soothing to a sore throat or to relieve cold symptoms; it is effective at clearing phlegm. I keep a piece in my car, to chew before public speaking, as it helps me keep a clear voice. I have met professional singers who do the same, and the rhizome is still distributed at powwows among singers as a voice tonic. Calamus candy was traditionally made from sections of peeled rhizome boiled in a sugar syrup, then dried. Although these candies may be a pleasant nibble, I think of them more like strong mints or cough drops. The syrup left over from boiling the rhizomes can be used as a flavoring; some people like it in alcoholic drinks.

I don't imagine that sweet flag root does all the things for which it has been given credit, but it must do some of them. Fortunately, this herb has been studied far more than most wild medicinals. Research has shown that it acts as an antispasmodic on intestinal muscles (at least on rabbits and guinea pigs), and is effective against many common bacteria and fungi, as well as the amoeba *Paramecium caudatum*, and several insects, including lice and bedbugs. It kills the prevalent parasitic nematode *Ascaris lumbricoides*, which always curries favor with me. These findings confirm that many of the traditional medicinal uses of the plant were well-founded. (Again, for an overview of this research, see Motley 1994).

There is another issue that some of you may be wondering about: the claim, sometimes encountered, that calamus root in massive doses is hallucinogenic. I can find nothing to substantiate this claim. Herbalist Jim McDonald, who has great respect for this plant (and whose website, herbcraft.org, contains a fantastic article about its medicinal characteristics), tells me that this is a gross exaggeration. This is one hypothesis I have no interest in testing.

Perhaps that diversion was too long-winded for a book on edible wild plants, but I thought you might want to know. The rhizome is primarily medicinal, and secondarily a flavoring; it is not a food. But calamus is also an excellent food plant, obscure and underused by foragers.

The **base of the leaves and stem** in the center of the leaf cluster, early in the growing season, are homologous to the "heart" or shoot base eaten on cattails at the same time of year. Follow the calamus leaf cluster down to the rhizome with your hand, then pinch or break it off. Remove the leaves on the outside

Above top This is the good part inside one of those young calamus leaf clusters from page 76. Note the purplish tint near the base. The flavor of the green inner leaf is much milder than the SLOTSM at the base. **Above bottom** Young leaf cluster of iris. Purple tint is absent, as is a middle ridge. Note also the white roots and broader leaves.

of the cluster until you have exposed the tender interior, which will be white and pink rather than green. This part of sweet flag has just a slim touch of the rhizome's spicy flavor. I like to nibble these hearts raw, all by themselves, right after I pluck them from the frigid water. Sliced and tossed into a salad, they add a delectable and indescribable flavor that seamlessly melds the concepts of *wild*, *exotic*, and *gourmet*. They can also be used in cooked dishes, as long as you are careful not to mix discordant flavors.

As one gets close to the bottom, the leaf bases taste more like the rhizomes. If this part is too strong for your liking, cut off the lowest inch or two and leave it out of your salad. You can learn to collect the sweet flag hearts by pinching or cutting a tad higher than the rhizome, leaving the strongest-flavored part behind—and if you do it right, you can even leave the outermost leaves growing in place, thus doing less damage to the plant.

The green parts of calamus have a flavor quite different from the rhizomes— they exude the sweet essence mentioned earlier, for which the plant is named. But unfortunately, the **leaves** are too tough to eat—green parts of the blade are never tender. You can chew one up and suck out some of the marvelous flavor, and then spit out the cud. I readily admit to doing this several times every summer. But I finally discovered a way to use that flavor in a manner acceptable to the civilized majority. Profoundly acceptable, in fact. Take some fresh, clean calamus leaves (from above the high-water level), chop them into short sections, and put them in a blender with cold water. Blend thoroughly, then strain the liquid through a cheesecloth or jelly bag. It should come out bright yellow-green and frothy. Now, that calamus-flavored water will be nothing special by itself. Scarcely worth drinking, in fact. But if you want the most delicious and memorable lemonade to ever pass your lips, stir some lemon juice and sugar into it.

I did save the best for last. There is one green part tender enough to actually eat: the immature **flower spike**. You need to get them while the flowers are still in the bud stage; if they are blooming or fruiting, they are too old and tough. Look for spikes that are obviously less than full size. If they are approaching bloom, you can test them by pressing hard with a finger; if whitish contents squirt out of the flower buds, they are still tender. The ideal spikes will be firm but not fibrous, and a little slimy. And a warning to the Chicken Feathers Guy: Spikes with mature fruit become very tough, and their flavor morphs into that of the rhizome.

Immature calamus spikes are one of the most unique vegetables in the world. There is literally nothing that you have ever eaten that is even remotely similar. There will never be a more appropriate moment to utter that favorite French culinary phrase, *je ne sais quoi*. For a true foodie, this experience alone will be worth the price of this book.

A handful of immature calamus spikes at exactly the stage where I like to eat them. Two of them are actually releasing pollen, but early in bloom like this they are still tender.

Calamus spikes are fun to nibble raw, and are good in salad. The sweet aroma dies down considerably upon cooking, making it rather easy to combine it with other vegetables without overpowering them. We like it in chicken soup or venison stew, where its mild sweetness fits right in with traditional herbs such as thyme, basil, and savory. It is also great in a Chinese-style vegetable stir-fry.

THE OLD, THE NEW, AND THE FORBIDDEN CALAMUS

There are two forms of Calamus found in North America, one native and one introduced. Most sources list them as a single species, both forms being encompassed by the name *Acorus calamus*, although it has long been recognized that the populations native to North America have some differences from the Old-World plants. Native North American calamus is a diploid, meaning it has two times the basal chromosome number—in this case, 24 chromosomes. The introduced plants are triploid, having 36 chromosomes. (Some Asian populations are tetraploid, having 48). Some botanists use *A. calamus* to cover the various populations with differing chromosome counts, but most recent North American floras recognize our native stock as a separate species, *Acorus americanus*, per Thompson (1995). Unfortunately, most floras inadequately explain how to tell them apart, because the botany world is just beginning to pay attention to the difference.

A colony of Old-World calamus in a roadside ditch in southern Missouri, south of the native range. This is not typical habitat for native populations. Note the somewhat broader leaves and more robust aspect.

Here's how to differentiate them at any time: The native diploid *A. americanus* has the leaf gradually thickening toward the center, which has a gentle ridge running its length. The introduced (triploid) *A. calamus* has the leaf abruptly thickening into a sharp, keel-like ridge in the center. The leaves of introduced calamus often have wavy edges, while those of native calamus do not. The native sweet flag averages a bit smaller than the imported plant in all respects. Although the leaf cross section has been poorly described in many sources (those descriptions refer to dried leaves in the herbarium) it's easy to tell in the field. Just check out the photos.

Why am I boring you with these technical details? Well, back in 1960, the US Food and Drug Administration decided that calamus was unsafe, due to the presence of a carcinogen known as beta-asarone, and prohibited its use in food or medicine (21 CFR Sect. 180). (This was back when trans fats were good for us, butter and lard were serious health hazards, and heart attacks were caused by eating red meat.) I find it highly dubious that the beta-asarone in this herb, consumed in the normal dosages that were meted out to millions of

Below top Cross section of a native North American calamus leaf *A. americanus*. Note the gradual taper to a gentle ridge. You can see a few of the more prominent veins as whitish spots. **Below bottom** Cross section of an introduced Old-World calamus leaf *A. calamus*. Note the rippling on the long side, and much more sudden and sharper ridge. Photo by Todd Elliott.

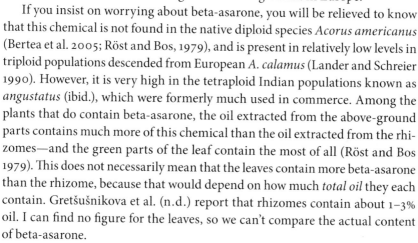

Above Close up of the surface of American calamus leaves. The central ridge is not prominent on either side, but you can see 2–3 slightly darker veins on each side of the ridge. **Right** Close up of the surface of a European calamus leaf. See how the central ridge is much more prominent. Photo by Todd Elliott.

people over thousands of years among hundreds of cultures on two continents, is dangerous. About half of all chemicals tested are found carcinogenic (Ames and Gold 2000). Does a piece of calamus root pose more risk than an acetaminophen tablet or french fries? I don't know, but it's still legal as a food ingredient in Europe.

If you insist on worrying about beta-asarone, you will be relieved to know that this chemical is not found in the native diploid species *Acorus americanus* (Bertea et al. 2005; Röst and Bos, 1979), and is present in relatively low levels in triploid populations descended from European *A. calamus* (Lander and Schreier 1990). However, it is very high in the tetraploid Indian populations known as *angustatus* (ibid.), which were formerly much used in commerce. Among the plants that do contain beta-asarone, the oil extracted from the above-ground parts contains much more of this chemical than the oil extracted from the rhizomes—and the green parts of the leaf contain the most of all (Röst and Bos 1979). This does not necessarily mean that the leaves contain more beta-asarone than the rhizome, because that would depend on how much *total oil* they each contain. Gretšušnikova et al. (n.d.) report that rhizomes contain about 1–3% oil. I can find no figure for the leaves, so we can't compare the actual content of beta-asarone.

Sweet flag sums up all the best reasons to forage. It is a gift to the world, a plant of a thousand uses, an awe-rendering reminder of the simple miracle of life that surrounds us. And shrugged off, forbidden, almost forgotten by the modern world, as if the only potent chemical force allowed is that made in a factory. Known for millennia, cherished by many, held sacred with good reason: a friend to all people. And now, you get to go out to the boat landing, sniff it, and bring some home.

Caraway

Carum carvi

his is not a chapter about flavoring rye bread. We have forgotten caraway—
even most devout gardeners and produce-savvy chefs could tell you nothing
about the plant that produces those aromatic schizocarps. But Paris is more
than the Eiffel Tower, deer are more than antlers, and caraway is more than
those brown seeds in a pumpernickel chunk. A cultural culinary amnesia has
robbed us of this herb's sweet root, tender stem, and delicately flavored leaf.
These things have been eaten for ages, but are not easy to package, store, and
ship—so in this age, when food is either a commodity or nothing, the best parts
of caraway have become the forgotten parts. But caraway is not just a spice: It's
two vegetables and a seasoning with a spice on top, and it deserves respect for
all of its body parts.

Few people consider caraway a root vegetable, but look at that. Note the ribbon-like petiole bases.

DESCRIPTION

Caraway has a rosette of 6–13 basal leaves. These are lacy and divided two or three times; all of the lobes or divisions are long and narrow. The leaf is 6–18 inches (15–45 cm) long, and narrow in outline. It has a fluffy appearance because the divisions are not in plane with each other. The leaf undersides are tinted silver-gray. The petioles are solid, V-channeled, and light green; at ground level they become broad, flat, and whitish. In competition with other plants, the leaves stand erect, but in the open they lie flat. Basal leaves mostly wither by fruiting.

Stem leaves are alternate, similar in form to the basal leaves but smaller. Petioles of stem leaves are thin and ribbon-like at the base and very light in color, with prominent ridged veins; they soon taper to a typical channeled petiole. In all caraway leaves the divisions begin subdividing immediately where they attach the rachis—this feature helps separate them from many similar members of the carrot family.

Flowering plants grow a zigzag, branching stalk 12–32 inches (30–80 cm) tall. The stems are smooth and solid (sometimes with a pinhole hollow in the upper parts), light green and glaucous, finely ridged and striped with darker green. A cross section of the shoot shows 3 color zones: light in the center, darker green around that, and the outer layer again light green. At maturity, the branches bear numerous compound umbels at their tips, 2–2.8 inches (5–7 cm) wide, composed of many tiny, 5-petaled white flowers. The umbels have a whorl of linear bracts beneath them, which are often hidden by being pressed against the rays. These knee-high flowering plants can best be spotted when flowering, which occurs in late spring or early summer in the northern United States, but in mid to late summer in much of Canada or at high elevations. The flowers develop into the familiar fruits, about an eighth inch (3 mm) long, curved, brown, with lengthwise ridges, and splitting in two. All parts of the plant are hairless.

Mature caraway plant, about knee-high. Note the branchy, nearly leafless top that spreads almost as wide as tall.

Close up of caraway leaf. Note how the divisions are out of plane with the rachis and each other, and the central rachis is very dominant (much larger than any division). Also, see how the divisions begin subdividing immediately where they attach to the rachis.

There are some other plants that might be confused with caraway, most of which are edible. It can be told from yarrow and wild carrot—two common weeds with pinnately divided leaves that sometimes share its habitat—by its complete lack of hairs. There are three genera in the carrot family, each with multiple species (most of which are known to be edible), that have multi-compound leaves like caraway: *Lomatium*, *Perideridia*, and *Anthriscus*. All of these have leaves that are broader in outline than those of caraway with rachises that divide into major divisions. Caraway leaves have a dominant central rachis with strictly pinnate first divisions; their leaf rachises never branch or divide into major or equal parts.

Poison hemlock *Conium maculatum* is a much larger plant with a very loose resemblance to caraway. It overlaps caraway in habitat, but rarely in range. Poison hemlock's stems are hollow, purple-spotted, and densely coated with white powder. Its leaves are triangular in outline and much larger than those of caraway. Its rachises have major divisions, the leaves are three to four times compound, and the ultimate leaf divisions are not linear. Poison hemlock's petioles are hollow, stiff, and rounded or roughly triangular in cross section.

A less common introduced and poisonous plant is fool's parsley *Aethusa cynapium*. This species has shiny leaves with rachises that divide into three major parts and are broadly triangular in outline.

HABITAT

Caraway is not native to North America, but it has long been here as a weed, originally spread by homestead gardeners in the days when it was more convenient to grow an herb than to buy it. Caraway prefers cool summers and full sun; it is most often seen in poor, moist soil—from those heavy with clay to those composed mostly of gravel and stone. Where the growing season is very short, even well-drained soils have little time to dry out, and it is in precisely this

Caraway *Carum carvi* is most common in the northern half of this range, and in the Rocky Mountains.

situation that caraway does best. While it is occasionally found on level ground or moist depressions, caraway is more typical of slopes—perhaps only because the erosion tends to create good germination sites.

Most commonly, caraway is seen as a weed of hayfields, lightly used pastures, ditches, and roadsides. It may also be found in abandoned farmland, meadows, vacant lots, and backyards. In some regions, caraway is ubiquitous. It is among the most common weeds over much of Newfoundland and the Maritime Provinces of Canada. Great patches of it can be seen on the north shore of Lake Superior along Highway 61 in Minnesota. It decorates many hay meadows of the northern Plains and New England, and thrives in the vicinity of some old mining towns of the Rockies.

HARVEST AND PREPARATION

Caraway is a biennial; the rosette stores energy in a thick taproot for one or two growing seasons before blooming. This taproot is nearly white and resembles a wild carrot or parsnip in both appearance and texture. Caraway roots are widest near the top and taper quickly; the side roots tend to be minor. They average somewhat larger than wild carrots. The flavor is sweet and aromatic with a lightly bitter aftertaste; although clearly different from carrot and parsnip, they let you know they are related.

Caraway roots are harvested in fall or spring—not winter, because the lands where caraway grows have a long period of snow and frozen soil. They are good in soups, casseroles, or in other ways you'd employ parsnips. If you get a bunch they can be easily stored in a root cellar or wrapped up in the refrigerator.

Left Caraway umbel in fruit. The schizocarps are mature, but not yet dry. **Right** Blooming caraway umbel. Notice how each petal has a sharp tip that is folded in toward the center, making the petal look almost heart-shaped. This feature is not exclusive to caraway, but it helps narrow down the field.

(I discovered by accident, when I left a cleaned root on my dashboard, that I enjoy them dried as well.)

Since caraway is a non-native weed, there is no need to worry about the ecological consequences of overharvesting it. But experience might show you a forager's secret: As with most biennials, harvesting a portion of the roots in a colony helps maintain the population. The soil loosened by the excavation of the root becomes a perfect germination site for new caraway plants, so long as there remains a seed source. And that clod of dirt that tumbles off your shovel blade into the grass nearby: it, too, will weather into a fine germination site. In the absence of disturbance, caraway will lose ground to perennial plants.

In spring, the energy from the root will be used to produce a tuft of basal leaves and a flowering stalk. The tender spring leaves can be chopped and used as an herb as one would use parsley: sprinkled

Caraway shoots in spring, the stems very tender and about 6" tall. This is the ideal time to get them. All of the attached upper leaves are also tender. Note the broad, light-colored, ribbon-like petiole bases; this unusual feature is most prominent on the lower leaves of the bolting stem of second-year plants. They taper into a petiole that is merely channeled.

Caraway seeds; the schizocarps have dried and schizzed. Some people think there's nothing else to a caraway plant.

into casseroles, salads, soups, or mashed potatoes, or mixed with boiled and buttered root vegetables. The flavor of these greens is not strong like caraway seed; it has only a mild hint of that taste.

My favorite part of caraway to eat is the young stalk when it is 5–10 inches (12–25 cm) tall. These stalks are generally 0.2–0.4 inch (5–10 mm) thick. They are tender and sweet, with the same flavor as the greens, only milder. These make a good snack raw, and they can also be sliced thin into salads. Tender stems are excellent sautéed, and chopped into sections they make a nice soup vegetable. Of course, the stems have leafy greens attached, and they can all be used together in most dishes. As the plants mature and approach flowering, they become fibrous, but the leaves can still be used as a seasoning if they are finely chopped.

I learned from Stephen Barstow's fantastic book *Around the World in 80 Plants* that fresh wild caraway greens of spring have long been used in Norway to make a traditional soup called *karvekaalsuppe*. A heap of finely chopped spring caraway greens is wilted in butter, then cooked in beef or fish stock, thickened with a little flour and boiled for about 20 minutes. After reading this I visited my cherished local caraway patch and made a pot for my family. Not only was it an elegantly simple recipe, but it was avidly slurped down by everyone.

Finally, we get to the top of the caraway plant, to the end of its life, to those seeds—or technically, schizocarps—that mature (and break into mericarps) upon its death. These are quite easy and fun to harvest, stripping them by hand. In fact, I'm pretty comfortable guaranteeing that, if you find the plant, even with this fair warning, you will go overboard and collect far more than you have any use for. The seeds can be readily dried in any open container at room temperature; spread them in a thin layer and stir occasionally for a week or so. Wild caraway seeds can be used just like the cultivated ones. They are most commonly used to season rye bread, sauerkraut, and certain cheeses and alcoholic drinks. Some people subsist happily on a diet just like that—but aren't you glad there's more to this lacy weed than the seed?

Chickweed, Stitchwort

Genus *Stellaria*

"It tastes like corn silk," I say.

Some people besides me have actually eaten corn silk, and so murmur their agreement as their eager teeth press green juice from the delicate leaves between them. Other people, whose mouths have no memory of corn silk, take our word for it—although they might inquire just what, exactly, corn silk is. And here is what I tell them, as I hand them a generous fistful of prime chickweed: "It's the soft, golden, stringy stuff under the husks of corn, and it tastes like *this*—it's only good before the corn is ripe."

Some people didn't grow up like me, nutritionally deficient, sneaking across the road like a raccoon to vandalize immature ears of field corn in mid summer, running down the narrow rows with rough corn leaves slapping my face and the thick scent of pollen in my nose, fleeing a phantom farmer (who in reality would probably be glad to feed me a real dinner), until finally stopping for the naughty deed, peeling back the squeaking husks to get at the soft silk pressed underneath, and maybe even the sweet unripe kernels.

A lush clump of common chickweed at the perfect stage for eating.

I don't really pity the people who missed out on all this. After all, the corn-silk substitute that I recommend actually tastes better than the real thing. It is immensely more nutritious, is not genetically modified, comes with less exercise and no guilty conscience, and in the right places is even free of herbicides and insecticides. And it doesn't feel like someone's hair in your mouth.

Chickweed: It's like corn silk, but better.

DESCRIPTION

Chickweeds are small, limp herbs with uniformly thin stems, often forming dense mats. They trail along the ground where vegetation is sparse, but may stand erect where it is dense. Chickweeds are often *decumbent*—growing along the ground at first, but turning upward at the tip. The leaves are simple and paired with no teeth or lobes; the tips are pointed but not acuminate, and the surfaces are hairless. The leaves have a few secondary veins arising along a depressed midvein.

The best identifying characteristic is the flowers, which are surprisingly similar among the various species. They are symmetrical, with five sepals and five white petals—but each petal is cleft nearly to the bottom, so that at a glance there appears to be ten of them. (However, the flowers of some species may lack petals.) The flowers are borne individually on very thin pedicels, or in sparse clusters with forking stems.

Right The line of hairs on only one side of the stem is diagnostic of common chickweed. **Below Not chickweed.** Scarlet pimpernel, a plant sometimes confused with chickweed.

At a glance, scarlet pimpernel *Anagallis arvensis* resembles common chickweed. The flowers of pimpernel are very different: The petals are broadly ovate, not cleft, and pink to red. Even unopened buds can be differentiated from chickweed because they are borne one per leaf axil—not in terminal clusters. The stems of scarlet pimpernel have four unequal angles, each corner winged. The leaves are broadly ovate and always sessile, and have all of their major secondary veins arising at the base. Scarlet pimpernel is not often considered edible, but it isn't dangerous, either; the taste is unpleasant.

HARVEST AND PREPARATION

Harvest the tips of chickweed stems, as far down as they are tender; if you are not selective, you will end up with a wiry mouthful. You can pinch or pluck chickweed by hand, which helps you feel where they are tender and tough. However, you'll go much faster if you use a pair of scissors, grabbing the tops with one hand while using the other to snip them off a few inches lower. As with any low-growing plant, beware of dirt.

Chickweeds, collectively.

The flavor of chickweed is mild and slightly sweet, making it suitable as the base for a salad. It can be chopped or pureed into soups, and adds pleasant body to the broth. (The ultra-thin leaves disintegrate readily and disappear in any cooked dish.) Chickweed is also a good green for a smoothie. You can throw a handful onto a sandwich or taco, or just pop a sprig into your mouth as a snack. When you do this, let several chickweed stems dangle conspicuously from your mouth and bring them in bit by bit, making lateral bovine chewing motions, preferably in front of a crowded storefront window.

Chickweeds have two distinct forms or phases of growth. In the cool weather of autumn, winter, and early spring, they focus on producing lots of stems with large, closely spaced leaves. The most succulent growth is found during this vegetative phase; you might get eight or more tender inches at the end of each stem, and can often quickly collect large quantities of the greens. Regions with moist, mild winters are ideal for producing robust chickweed.

In the heart of the growing season, chickweeds shift their focus to flowering and producing seed; their stems grow less rapidly and their leaves become smaller and more spaced out. During the flowering phase, you need to select the tender tips more carefully and cut shorter sections; look for non-flowering branch tips.

Left Sometimes common chickweed is incredibly small like this. Right Common chickweed, flowers and fruit. Note that even the pedicels have the single line of hairs.

While the foregoing applies generally to the chickweeds, there are significant and interesting differences between the many species. More specific information is found in the accounts below.

Common chickweed is the best known member of this group. But "common chickweed" is a flagship name actually covering three similar species: *S. media, S. neglecta,* and *S. pallida.* The species *neglecta* is, on average, a larger and more robust plant. On the other hand, *pallida* is a tiny little thing, hardly worth your time. The larger two species usually have petals, but the flowers of *S. pallida* usually do not. Even botanists have tended to lump these species together, so their abundance and distribution is not well known. For the present discussion we'll speak of them as one. The diagnostic characteristic of common chickweeds is the thin line of short, twisted hairs on one side of the stem only. The location of this line of hairs often changes between nodes.

Common chickweed is considered an annual, but it sometimes persists through the winter—even under snow—and resumes growth in spring. It is quite variable in size. Some plants have leaves only an eighth of an inch (3 mm) long, while the largest ones may be nearly 2 inches (5 cm), with stems 2 feet (60 cm) long. The leaf is very thin and broadly ovate with the tip obtusely to sharply pointed. Leaves are hairless except sometimes on the margins. Upper stem leaves are usually sessile, but lower leaves often have petioles nearly as long as the blade.

This cosmopolitan, introduced weed is found throughout North America in both urban and rural areas—although it is less common northward, and more common in cities. Common chickweed likes rich, disturbed ground with ample moisture, but unlike many weeds, it can tolerate heavy shade. This plant commonly shows up in gardens, flower beds, dirt piles, and raised planting boxes, along fences, and beside footpaths and building foundations. It is rarely found in newly tilled soil, preferring out-of-the-way places that remain both untilled and seldom trodden. The young greens are superb.

Above left The flowers of water chickweed. **Above right** The growing tips of water chickweed in early summer. On these pictured, I would just eat the terminal two or three sets of leaves. **Left** The stems of water chickweed are either not hairy, or have hairs all around, like these.

    Water or **giant chickweed** *Stellaria aquatica* (sometimes placed in its own genus, in which case it is known as *Myosoton aquaticum*) is another annual-ish species, often remaining alive and green under the snow. It is not native to North America. Water chickweed has somehow been lost in the shadow of its more famous cousin—there has been virtually nothing ever written about this plant in the wild food literature. Yet water chickweed is a delicious green in its own right, and far more common than common chickweed in some parts of the country. It thrives under similar conditions to common chickweed, but persists more tenaciously as succession takes place. Although it is sometimes found in urban parks and backyards, it might be thought of as a sort of "country cousin" to the common chickweed; it is often abundant in farm woodlots, pastures, and even in deep woods, where it does especially well in moist depressions, pond edges, and floodplains, beside springs and streams, and along logging roads and trails.

    Water chickweed looks a lot like common chickweed but is in most respects larger, and it tends to grow less erect. If you look closely, you will see that water chickweed's stems—if they are hairy at all—have fine hairs all over, and the petioles have long cilia on their margins.

    For eating, water chickweed is nearly as good as common chickweed, but its tender stem tips are not as long.

Starry or **giant Chickweed** *Stellaria pubera* is a perennial, native plant of the Southeast, where it inhabits hardwood forests, especially along streams and rivers, in ravines, or where there has been disturbance such as logging. This species is characterized by its larger, showier flowers than other chickweeds have. Starry chickweed is available in a habitat where other chickweeds are generally not found, and this makes it particularly useful. It is common, but rarely forms large, dense colonies. The fact that this and the former species are both often called "giant chickweed" creates a good deal of confusion among foragers.

Starry chickweed looks remarkably different in its vegetative and flowering phases. The vegetative shoots are tall and erect, with leaves several times larger than those of the flowering stems; they look quite like honeysuckle shoots. The flowering stems are a bit tough, but the vegetative stems are excellent.

Stitchwort is the common name for *S. longifolia* and *S. graminea*, the former native and the latter introduced. These species are so similar that few will care to differentiate them—we'll speak of them collectively. (There

Right This star chickweed plant simultaneously shows the vegetative phase (the tall stem on the left) and the flowering phase (on the right). The vegetative phase is the better one to eat. **Below** Star chickweed is very showy, but it does not always grow in dense clumps like this.

Top A mat of stitchwort in early spring.
Left Close up of young stitchwort at the ideal
stage for eating. Note the squared stem and
strongly keeled midvein. **Right** Stitchwort flower
and flower buds. Note the squared stem.

are actually several more native stitchworts, all of which are edible, but the two
mentioned above are the most widespread and common.)

Stitchwort is a perennial with a tough root system that grows in meadows,
pastures, fields, ditches, roadsides, yards, gardens, and other sunny, grassy spots
where other chickweeds wouldn't have a chance. Stitchwort spends the early
spring close to the Earth where frost is less intense and the inevitable snows
will not hurt it, happily photosynthesizing in the cold weather when moisture
is ample, shade is absent, and most other plants are dormant. When warm
weather comes in later spring, it stands upright; and when summer finally
arrives, stitchwort transforms to the flowering phase, scarcely recognizable as
the same plant. The stems become thread-like (hence the name), holding up
pairs of tiny, narrow leaves with several inches between them. These ultra-thin
stems weave between the stalks of neighboring plants for support. Long, delicate

Mouse-ear chickweed (genus *Cerastium*).
These are edible, but not very exciting.

pedicels lean into the sunshine to post a tiny flower here and there in openings among the meadow forbs and grasses. If the soil becomes too dry by late summer, the wiry flowering stems wither and die, and the patient stitchwort lies quiescent until moist, sunny conditions return in fall, at which time it resumes the creeping phase.

Some other members of the pink family, such as Deptford pink *Dianthus armeria,* can appear similar to stitchwort before blooming. These may be distasteful but are not dangerously toxic. To verify that you've found stitchwort, check for squared stems and a ground-hugging mat. Also, another genus of plants, *Minuartia,* is sometimes called stitchwort. These are tiny, tough plants, mostly with whorled leaves.

Spring is the primary time to gather stitchwort, with a secondary collection season in autumn. The paired leaves are sessile, relatively thick, elliptic to lanceolate, less than an inch (2.5 cm) long, down-curved along the margin, with a sharp and prominent midvein ridge underneath. Unlike other chickweeds, the stems are squared. In mid spring the creeping stems turn up at the tip and stand erect, but remain in their vegetative form. These erect vegetative stems are small but often numerous; with the aid of scissors they can be collected with reasonable efficiency. I think they taste even better than common chickweed, and I love them in salads.

Other chickweeds: The four chickweeds listed above are common, widespread, and delicious. However, there are nearly thirty additional species in North America, and all are considered edible, although I have not personally eaten each kind.

Another group that should be mentioned is the mouse-ear chickweeds of the closely related genus *Cerastium.* Mouse-ear chickweeds share most of the characteristics of the *Stellaria* chickweeds, but tend to be smaller, with short, blunt or rounded leaves that are sessile and hairy. Mouse-ear chickweeds are common in parks, lawns, flower beds, sidewalk cracks, vacant lots, and other disturbed sites, and occasionally in wilder settings—I'm sure you've seen them. They are edible, but none are as good as any of the real chickweeds.

Chickweed is a fantastic green that is simple to use. Good thing there are so many kinds, in so many places.

Chufa (Nut Sedge)

Cyperus esculentus

look out my dining room window, from this bowl of grayish, sweetish gruel that my children and I pass between us, and across our little orchard to a windswept snowy field beyond the fence. No trace of vegetation rises above the waves and drifts that encrust this gentle slope, cut in half by a curving ravine. But we remember what is frozen in that smothered dirt—with the vivid kind of reverie that only cold, muddy fingers and sharp autumn winds can manufacture. And the soothing heartiness that we slurp from our spoon brings a timeless comfort as we stare at the place where this breakfast came from, and where a thousand more such breakfasts wait for our fingers. Earth almonds, as they are sometimes called. Millions and millions of them, more than we would ever care to gather.

The man who farms the field just south of my orchard is a nice fellow, so I don't mean to rejoice in his troubles. But one spring, which was very late and wet, left a two-acre low spot in his field where the corn didn't germinate. In its place sprouted a thick crop of a weed that adores waterlogged low spots

The small tubers of chufa or yellow nut-sedge, after being collected in December and rinsed. The thin rhizomes are not attached, as these tend to wither away after the tubers mature. Note how the tubers on the right are flattened—these were from clay.

in crop fields: chufa. Farmers know the plant as nut sedge, and many of them know it well—but they are no more excited to eat it than they are to eat potato bugs or pigeons.

I didn't always fully believe in chufa. Euell Gibbons described it, in *Stalking the Healthful Herbs*, as tasting "in between the flavors of coconut and almond," noting that "as it is chewed it yields copious amounts of sweet white milk" and adding that it was "one of the finest tasting and most nourishing wild bread-stuffs I ever tried." This makes it sound pretty good. Gibbons also related that "where the soil is light, sandy, and easy to dig, the chufa is likely to bear huge crops of larger tubers only an inch or so below the surface. . . . One can some-times merely grasp all the grasslike leaves and stout stems and pull up the plant, bringing up at least three-fourths of the nuts with it, without digging at all." A plant given such accolades arouses suspicion.

For me, chufa didn't live up to all that. I'd find an occasional clump of it growing in the flower garden at the library, in the median strip of a brand-new four-lane, or even in its natural habitat on a sandy riverbank. From these scat-tered specimens I'd get a small palmful of tubers so tiny that I couldn't taste them apart from the dirty fingers that popped them into my mouth. Then one spring, a hayfield down the road was plowed and planted with soybeans, and

I noticed that by mid summer the chufa was growing there thicker than the beans. And then, the next sum-mer, it was the field next door, with a solid carpet of the grassy stems over more than an acre. Enough chufa, at last, to really eat.

I waited until November, when the berries were all picked, the nuts collected, the garden chores done—when root vegetables are about all that's left for a Northwoods forager to gather. We went as a family to seek the dead brown chufa tops, with a shovel and four bowls, and started turning

Young chufa plants in early summer. They look like grass at a glance, but are very light in color, and the leaf bundles and stems are three-sided. By late summer, chufa stands out among crop weeds in that it almost never exceeds three feet in height.

over clods of dirt and picking through them for the tiny starchy treasures—like wild turkeys, minus the head bobbing. Although our hands got cold, it was hard to stop, and only the weight of other chores drew us home. We dumped our individual bowls into the big one, and I marveled at the heap of muddy, crinkled, tan globs we had collected. A quart. Not a ton of food, but a nice heap for a few meals, to get an idea of what chufa is all about.

Sitting now by the sunny window and warming my throat with a delicious chufa porridge, I can't wait for all that snow to melt, and the ground to thaw, so I can get wet, muddy, semi-numb fingers again. I believe in chufa, and I like it.

DESCRIPTION

Chufa in crop fields is often easy to spot from a distance: clumps of grass-like plants that are *unusually light green* and *shorter than most weeds*. When you see this in a low spot where moisture often accumulates, it is time to investigate further. Chufa is a perennial sedge with numerous light-green, grass-like leaves, 10–28 inches (25–70 cm) long, in a basal rosette. These are folded like a paper airplane, with three distinct angles in cross section, and a V-shaped depression in the middle. At the base these rosette leaves are packed into a tight, 3-sided cluster that is often maroon; a few inches above the ground, the leaves diverge. From the center of each rosette rises a straight, unbranched, unjointed, leafless, untapered stalk 12–32 inches (30–80 cm) tall. The stalk has 3 sides, each with a shallow groove or depression running its length. At the top of this stalk is an umbel-like inflorescence subtended by 3–8 wide-spreading leaves

of very unequal length. Because of the form of their inflorescence, members of the genus *Cyperus* are often called "umbrella sedges."

Chufa has several thin, tan rhizomes radiating from the base, each terminating in a single, small, hard tuber ranging from the size of a pea to almost an inch (2.5 cm) long. In loose soil, most chufa tubers are plump and spherical or oblong, but in heavy soil with a lot of clay or fine silt, the tubers are usually flattened. Many are turtle-shaped. At the base of

Chufa top in full bloom, mid summer.

The fruiting top of *C. strigosus*, the false chufa. At a glance it looks very similar.

the chufa is a little scar where the rhizome was attached. At the opposite end is a tiny bud; when the tuber is dormant this bud is hidden in a tuft of dark brown, bristle-like scales (reduced leaves). The tuber has 3–6 faintly raised and darkened rings running all the way around, perpendicular to the direction of growth; bristles are attached to these. The surface of the tuber is primarily smooth, ranging from light orange-brown to dark red-brown, with scattered, tiny spots like the eyes of a potato. The skin is thin but semi-tough. Inside, the chufa is whitish, with a texture like fresh coconut, but harder.

Cyperus rotundus, a common weed in the southern United States and throughout much of the world, has multiple tubers that form a "chain" along the rhizomes. The rhizome tips become hardened and hazardously sharp, but they do not enlarge into tubers. The spikes atop *C. rotundus* are fewer and much sparser than those of chufa. The tubers are reported in some sources to be bitter and somewhat toxic—but edible in others. I have never tried them. Hillman et al. (1989) have found great quantities of them in the archaeological site of Wadi Kubbaniya in Upper Egypt, where the authors believe that 17,000 years ago, these were a staple food, eaten after some sort of processing. *C. rotundus* tubers were used extensively in ancient Greece to produce an oil that was used for ointments and perfumes (Negbi 1992).

Although chufa does not resemble any poisonous plant, it can be hard to tell from the many other umbrella sedges. This isn't dangerous—it's just exasperating. I suspect that this is why so few foragers collect chufa, despite its glowing accolades and auspicious history. One species to watch out for is *C. strigosus*, the false nut-sedge or false chufa, which often grows right beside chufa. There's nothing dangerous about it; it just doesn't grow any rhizomes or tubers. Check out the photos here and on page 102 for comparison.

To learn to identify chufa by the top alone, it'll help to know what the parts of the inflorescence are called. Look at the photo of a chufa umbel on page 100. The numerous stems emanating from the base are called rays. Each ray terminates in a spike, which consists of a central stem (rachis) that bears numerous side branches. These side branches are called spikelets. Now look at the close-up on page 102. You'll see that each spikelet is composed of several overlapping scale-like structures—these are the florets (individual flowers or, later, fruits). With that understood, I'll give you a set of characteristics that, taken together, will allow you to separate chufa from other similar-looking umbrella sedges by the inflorescence alone:

Left Close up of a chufa spike in fruit in autumn. The spikelets are well-spaced and flattened. **Right** *C. strigosus*, close up of the spike. Note that the spikelets are packed so closely along the rachis that they nearly touch at the base, the spikelets radiate evenly in all directions like a bottle brush, but most of them lean toward the tip or base, and the spikelets usually appear needle-tipped because one sharp scale projects well beyond the others.

1. Chufa's rays are very irregular in length.
2. The longer rays are naked near the base.
3. Naked rays are smooth, not rough or hairy.
4. A few of the rays or rachises are branched.
5. The whole spike is usually slightly flattened (like a bottle-brush that got stepped on).
6. Except at the ends, spikelets are at right angles to the rachis, not angled toward or away from the base.
7. Spikelets are yellow-brown when ripe, not dark brown or tinged with purple or red.
8. Spikelets are distinctly flattened.
9. Spikelets are not crowded or touching at the base.

HABITAT

Chufa's natural habitat is primarily open areas in river floodplains, including mudflats, sandbars, dried-up backwaters, openings in floodplain forests, and the upper margins of beaches. Chufa is also common in anthropogenic weedy situations, such as crop fields, gardens, and construction sites. It is one of the most prevalent weeds in the Southeast, where it is much loathed by farmers. It becomes locally problematic throughout most of its range wherever the soil moisture is high. It can persist at low density for years, only to explode in numbers during a rainy summer when other weeds that like drier conditions are suppressed. Despite its proclivity for wet, mucky soil, chufa will grow in sandy locations as long as it's not too dry. I have seen it growing thickly in highway medians and shoulders after road construction.

Chufa is not just a competitor with crops—it is also allelopathic. We don't know which wild plants it chemically inhibits, but Drost and Doll (1980) have shown it to be allelopathic to both corn and soybeans.

Besides producing tubers, chufa also invests in heavy seed production. Tubers can remain dormant for at least three years, and seeds probably much longer. This dual strategy allows it to spread rapidly, and to persist in competition with perennials once it spreads—hence it is a

Chufa *Cyperus esculentus.* Most common in the southern 2/3 of the range.

very successful weed. If you are seeking chufa to collect, look for rich soil on low, flat ground, in an area where the soil is regularly disturbed by agriculture or flooding. Here it tends to be abundant. Sandy soil makes it easier to collect, but the plant seems to do well in all soils but heavy clay. Farmers might look at you funny, but they are usually eager to grant permission to collect. Just make sure you call it nut sedge; they've probably never heard of chufa.

Some Chufa History

Chufa has been used as food for untold millennia. It was domesticated in the Old World several thousand years ago. Evidence suggests that this first occurred in Egypt (Zohary and Hopf 1988), or the White Nile region of what is today called Sudan (Zeven and Zhukovsky 1975). It was one of the oldest domestic crops used in ancient Egypt, where it has been found regularly in archaeological sites from the 4th millennium BC onward (Negbi 1992). During the earlier millennia, it appears that the cultivated crop was confined to Egypt (Zohary and Hopf 1988), although wild chufa was used elsewhere.

Although the literature often gives the impression that *Cyperus esculentus* is a tropical and subtropical Old World plant whose presence in North America is the result of introduction, field botanists have long recognized it as native here. I can readily find it in natural habitats along wild, undeveloped floodplains, such as that of the Bad River near the south shore of Lake Superior. Chufa was cultivated by the Owens Valley Paiute of California, for whom it was a staple food (Lawton et al. 1976). The Paiute built extensive irrigation systems to water their fields of chufa and blue dicks (genus *Dicholostemma*), from which they harvested the tubers and bulbs every other year.

Today domestic chufa remains a popular food in Spain, Portugal, Morocco, and much of West Africa; thousands of acres are under cultivation. The tubers are sold dried, ground into flour, or in the form of a prepared milk. In Spain, millions of pounds of them yearly are ground and brewed into a beverage called *horchata de chufa*. The tubers are also pressed commercially for oil.

In the United States, chufa is currently experiencing a boom in popularity under the name "tiger nut." The tubers or flour can be purchased online or in many health food stores, and the tubers are also sold in some garden catalogs for growing at home. The weed has also experienced a boom; since about 1950 it has become much more prevalent as an agricultural pest in North America (DeFelice 2002), and it is a common lawn weed in some regions.

Domesticated versus Wild Chufa

Domesticated chufa has been greatly changed through thousands of years of intense selective pressure under cultivation, producing a crop that is easily distinguished from its wild progenitor. Domestic chufas average several times larger than the wild ones. While wild chufas are produced 3–10 inches from the parent plant at the ends of long rhizomes, domestic chufas are clustered right near the plant's base on very short rhizomes, and are thus much easier to harvest. Wild chufa produces lots of seed, while the domestic plant puts almost all of its energy into the tubers—it rarely ever flowers, especially at northern latitudes. The domestic tubers cannot survive freezing, while the wild plants make it through weather at –50°F. Domestic chufas have a greater percentage of oil and sugar than their wild cousins (DeFelice 2002). They are also softer and less woody.

While the domestic strains of chufa have been improved in the ways mentioned, the wild plant is still a good food source. Unfortunately, much that has been written about chufa does not specify whether it pertains to the wild or domesticated form, resulting in frequent confusion and misinformation. In this account, unless otherwise mentioned, I am talking about the qualities and uses of the wild plant.

HARVEST AND PREPARATION

Chufa tubers can be dug from fall through early spring—in other words, when the tops are dormant. In the southern third of the United States they can be gathered all winter long. They form later than many underground storage organs, and so should generally be left alone until later in the autumn or early winter. I wait until the tops are brown and dead; if they are still green, many of the tubers will not yet be fully formed. If you can remember where the plants are, or can identify them by the withered stalks, early spring is also a good time to collect chufa. It does not begin growing until the weather is warm, in late spring or early summer.

Above This patch of chufa covers a few acres in a low field. The plants are in full fruit in late October and are mostly lodged over. Not all the tubers have filled out yet. **Right** Chufas imbedded in a clod of soil that I've turned over in the same field in early December.

In loose, sandy soil you can grab the whole plant and pull up, using a shovel or garden fork to loosen the soil at the same time. Gently shake the sand loose, then pick the tubers off by hand. In heavier soil you will have to use a shovel or fork to dig out and turn over a clod of dirt, then break it apart with your fingers as you pick out individual tubers. In heavy soil the tubers tend to be smaller. Thus, soil type has a great impact on the efficiency of your chufa harvest. Chufa tubers can reach extraordinary densities under a healthy colony—Taylor and Smith (2003) found up to 1,550 tubers per square meter in some plots.

There will be thread-like roots attached to your tubers, along with the dark bristles and an occasional rhizome. And of course, they will be dirty. Put them in a large bowl of water, rub vigorously between your palms, and rinse; do this repeatedly to get them clean. No matter how many times you rub and rinse, there will always be some scaly material that comes loose, so eventually you have to call it clean enough and stop. A few bristles won't hurt anything.

There will also be a few pebbles mixed in with your chufas—my last batch had 23 pebbles, in fact—so inspect them carefully. It works well to put them onto a white ceramic plate, one handful at a time, in good lighting, to sort out any bits of stone. Move the tubers around and listen for the clink or scrape of stone on glass. ***Don't skip this step unless you want dentures.***

One analysis of wild chufas from Mississippi (Billingsly and Arner 1970) showed 8% protein, 5% fiber, and 21% fat. The remainder is mostly a mixture of starch and sugars. This makes them quite suitable as a caloric staple. Although wild chufas are surprisingly woody, the dark ones are especially hard, while the light orange-brown ones are less so, and also sweeter.

It is very easy to dehydrate chufas, and they hardly shrink at all. You can dry them in the sun, or use a dehydrator or an oven, but most of that is overkill. It works well enough to spread them shallowly in a tray or pan and lay them in a dry place, stirring every now and then. Once dry, they keep very well. You can rehydrate them by soaking for a day or two in the fridge. Dried chufas can be ground into flour; however, this is too coarse for my liking in most applications.

I take fresh or rehydrated chufas, cover them with water, puree them in a blender, then strain them through a cloth or nutmilk bag. This separates the roughage from the digestible stuff, which breaks up and dissolves more readily. Everything I like to do with chufa starts with this strained milk. You can simply heat it up and drink it warm, sweetened and spiced if you like. This is the traditional *horchata de chufa*, and there's a good reason people have been making it for thousands of years—it's delicious. However, if you heat it past about 140°F, the starches will dissolve and it turns into a slimy, gravy-like stuff. (This is not an issue with most nutmilks, because most nuts have little to no starch.) Add some salty broth to this and whisk while heating, and it makes the best wild gravy you'll ever find.

Thick chufa milk can also be cooked as a hot cereal or porridge. For this, it's nice to squeeze the milk through something like a jelly bag with slightly larger holes, so that a few coarser particles get through to give the gruel some texture. I like to use the chufa porridge as a base in which other seeds are cooked. Try chufa with buckwheat, chia, or oatmeal. For a most fantastic breakfast, make chufa gruel and mix in a generous heap of hickory nutmeats chopped fine in a food processor, then add a little maple syrup and cinnamon.

Chufa didn't live up to my original expectations. The tubers were harder, smaller, less sweet, and more painstaking to gather than I had been led to believe. They didn't make as good a flour as I had hoped. And then I looked to tradition, seeing what millions before me had done with earth almonds, and began to understand the difference between the wild and domestic ones. This tiny tuber measures up marvelously to my new expectations. Hopefully it will for you, too.

Creeping Bellflower

Campanula rapunculoides

"I brought you something," François told me, smiling and pulling out a gallon plastic bag full of creamy roots. "*Campanules*. I dug these yesterday." I had asked François about rampion, a cultivated root vegetable once regularly grown in Europe, made famous by the fairy tale of Rapunzel, a beautiful girl who was named for the plant (*rapunzel* in German) that her mother craved during pregnancy. In fact, she wanted it so desperately that her husband agreed to give up the child so that his wife could have more of the coveted vegetable.

François had eaten the real rampion a few times as a child in France, and told me that it was delicious but had fallen into disuse because it grew so deep in the soil that it was extremely laborious to harvest. Then I asked him about its smaller but much more common relative, the creeping bellflower—or as he knew it, *la campanule*. I had read that the roots were edible, but I'd never tried them, although from time to time I saw the plant growing in some vacant lot or backyard. François had tried them, and he was excited to share. He cooked and served these in the simplest fashion: boiled them in salted water, then spread some butter on them. They were delicious. I knew that I would have to find some of my own *campanule*.

I returned home determined to find a colony of creeping bellflower. Two weeks later, as I was running by a nearby lake, I noticed a few bellflower stalks blooming in the ditch

Creeping bellflower in bloom, growing at the edge of a gravel parking lot. Although these stand erect, the flowering stems often lean later in summer.

beside the road. The next day, as I ran a different route, I found two more little patches along the roadside, also in spots I had passed dozens of times. Later in the week, on the way to the post office, I spotted a huge colony in a vacant lot a block from the local grade school. Not long after that, I was mowing the lawn and noticed a nice colony of creeping bellflower mixed with the roses and goutweed along the edge of *my* yard, where the previous owners had planted it. Somehow, getting hungry for the plant made it spontaneously generate. Since that day I seem to find it whenever I'm not looking for it. I bet there's a bunch growing near you, too.

DESCRIPTION

Creeping bellflower is a perennial herb with a creeping network of roots and rhizomes, forming dense colonies where the conditions are ideal. In the spring, before the flowering stalks appear, a creeping bellflower colony has a carpet of basal leaves. These leaves are heart-shaped, hairy, coarsely toothed, and 2–5 inches (5–13 cm) long. Each leaf is borne on a long, channeled petiole. At any stage, but most notably when young and tender, the leaves and stems of creeping bellflower have a milky sap that can be observed when the plants are broken— although it is not as copious as the latex of some plants, and you may have to wait a few seconds to see it accumulate on the broken stem.

In late spring the erect flower stalks begin to appear, scattered among the basal leaves. The leaves of the flower stalks are alternate, and change dramatically as you move away from the ground. The lower ones are similar to the basal leaves, but upper stem leaves are on very short petioles or are completely sessile. Their shape becomes narrowly triangular, and the leaves get much smaller—typically just an inch (2.5 cm) or so long. The upper leaves also become far less hairy.

The stems of creeping bellflower, at first, are erect; but as they reach their full height of 2–3 feet (60–90 cm) and begin blooming in mid summer, they usually lean or arch to the side. The stems are rarely more than a quarter inch (6mm) thick. They are unbranched, solid, rounded, and smooth except for a faint

Basal leaves of creeping bellflower in summer.

ridge running down from each node. The stems are green in the shoot phase, but at maturity, the bases of the stems usually turn to a deep burgundy.

The upper half or more of the stem may bear flowers. These are blue, with 5 fused petals that spread at the tip to make a bell-like shape, and 5 much shorter green sepals. The flowers are produced on short, drooping pedicels, hanging mostly off to one side of the stem, either singly or in small clusters.

HABITAT

Creeping bellflower is a plant, like the day lily and lilac, that marks old homesteads, sometimes persisting when nothing is left of the house and barn but a few rows of loose stones and a trace of dissolved mortar. Bellflower will escape from ornamental plantings and spread into anthropogenic habitats such as roadsides, meadows, parks, cemeteries, lightly used pastures, vacant lots, and farmfield borders. It likes rich, moist, but well-drained soil and can thrive in full sun to moderate shade. It does not survive in heavy shade, and in full sun it often gets shaded out

Creeping bellflower *Campanula rapunculoides*. Within this range, this plant is found exclusively in areas of human habitation.

by taller perennials. Creeping bellflower is rarely found in any native plant community, and if so is usually localized near human habitation, and not very prolific. It is of little concern as an invasive.

HARVEST AND PREPARATION

There are four good edible parts of the creeping bellflower. Best known are the **roots**, which are a little bit different than most edible roots. At the base of the bellflower stalk, you won't find a stout, fleshy taproot; there will just be some inconspicuous rhizomes less than an eighth of an inch (3 mm) thick. These rhizomes travel from one to several inches, working their way diagonally into the soil. At the ends of these short rhizomes there will be an enlarged root, shaped like a typical taproot but often curvy. The larger bellflower roots will be about an inch thick and nine or ten inches long, but most are smaller.

You can dig up bellflower roots at any time, but the peak of growth of the flowering stalks in mid to late summer is the worst time, because most of the energy will have been sucked out of the roots to feed the tops. Autumn through spring is the best time. I just dig up a large shovelful of dirt in the middle of a colony, trying to get the base of a large stem near the center of my scoop. The rhizomes crisscross in all directions through the dirt, and the roots could be

Roots of creeping bellflower.

anywhere among the plants. I pull out the larger roots and replant the small ones, packing the dirt back into the hole.

Since this bellflower is not native, overharvest is not an ecological issue. Indeed, people complain that the plant takes over the yard and is impossible to eradicate once it gets established. I once heard an invasive plant specialist declare that creeping bellflower cannot be eradicated without extreme measures, and that it takes many years to do so. People who say this aren't bellflower eaters. I took these exaggerators at their word and in one summer, with just the effort of a few good meals, completely eradicated the bellflower patch at the edge of my yard. In the three years since then, not a single sprig has shown itself. So if you want to keep coming back to a spot for harvest, take it easy and be sure to leave most of the colony untouched. The plant is a creeping perennial, but it actually doesn't have superpowers. If you decide that you need to get rid of creeping bellflower, you don't need to resort to using poisons. You'll need to dig most of the roots, and then follow that up by repeatedly harvesting leaves and shoots. It's actually not hard for a bellflower eater to do.

Creeping bellflower roots are not good raw. Once cooked, they become mild, tender, and slightly sweet, but not aromatic in the fashion of carrots or parsnips. Their flesh is light in color and only slightly fibrous. The most similar vegetable I can think of is salsify. Like salsify, bellflower roots are delicious just boiled, buttered, and seasoned as a vegetable; or they can be used in a thousand different soups, pot pies, or hot dishes. The skins may be slightly tough on some roots. To combat this you can peel them, or slice them crosswise into thin medallions.

Early spring leaves of creeping bellflower at the perfect size. These are good raw or cooked.

Although not as well-known as the roots, **bellflower leaves** are also edible—it would be worth growing for its greens alone. Collected while tender and light green in spring, the basal leaves of bellflower have a mild, pleasant flavor that is distinct and hard to describe—almost like comfrey crossed with lettuce, but with a hint of walleye fillet. They can be cooked as well—since learning of this plant's edibility, I have enjoyed the greens fried every spring. Bellflower grows profusely, and a large salad bowl can often be filled with the highest-caliber leaves in one kneel-down.

In late spring and early summer, bellflower sends up the **shoots** that will form the flowering stalk. These shoots are tender, mild, and superb in flavor, when 8–10 inches (20–25 cm) tall or less. They can be eaten raw or cooked along with the attached leaves. The **flowers and flower buds** can also be eaten. They are not very substantial but have a pleasant, mild flavor and make an attractive garnish.

Later in spring, the shoots of the flower stalks appear. Along with all of the attached leaves, these are a delicious, tender green that can easily be collected in quantity.

EDIBLE RELATIVES

There are several other members of the genus *Campanula* that grow wild in North America; some are native and some have been introduced. Several of these species are documented as traditional foods for Native Americans, while others were used as vegetables in Europe and Asia. All are considered edible. I have eaten and enjoyed the greens of harebell *Campanula rotundifolia* and American bellflower *C. americana*.

The creeping bellflower was once a very popular flower for the perennial garden or as a ground cover, commonly planted in shady yards, both urban and rural. In recent decades, however, this plant has fallen dramatically out of favor. It is now very hard to find for sale in nurseries. Many states and provinces list it as an invasive species, and some, like my home state of Wisconsin, have made it illegal to plant.

Gardening author Liz Primeau (2013) shares her unenthusiastic opinion: "Creeping bellflower, botanically known as *Campanula rapunculoides*, is one evil plant. Frankly, it's a garden cancer, spreading rampantly everywhere and entwining itself around the roots of any plant in its way. . . . Positive comments usually come from new gardeners unfamiliar with its wantonly evil ways." She goes on to call it "the despicable bellflower," "the blasted plant," "the bad guy," and "this nasty plant." She suggests using herbicides to kill it, even where that is illegal.

And to think: All this hatred directed at a plant *because it grows*.

I can't relate to this criticism. Bellflower is worth growing for its beauty alone. How convenient that it also provides four excellent vegetables. If it takes over the lawn, good. We have too much lawn anyway. While I am very concerned about invasive plants, creeping bellflower does not show up on my list of problem species. Although I know of dozens of colonies of this plant, I have never seen it become a problematic invasive. It invades backyards, gardens, and human-disturbed lands; I have never seen it take over areas of native vegetation.

The tradition of planting bellflower on the homestead, brought here from the Old World, hearkens back to a time when food was valuable and famine was real. There are people alive today who lived through that, and some of them got hungry enough to dig up their pretty bellflowers. I don't have homeowner's insurance, but I planted a patch of bellflower around a wild plum tree in my orchard (when it was still legal to do so). That's the kind of old-fashioned insurance policy that I like.

Fennel

Foeniculum vulgare

My wife insisted that she just felt sick to her stomach, but I was pretty sure she was pregnant. The whole camping trip we debated our cases, even as it became increasingly improbable that any mere illness could last so long. We were camped atop a bluff along the Pacific about halfway between San Francisco and Los Angeles in October, and as I walked down to the water I marveled at the dense clumps of towering fennel stalks along the trail. I decided to

Luscious fennel shoots at the perfect stage to gather. This is one of the most common weeds along the Pacific coast, especially near urban areas.

gather some seeds for the spice rack, pulled a bread bag out of my pocket, and filled it with a few ounces of fennel schizocarps. When we packed up camp and drove away, Melissa told me that those noxious fennel seeds needed to be double-bagged and put into the trunk if I wanted to take them home. I obeyed, noting that the smell of fennel had never bothered her before.

Our new best friend was born eight and a half months later.

DESCRIPTION

Fennel is a perennial growing from a multi-crowned network of roots. It forms thick clumps that may produce a dozen or more stems. The dried, dead, dark-brown stalks from the previous growing season persist, signaling where to look for the new shoots nestled at their base. Each stem has a few basal leaves, but these do not form a rosette as is the case with most other members of the carrot family. Instead, the leaves have an elongated fleshy sheath at the base that wraps fully around the stem for 3–10 inches (8–25 cm). Several such leaves are layered around the lower stem, arranged on two opposing sides, making the cluster elliptic in cross section. Small plants without stalks, however, have a basal rosette.

The leaf is pinnately divided multiple times, resulting in numerous thread-like leaflets or divisions up to 2 inches (5 cm) long. The stem leaves are alternate.

A clump of fennel without stalks consisting of several adjacent root crowns. Note the thread-like leaf divisions and dominant central rachis. A few of the lighter green, more compact leaves are immature and would be good to chop fine and use for flavoring.

Above left These are the clustered leaf bases around the stem of mature, wild fennel plants. They do not form the bulb of domestic fennel.**Above right** Domestic fennel from the grocery store, showing the bulb of enlarged leaf bases. This is an acceptable substitute if you can't find the wild stuff or it's out of season.

They are similar to the basal leaves, but become smaller, and the petioles shorter, as you go up the stalk.

The stalks grow erect and typically reach 4.5–7.5 feet (1.5–2.3 m) at maturity. They are lanky plants, growing much taller than wide, and branching mostly in the upper third. The skin is smooth, hairless, green or dark blue-green, and glaucous with a light bloom. Inside, the stem is solid.

The plant produces many compound umbels at every branch tip and from upper leaf axils. There are no bracts beneath either the first or second juncture of the umbel. The umbels contain numerous tiny yellow flowers with 5 blunt petals that are wider toward the tip. These produce oblong, slightly flattened fruits, dark brown striped with lighter brown, about 4 mm long.

Wild fennel is an escaped, feral version of cultivated fennel, but there is one important difference. The common strain of fennel commercially available, called "Florence fennel," is bred to have an enlarged sheath at the base of the petiole. These enlarged sheaths, clustered together and wrapped around an embryonic stem, form that baseball-sized mass at the base of the fennel you see in the grocery store. This is generally called the "bulb." Many authors assert that this designation is "incorrect," but don't explain why. A bulb is a structure formed by leaves that are modified into a storage organ. Cultivated fennel's bulb fits that description. So what are we supposed to call it—a mass of enlarged petiole sheath bases, or a bulb?

Wild fennel doesn't have this bulb, however. The petiole bases are still massed together and ensheath each other, but they are elongated, enlarged scarcely, and are more fibrous. In all other respects, wild fennel is essentially identical to the domesticated form, but better (Hoinkernoodle et al. 2016).

Fennel grows in many of the same places where its deadly relative, poison hemlock *Conium maculatum*, is common. Although these species are both in the same family, they are very easy to tell apart. Poison hemlock's flowers are white, not yellow. Its stems are hollow, not solid—and they are covered copiously with white powder. Poison hemlock stinks; fennel smells wonderful. At any time, these plants can be distinguished by their leaves: Poison hemlock has small leaflets that are pinnately toothed or lobed, while fennel's leaf divisions are thread-like.

HABITAT

Fennel likes dry, often rocky, disturbed soil in full sun. As an introduced weed of Eurasian origin, it is distributed erratically about the continent—but it has a decided preference for mild climates and the coasts. It is somewhat regular along the Atlantic, but scattered and rare over most of the continent's interior, mostly confined to urban areas. Fennel is remarkably abundant along much of the West Coast. It likes steep slopes, roadsides, vacant lots, meadows, parks, barnyards, rubble dumps, and other disturbed places. It is abundant in and around most major cities along the Pacific.

Fennel *Foeniculum vulgare*. Blue along west coast represents area of greatest abundance. Blue along east coast represents area where fennel is common to uncommon. Red in continent's interior represents area where fennel is uncommon to rare.

Mature fennel, going to seed, along a hiking trail in autumn. The leaves have all withered.

HARVEST AND PREPARATION

If you have not used fennel—wild or domestic—in your cooking, I encourage you to try it. Many people, familiar with the seeds, fear that the vegetable will taste too strong, but in fact it is much milder. Especially when cooked, fennel blends well with other ingredients, and is never overpowering unless misused. The exquisite flavor of domestic fennel is also present in the wild plant—only more so. You can collect any part of the plant that is tender and use it as a vegetable or flavoring. The young leaves can be chopped fine, like dill, and mixed with cooked whole grains or vegetables to add color and flavor. The larger petioles, before they have reached full size, can be peeled with a carrot peeler to remove the fibrous outer layer, and then used as a vegetable like celery. They are crisp but tender, and sweet. When the leaves are very young, you can even include the inflated sheaths at the base, although they will be far less substantial than what you get from domestic fennel.

The premiere part of wild fennel, however, is the young stalk. Collect these ideally when they are 10–22 inches (25–55 cm) tall, and still tender and flexible. Even at two or three feet tall, as long as the top remains yet unbranched, some portion of the stem's top will be tender—you just need to feel and select carefully. These young fennel stalks should be peeled of their stringy skins, which is not a tedious task. This will leave an interior that is crisp but tender,

juicy and sweet, with a mild fennel flavor. They can be used in salads, soups, or any other recipe in place of domestic fennel, with great results. Served in a veggie tray at your next party, they are sure to attract some comments.

Here is a forager's secret: These peeled shoots are superior to any form of fennel that you will find for sale. You see, fennel stalks are of fleeting perfection, with a short shelf life, and this is not conducive to growing in mass quantities and shipping around the continent on

In spring, look for last year's dark, dead stalks to guide you to the tender shoots. Fennel often grows enormous root systems in areas with mild winters.

Above top Mature fennel stalk in summer. Note the dark, blue-green, slightly ribbed stem contrasting with the lighter green sheath. Also notice how the tiny fennel seedlings in the background, such as under Abe's pinkie, have true rosettes. **Above left** These are the baby fennel leaves wrapped in the sheaths of a shoot about to bolt. Chop these fine and put them on new potatoes or in tzaziki sauce. All other uses are strictly forbidden. Just kidding. **Above right** With wild fennel, you're mostly after the stalk, not the leaf bases and sheaths. Here is the delicious, tender SLOTSM at the base of the fennel shoot. **Below** Perfect young fennel shoots, peeled and unpeeled. These are way more tender than domestic fennel bulbs, and milder in flavor.

Fennel in bloom. The tiny petals curl inward.

refrigerated trailers, then sitting in the produce aisle for 17 days under intermittent mist. This is why the modern palate is ignorant not only of fennel stalks, but of young stalks as an entire class of vegetables. Carrot, burdock, caraway, salsify—these are all grown commercially for the part with the best shelf life, while we ignore their excellent stalks. Most vegetables whose primary product is the young stalk have fallen into disuse, or have never been commercially successful here: poke, mitsuba, cow parsnip. But we foragers, thankfully, can get that fennel stalk on the grill in 20 minutes, or down the gullet in 20 seconds. I'm telling you: Wild food is *the best food on Earth.*

The time to get the young leaves and shoots of fennel is generally early spring. In the mild climate of coastal California, the season for fennel is long and erratic, with some plants sending up shoots throughout the winter, but the peak of this activity still occurring in February, March, or April. If you miss the earliest growth stage for fennel one year, don't despair. As the stalks begin

Fennel in fruit. Green ones, such as on the left, are delicious—ephemeral forager's treasures that cannot be purchased. Those to the right are mature but not dry, thus they have not yet schizzed into the smaller halves you can get in a jar at the store.

to branch, you can pluck off the tender tips—those with the flower buds yet unopened. These are small and stronger in flavor, but you can chop them fine and use them in any dish where you'd appreciate the flavor.

Once fennel blooms, it's time to make use of the flowers, which have a milder taste than the seeds, but a stronger one than the stems or leaves. The whole umbels can be chopped up and added to soups, salads, or fried vegetables. Or you can just eat them as a breath-freshening snack.

Some authors report collecting the pollen by bending the flowering umbels over a bag or bucket and tapping them. Or, you can snip off the newly opened umbels, dry them, and then rub them over a screen strainer to sift out the pollen and perhaps a few stray petals and stuff. The pollen, once dried, is said to store well, and can be used as a delicious flavoring in sweet baked goods. I have not done this, but I will try it when the chance next arises, because the thought of it makes my mouth water.

Finally, there is that well-known part of the fennel plant that most everyone has tasted in Italian sausage: the seeds. (Now really, to satisfy the technicality police, who are already deeply distracted by my comments regarding the bulb, I should acknowledge that the things sold in little glass jars as "fennel seed" are really dry fruits, known a schizocarps, that have split into two mericarps, each of which encloses one seed. I really enjoy the term "schizocarp," but the general population is adamant about calling them seeds, so I will comply with the public pressure.) After maturing, wild fennel seeds can be collected, dried, stored, and used as a seasoning just like cultivated fennel seeds. I must admit something about those fennel seeds I gathered before my daughter was born—half of them are still in the cupboard in a jar. That's because I don't make Italian sausage. I did put a pinch into a rabbit stew just last week, but a more creative cook would empty the jar sooner. For many culinary purposes, or just nibbling, I prefer the fresh, moist, barely ripe or under-ripe seeds. The seeds are also nice in tea blends, as is the greenery.

Isn't it nice to know that this noxious roadside weed is also a gourmet vegetable? This is one wild food you will not be faulted for collecting, even by the anti-foraging conservationists; it is an aggressive invasive weed that has been crowding out guard rails and broken concrete, plus other invasive weeds, for decades. The world will supposedly be a better place if you eat it. Your kitchen will definitely be.

Garlic, Field and Wild

Allium vineale and *A. canadense*

Wisconsin is not within the range of field garlic; there are no herbarium records of *Allium vineale* from the state. But nobody told that to the field garlic, so it decided to grow in the clearing on top of the hill in my sugarbush, almost 300 miles from the nearest known population. I suppose it came in a clod of dirt stuck to a piece of construction machinery when this clearing was made, almost 50 years ago. There are two important lessons to draw from this. First, you can't always rely on range maps. Second, you can't trust invasive plants to stay put.

There are numerous species of alliaceous vegetable (the group that contains onion, chive, garlic, leek, etc.) growing wild in North America, both native and introduced. The one most readily available to the greatest number of foragers is certainly the introduced field garlic. This plant loves growing in developed land-scapes, from the countryside to the interior of our largest cities. It goes out of its way to get in your way. Try sitting outside for lunch to enjoy a sunny spring day, and you'll probably crush some with your butt. You probably mow it with your lawn. It abounds in the weedy edges of parks and backyards, where your dog waters it. Farmers try to rid their fields and pastures of an inexhaustible supply of the stuff. You won't be able to get rid of your field garlic patch either, but you may as well see if you can put a dent in it.

Our native wild garlic is rarely found in urban lawns, and does not make it west of the Plains. But like field garlic, it is fairly large, widespread, frequently abundant, and easily har-vested sustainably.

Gotcho skillet ready?

A handful of field garlic bulbs in early summer, as the plants are going dormant.

DESCRIPTION AND LIFE CYCLE

We have no common name for the alliaceous vegetables collectively, and no good system for naming the great variety of wild species, so I will call the group "onions." All the wild onions are edible, and can be identified by having some version of the familiar onion or garlic scent. All leaves of onions are basal (although some sheath the stem before coming free) and linear without conspicuous veins. The scapes are naked and unbranched, terminating in a single umbel. The flowers have 6 tepals, and are white, purple, or pink. One or more is found in almost every part of North America. The Mountain West and Pacific Coast have the greatest diversity of species.

Field garlic has an interesting and unique life cycle as a winter perennial. It is completely dormant in summer, but grows the rest of the year. This strategy takes advantage of important resources while other plants are dormant. In autumn, the thread-like leaves appear in clumps among the grasses. You may see it in lawns at this time, its often curly, twisted, dark green leaves rising a few inches higher than the turf around it. Whenever the ground is thawed and free of snow, it gets to do a little photosynthesizing, with ample soil moisture and greatly reduced competition for sunlight. When spring comes, it has a big

Below left Knee-high field garlic in mid spring at the edge of a pasture. **Below right** Field garlic heads in spring, showing the sheaths around the developing bulblets and maybe flowers.

jumpstart on its competitors, and it starts vigorous growth very early—really, in late winter. At this time, when the grass is brown, it is very noticeable, and you can see that it is a major component of many lawns. Early in spring, the leaves straighten out, and by mid to late spring, mature plants of field garlic reach 2–3 feet (60–90 cm) in height—at least, where they haven't been mowed.

Each plant produces three to five leaves, all of them in the lower third, that have sheaths at the base, wrapping around the stem and each other. The leaves are narrow, rounded, and hollow, so you can use the older ones to make onion straws, which are not good for drinking milk. The outermost leaves in the cluster are the shortest and lean the most; they wither away in advance of the innermost leaf, which is the tallest, standing erect and diverging only slightly from the flower scape.

Each mature bulb produces a single unbranched flower stalk known as a scape. The scape is rounded, erect, and stands 18–30 inches (45–75 cm) high. At the top is an umbel of 30–50 small, white to pink, 6-part flowers. Before blooming, this umbel is tightly wrapped in a sheath, forming a long, pointed bud that is maroon at the base. As the plant blooms, its leaves begin to wilt for the season, commencing at the tips. Rather than pollinating and producing seed, most or all of the flowers in a field garlic umbel will turn into a bulblet—a vegetative reproductive organ that is a clone of the parent plant. The bulblets are about the size of a wheat kernel. Each one will sprout a thin, squiggly leaf while still attached to the scape, forming a curious nappy-headed thing. The weight of these growing

bulblets causes the stem to lean over and place them on the ground, planting a whole pile of them in one spot.

This ingenious and effective reproduction strategy allows field garlic to proliferate rapidly, but it also has three more kinds of bulbs. There is the *central bulb*, which is not wrapped in a leaf sheath, and from which the scape grows. New plants usually have

A grasslike clump of young, tiny, field garlic in spring.

just this central bulb in their first season or two. Healthy plants produce offset bulbs beside the central bulb; these eventually separate to become new plants. There are two kinds of offset bulbs. Big ones, close to the center and surrounded by a thin leaf sheath, are called *soft offsets*—only one of them is produced. Smaller ones, often slightly crescent-shaped, usually further from the center, and surrounded by a thick and tough leaf sheath, are called *hard offsets*—up to three might be produced, and these can remain dormant for several years. The larger offset bulbs of mature plants are about an inch (2.5 cm) long, and almost as thick.

The one worrisome plant that could be confused with field garlic, at a glance, is star-of-Bethlehem *Ornithogalum umbellatum*. This toxic plant has similarly linear leaves that come up in urban lawns, enjoying much the same growing conditions as field garlic. However, its leaves do not have the characteristic onion scent. Star-of-Bethlehem is a smaller plant and, unlike field garlic, has slimy sap in its leaves. The leaves are thicker at the tips, broadly U-shaped rather than hollow, and less erect. The bulbs wrap around the green leaves, which extend through the bulb's center all the way to the root crown below.

Bulbs and attached leaves of *Ornithogalum ubellatum*, star-of-Bethlehem, in early spring. **Not edible!** (unless carefully detoxified). These often grow in clumps like field garlic. Note the thicker leaves with a silvery channel, the fact that they are green all the way to the bulb (and inside it) and never ensheath each other.

HABITAT

Field garlic *A. vineale* thrives in sunny or semi-shaded grassy areas where the soil has been disturbed, or the native vegetation degraded. It likes relatively rich and moist soil. It can be found in pastures, stream valleys, crop fields, and disturbed woodlots in most agricultural countrysides. It thrives in lawns, parks, vacant lots, and in many of those sites ambiguously called "urban waste places." Field garlic seems to have trouble competing with tall, tough perennials such as goldenrod, tansy, and milkweed that dominate old fields and meadows. Nor does it do well in dense, wild forests. This is by far the weediest of our wild onions.

Native wild garlic *A. canadense* is found in fields and woods with rich, moist soil, being

Field garlic *Allium vineale* may be found scattered outside this mapped range.

Wild garlic *Allium canadense.*

Field garlic, spring bulbs from a clump of small plants. Most of these young plants just have the central bulb, although a few offsets can be seen. This photo was taken the same day as the *Ornithogalum* bulbs on the opposite page.

especially fond of low but not swampy woods, small floodplains, lightly used pastures, and rich valleys. Despite its Latin name, this species reaches only into southernmost Canada; but it is widespread through almost all of the forested region of the eastern United States. It is locally quite abundant, sometimes forming thick carpets over the forest floor. It does not colonize lawns and urban areas as readily as its imported counterpart, but you can have it in a lawn with moist, rich soil if you wait until early summer for the first mowing.

HARVEST AND PREPARATION (FIELD GARLIC)

The unique pungency that identifies the genus *Allium* was apparently intended as an herbivore repellent, but instead it has consistently attracted the attention of the world's most prolific mammalian omnivore. Onions are used in the cuisine of nearly every culture on Earth, forming a keystone flavor, unique and irreplaceable, in thousands of dishes. Field garlic is at once the largest and most prolific of our wild onions, but also the toughest in texture. Getting the best culinary use from it requires understanding and working around this latter quality.

In early spring you can take some shears to the lawn, seek those curly-haired sections, and snip off the young leaves. These can be used like chives—although they are never as tender, and get tougher with age. The leaves are coarser and stiffer than those of our native wild onions. You probably don't want the larger leaves chopped into your potato salad in place of scallions. You can, however, still take advantage of their excellent flavor in broths. Just cut a bundle of the leaves and stems, tie them together with cotton string, and place them into a boiling pot of soup to impart their essence. Pull the bundle out sometimes before serving. (In addition to using field garlic, you can make a good vegetable broth with all kinds of overgrown leaves and stems that are too tough for eating but still retain great flavor. Wild carrot, American chervil, honewort, cow parsley, nettles, mallow, and wood sorrel are a few examples. After boiling to extract the flavor, just strain the broth and give the spent greenery to Mr. Chicken Feathers.)

Later in spring, you can chop up a handful of the flower buds and use them wherever you want a fresh garlicky taste.

And finally, as the leaves and tops die back in late spring or early summer, when the dead tops are still evident and their location fresh in your memory, it is time to dig the bulbs. (You can also get them through the summer and early autumn, if you know where they are.) All bulb types are edible, but the best one is the soft offset—it is the largest, tenderest, and easiest to peel. The bulbs are milder than garlic, but stronger than a white onion. The literature focusing on this plant as a pernicious and destructive agricultural weed invariably claims that the flavor is poor. Most foragers, however, find it pretty good.

As this plant is a non-native that is extremely successful, conservation is not an issue with harvesting it. Indeed, in many parks and woodlots it is crowding out the native *Allium canadense*, in which case it would be a responsible act of stewardship to remove every field garlic plant that you find.

NATIVE WILD GARLIC

Allium canadense is most often called wild garlic, but also frequently called wild onion. How creative. Wild garlic shares a reproductive characteristic with field garlic and domestic garlics, in that most of its flowers turn into bulblets, which fall off and disperse to grow into new plants. (In some southern populations, however, the plants form few or no bulblets.) It differs from those other garlics in that it does not form offset bulbs or cloves; its original bulb is replenished by the dying top and goes dormant to grow again the next year. The bulb is only about half an inch (13 mm) long, white, symmetrical, and of a broad teardrop shape. Wild garlic starts off in early spring much like field garlic—but the young leaves of wild garlic are

Right The early spring leaves of *Allium canadense*, one of our best tasting and tenderest wild onions. **Below** *Allium canadense* just before blooming. Note the light green sheaths around the heads. The whole plant can be chopped into food at this stage.

Left top The blooming top of *Allium canadense*, showing bulblets and flowers. In some southern populations, there are no bulblets. **Left bottom** Bulbs of *Allium canadense* in summer when they are fully dormant. These are uniform in shape because, unlike field garlic, they never form offsets.

fleshier, solid, broadly U-shaped in cross section, and much more tender. There are generally 3 leaves per mature stem. This plant blooms in late spring, and at maturity it stands 14–30 inches (35–75 cm) tall. Before opening, the flower cluster is wrapped in an inflated sheath forming a broad, light green bud.

Native wild garlic should be collected with care to avoid overharvest: Thin out a small portion of the colony, and carefully spread the bulblets to ideal sites where the plant is absent. The disturbed soil from digging bulbs actually creates ideal growth conditions for new plants to propagate from bulblets—this is why it does so well in floodplains and at slope bases. As long as a good portion of the plants are left, wild garlic will thrive after harvest. Any responsible forager who has a favorite patch should invest some time removing the garlic mustard and buckthorn that are most likely crowding it out.

Although the bulbs of wild garlic are small, they have a wonderful flavor when used like garlic. They are milder than domestic garlic, however. Any part of the top that is tender can be used in cooking as well, and almost everyone prefers the greens of this native species to those of field garlic because they are so tender and have a milder flavor.

I suppose we could live just fine without alliaceous vegetables, but why? Every forager needs a wild onion in his or her life.

Gooseberry

Genus *Ribes* (in part)

One summer evening when I was ten years old, I was walking through the streets and alleys of our town, three miles from home, looking for something to eat. I stopped to stare at the lush panoply of produce in a front yard that was obviously cared for by an avid horticulturist. A couple weeks earlier I had gorged on cherries from the backyard of this same house, which was accessible from a brushy ravine. From the sidewalk, marauding seemed ill advised. But right in front of me was a bush with plump green berries, each round as a basketball, light green, and translucent. I had never seen such a thing, and stared in wonderment.

A pleasant voice startled me with the question, "Have you ever tried a gooseberry, Sam?" The old man smiled at me from his porch. So much for sneakiness. I told him no, intrigued and a little stunned. He approached. I had no idea who this guy was, but I sensed that he knew I had been in his yard before. "Right here, Sam," he said, parting the branches and pointing to a loaded gooseberry limb.

Gooseberry *Ribes missouriense* showing ripe and unripe fruit. This is a species of dry soil in savannahs, open woodlands, and borders.

"Is it ripe?" I asked.

"Yes. They ripen green like that."

I ate a few and went on my way. But everything about that bush—the spherical, translucent, lined fruit; the beak-like clump of dried stuff projecting from the end; the blunt-lobed, maple-like leaves—was imprinted in my hungry brain.

Shortly, I discovered that I didn't have to sneak gooseberries from other people's gardens; they were growing in thickets along most of the fencelines in the area. They weren't as large, nor as sweet, and they ripened to a deep purple. Since cows avoided the thorny bushes, some of the pastures in our neighborhood had been turned into virtual gooseberry orchards. And then I found another prickly-fruited kind in the woodlot across the hayfield south of our house. I came to realize that this exotic berry was actually pretty mundane. But I never figured out who that old man was, or how he knew my name.

Swamp gooseberry *Ribes hirtellum* softens but acquires only a faint purplish hue upon ripening. This is a species of openings in moist forest or swamp edges. I love how you can see right inside the fruit.

DESCRIPTION

Gooseberries are a large and variable group containing more than a dozen species in North America; their flavor, use, and appearance are all similar. Gooseberries are medium-sized woody shrubs with multiple stems, standing typically 2–6 feet (60–180 cm) tall. The leaves are small, alternate or in clumps, simple, and palmately lobed—similar in shape to a maple leaf. The flowers have 5 spreading petals and 5 sepals, and they ripen into soft, fleshy, juicy, globe-shaped berries with numerous seeds inside. The berries are a little translucent, at least when unripe. They dangle from a thin, wiry stem. The green fruit has veins visible under the skin, running from the base to the tip. The brown, dried-up remains of flower parts stay attached to the end of the fruit, like a withered beak.

The genus *Ribes* includes both gooseberries and currants. Generally, gooseberries have spiny stems and fruits that grow singly, while currants have unarmed stems and fruits in small bunches. Some gooseberries produce numerous spines all along the stem, while others bear them only at leaf nodes. A more technical difference between these groups is that currants have a jointed pedicel that breaks off as the fruit ripens, while gooseberries have unjointed pedicels that stick to the ripe fruit when it is picked. While this account focuses on the gooseberries, all of the currants are also edible, so there is no danger in confusing the two groups.

HABITAT

Gooseberries are found in most forested regions of North America: coastal rain forests, Rocky Mountain forests, boreal forests, eastern hardwood forests, the mixed forests of the Great Lakes, wooded ravines on the Great Plains. In general, these bushes like openings that allow a little sunlight through the canopy, and are often abundant on forest edges, along roads, or in wooded pastures and abandoned fields. They like river floodplains

Composite range of gooseberries.

and slopes, and are often found on the margins of wetlands or along waterways.

Members of the genus *Ribes* are alternate hosts for the white pine blister rust, a fungal disease that has decimated several important timber trees. Because of this, the government carried out extensive *Ribes* eradication programs for decades in some regions, making gooseberries difficult to find in certain areas, especially in the Northeast.

HARVEST AND PREPARATION

Gooseberries flower in spring and ripen in mid summer; picking them is moderately fast. I love to pop them with my teeth and savor their sweet-tart flavor. However, cooking seems to accentuate the toughness of their stems and skins by softening everything else. To make most products, I like to run the berries through a fruit strainer to remove the skins and stems. The resulting puree makes an excellent jam. I think it is too tart to make good fruit leather by itself, but if you mix it 50/50 with unsweetened apple puree, you will get a leather with great flavor and texture. Gooseberry puree can also be used in pies or other desserts, but I recommend mixing it with a milder, sweeter fruit such as apple or blueberry.

As a teenager I developed a special fondness for an unusual use of wild gooseberries that I call "green goose lemonade." When camping during that period of early summer when berries were not yet available, I craved something fruity with my boiled greens, roasted fish, peanut butter, and ramen noodles. I liked to nibble tart, under-ripe gooseberries, but they were literally hard to swallow, because the most common species I encountered was *Ribes cynosbati*, with

A bush of *Ribes missouriense* in a pasture. Note numerous more in the background. This is one of the best places to pick gooseberries.

Above Green, unripe berries of prickly gooseberry *R. cynosbati*, a plant of rich hardwood forests. These are perfect for green goose lemonade. Below Ripe fruit of prickly gooseberry turns light purple, is delicious (less tart than most species) and can be quite large (this one 0.6 inch in diameter).

prickly fruit. So I gathered a few cups of green gooseberries, smashed them up in a pot, put them in a quart bottle, filled the bottle with cold water, and let it sit for half an hour or so. The tangy liquid that resulted was refreshing like lemonade—a precious camp luxury.

Today I still enjoy making green goose lemonade, but am more likely to prepare it at home with the aid of a blender. Two cups of berries to a quart of cold water makes a delightful beverage; blend for about 15 seconds to break up the skins and release the juices, but not long enough to make a smooth slurry. Strain the liquid and sweeten it if you like—even try mixing in a bit of lemon. This is one of the best lemonade-like drinks I've ever tasted, and it's best when made from unripe berries, with no more than a few ripe ones for the beautiful pink tint they add.

Lemonade, jam, and fruit leather: three great reasons to get out in the midsummer heat and brave the thorny thickets of gooseberry. How wonderful to get all of this, without even having to steal.

Hickory (Including Pecan)

Genus *Carya*

Around Thanksgiving the year I was in eighth grade, a friend and I found a loaded shagbark hickory on a Saturday hike. I turned my sweatshirt into a gunnysack by tying one end with a strip of elm bark, and we stuffed it with eight gallons of nuts. A few weeks later there was an end-of-semester ice cream party coming up in our algebra class, and our teacher had asked each student to bring one sundae topping. My brilliant idea was to share the bounty of my wild delicacy. Like most teenagers, I procrastinated, but on the last night before the party I set upon the task and realized that I had no idea how to seriously crack and shell hickory nuts. Using a traditional handheld nutcracker, and a nail for a nutpick, I stayed up past midnight, and in three hours I managed to separate almost a cup of nutmeats.

The next day I brought my precious gourmet ice cream topping to school in a plastic bag, visions of its glorious reception coursing through my mind. "Wow,

Nobody should pass through life without imbibing the mouth-watering, honey-rich scent of freshly hulled shagbark hickory nuts.

these are great! Like pecans, only way better. Did you really *collect* these?" my classmates would ask in astonishment.

As kids came into algebra class and placed their bottles of chocolate syrup and cans of strawberry sparkles on a table by the big window, my fantasy began to crumble. I had no suitable container, just a lousy baggie. Our teacher said, "Hickory nuts? What are hickory nuts?" Her disdain for me and my few odd friends was often a palpable part of class. But she was kind enough to scrounge up a cup to make the suspect topping look more presentable, filling it reluctantly as she asked, "Now, you're sure these are safe?" One girl in class screeched, "Ewww! I'm not eating something that Sam touched."

Nobody ate the hickory nuts. Nobody even *tried* them. I was heartbroken— but lucky, because I got to eat the whole cupful, and they were fantastic on ice cream.

DESCRIPTION

As a group hickories are easy to identify. They are medium to large trees with erect, dominant, straight, single trunks. They have smooth, very dark gray bark as saplings; scattered thin, sinuous, lighter gray lines contrast with this background. With age the bark separates into longitudinal ridges or strips. Hickories have pinnately compound leaves that grow alternately on thick twigs with large terminal buds. There are 5–9 leaflets on most species, although a few have more than that. The leaflets have fine, forward-pointing teeth

An open-grown pignut hickory *Carya glabra* in October. Most people just call this delicious species "hickory nut tree."

Hickories have pinnately compound leaves, like their close relatives the walnuts. With most species, the leaflets get larger toward the end, and the terminal leaflet is prominent. (This leaf is of mockernut *Carya tomentosa*, another species that laypeople generally call "hickory nut tree."

on their margins and are dark green, thick, and rather tough, with a glossy upper surface. The leaflets of most hickories get much larger toward the end of the leaf, and the terminal leaflet is prominent.

The tiny, no-nonsense flowers are wind-pollinated and contain just the sexual parts. They appear in late spring, both genders on the same tree, the male hanging in long catkins, the female on short spikes of 2–4 flowers. The female flowers ripen into fruits 1–3 inches (2.5–8 cm) long, each containing a single nut. The distinctive hickory fruit has a green fleshy husk that turns brownish upon maturity; it is divided into sections called valves. Four is the most common number of valves, but five is also frequent; pignuts may have only two or three. On some species the seams between the valves are grooved, while on others they are marked with a ridge; otherwise the surface of the husk is smooth. The valves of some hickories peel back from the nut entirely when ripe, while others peel only partway.

The nut itself is bilaterally symmetrical, with suture lines dividing the shell in two, although these may be hard to see until the nut begins to dry. The nut has a nipple-like projection at the end, with a dark mass of floral remains at its tip—these often break off from handling. Some hickory nuts have a sharp point at the base as well. The shell is hard and rigid. Its surface is light in color and smooth, except sometimes for a few angles that form low ridges. (Water hickory is an exception to this: Its shell is dark and corrugated, like that of a walnut). The meats are brain-like, with multiple lobes and crevices matching the convolutions of the shell's interior.

Some of the lobes of a hickory nut meat are narrowed at the base and widened at the tip, thus locking themselves into crevices in the shell. The extent to which lobes are locked into the shell is the most important determinant of how easily the nuts of the various species can be shelled out. The two that lack locked lobes—shagbark and pecan—are not coincidentally the most commonly eaten hickory nuts.

Right Pecan in bloom during late spring; the drooping catkins have male flowers, while the female flowers are in small groups attached to the twigs. **Below** Typical specimens of four important hickories I collected the same day, about life size. Above left is yellowbud, above right is mockernut, below left is shellbark, below right is shagbark.

HABITAT

The 11 or so species of North American hickory have different habitat preferences, but as a group they inhabit most major forest types in the East. They are most prevalent on well-drained sites with rich soil, where they often co-dominate with oaks, ash, beech, pine, sweet gum, black cherry, and maple. Hickories are also highly associated with each other; stands frequently contain three or more species together.

COLLECTING

All species of hickory nut ripen in autumn sometime between late September and December—typically a month later in the South than in the North. They may hold their nuts for several weeks after ripening, and occasional trees will hold them through much of the winter, especially in bumper-crop and wet years. Some nuts may fall early due to poor development, disease, or insects;

thus the early part of the season is characterized by a higher proportion of bad nuts under the trees. If the majority of the nuts are falling to the ground, they are ripe. However, they may also be ripe upon the tree; you can tell this because their husks will begin to split open and loosen, and because they will detach from the twigs with relative ease.

I most commonly collect hickory nuts that have fallen to the ground on their own. I am selective with hickory nuts—on some trees, the nuts are larger and have a better shape for cracking. Keep in mind that you will spend several times more labor cracking and separating the nuts than collecting them, so being picky pays off. And since it is easier to crack and sort a uniform batch, I like to keep the nuts from each tree in a separate bag. If possible, crack a sample of nuts beneath each tree from which you collect, in case they consist mostly of empty shells or rotten nutmeats. Look for hickory nuts under trees with ample sunlight, as these produce the best crops. Park, pasture, fenceline, and road-side trees, those along forest edges and in clearings, and trees left after logging are all good candidates. Interior forest hickories rarely produce a good crop.

Sometimes I knock the nuts off the tree. Hickories up to about 10 inches (25 cm) in diameter can be given a sharp blow with the thickest, heaviest stick you can swing, and the vibration will often cause a surprising number of nuts to drop. Another good but hazardous way to get nuts down is with a throwing stick about four feet long and an inch thick. It is often possible to knock down dozens or even hundreds with a single toss. You'll probably want four or five such sticks because they have a tendency to get stuck in the branches. The final way to loosen the nuts—most effective but also most dangerous—is to climb the tree and shake the limbs. Do this only if you, like me, are a certified monkey and desperately need hickory nuts.

Some of the nuts will be in their husks, and others will have come free. If I have to remove husks, I usually do it outside by stepping on the husks or by filling a gunnysack and flailing it against a tree. You can also smack each nut with a hammer, or pry them off with your fingers.

Remember **The Nut Law:** *An adhering husk means a bad nut.* The fact that a nut is contained within a husk does not mean that it's bad; but if one valve tenaciously resists your attempt to remove it, toss the nut. Any further effort will yield nothing but sore fingers. With most hickory species (but not pignut or yellowbud), the husk falls off rather easily when ripe, often dislodging upon impact as the nut falls. Or the husk may open up on the tree, letting the nut drop out cleanly. Under-ripe nuts do not peel easily, even if they are good. Drying the nuts, or letting them sit for a few days in a sack, helps loosen the hulls. Occasional trees have husks that hold more tightly, so you will need to figure out what is normal for a particular tree before you can determine what is an adhering husk.

FLOATING

After collecting and removing any husks, you can "float" the nuts by placing about a gallon of them into a 5-gallon bucket with 4 gallons of water. Stir the nuts vigorously and then wait 20 seconds or so. Hopefully, most of the nuts will settle to the bottom, and a small portion will float. The floating nuts are usually bad ones and can be discarded.

However, *floating will not work with nuts that have dried out*—those all float. This happens when good nuts sit for a few weeks in a sunny spot during dry weather. This is especially common in parks, cemeteries, yards, and other localities with manicured lawns. You'll have to crack a sample of the floaters to assess their quality. If most of them are good, you'll have to separate high floaters (with 20–40% of the shell above the surface) from low floaters (which usually have less than 10% above the surface, or hover just beneath the surface). The high floaters are bad; the low floaters are likely good. When separating high and low floaters, you want smaller batches of nuts in the bucket, so that none of them have another nut beneath them pushing them up and affecting their floating position.

Besides helping you separate the bad nuts that visual inspection missed, floating also rinses off sand or dirt. However, do not soak them in the bucket for more than is necessary to clean and sort them—longer soaking promotes spoiling in storage. Floating is not a must. If my original tests under the tree showed a preponderance of good nuts, and the nuts were clean, and I plan on cracking and shelling them, I do not float them. I always float dirty nuts, those that showed lots of insect damage or spoiling, or those I intend to make into hickory milk.

STORING

Once floated, the nuts go in a gunnysack, shallow tub, or box where I can shake them once every day or two to facilitate even drying. You want the surface dry; don't dehydrate so much that they crack along the seams. Hickory nuts in the shell thus prepared will easily last 3 months at room temperature, and until the early part of the following summer if kept in a cool place such as a basement, enclosed porch, or cool closet. They will last longer still in a cool and moist place such as a cellar or refrigerator. They will last indefinitely in the freezer, after or before shelling.

A hickory nut is a living organism, and it will keep as long as it remains alive. Excessive heat will kill them, such as when roasted or left in a hot car for too long. Although they survive freezing temperatures in the outdoors, extreme cold (such as in a freezer) will also kill them. Dehydration will kill them, as will physical injury like cracking the shell. Once the nut is killed, it does not go bad immediately, but its flavor begins to change, it slowly loses quality, and it eventually goes bad. Ideally, you want them slightly dry, so the nutmeats shrink away from the shell to facilitate shelling—but not so dry that the nut dies. However, very dry storage is fine if you will use them up or freeze them within a few months.

Once removed from the shell, hickory nuts lose quality rapidly and will eventually go rancid. They should be used within two weeks (and preferably just a few days) or kept in a freezer.

MASTING

Hickories have erratic yearly production; this variability is key to their ecology. The bumper-crop years are called "mast years." If the trees produced an identical crop each fall, the populations of nut-eating mammals and insects would stabilize at a level where virtually all the nuts would get eaten every year; the trees would spend a great deal of energy for very little reproductive gain. By fluctuating, the hickories assure that occasionally a crop failure will be followed by a bumper crop. The crop failure causes a drastic crash in the population of nut predators, so that a subsequent bumper crop far exceeds the appetites of the insects and larger nut-eaters, assuring that some nuts are left to germinate. Since hickories are long-lived, such a mast year does not need to occur frequently to ensure reproduction.

After a heavy crop, the trees have less energy to invest in flowering and fruiting, making successive bumper crops unlikely; but hickories do not have a regular or genetically pre-programmed cycle of masting. Previous crops, the weather at the time of flowering (affecting pollination), and to a lesser extent the weather during the growing season—all have their role in determining the nut crop. All of the hickory species in one area sometimes crop well together, but sometimes they do not. If the hickory crop is poor in one location, check other locations where the weather or flowering times may have been different. Check north slopes versus south slopes, valleys versus ridges, high versus low elevation.

Hickories have a symbiotic relationship with gray and fox squirrels, who carry the nuts away from the parent tree, often long distances, and bury them in the soil, singly or in small groups, for winter storage. Other rodents consume hickory nuts, but store them in caches where they rarely have the opportunity to grow. Squirrels often hoard more than they can recover and eat. Plus, many squirrels die each winter—each one leaving behind hundreds of well-planted nuts.

GRUBS AND OTHER INSECT PESTS

Hickory nuts are notably affected by several insect pests. Among them are the pecan casebearer *Acrobasis nuxvorella* and hickory shuckworm *Cydia caryana*, both of which have three generations per summer—the early ones destroying young nuts, and the later ones eating the hulls but not always killing the nut. The hickory curculio *Conotrachelus hicoriae* has only one generation per summer, the egg being deposited in mid to late summer, and the grub eating the kernel and causing premature drop in late summer. The most serious, and most familiar, pest of hickory is the hickory weevil *Curculio caryae*. These bastards emerge in late summer and feed on the almost-developed nuts, causing the kernels to shrivel and blacken. Then they lay their eggs in other kernels, and the larvae feed on the nutmeat over about a month as it ripens. They chew their way out of the nut in autumn, burrow into the soil, and remain there for one or two years before emerging as adults (G. Smith et al. 1995).

In some years, insects destroy most of the hickory crop. When there are consecutive years of moderate to good crops, the grub numbers are high. Conversely, two or three years of light hickory crops will result in low numbers of grubs. The various species of hickory are not equally affected by the hickory weevil: Shagbark, pignut, and black hickories seem most susceptible. The thick shells of shellbark seem to afford substantial protection, and grubs are uncommon. Pecans and yellowbuds are usually infected at very low rates. In colder regions (only shagbark and yellowbud are found far enough north for this to apply) the weevils are absent, probably because of low winter soil temperatures.

Strategies for avoiding grubs are simple. As you pick, discard any nuts with holes in them. If there are a lot of grubby nuts, be sure to float the batch. If you are collecting early in the season (typically, this means when the trees still have leaves), many nuts will have grubs that have not yet chewed their exit holes. In this case, if the grub numbers are high, you should re-sort or float the nuts a few weeks later, after the rest of the grubs have emerged. If you wait until late autumn or early winter to collect your nuts, the weevil larvae will have finished their work and exited, and there will be few still containing grubs—but you can wait this long only if there is a heavy crop.

Hickory grubs *Curculio caryae*.

Above left Shagbark hickory nut, cracked to show the X on its side. When you get this X on both sides, the meat will come out in two nice halves. **Above right** The extracted nutmeats and shells. Note that shagbark lacks deep convolutions or "locked lobes."

CRACKING AND SHELLING SWEET HICKORIES

Shagbark and shellbark are the most popular hard-shelled hickory nuts. Mockernut, black, and pignut hickories have good flavor, but the form of the nuts makes cracking and shelling more laborious; while these species can be treated according to the instructions here, they are best used to make hickory milk.

Hickory nuts are cracked with a hammer, a vise, or occasionally, a special nutcracker designed for the job. A regular handheld nutcracker will not suffice. With any method, force is applied to the narrow sides of the nut, and nuts with a somewhat flattened shape will usually crack better than those that are closer to spherical. If the cracking is going well, you'll see an X shape on the narrow sides of the shell, indicating that it is separated into four pieces. When the nut cracks like this, it is usually possible to quickly remove the meat in two halves or four quarters.

The choice of hammer or vise largely reflects personal preference. A hammer is cheap and convenient for occasional small batches, and is easy to keep in the kitchen, but it is more likely to over-shatter the nuts, or your fingers. I prefer a drywall hammer because the wide face reduces the shock to the fingers, and the convex, textured surface seems to catch the nutshell better. If you use a hammer, you need to hold the nut while you strike it, for both safety and practicality. Those unskilled or uncomfortable with a hammer should not use one.

A textured contact surface also makes the nuts less likely to slip in a tabletop vise. It is also nice if the crank immediately moves the jaw of the vise, as opposed to those models where it takes a quarter or half turn before the gears engage—the quick reaction makes it much faster to repeatedly open and close the vise. Keep a clean bucket under the vise so you can open it just far enough to let the cracked nut fall out, then slide in the next one. When cracking

Hickory nut being cracked in a vise. This one didn't crack with good form, because it is black hickory.

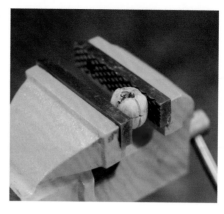

with a vise, it is especially helpful to have the nuts sorted into batches by size so you don't have to repeatedly adjust the width of the jaws. A vise is slower than a hammer, but it usually achieves more perfect breaking of the shell, and thus saves time when shelling is accounted for.

The most serious hickory nut crackers—the ones who shell nuts for sale—usually use a vise. They also employ elaborate pre-cracking processes to make shelling easier. These include some combination of drying (to get the meats to shrink), soaking (to get the shells to expand and become pliable), and freezing (to make moist shells brittle). The nuts may be cracked when frozen, then allowed to thaw before separating. Some processes may detract from the quality of the shelled meats, however.

Regardless of the method used to crack the nuts, you will spend much more time removing the nutmeats from the shells than you will spend cracking them. You'll definitely want a nutpick for this. The nutpicks that come with nutcrackers you buy have poor ergonomics and don't work well for hickory nuts, so I make my own. I cut a 5/8-inch hardwood dowel into 3-inch sections, then drive an eightpenny finish nail about an inch into one end of the dowel piece. (You may want to drill a very thin pilot hole to prevent splitting the dowel.) Then I snip off the head of the nail, peen it with a small hammer until it is flattened and slightly curved, and clean up the edges by dragging them on a mill file. A pick like those shown here is immensely better than the store-bought variety. The wide, thin end can be slid behind the kernel halves to pry them out of the shell

Below left Handmade nutpicks designed for hickory. **Below right** Wire cutters being used to extract hickory meats.

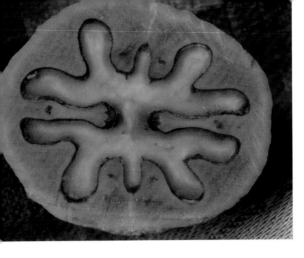

Nut of black hickory sawn to show four locked lobes per half. A "locked lobe" is either curved or bulging at the tip so that it cannot be extracted without breaking it. The only hickories that don't have locked lobes are shagbark, pecan, and an occasional shellbark—and it's no coincidence that these are the most popular hickory nuts for shelling.

without breaking them into numerous little pieces. The size should be tailored to your species: We have a big, wide one for shellbarks, a medium one for shagbarks, and a narrow, more pointed one for mockernuts, black, and pignuts.

Another good tool for shelling hickory nuts is a small pair of wire cutters. This often allows you to make one strategic snip and get out a much larger piece of nutmeat, and eliminates the need to use a hammer or vise for re-cracking those that didn't break right the first time.

One of the most important things you can do to increase your shelling efficiency is to feed the chickadees. Be willing to set down a piece of shell that contains one tiny morsel of meat deep inside a remote crevice. Just let it go in the shell pile, and move on to an easy chunk. The faster you can make this decision, and the less emotional pain it brings you, the easier it will be to shell the nuts. Being willing to leave 10% or 15% of the kernels behind can triple your labor efficiency. If it helps you let go, collect an extra gallon or two "for the birds" every fall.

In our house, shelling hickory nuts is a pleasant morning ritual while breakfast cooks. But it can be daunting to those just learning the skill. In principle, shelling nuts is simple, but experience makes a huge difference for both speed and quality. New hickory shellers go at just a fraction of the speed and get many times more shell pieces in with their meats. If you work past this stage you'll find it a much easier task.

Once separated, hickory nutmeats are hard *not* to use. In our house they disappear within a few hours, and if I want them for a recipe I have to hide them. That's because they are the world's most delicious nut. The flavor of wild pecans is like that of commercial pecans, only better. Shagbarks and shellbarks are better still, and can be used in any of the same ways with superior results. Hickory nut pie, breads, cookies, and ice cream are a few popular ways. We eat most of ours in hot cereal or just plain as a snack. Mixed with dried berries they make a hearty trail food, greatly appreciated on a long winter walk. Hickory nuts are good in salads or pasta, or any place that you might use a commercial nut.

HICKORY MILK

For the native tribes of the Eastern Woodlands of North America, hickory nuts were once an important staple food: abundant, tasty, dense in calories, and easy to store for half a year or more. The biggest drawback of the hickory nut as a food source is the labor required to shell the nuts—a dilemma the native people solved by not shelling them. The tribes of the eastern forests seldom ate hickory nuts as Euro-Americans customarily do today. Instead, they pounded the whole nuts in a wooden mortar, breaking the shells and nutmeats both into tiny fragments. The pounded nuts were then boiled in a pot. In this process, the shells sink to the bottom, while the fine nut fragments and dissolved solids are suspended in the water. This nut-rich liquid, or hickory milk, is then ladled off the top. This is much more labor-efficient than cracking and shelling. Although once a daily ritual in thousands of villages from Ontario to Alabama, Oklahoma to Virginia, very few people make hickory milk or soup today. But it still works. And it's delicious.

There are numerous detailed reports from early explorers and colonists regarding this use of hickory nuts by Native Americans throughout the East. Today, the tradition probably remains strongest among the Cherokee of northeast Oklahoma and the southern Appalachians—although their use involves additional steps not mentioned in the older accounts. The Cherokee crack the nuts individually to check for bad ones, sift out larger nutshell pieces, and then pulverize the remainder until it can be formed into balls for storage or transport. These balls are called *ku-nu-che*, and are refrigerated or frozen for longer storage. They are broken up and rehydrated by boiling to form a hickory nut soup—hickory milk by another name. (Fritz et al. 2001.)

When we pick hickory nuts, we separate them into "crackers" and "milkers" according to their designated use. Nuts that are large and have a good shape for shelling are crackers. Nuts that are smaller, or have an irregular shape, or belong to species that are hard to shell, are milkers. We don't sort nut by nut; all the nuts from one tree go into the same bag. Making hickory milk allows you to use nuts that otherwise would not be worth collecting. You can use any sweet hickory to make milk, but I think shagbark, pignut, and black hickory are best, in that order. The thick shells of some species will eat up a wooden mortar. Pecans have bitter material between the shell and kernel that will detract from the milk's flavor.

A good quality batch of nuts is imperative when making hickory milk. You need to pre-crack each nut to check its quality before throwing it in the mortar for further smashing—unless you have a batch of nuts known to be of supreme quality. If I have not recently used them, I'll test a batch by cracking 15–20 nuts. If I find a single bad nut in a sample of that size, I am suspicious and check another 20; if there's more than one I will definitely not use those nuts for milk. A perfect batch of hickory nuts is not as hard to get as it may sound. Just before writing this, I went and cracked 230 mockernuts from a bag that I picked two months ago; 3 of them were bad. And this was a batch that I did *not* float—all three of these bad nuts were empties, which would have definitely been removed by floating.

All bad hickory nuts are not created equal. Shells that have nothing but a dry, shriveled, aborted kernel inside are not dangerous and don't ruin the flavor of your milk. Neither does an occasional grub-eaten nut, even if the idea of insect frass is profoundly unappetizing. However, the highest degree of badness in a hickory nut is something to be concerned about. This happens to nuts that start out good but spoil or mold inside the shell during storage. This is accompanied by changes in color—sometimes to bluish, sometimes to dark yellowish or light brown—and by characteristic flavors that experienced hickory eaters learn to be wary of. Some spoiled nuts taste terrible and are instinctively spit out, but other forms of spoilage create a distinctively odd but not terrible flavor that you might unwittingly swallow. These nuts can be highly toxic; only one is sufficient to cause deafening tinnitus and extreme dizziness that can last a few hours. You don't want even one of those in your hickory milk—and floating will not find them. As soon as you find one, your whole gunnysack or bucket—probably your whole year's supply—is suspect. If you suspect bad nuts in your batch, be sure to pre-crack each one and check it before pounding in the mortar.

No matter how you store your cracking nuts, nuts for milking should be stored for the long term in a refrigerator, cool garage, or cellar to keep them alive. Any time they are used to make milk during autumn, you should float the batch before pounding, in case any additional ones have developed grubs. By winter the grubs will have run their course, so there is no need to float again. You can expect good nuts to stay good through the cool months, as long as you don't store them somewhere that is excessively hot or dry, or that fluctuates between extreme cold and warm. Hickory nuts for milking should also be clean. If they are sitting in mud or a slimy puddle when you collect them, they may be fine for cracking, but the woody shells will absorb off flavors that will boil out into the milk.

The nuts are pounded in a large mortar. I know one person who made a mortar from a piece of 3-inch pipe attached to a board, but most use a solid log section. Some people also use heavy cast iron kettles or other improvised pounding containers. If you use something with a large, open top, you'll need to pre-crack the nuts so they don't pop out when pounded. A mortar should preferably be made from a hard wood that has diffuse pores. Hard maple, yellow birch, and beech are ideal. A section of wood about 16–20 inches (40–50 cm) long and 9 inches (23 cm) in diameter is good. Peel the bark off the block. Prepare

Two mortars that I use for pounding hickory nuts.

two or three log sections; it only takes a few minutes longer than doing one. You can let two of them season, and make a mortar from the third one right away; you'll have a replacement if it cracks.

You need a pounding hole in the center of your mortar, ideally 3.5–4.5 inches (9–11 cm) in diameter and at least 6 inches (15 cm) deep—preferably 12 so the nuts don't jump out. The primitive way to get such a hole is to burn and scrape it out, but quite frankly, this option sucks. Much better is a large Forstner bit with a long shaft, mounted on a drill press. If you don't have a drill press, get in contact with a macho woodworking guy who likes showing off his power tools. (You'll still probably have to buy or rent the bit.) After your mortar is made, oil it liberally so that it dries slowly, to reduce cracking.

The pestle or pounder is much easier to make: Find a straight sapling slightly smaller than the mortar hole, preferably of a similar wood. Cut the pestle 5–6 feet long so that it can be used comfortably while standing upright, peel the bark, and shave down a portion to make a comfortable handhold. If it's too heavy to use, shave off more wood until you like the weight.

Place a handful of nuts in the mortar and then pound the heck out of them. You want all of the shells broken into small fragments so the nutmeats are easily released. The mashed nuts will form a sort of hard cake pressed to the bottom of the mortar, and you'll need a flat piece of wood or perhaps a long metal spoon or butterknife to scrape it loose. Then dump the mashed nuts into a pot.

Pulverized black hickory nuts ready to be boiled into milk or soup. Those on the left have been pounded but still have the large shell pieces. On the right are the same nuts with the larger shell bits sifted out. Sifting is nice when using those hickories, such as mockernut and black, that have very thick shells. I don't sift shagbark or pignuts.

After shells are sifted out, the nutmeats can be pounded further and made into balls like this, to wrap up and give as gifts to your friends who don't own a mortar. They can just plop it into boiling water for instant "hickmilk."

You can make a batch of hickory milk any size you want, but it seems silly to go through the trouble for anything less than a quart of nuts. To that quantity of crushed nuts I add about 2¼ quarts of water. (The ratio is a matter of preference—you may like yours thicker or thinner than I do.) Bring the mixture to a boil, stirring frequently to coax the kernel fragments from their shells.

When the hickory first begins boiling, a light-colored foam will appear on top. I call this "hickory cream." You can skim it off with a large spoon, taking as little liquid as possible with it, and set it aside. Hickory cream is thicker, richer, and more flavorful than the milk, but if you don't want to separate it, just stir a few moments and it will settle back into the milk.

After brief boiling, your hickory milk is ready to be ladled off. Turn the heat off and stir, then let the mixture sit for three seconds so the shell pieces can settle to the bottom. Dip a cup or ladle while the liquid is still agitated, being careful not to go too deep and pick up shell fragments, and pour the milk into another container. Stir repeatedly as necessary to keep the liquid moving as you continue ladling off the milk. Toward the end, tilt the pot to get as much liquid as possible. *Violà*: hickory milk.

You can drink it just like that, and it is good. It has some chunks in it, but they are good chunks. Stir in a little maple syrup and it is almost too good to be true. You can cook grain such as oatmeal, amaranth, rice, couscous, or polenta in hickory milk, and then season it either sweet or savory. Any leftover hickory milk should be refrigerated, as it will spoil quickly.

But wait a second! In the bottom of that pot there is still some liquid filling the spaces between a layer of shell fragments. Suspended within that liquid you can see more good

Boiling hickory milk. The foamy "cream" has already settled.

chunks, and you can also deduce the presence of invisible yet delicious solutes. You can dump this stuff in good conscience—at least as much meat is wasted with cracking and shelling. But if you have even a trace of Chicken Feathers syndrome, you must get those chunks and solutes. A strainer is not the answer: Larger nutmeat pieces will not go through, but many tiny chunks of shell will. I solve this dilemma by pouring another quart of water into the pot, then stirring and ladling off again. This second round of hickory milk will be very weak, but it will make you feel better to use it for cooking grain or as a base for soups.

BARK AND SAP

Hickory is famous for the flavor its wood imparts to smoking meats. "Hickory syrup" can be purchased from several retailers—it's used as a flavoring, especially in meat glazes. This product is not made from hickory sap, but rather from the outer bark boiled in a syrup of table sugar. The hickory bark provides flavoring but not calories.

However, hickories are in the walnut family, and walnuts run sweet sap in the spring that can be boiled down like maple sap to produce a sugary syrup. Fernald and Kinsey (1943) claim to have made sugar by tapping shellbarks in early spring and boiling down the sap. Pehr Kalm[3] reported from about 1750, "In some places in Canada and Albany the inhabitants collect as much of this sap as possible and cook sugar from it. . . . The hickory gives such small quantities of sap, however, that it does not compensate for the work." In early spring I have found sapsucker holes on yellowbud hickory that were exuding one or two large, thick globs of sugar that tasted almost exactly like maple sugar, but my limited attempts at tapping have been futile. My friend Rachel Mifsud, a foraging teacher from Michigan, tapped a shagbark and a pignut—getting a few ounces of very sweet sap from the shagbark. I conclude that this is a novelty use of hickory rather than a practical one.

NOTES ON THE SPECIES

There are 11 species of hickory native to eastern North America (a few more if you're a splitter.) While identifying the group is easy, telling the species apart is less so, but entirely possible. Unfortunately, the "common" names that books use for hickories are out of touch with actual usage. The tree that books call "bitternut" is actually normally called "pignut." The trees that books call "pignut," "mockernut," and "black hickory" are almost never called that—the average

---

3 Kalm's report on hickories, translated by Larsen in 1945, is a valuable and repeatedly cited source for information on uses of hickory.

fellow just calls them "hickory nut tree." Other species with more salient features are distinguished as "scalybark," "shagbark," "shellbark," "pecan," or "kingnut."

Dendrologists recognize two major groups of hickories, usually called the sweet or hard hickories, and the bitter or pecan hickories. The pecan hickories include pecan, water hickory, and yellowbud. All members of the pecan group have thin shells; they have more leaflets than other hickories, and two of them have very bitter kernels. However, these groups do not necessarily reflect genetic affinity. Within the genus *Carya*, there are two common chromosome counts: 32 (diploid) and 64 (tetraploid). The tetraploid hickories include mockernut, black, pignut, and *C. floridana*, while the diploid species include pecan, yellowbud, water, shagbark, shellbark, and nutmeg hickories (Stone 1997). Certain species sets hybridize regularly, and others occasionally—most often with those of the same chromosome count, although fertile crosses are reported between diploid and tetraploid species (Stone 1997).

A detailed account of the seven most important species follows.

Shagbark *Carya ovata*

This is one of our most common and widespread species, and it is probably the most commonly collected wild hickory; in my opinion it has the best flavor of them all. To confuse matters, the shagbark is often called "shellbark," even by some

foresters and botanists. While the use of the two names has been more standardized in recent decades,

Shagbark hickory *C. ovata*. Within this area, shagbark is most prevalent on limestone-derived soils.

one should always confirm the Latin name. Shagbark likes dry or well-drained soil, being especially common in limestone areas; it is associated with black walnut, white oak, white ash, black cherry, elm, and other hickories. Mature trees are recognized by their bark, which forms long, thin sheets or strips that hang loosely from the trunks, often for two feet or more, and the lower ends of these strips often curve away from the trunk. A few other North American trees (shellbark, nutmeg, and water hickory, plus silver and occasionally red maple) have shaggy bark like this, but

The trunk of a shagbark hickory. This one is shaggier than average. Nutmeg, water, and shellbark hickory may also be shaggy, as are silver and rarely red maples. This is the bark used to flavor "hickory syrup."

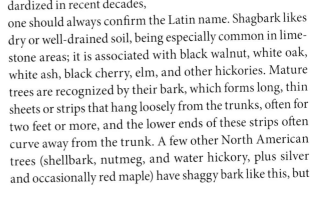

on no other species are the shags so wide, long, or prevalent. These distinctive shaggy trunks have served as a hallmark for nut collectors since time immemorial. Shagbark leaves have 5 or 7 leaflets (usually 5), and a large, plump terminal bud covered with dark scales.

Shagbark nuts have a thick, rigid husk separating into 4 or 5 parts, with no ridges at the seams. The valves of the husk separate fully when ripe and release the nut, either letting it fall naked from the tree, or shattering off it when the fruit hits the ground. The nutshells are angled and slightly to moderately flattened; they may be elongated or squat in shape, and can be blunt or pointed at either end. Inside the shell there are a few ridges that make valleys in the nutmeats, but there are no locked lobes. The shells are moderately thick.

While cracking and shelling this species is slow compared to commercial nuts, it is faster than any hickories but shellbark and pecan. Trees that produce large nuts with good cracking form are treasured by foragers. The smaller nuts are excellent for hickory milk. Shagbarks ripen in mid to late autumn and are highly susceptible to grubs. A loaded tree can produce one or two bushels of clean nuts in a good year.

Shellbark, Kingnut, Big Shagbark
Carya laciniosa

My first shellbark was memorable. A friend had moved to Carbondale, Illinois, for college, and when he came back around Christmas, he brought me one big hickory nut. I stared in wonderment at that goliath nut for several minutes before grabbing a hammer and putting it on the patio block near the woodstove

Shellbark or kingnut hickory *C. laciniosa*. Withinn this range, occurrence is very sporadic due to the specialized floodplain and rich, flat habitat.

Shellbark hickory nuts on the tree. Most of the leaves visible here have 7 leaflets, which is common in full sun.

Shellbark hickory leaves in the shade—they are enormous and have 9 leaflets. Although the names and bark are similar, this tree is easy to tell from shagbark by nuts or leaves, and the two almost never grow together.

where I had cracked my shagbarks for years. I held the nut in position and gave it a good whack on the narrow side. The nut didn't crack, but the patio block broke in half.

This uncommon Midwestern species is the premiere hickory nut. You'll know you've found a shellbark when you pick up a hickory nut so large it makes you gasp; shellbark nuts average 5 times as large as shagbarks, and larger than black walnuts. The nut's exterior form resembles that of shagbark, but the shell is proportionately thicker. The leaf of shellbark is much larger than that of shagbark, and it normally has 7 or 9 leaflets; the twigs are also thicker. Although the name suggests otherwise, shellbark's bark tends to have narrower shaggy strips than shagbark, and these are usually fewer and sometimes entirely absent on the lower 40 feet or so—especially on older trees. Old trees, near the base, often look like a pignut.

Shellbark is predominantly a tree of the lower Midwest. Although it can be confused with shagbark at a glance, the two almost never grow together. Shellbark's native habitat is the higher parts of river floodplains, river terraces, valleys, lower slopes, and flatlands with exceptionally rich soil; it is associated with pecan, swamp chestnut oak, Shumard oak, cherrybark oak, overcup oak, bur oak, coffeetree, red mulberry, pawpaw, black walnut, green ash, pumpkin ash, sugarberry, sweetgum, and honey locust. In other words, this tree is King of Foraging Paradise. Unfortunately, these

Trunk of a shellbark hickory. Young trees have shaggy bark essentially indistinguishable from shagbark, but older trunks tend to lose this feature, especially in shade. This ancient tree stands about 120' tall, and you'll notice that there are no shags until you get about 50' up the trunk.

Shellbark nuts from 3 different trees next to one black walnut. The small shellbark nut seen here would be very large for a shagbark; the average shellbark nut dwarfs that of any other hickory.

are exactly the locations most coveted as farmland, and as the countryside was heavily settled, most of the forests inhabited by shellbark were cleared for agriculture. Although the tree's numbers have been decimated, there are scattered individuals and occasional groves left.

Since shellbark valves sometimes cling stubbornly to the nut, I like to bring my drywall hammer with me, to smack the nuts right where they lay and dislodge the husks. Fortunately, shellbarks are affected minimally by hickory grubs. The thick shells take a lot of force to crack, but once this is accomplished, shellbarks are pretty fast to shell out. I sometimes wear a thin glove on the hand holding the nut when I crack them with a hammer, because the shell sends a formidable shock wave through the fingers the moment it cracks. A vise is especially advisable for cracking shellbarks. There tends to be two locked lobes per half, which makes the meat slightly harder to extract than that of shagbark, but the greater size more than makes up for the difference. In flavor this species is much like the shagbark—almost as good, in my opinion.

Mockernut *Carya tomentosa*

This widespread hickory is generally the most common species in the South, where it can be found in most types of well-drained hardwood or hardwood-pine forest. The bark of mockernut is deeply furrowed with interlacing ridges, but it is not shaggy. Mockernut's leaves are characterized by tufts of woolly hairs, especially on the rachis and the lower side of the midvein. The leaflets are large and broad, and there are 7 or 9 of them per leaf.

Mockernut hickory *C. tomentosa* is the most common hickory in the Southeast.

Top left Mockernut is pretty easy to identify by the dense tufts of soft hair on the rachis and midvein. **Bottom left** Mockernuts, a little smaller than average, with and without husks. Husks may or may not fully split open, but are always thick. **Right** Mockernut trunk. The bark typically has a pattern of crisscrossing ridges (like expanded-metal walkways), but it doesn't shag. This one was only 9" in diameter but dropped a bunch of huge nuts.

The nuts of this species are large, with thick valves. They are usually elongated, faintly flattened, and pointed at both ends, with angles on the shell; but sometimes they are short and squat. This is our second-largest hickory nut, but don't get too excited over that. It has been said that the "mocker" part of the name is derived from a Dutch word for a heavy hammer. Maybe so; I don't speak Dutch. But the name seems appropriate in English as well—a practical joke that Nature played on zealous foragers. I am, as I write this, the butt of that joke, with 16 gallons of mockernuts on the porch, which I curse every time

I shell. The problem with mockernuts is not thick shells or small nutmeats, as is often claimed; it is the presence of 4 or 5 tenaciously locked lobes per side. Even if you manage to expose a beautiful half-meat, your nutpick will pop it out with great trouble, and probably in 11 pieces. This makes mockernut one of the worst choices for cracking and shelling. If you insist on doing it, make your nutpick with a narrow tip to get in these deep crevices.

Hickory milk is a much more labor-efficient way to use mockernuts, but they are not ideal for this, either; the thick shells tend to eat up the pestle and the mortar. Despite its abundance and large size, mockernut is an exasperating hickory. (Update: By the next fall, I still had 8 gallons of those mockernuts left over, and happily fed them to the squirrels.)

Pignut *Carya glabra, C. ovalis*

This species (or two species, depending on which taxonomy you follow) is among our best hickories for eating, and many savvy foragers claim it as their favorite. The name "pignut" is deeply problematic. Although foresters, dendrologists, and field guides invariably call these trees "pignuts," most laypeople just call them "hickory nut." In

Pignut hickory *C. glabra/ovalis.*

actual practice, the name "pignut" is most often used for *Carya cordiformis*—the tree that books call "bitternut" or "yellowbud." (Pehr Kalm confirms that this has been the case since at least 1750.) Sloppy naturalists have been conflating these trees with such regularity that communication about them is now muddled to dysfunction. This is totally unnecessary, since pignut and bitternut are easy to distinguish by their nuts.

Pignut is a medium to large tree that dominates in some areas that are well drained and acidic. The leaves are small among hickories, with 5 or 7 leaflets. The bark has ridges between fissures; these ridges may be tight and low or loose, high and separating (even occasionally slightly shaggy) on older trees; but they never hang off in wide, flat, long strips like shagbark. The bark form is highly variable—one extreme resembles yellowbud almost exactly, while the other extreme can be easily mistaken for the lower portion of a shellbark's trunk or even sometimes a shagbark. The average trunk, however, has bark that is rather easily recognized.

The pignut's fruit is small and usually pear- or teardrop-shaped—a form sometimes shared only by black hickory. The elongated part of the fruit near the stem has a much thicker husk, and nestled inside this is usually an elongated sharp point attached to the nutshell. The husk valves are often held together by this thickened basal section of the fruit, so they don't fall away or peel off as

Top left Pignut leaves, with only five leaflets. They are often narrower than this, and may have 7 leaflets. **Bottom left** Despite the variable bark and non-descript leaves, pignut is easily identified by its nut: moderately thin husk, and moderately thick shell with the ridges faint to absent. Also, the fruit around the nut is usually pear-shaped and never winged. **Right** An average pignut trunk. This species has the greatest variability in bark form of our hickories—it can also be smoothish and shallowly fissured like yellowbud, or slightly shaggy (but with very narrow strips, and thicker than those of shagbark.)

readily as shagbark husks. The husks are generally thin, but stiffer and thicker than those of yellowbuds, without the raised, wing-like ridge where the valves meet. Pignut husks may have 4 valves like most other hickories, but sometimes have only 2 or 3.

Pignuts are small and slightly flattened in cross section. The shells are smooth and rounded except for 1 or 2 faint ridges that are usually present on each side. Pignuts have moderately thick, hard shells—similar to shagbark, but on average slightly thicker, although they shatter more easily. The kernels have 2 or 4 locked lobes per side. It is reported that some pignuts along the Gulf Coast have unusually large nuts (Stone 1997). I'd love to get my hands on some of these.

You will often hear that the kernels of pignuts are bitter, but such reports are primarily, if not wholly, the result of confusion with yellowbud hickory. I have collected and eaten quantities of pignuts from New York, Michigan, North Carolina, Georgia, Missouri, Arkansas, and Illinois and have yet to find a bitter one. Pignuts, in fact, are delicious. If you have the time to shell them, or find a tree with especially good size or shape, the kernels are fantastic. Pignuts are always an excellent choice for making hickory milk. Their only drawback is their high susceptibility to grubs.

Black hickory *Carya texana*

Black hickory is a close relative of mockernut and pignut, about halfway between the two in characteristics. It is a moderately sized tree of the south-central United States, found mostly on dry, well-drained ridges or sandy soils. Black hickory is very common in Missouri, Arkansas, Oklahoma, and surrounding areas, but it is

Black hickory *C. texana.*

almost never identified more specifically than "hickory nut" by those who use it.

The husks of this species are thin, but not as thin as those of pignut, and they are stiff. The outside of the husk is heavily covered with tiny yellowish scales—a good identifying feature that is easily overlooked. The nuts are plump and only slightly flattened, with thick shells, but not so thick as mockernut, and the outside of the shell tends to be smooth. The meats usually have 4 locked lobes per side and are thus difficult to separate from the cracked shells, but not quite so bad as mockernut. This nut is primarily a candidate for hickory milk, but larger ones are sometimes reasonable to crack and shell. Black hickory nuts have a great flavor.

The nuts of black hickory are plump, rounded, and usually ridged faintly; they have moderately thin husks and moderately to very thick shells. It's like a scrubby cross of pignut and mockernut, and a few trees are hard to separate from pignuts.

Pecan *Carya illinoinensis*

This is the champion among hickories in tree size, nut production, and ease of use. It is the state tree of Texas, where it is widespread and abundant. Although its distribution is smaller than that of some of our other species, pecan was an important food for native people wherever it grew. Pecan stands out among hickories, looking in some ways more like a walnut. The tree has deeply furrowed bark that is a lighter gray than other hickories, a wide crown, and 11–21 long, narrow leaflets. Several bushels of nuts can be produced by one large tree.

Pecan *Carya illinoinensis*. Native range shown in blue; area of widespread introduction and occasional naturalization shown in lighter blue.

Wild pecans tend to be much smaller than the cultivated pecans we are accustomed to seeing in the grocery store. They also taste much better. The nuts are easy to identify: They are elongated, cylindrical, pointed, and have thin husks

A loaded pecan branch. The leaves are longer than those of most other hickories, and the terminal leaflets are not enlarged.

Top left Wild pecans on the tree. This is our most elongated hickory nut. **Bottom left** Wild pecans are smaller than the average nuts you'd find in the store, but are otherwise identical, and usually taste better. **Right** Typical trunk of an old pecan growing in a park along a river.

and smooth, thin shells. The husks split fully open when ripe, often dropping naked nuts to the ground while the husks remain on the twigs. Pecans are the easiest of the hickories to crack and shell, and their flavor is among the best. The nuts suffer from weevil damage much less than most species. Considering all of this, one can see why the pecan was the hickory chosen for cultivation.

Pecans are most common in Texas, Oklahoma, and Louisiana, where they ripen primarily in November and December. Further north they are locally abundant along river systems, ripening somewhat earlier. Pecans are naturally found in rich valleys and the higher parts of river floodplains, along with such trees as cottonwood, elm, black walnut, red mulberry, and sugarberry; shellbark, yellowbud, and water hickories; and bur, Shumard, overcup, water, willow, and cherrybark oaks. Although most of these stands have been cleared for agriculture, the pecan, like most floodplain trees, has done well colonizing fencerows, field edges, and other disturbed areas. It is also widely planted as a shade tree, even well outside of its natural range, and the loads of nuts that it drops on city streets and in backyards are largely ignored. In the heart of its range, pecan is ubiquitous as a street and yard tree.

Pecans keep better than most hickory nuts. They are also very easy to crack with a simple handheld nutcracker. Another way is to set the nut on a cutting board or countertop and smash them with the bottom of a mason jar. Gently—you don't need shattered glass in the kitchen. You can crack pecans extremely fast in a Davebilt nutcracker, if you have one, but I find them easier to shell when cracked by hand, so I don't use my Davebilt on them.

The most important reason that pecans have become commercialized is the form of the nut: It is easy to shell mechanically. The shells have minimal convolutions inside, so the meats come out easily, in large pieces. If you live in pecan-growing regions, you might be able to find a commercial cracking and shelling facility that, for a fee, will shell out a few bushels for you. In years of a bumper crop, this is almost too good to be true. Just remember to keep the shelled pecans in a refrigerator, or preferably a freezer, for the best flavor.

Yellowbud (Bitternut) *Carya cordiformis*: The Oil-Nut Hickory

This is the most abundant and widespread of all the hickories. It likes the rich, moist soils of valleys and high floodplains but is also found in well-drained uplands with trees such as red oak, white ash, sugar maple, beech, slippery elm, and shagbark. Although listed in field guides as bitternut or yellowbud hickory, laypeople most commonly call it "pignut," which leads to great confusion. I prefer to use "yellowbud" because the name "bitternut" is endlessly confused with "butternut," in both print and speech.

Yellowbud or bitternut hickory
C. cordiformis.

The bark of yellowbud remains rather smooth well into maturity, although it eventually develops shallow fissures and, on the largest trees, small plates. The leaflets, typically 7–11 in number, are thin and narrow compared to most species. Yellowbud can be easily identified by its naked, sulfur-yellow buds—a feature distinguishing it from all other North American trees. The nut is enclosed in the thinnest husk of any hickory, with 4 wing-like ridges where the valves meet. The valves separate only partially at maturity—sometimes hardly at all—and commonly the separation occurs in the middle of the seam, while the valve tips remain attached. The husk commonly remains attached to the nut until it turns black and rots off. The nut itself is about as wide as long and only slightly flattened, sometimes heart-shaped at the tip, without angles on the shell. The shell is very thin, even thinner than a pecan shell, and is much convoluted on the inside, giving the meat a decidedly brain-like appearance.

Top left Yellowbud hickory with ripe nut. The leaves look halfway between pecan and shagbark. Note the ridged husk. **Bottom left** This is the distinct yellow bud of yellowbud hickory. **Right** The bark of mature yellowbud hickory is has thin, smooth-topped, criscrossing ridges (occasional old-growth trees get small, light gray, peeling chips).

The yellowbud's kernel is high in tannin and very bitter as a result. Although the literature often reports that the nuts of this species are not eaten by wildlife, this is false. Yellowbuds are an incredibly important and highly sought food source for all species that eat other hickory nuts, and (due to the thin shells) some that don't. I have watched white-tailed deer and black bears eat them avidly, and they are relished by red, gray, fox, and flying squirrels as well as chipmunks and deer mice. The year I write this, the yellowbud crop in our woods was fairly good, but since the acorns failed, the yellowbud trees were completely cleaned off before any nuts hit the ground.

You can crack and shell yellowbuds, and doing so is faster than most species of hickory nut because of the thin shells. The nutmeats can be leached in 4–5 changes of boiling water over a period of several hours, after which they taste something like cooked beans. These leached nuts are actually an easily harvested source of calories, but they suffer from what I call a "comparison dilemma"— since other hickory nuts do not have to be leached, these are frowned upon. This nut is thus widely despised by modern foragers.

This hickory's yellow buds have a unique fragrance and strong flavor that reminds me of nutmeg, and we have experimented some with the use of these

Left Husks of yellowbud hickory are very thin, as are the shells (thinner than pecan shells). The valves may separate much of the way, or scarcely at all, but they do not fall of the nut. Right Clean, perfect nuts of yellowbud, ready to go into the oil press. This species, the maligned and unappreciated bastard stepchild of the hickories, has the greatest potential as a sustainable forest crop.

as a seasoning. The young, newly emerging leaves, dried and crushed, can be made into a tea. According to Pehr Kalm ([1750] 1945), Benjamin Franklin drank this tea and considered it his favorite American substitute for Oriental tea. I'm not as fond of it as Ben was.

The best use of yellowbuds, however, is in making oil. One of the hardest tasks of the forager is to find a wild source of vegetable oil. Oily seeds have long been highly sought after by foraging people. Yellowbud hickory nuts are about 55% kernel by weight, which is the highest percentage of all wild hickories, comparing favorably with selected pecan cultivars. The meats contain about 75% oil. Tannin, which accounts for the bitterness in hickory nuts (as well as acorns and olives), is not oil-soluble, so the oil contains no hint of bitterness.

I believe that yellowbud hickory is the best wild source of edible vegetable oil in North America. It is our most abundant and widespread hickory, and it produces enormous nut crops. (I know of one open-grown tree that produced more than 40 gallons of clean nuts in 2016.) This is quite incredible when you consider that a gallon of bitternuts has the same meat content of 2 gallons of shagbark nuts. Five gallons of nuts in the shell produces about 3 quarts of finished oil. All hickories contain delicious oil, but only yellowbud and pecan have thin shells and shell-to-kernel ratios that make it practical to use an expeller press without shelling them first. This advantage outweighs any other consideration in the pressing for oil.

Most people do not have a commercial expeller press, of course. But there is a real opportunity here for a woodsy entrepreneur, with a relatively small investment, to establish a sustainable, local, native, and healthy oil crop. Other than me (I have been pressing yellowbud hickory oil on a small commercial scale since 2014), there is currently no hickory oil industry in North America. I can find no reference to the domestic manufacture of hickory oil after about 1800. However, there is a commercial hickory oil industry in Southeast Asia—the only other part of the world where these nuts are native.

Thomas Ash (1682) reports thus of Native American production of hickory oil in what is now North Carolina:

> The Wild Wallnut, or Hiquery-tree, gives the Indians, by boyling its Kernel, a wholesome Oyl, from whom the English frequently supply themselves for their Kitchen uses. . . . Whilst new it has a pleasant Taste, but after six Months, it decays and grows acid. I believe it might make a good Oyl, and of as general an use as that of the Olive, if it were better purified and rectified.

For small-scale oil extraction, the best option I have found is boiling, following the example of the Indians. To do this, smash the nuts in a wooden mortar, just as if you were making hickory milk. The shells (of yellowbuds only!) are also thin enough to be broken in a powerful blender, if you don't have a mortar. Then, boil the mashed nuts for a long time—preferably several hours, or a few days—to let the oils out of the kernel. An oil slick will form on top of the pot. When you decide it has boiled long enough, skim the oil-rich liquid off the top, trying to get as little water as possible. Take your oily water and strain it through a cloth or fine strainer to get out any chunks. If you have a large amount of oil, you can put the mixture into a deep container (such as a mason jar) and let the oil rise and the water settle, and then use a dropper to pull the pure oil off the top. You can also cook away the water; the dissolved solids, including tannin, will form a cake at the bottom of the pan. When your water has boiled off, strain the oil again to get rid of any coagulated chunks. It is important to get rid of all the water, as it is bitter and will give the oil a short shelf life. This boiled hickory oil is pleasant with a light-yellow color, but unfortunately it doesn't have the fresh, intense flavor of cold-pressed oil. Hickory oil does not keep for long at room temperature and should be refrigerated.

That gorgeous, golden, delicious liquid is yellowbud hickory oil.

This ancient shagbark has witnessed the passing of passenger pigeons and American parrots, served as a scratching post for bison and shade for elk, and dropped nuts for the Sauk people. Some things, thank God, did not change.

The hickory nut is the quintessential American wild edible. For thousands of years it provided the residents of our eastern forests with a food as basic and vital as dairy products in our modern diets. Although the European latecomers who settled here never made hickory a staple, the nuts became a regular and highly appreciated food on pioneer homesteads. A few generations back, the hickory nut was almost universally used in those rural districts where it is found. Nut collecting was a common fall activity for families or a serious chore that children were set upon. The tree figures deeply in American lore as an emblem of strength, toughness, and value: the stuff of tool handles, wagon wheels, longbows, wedges; the finest of firewoods. Still today, most Easterners have heard of the hickory nut, and arguably the best of our hickories, the pecan, has become a major commercial crop available in every grocery store on the continent.

In recent decades, however, hickories have fallen into disuse. Ancient trees left in crop fields by our forebears are now mere decorations—or obstructions to the farmer's machinery. They have outlived the era of bark-covered wigwams in clearings, of log cabins surrounded by stump-studded pastures. These stately pasture hickories were tall and bountiful in the era of white-painted farmhouses with outdoor privies, when they were the focus of Sunday congregations of basket-toting families. You can still sometimes find the cracked and shelled nuts for sale at a farmers' market or a roadside stand, a tradition kept alive by some semi-retired farmer who hates the feel of idle hands. But the rows of shagbarks judiciously left beside country lanes are today nameless to most commuters, the fallen nuts but litter.

Those rigid trunks and regal crowns are not just relics of a bygone era; they are a gateway to it. The frost and wind of *this* autumn are just like *that* autumn so long ago. The roadside litter that pops under the tires of the sightseer's SUV reminds us of a time when good food was worth our time, when staring at a screen wasn't the only way to spend a spare hour. The hickory begs us to notice that such a time is now.

Hops

Humulus lupulus

"Ooohh, hops!" Mike shouted. He looked over his shoulder, swerved to the roadside while hitting the brakes, and then backed up fifty yards. He jumped out of the car as soon as it was stopped and bolted over to the fenceline, returning shortly with a big smile and a handful of something green. "Do you like the smell of hops?" he asked, shoving his hand toward my face. I didn't know. I grabbed one of the green clusters of papery scales and held it to my nose for a long sniff, discovering that I do like the smell of hops.

Something about hops gets people excited. My heart still leaps a little each time I happen upon a clump of it growing along a stream or fence line. Since I don't make beer, I had no use for the plant, other than to occasionally pull down a vine and inhale the exotic scent of a fruit cluster. But something about hops would always draw me to it. Then I learned to eat hops shoots, which drew me even closer—this time with my mouth open.

The cones of wild hops growing along my orchard fence.

DESCRIPTION

Hops is a thin, perennial, herbaceous vine that grows many stems (sometimes a dozen or more) from a tough root crown. The vines are only about a eighth of an inch (3 mm) thick—rarely twice as thick on very rich soil in full sunlight—but they commonly grow 12–25 feet (4–8 m) long. The vines branch only rarely and lack tendrils, and so grow by twining, wrapping around tree trunks, branches, bushes, herbs, and often braiding themselves around each other. The stems are uniformly green and do not taper. They are round in cross section, with 6 ridges, roughened by short spurs pointing toward the base. The raspy texture of the hops stem helps separate this plant from another thin herbaceous vine that is often found near it, and which has a similar name, hopniss. Hopniss has thin stems with no ridges or spurs, and it has a compound leaf (the hops leaf is simple). Hops is also often found near clematis—which has a rough but not raspy stem, and which has compound leaves in pairs held at enlarged nodes.

The herbaceous vines of hops are traditionally called "bines," an archaic word etymologically related to "bind." Call them that if you wish. Some hop growers assert that *bines* climb by twining, while *vines* use tendrils, but this is a false dichotomy that neither botanical nor common language recognizes. The word "bine" has largely disappeared from the language except in reference to hops and wood*bine*—only one of which climbs by twining.

Hops leaves are paired and widely spaced, sometimes with a foot or more between pairs. They have 3 or 5 main veins from the base. Typically the leaves are deeply 3-lobed or 5-lobed, but the upper leaves are sometimes unlobed. The margins are not toothed. Leaves are 4–6 inches (10–15 cm) long and almost as wide. The leaf's upper surface is roughened by scattered, stiff hairs, while the underside is much smoother— hairless or with scattered minute hairs. The petiole is about 80% of the length of the blade, and raspy like the stems.

The leaf of native hops in eastern North America can have three lobes, like this one, or five—and rarely is unlobed. It is almost identical to cultivated hops from the Old World, which is the same species.

As one travels south and west, the hops native to North America has more deeply lobed leaves, and more lobes, like these from Colorado. Note the nice shoot on the right side. (Photo by Briana Wiles)

Humulus lupulus has been divided into several subspecies, based mostly on characteristics of the leaf—and of course, this has been done with some degree of confusion and disagreement. Some authors find these differences great enough to separate one or more of these populations as species. I will not wade deeply into this taxonomic discussion, as it is not particularly relevant to the forager. The Eurasian subspecies grown commercially is *H. l. lupulus*. The hops native to eastern North America appears very similar to the European; its mature leaves normally have 3 major lobes, and 3 major veins from the base (although 5 lobes is common, especially on the earliest spring leaves). As one travels west across the continent, however, our native hops becomes progressively more distinct, and the leaves more lobed. At the southwestern end of its range, hops has leaves that are very deeply lobed, with 5 major veins and 5–9 lobes per leaf.

Hops is usually a dioecious plant; individuals tend to be male or female, not bearing both kinds of flower. The female flowers are small and hidden by overlapping leafy bracts in a tight spike—this is the familiar, scaly, cone-like structure for which hops is grown commercially. The male flowers are greenish white, with 5 spreading sepals, less than a quarter inch (6 mm) across, in naked axillary panicles a few inches long; these fall off after pollination and are rarely noticed. The fruit is a papery capsule holding one seed, borne in a tight, cone-like cluster 1–2.5 inches (2.5–6 cm) long, green at first but later turning brown.

The above description refers to the native hops and the Eurasian cultivars that have been planted here, all of which belong to the species *Humulus lupulus*. There is also an introduced invasive species, Japanese hops *H. japonicus*, which is widespread and spotty in the United States, but locally abundant. Unlike its native relative, Japanese hops is an annual. It can be told apart by its leaves having more lobes (usually 5–7), which tend to broaden toward the tip. Japanese hops also has more than 3 main veins from the base. The best distinguishing feature is that Japanese hops has stiff, raspy hairs along the major veins on the undersurface; the same veins on true hops have small, soft hairs or none at all. The flowers of Japanese hops lack the resinous glands, and thus most of the scent, of true hops.

HABITAT

The same species of hops that is native to Asia, and that is cultivated for beer making, *Humulus lupulus*, is also native to North America (Small 1980). This surprises many people, who assume that it is only found here as an escape from cultivation. The myth that hops is not native is prevalent and quite tenacious, and is especially perpetuated by the brewing community. While it is true that hops has sometimes escaped from cultivation, this does not account for its widespread occurrence in North America. Native hops has a broad range and is quite common.

Hops likes rich, moist soil, especially where it is sandy. It thrives in full sun but also can be found in lightly shaded localities. The primary natural habitat of hops is river floodplains and swampy or brushy streamsides and valleys. It can also be found at the bases of steep slopes or cliffs, shrub swamps on sandy soil, and the margins of ponds and lakes. Human disturbance has greatly increased the habitat available to this vine, which now thrives along roadsides, fencelines, and forest borders—like other floodplain species. Associated plants include black elderberry, stinging nettle, jerusalem-artichoke, hopniss, cow parsnip, carrion flower, sochan, and clematis.

Hops *H. lupulus*. Some portions of this range, such as the Southeast, represent introduced populations exclusively—in these areas hops is much less common. In most of the range, most or all of the populations are native.

HARVEST AND PREPARATION

The food source provided by hops is the young shoot or the rapidly growing tip of the vine. These can be collected from mid spring through early summer. You can tell they are still tender because they will snap when bent sharply, pinched, or pulled. The bark of older hops stems becomes very fibrous; young shoots are not tough at all. The leaves of the tender tips are also not fully formed. Because hops grows very fast, these shoots may be tender for as much as 26 inches (8–14 inches is more common). The largest, thickest shoots are found where growing conditions are ideal. Although each shoot is thin—pencil-thick would be considered very robust—there are often a great number of stems in an area, making it possible to collect a serving in just a minute or two. The plants are reported to cause contact dermatitis in some individuals (Foster and Duke 2000).

Hops is primarily grown decoratively, or on a large scale for the brewing industry; however, the edible shoots have traditionally been an important secondary product of the plant. They are available in markets in many hop growing regions. The shoots are popular in Belgian cooking (Van Wyk 2005), and are often used in omelets in France (Couplan 2009).

I like hops shoots raw, but in this state they must be chewed thoroughly because of their raspy surface. The flavor and texture both remind me of green beans. Steamed or boiled, the surface texture becomes gentler and the shoots are an excellent vegetable. From the first time I tasted a hops shoot, I have eagerly sought them every spring, and have transplanted some from a nearby stream to grow along my orchard fence.

The tender new growth of Japanese hops *H. japonicus* can be used as a vegetable, just as with true hops. However, since this plant is annual, it never has the extremely fast growth spurt seen in *H. lupulus*, so the tender portion is never as large or as tender. It's not bad, but neither is it fantastic like true hops—and it is more difficult to collect in quantity.

Hops is used in brewing beer to add its aroma and characteristic bitterness, as well as to inhibit bacterial growth. This is a relatively recent innovation; before hops, various herb mixtures had been used for this purpose for thousands of years. A few decades ago, when

Hops shoots in typical habitat along a river. 14–20 inches are tender. Note the five-lobed leaves.

Japanese hops, an invasive annual, also edible but not nearly as good. This species may have a few tender leaves near the tip, but doesn't produce a shoot.

I pointed out wild hops to home beer makers, they scoffed at the notion of ruining their brew with its skunky, unrefined flavor. Most brewing books condemn the idea with gusto. But obviously, wild hops was good enough to use in the distant past, or it would not have been brought into cultivation. To the unrefined nose of a non-brewer like me, they smell pretty darn similar. Now, wild hops is the rage in certain brewing circles; there are several microbrews that actually *advertise* the use of native wild hops in their product.

Even if you don't like beer or don't want the alcohol, the flower clusters and their essence may be of use: They have long been used as a tonic, diuretic, digestive aid, sedative, and sleep aid. For this purpose, you can steep a simple infusion (tea) of the flower or young fruit clusters in warm water. Too much of it can give you a headache, though, just like beer.

There are two little-known, additional edible parts of hops. The oily seeds are soft and have good flavor. They are surrounded by a thin shell, which I just chew up. Unfortunately, they are hard to gather in quantity, and are often coated with some of the strong-flavored resin from the scales around them. I don't think these are a very practical food source. The roots have reportedly been eaten in Japan and China (Couplan 2009), but the ones I dig seem prohibitively tough.

Mixed in the tangled brush along some ravine that you have passed a hundred times, there is a beautiful, exotic-looking vine, hiding among the meadow rue and cow parsnip between the bushes. Look in there, hard. Get in there, deep. When you finally find it, follow the raspy twining bundle to its base. You'll have a secret spot that only the rabbits will share. And every spring thereafter, so long as you treat it well, you'll be able to return and nibble a few of those juicy shoots that the rabbits thought they had to themselves.

Japanese Knotweed, Giant Knotweed

Polygonum cuspidatum (Fallopia japonica), P. sachalinense

As a youngster I read every book in our library about pandas, and it got me thinking about how simple and easy life would be if all I needed to do was lollygag in a bamboo thicket. But there is no bamboo in Wisconsin. Then one spring day I came across an enormous thicket of a bamboo-like plant growing between a four-lane highway and its exit ramp. I knew it wasn't actually bamboo, because I had bamboo-cane sword fights with kids in my neighborhood and knew that real bamboo was tough as heck; this stuff was brittle enough to crush in my fist. Still, it looked kind of like bamboo. I figured this was my best chance to experience the life of a panda, so I crawled in amongst the dry, dead stems and built myself a nest. I lollygagged with the peace of

Perfect spring shoots of Japanese knotweed.

mind that, despite my proximity to the highway, nobody knew I was there and no poachers would shoot me for my pied pelt.

It was pretty cool being a panda, so I came back to my little thicket from time to time. One day I noticed that there were new shoots coming up. "Bamboo shoots! That's what pandas eat," I thought. Of course, I knew they really weren't bamboo, but just for pretend, I picked one and chewed on it cautiously. (I know, eating a plant without identifying it is a terrible idea.) It tasted like rhubarb. I gradually grew bolder and bolder with my nibbling, until eventually I just considered these "bamboo shoots" another feral snack in my repertoire. My taste for them outlived my penchant for playing panda, and eventually, I even learned the name of the plant: Japanese knotweed.

DESCRIPTION

Japanese knotweed is an enormous perennial herb that forms dense colonies. I have seen patches covering several acres, although typical clones are smaller. The stems are arching, hollow like bamboo, and have a wall inside at each leaf

A typical colony of Japanese knotweed in midsummer.

A mature clump of giant knotweed. Note the larger, drooping leaves, pleated along the prominent secondary veins.

node, separating it into jointed segments. The surface of the stalk is smooth with gentle ridges, hairless, and reddish-purple mixed with green. The stalks are typically 0.8–1.6 inches (2–4 cm) thick at the base and stand 5–9 feet (1.5–3 m) tall, branching minimally and only near the tip.

The leaves are alternate and large, 4–12 inches (10–30 cm) long and about two-thirds as wide, growing on petioles about 15% of the blade length. They are very broadly ovate to heart-shaped, with entire margins. Leaves are hairless above but may have scattered, tiny hairs below. The flowers are tiny and whitish, appearing in late summer in dense panicles from the upper leaf axils; there are also somewhat larger terminal panicles.

Japanese knotweed leaves.

Japanese knotweed is a showy bloomer in late summer.

The two species in this section are very similar, and few people differentiate them. The giant knotweed *Polygonatum sachalinense* is larger in all respects, with larger, more elongated leaves that are distinctly heart-shaped at the base. Giant knotweed's leaves droop, and they have more numerous and more prominent secondary veins. The stems of giant knotweed tend to be pure green with numerous small channels roughly equal in size; Japanese knotweed stems typically have purple mottling and a few deeper, larger channels. Both species are used similarly as food, and hybrids between the two are also quite common. I prefer the giant knotweed where I can find it—not only is it larger, but the shoot walls are thicker and the flavor is slightly better.

The scientific name of Japanese knotweed varies from source to source. It is sometimes listed as *Polygonum cuspidatum* and at other times *Fallopia japonica*, with an occasional *Reynoutria japonica* thrown in the mix by those who really want to split up the knotweeds.

HABITAT

Japanese knotweed is not native to North America, so it is hard to predict its occurrence; however, it can be found in almost every state. In some regions one sees occasional colonies of it scattered here and there on country roadsides; in other areas it is a pernicious weed found around every corner, forming massive pure colonies covering acres, to the exclusion of all other vegetation. Although it will grow on almost any soil that is not water-logged or exceedingly dry, it prefers sand or loam to clay. The most thriving patches are found in well-drained but rich soil in full sun—it does not survive in heavy shade.

HARVEST AND PREPARATION

Gather the tender young shoots of this plant when they are still in the spear-like stage and the leaves are not yet fully formed. Ideal height is 8–20 inches, but you can get them when smaller, and you can also pick the top section of much larger shoots, keeping to the portion that is tender. Use a knife or scissors if you want, but it is easy enough to just bend them until they snap—especially the youngest ones. In fact, this is how I get only the tender parts: I grab the shoot at the base and pull to the side. If it doesn't snap off with a sudden pop, it's not tender, and I move up a node or two and pull again until it does pop off.

Composite range of Japanese knotweed *Fallopia japonica* and giant knotweed *F. sachalinense*. Occasional colonies are to be expected outside the mapped range.

Knotweed shoots appear in mid spring among the dead stalks of last year's growth, an army of phyto-soldiers holding conquered territory while their rhizomes advance unseen in their Napoleonesque cause of taking over the continent. Hyperbole, perhaps—but such that will ring true to anyone who has tried to keep claim on her backyard as knotweed invaded. If you have Japanese knotweed around, you probably have much more than you could possibly eat. This is a plant for which conservation is irrelevant.

Japanese knotweed shoots peel best the moment you pick them, and when very young.

When you harvest knotweed, be careful what you do with leftover parts. Cut stems can root easily to form new colonies, so make sure they are completely dead (through drying, freezing, cooking, or feeding to livestock) before discarding them.

Giant knotweed shoot, a little further along than the Japanese knotweed shoots shown earlier, but still tender.

Knotweed shoots are sour, like rhubarb or dock petioles, and are used similarly as a tangy vegetable. I like to peel the slightly bitter skin before eating them. Although you don't have to, virtually anything made from knotweed will have better flavor if the shoots are peeled. This is most true if you are extending the season a bit by plucking the top few inches off older shoots. It is easiest to peel with your fingers, grabbing the skin at the cut end of the shoot; a vegetable peeler takes off half the volume. Younger shoots peel more easily, as do shoots peeled in the field, just seconds after picking. Peeled knotweed stalks are often blanched and then soaked overnight to reduce their acidity—although I don't do that.

Being available in huge quantity, but only for a brief time in spring, makes these shoots ideal for storing. Knotweed shoots are acidic enough to can in a water bath, but they turn to a soft, sloppy, slimy mass. They can also be frozen after blanching. In Japan, peeled raw shoots are traditionally stored with enormous amounts of salt, which keeps the fresh, crisp texture; they are soaked in fresh water for 8–12 hours to remove the salt before use. For the most part, I just enjoy them in season.

I enjoy eating a knotweed shoot raw, and some people dip them in sugar, as is done with rhubarb. The shoots can be sliced crosswise and used raw in salads. You can add them to stir-fry (in which case I like them sliced small so that the sour doesn't overpower any single bite, and thrown in at the end so they don't get too soft). They also make a nice vegetable for soups, adding a pleasant tang. Japanese knotweed pie is a commonly touted way to use the stalks. It is often likened to rhubarb pie, but having had both many times, I don't think the knotweed measures up. Karen Monger (2015) suggests making a leather from knotweed stalks. Inspired by her idea, I chopped some peeled shoots and steamed them until soft, then pureed in a blender. I mixed this 50/50 with unsweetened applesauce, spread it on trays, and dehydrated it. Pretty good. Alan Bergo, a chef in Minneapolis who incorporates wild food into his cuisine, makes a knotweed sorbet (also mixed with apple) that is fantastic. Ellen Zachos makes knotweed wine and a lovely pink syrup by boiling the stems.

Japanese knotweed has received much attention for the extremely high concentration of resveratrol in its rhizome, from which it is extracted commercially. (This is the chemical found in grape skins and red wine that may or may not make you become French and live almost forever.) I have found no analyses of the resveratrol content of the young shoots, but you might like to eat some, just in case.

Anyone who thinks that wild vegetables are rare, delicate, difficult to find, and small should get lost in a Japanese knotweed patch.

Kentucky Coffeetree (Coffeenut)

Gymnocladus dioicus

discovered Kentucky coffeetree as an adult. I read of the tree at a young age and knew that it grew in river floodplains and rich valleys, where I kept an eye out for it over the years. Yet it remained one of the last trees native to my home state that I had yet to find in the wild. Then, one early November day, driving along the lower Wisconsin River, my wife and I stopped at some little nameless ravine that was a mini-paradise of wild food. There were hopniss vines in thick tangles over elderberry bushes and angelica beside the road; going up the hill, these gave way to ground beans under the light shade of oaks and hickories. Wild grapes weighed down small elms at the edge of a clearing. Mulberries leaned out toward the road. All around was a panoply of edible herbs, fruits, and nuts. As I walked through the woods toward a slough of the river, a tree with unusual scaly bark caught my eye.

Everything you need to identify coffeenut is here: the scaly bark, the giant twice-compound leaves, and the wide, stout pods.

"Is that a honey locust?" I puzzled aloud. "It's got no thorns." The tree was the tallest one around, perhaps ninety feet, and its trunk was thicker than any other tree in the grove. I pressed my palm to the rough bark and looked up at the thick twigs in the canopy.

"Holy cow, Melissa, this is a Kentucky coffeetree!" I screamed as if I had just found Elvis. She gave me a look as if to say, "Yeah, so?"

"I've been looking for this tree my whole life," I said in defense of my exuberance. She came over and pretended to admire it with me so that I didn't feel bad.

After marveling at the tree for a few minutes I went down to the slough, where I found some water parsnips and began to dig them out. I was on my knees, up to my wrists in muck, when Melissa shoved a branch in my face and asked, "Hey Sam, what are *these*?"

They were the biggest, baddest legume pods I'd ever seen, hanging from the finger-thick twigs of a broken branch. After a moment I pieced it all together. "Those are Kentucky coffeetree pods," I said, in a nonchalant voice that implied, "See, I told you it was a cool tree."

"These *are* cool," she said.

"Where'd you find that?"

"Right there." She pointed a bit up the hill. We looked up and could see some more pods hanging on a smaller Kentucky coffeetree that leaned toward the slough.

The tree had no branches for thirty feet. "Not the best tree to climb," I said. We pulled the dozen or so pods off of her branch and put them in a cloth bag for later experiments. Our adventure began right there.

DESCRIPTION

Kentucky coffeetree is a medium to large tree, usually tall with a narrow crown and devoid of branches near the ground. The bark is dark brown or reddish-brown and covered uniformly with thin, hard, curled plates that look something like burnt potato chips. The tops are sparse due to unusually thick twigs, and may look dead due to the tiny, inconspicuous buds sunken into depressions near the heart-shaped leaf scar.

Coffeetree's leaves are twice-compound; the whole leaf is typically 24–34 inches (60–85 cm) long, making it among the largest of any tree in North America. The leaflets are about 2 inches (5 cm) long and elliptic, and have smooth margins. The genus name *Gymnocladus* means "naked branch," referring to the apparent absence of winter buds. When coffeenut drops its foliage in autumn, the naked leaf rachises often remain attached to the twig tips for several weeks, resulting in an odd whiskery look that helps distinguish the tree. It blooms in early summer, with several flowers on a raceme or panicle 6–8 inches

Coffeenuts and their pods, showing the sticky green pulp inside.

(15–20 cm) long. Each flower is light whitish-green and less than a half inch (13 mm) long with 5 sepals and usually five hairy petals.

In the autumn or winter, when the pods are ripe and the leaves have dropped, coffeetrees stand out so well that the savvy can spot them from far off. I once spotted a loaded coffeetree from the car in January, so I turned around, backtracked, and parked. As I exited the car and headed toward the tree with a bag in hand, all of the pods flew away. Turns out they were starlings, and the tree was a cottonwood.

No other North American tree has pods as massive as those of coffeetree. They are 3–9 inches (8–23 cm) long and one-third as wide—almost D-shaped—and more than a half inch (13 mm) thick. The average pod contain 3–5 seeds, although large ones may hold 7 or, rarely, more. Inside the pods there is a sticky greenish pulp that is at once very sugary and very acrid—and reported to be toxic. The distinct seed is dark brown, smooth, and almost circular in outline but flattened, usually in an asymmetrical way—kind of like a deformed M&M. They have an extremely tough but thin shell and are 0.5–0.7 inches (13–18 mm) across.

The tree most commonly confused with coffeetree is honey locust, a relative that shares much of its range and prefers similar habitat. Honey locust has much

Coffeenut drops its leaves early, and stands out from far off, the treetop pods like a flock of blackbirds.

thinner pods, which usually twist, and the seeds are kidney-shaped and far smaller. Wild honey locusts are usually protected by fierce clusters of branching thorns scattered about the trunk; coffeetree is unarmed.

HABITAT

Kentucky coffeetree is found in the central part of the Eastern Woodlands of North America, and extends west into the Great Plains in riparian forests. In no region is this species dominant, and in some it is rare, but in certain areas it is reasonably common. Nowhere have I seen it more abundant than in ravines in the semi-arid country of western Oklahoma, along the Canadian River and its tributaries. However, its optimal habitat is exactly that preferred by a common bipedal ape: the rich soil of high river floodplains and valleys. Therefore most good coffeetree habitat has been turned into farmland. In its natural habitat it is likely to be in the company of black walnut, sycamore,

Kentucky coffeetree *Gymnocladus dioicus* is very sporadic in occurrence, but is most common in Oklahoma and Missouri, and in the Ohio, Missouri, and Mississippi River valleys. These are common as street trees outside the mapped range and are currently being heavily planted to replace dying ash.

elm, cottonwood, ash, hackberry, American mulberry, shellbark hickory, pecan, yellowbud hickory, or honey locust. Coffeenut also does quite well at colonizing old fields, so it sometimes appears in second-growth stands near its normal habitat. And it is a common-enough ornamental tree to be found in nearly every urban area in the eastern United States.

We watch in horror as the ash trees die by the millions. But for every action there is a reaction: Kentucky coffeetree will benefit from the reduced competition in floodplain forests. And this species has been anointed as the best replacement for green ash as a street tree. You can expect to see the availability of coffeenut increase exponentially over the next few decades.

HARVEST AND PREPARATION

Not surprisingly, Kentucky coffeetree is used to brew a coffee-like drink. It is widely reported that early European settlers in Kentucky used it this way, a practice they probably learned from Native Americans. Why Kentucky? The Bluegrass region contained coveted, rich farmland, but it was surrounded by rugged, wild country on all sides. This made it largely inaccessible by wagon road and ship, rendering outside commodities hard to transport and extremely expensive. William Clark, a Kentucky resident and co-captain of the most famous

Roasted and shelled coffeenuts, ready to be ground and brewed.

military expedition in US history, simply called it "coffee nut" in his journals; the cumbersome modifier "Kentucky" became standard somewhat later.

The literature is almost unanimous in reporting that the drink brewed from *Gymnocladus dioicus* is distasteful. Donald Culross Peattie, in his *Trees of Eastern and Central North America*, pejoratively stated that it "can only by imagination and forbearance be called coffee." However, few of these authors have actually tasted the drink—their simplistic presumption appears to be based solely on the fact that people stopped drinking it, as if economics and addiction have no impact on human behavior. I have tried many of the coffee-like drinks reported in the wild food literature, and Kentucky coffeetree is my clear favorite for both flavor and practicality. I have served it to hundreds of people, most of whom gave favorable reviews. Even my wife, a coffee addict, likes it.

Coffeenuts ripen in fall. You can get them as early as late September, but you may as well wait until November. Or later. They hang on all winter and into the next spring, in case you're a procrastinator. You can usually pick some up off the ground, especially after a storm. But I often resort to climbing or throwing sticks to get them down. Coffeetrees are erratic producers. In good years they are totally loaded; in many years they are barren. Most trees are either male or female, so many of them will never fruit. Stock up when there's a bumper crop, as the beans store perfectly for years. You can collect enough pods to yield a pound of seeds in just a few minutes. You can dry the whole pods and remove the beans later, or you can remove the beans immediately—in either state they are not going to spoil unless you leave them wet.

After the beans have dried, I place them in a covered casserole pan and roast them in the oven at about 350 degrees until I hear several of them pop, at which time I turn off the oven, letting the beans continue to roast as the oven cools off. Experience tells you how long you need to roast them; higher temperatures necessitate shorter cooking times. Also, beans that are drier are less likely to explode, especially at lower temperatures. Exploded beans turn to a dark-reddish-brown powdery mass. The roasting process is forgiving of variation; the important thing is that the meat inside the shell turns brown. This may take from 40 minutes to 3 hours.

Once the coffee beans have cooled down, I crack them with a handheld nutcracker to get the kernels out. (They are nearly impossible to crack before roasting.) I like my coffee beans to be dark brown, so as I crack I sort out those that need additional roasting to reach the desired color.

Roasted beans can be ground in a regular electric or hand-cranked coffee grinder, or a flour or corn mill. Decide how strong you like your brew and adjust your ratio accordingly; it takes a little more coffeenut grounds, in proportion to the water, than it takes with true coffee. I usually brew my Kentucky coffeetree by bringing the grounds and water to a boil and letting it roll for a minute or two, then pouring the mixture into a French press. This extracts more flavor from the grounds. If you use a drip coffee maker, you may have a problem with the basket overflowing—the beans tend to grind very fine and clog up the filter, so it takes forever to percolate.

Coffeetree coffee is about as dark as real coffee—if you brew it that strong. I don't like it black, but with a touch of milk and a dash of maple syrup, it is a happy way to wash down breakfast.

There are a few ethnographic reports of Native Americans using the beans as a food after roasting (but apparently not to the point of dark brown). Huron Smith (1928, p. 260) reports, "Keosatok said that the round seeds of the ripened pods were roasted and eaten as a nut by his people a long time ago, and that sometimes the seeds were 'cooked too done' and then ground up and boiled to make coffee." Melvin Gilmore (1919, p. 38) states, "The Pawnee roast the seeds and eat them as chestnuts are eaten. A Winnebago said that the seeds after being pounded in a mortar were used for food."

The roasted beans have a strong, almost chocolate or carob-like flavor. If the beans are roasted to light brown so they retain some moisture and remain soft enough to chew, they make a pleasant nibble, but I have never eaten more than three or four at a time. I suppose there are some creative ways to use the flour from such beans in baking, but it should be used in moderation, as a flavoring rather than a main ingredient. (Since there are potential toxicity issues and our ethnographic reports do not give any detail about how the roasted seeds were used in food, I advise caution.)

COFFEETREE LORE

For a tree so scarce, coffeenut has disproportionately captured people's imagination and curiosity. Kentucky coffeetree was adopted as the state tree of Kentucky in 1976 after much promotion by its backers, replacing the tulip poplar that had been so designated 20 years earlier. The anti-coffeetree contingent managed to get it officially dethroned in 1994, restoring the honor to the tuliptree. George Rogers Clark, a famous general for the American army during the Revolutionary War (and older brother to William Clark), sent coffeenuts from Kentucky to Thomas Jefferson in Virginia, where the tree was absent, and recommended its cultivation.

Most of what has been written about coffeetree, however, pertains to two interesting and related theories about its ecology. The first of these is that its primary dispersal agents—perhaps ground sloths or mastodons—have been extinct for thousands of years (Barlow 2000). This makes perfect sense, since the sugary pods are obviously designed to attract some kind of large herbivore, and the hard seeds do not readily germinate unless mechanically damaged or soaked in an acid solution. Losing its primary symbiotic partners has probably caused the tree to decline greatly in abundance, and become confined to a more limited and specialized habitat.

Some authors, however, have carried this line of thinking too far, claiming that water is the only natural dispersal agent today, and therefore the tree's current distribution must be due to human propagation. VanNatta (2009) and Curtis (1959) claim that coffeetree in Wisconsin is associated exclusively with old village sites, but provide no analysis to support this observation. The same argument could be made of any river terrace species, because that is where humans settle. In fact, there is nothing unusual about coffeetree's distribution. These authors invoke the use of coffeenuts in a dice game to support this theory. Such dice games were well documented among Native Americans, but no reports mention coffeenuts being used—the dice were made from plum or peach pits.

Although coffeenut is found near rivers, it rarely grows in areas that are frequently subject to flooding. Instead, it tends to grow in the rich soil above the regular floodplain. It is a sun-loving tree that needs the combination of rich soil, fire protection, and disturbance. River systems provide all three of these; water is incidental and has little role in dispersal. Outside of major river courses, coffeetree is most abundant in steep, hilly country with rich soil, or in oasis-like woodlots in semi-arid open country. These associations support the idea of disturbance and access to sunlight being the limiting ecological factors. Although it is often repeated that no animals eat the fruit, the sugary pods are eaten by white-tailed deer, which are probably the main dispersal agent today.

Deer often swallow and later regurgitate nuts; they probably ingest coffeenuts with the pods, then spit out the seeds later while chewing their cud. The tree may be, as some ecologists suggest, sinking toward eventual extinction (of course, we all are) without more effective dispersers—so foragers might want to take over that role.

Whether or not coffeenut dice were used for gambling in the past, we like to play a guessing game with coffeenuts in our house, and it turns the task of collecting the pods and shelling out the beans into great fun. With a pile of pods in the center of a circle of players, we take turns holding one up for all the players to see. Each player guesses aloud the number of beans in the pod, then the pod is opened up. Beans are allotted to all the players who guess correctly. The player with the most beans after all the pods have been opened wins.

IS KENTUCKY COFFEETREE TOXIC? A STIMULANT?

Although numerous books (and now websites) have reported for a century that the seeds of Kentucky coffeetree are toxic and contain the nicotine-like alkaloid cystisine, these reports are hearsay: No chemical assays had been done to test them for toxins until recently. Biochemist Richard Fitch of Indiana University led a group of researchers who analyzed the plant and did not find cystisine in the seeds, or any other part of the plant (Fitch et al. 2009). Fitch's group did, however, identify a new alkaloid in the seeds of *Gymnocladus dioicus*, which they named "dioicine." He characterizes this alkaloid as "moderately toxic to animals," "unstable," and subject to "facile hydrolysis" (Fitch, n.d.). The levels of the toxin dioicine, and its potency, are not clear, but its nature suggests that it would be broken down through the process of roasting the seeds and boiling to brew the drink. (Roasted seeds were unfortunately not tested.)

Chemical assays are good for telling us if their targeted compounds are present in a substance, but they don't tell us whether or not that substance should be consumed—this is a complex question involving numerous considerations (see pp. 277–279). Tradition has proven itself much more reliable than laboratory analysis in establishing the safety of foods. There are no documented reports of the seeds, or a beverage brewed from them, causing poisoning in humans. Not a single anecdote of deleterious experience has been brought to my attention. In the absence of any known problems, our limited information regarding the chemistry of the seeds is insufficient to overturn an ancient tradition.

Interestingly, Fitch suggests that the alkaloid dioicine, after being hydrolyzed, will likely degrade into one or more compounds that produce stimulating effects similar to caffeine (Fitch et al. 2009). I do not notice any stimulant effect from the drink, nor have I spoken to anyone who reports such a thing. It would be interesting to see research shed further light on this issue.

In 2003, two professors from Northern Kentucky University published a paper called "Notes on 'Coffee' from the Kentucky Coffeetree (*Gymnocladus dioicus, Fabaceae*)" in the journal *SIDA Contributions to Botany* (Spaeth and Thieret 2003). In this piece, the authors argue that the use of Kentucky coffeetree as a coffee substitute in pioneer times has been exaggerated, which is apparently proved by the fact that the French botanist André Michaux (1746–1802) used the words "small number of persons" in his account of the practice. Spaeth and Thieret also cast doubt upon the idea that Native Americans taught European settlers to use these seeds in brewing a drink. (It is unsurprising that such use is not ethnographically recorded from this region, since there is *no ethnography* for any native peoples of Kentucky, Illinois, Indiana, or Ohio.) The authors reachily suggest that pioneers might have resorted to this brew because "coffee was seen as a mark of effeminacy."

Spaeth and Thieret conducted research to test their hypothesis that the coffee made from these seeds really sucks. They don't record what time of year the seeds were collected, if or how much they were dried, how dark the seeds were roasted, or how long the grounds were steeped before the drink was sampled. Then they performed a taste test, serving the drink, black and unsweetened, to 20 of their acquaintances. While many of them likened it to coffee, "no one claimed to enjoy the taste or the experience." The authors do not record how the tasters were selected, what they were told before tasting, or the protocol for giving samples or recording responses. (You would only do that stuff if you wanted unbiased and meaningful responses.) The authors then try to scare readers away from the beverage by noting that toxic compounds are reportedly present in the seeds. (If they really believed the drink to be dangerous, they should not have served it.)

Spaeth and Thieret's paper would have been more appropriately titled "Kentucky Coffeetree Sucks," and might have been worthy of a blog called *Partying Botanists*, but its inclusion in a peer-reviewed journal is shocking. The authors conclude their report with the remark, "The Kentucky coffeetree is of essentially no present-day concern as a beverage plant." Despite their professional opinions, I encourage you to try the drink yourself. You might enjoy it.

Maple

Genus *Acer*

There is incredible excitement in the anticipation of invisible things: ice fishing, a baby growing deep in mama's belly. To most people the silent winter
trunks of a hardwood forest are dull blocks of frozen wood. To me they are
pregnant, powerful, delicious. There is something magical about sugar water
running from a hole in a tree—the millions of gallons of sweet sap silently
working its way skyward through the hard trunks of a maple grove. Sugaring
turns the forager's calendar on its head; that lull of late winter, when the woods
seems to languish as it waits for spring, is for us tree-tappers the busiest and
largest harvest of the year. We begin in deep snow, shoveling paths to the shack
and hauling our pails and wood in sleds. We work through snow, sleet, rain,
and more snow; through those glorious sunny days when forgotten stumps
and dropped gloves reappear as fading snowbanks become rivulets that etch
the landscape another centimeter deep. We smell the first wild leeks, bruised
underfoot as sap pails bump our calves. We hear the first lonely peeper singing
on a newly brown south slope, and herald the first woodcock peenting at dusk

Maple syrup the old-fashioned way.

when we step away from the cooker for some chore. Other foragers fidget and pine for spring through that ruthless season when winter, like a capricious lover, can't make up its mind to let go. But sugar makers hear and smell every little change of the season in the fresh air of the maple woods; before we know it, springtime has conquered the countryside, and it's time to close up shop. With cracked fingers and weary arms we wash and stack the last buckets, happy to be leaving the sugarbush to the red-eyed vireos for the summer. But sometime after next Christmas, we'll start daydreaming again about that first big thaw at the end of winter.

I did not come to sugaring the easy way. Like most children, I sucked on icicles. Icicles that form on a roof below a chimney taste very bad. However, at a young age I discovered that icicles which form in March on the cut branches of maples are delicious. After a few years it dawned on me that this sapsicle sweetness was the essence of maple syrup. Which gave me an idea. Soon, every low-hanging maple limb in my neighborhood suffered a broken branch or two. In the morning, before school, I'd run out to check for sapsicles, putting them into a bucket to melt in my bedroom. After school I'd put the sap into a sauce pan and boil it down on the kitchen range, sometimes netting a few tablespoons of syrup. If you ever think traditional maple syrup making is too labor-intensive or weather-dependent, try doing it this way.

I have never been a conformist, but after a couple years of making maple syrup with this ridiculous strategy, it dawned on me that other people had already devised a better way. I found some old copper water pipes, cut them with a hack saw, and filed the edges of one end sharp to make spigots. I drilled holes in the two big silver maples in our front yard, and also in several boxelders in an empty lot along a stream about a mile away. (Yes, I carried sap buckets *that far.*) I put out eleven taps and, despite steaming up the kitchen late into the night, got more sap than I could possibly boil off. In a few days I had produced something that I had before only dreamed of: a few jars of real maple syrup. Since then I've worked my way up to manufactured sap spigots, a raised-flue evaporator, and 2,000 buckets—but I've kept the giddiness that got me started.

IDENTIFYING AND CHOOSING MAPLES

Any maples can be tapped for syrup if they are large enough, but sugar maple *Acer saccharum* and black maple *A. nigrum* are considered the most desirable. In the timber trade, these two species are collectively called "hard maple." They account for the vast majority of maple syrup produced in North America. It is often said that of the two, black maple is a slightly better sugar tree, but I have never seen any research demonstrating this, and very few people can tell them apart. Many falsely believe they can be differentiated by bark color, but this trait plays no role in identifying them. Many syrup regions have one species or the other; some have both, but they tend to be separated by habitat. Black maple likes more well-drained sites with coarser soil, especially ridge tops and south slopes. Sugar maple prefers moister soil and north slopes. In practice there is no reason to differentiate them, so hereafter I'll refer to both species collectively as "sugar maple."

Left top Sugar maple leaves. **Right top** Black maple leaves in midsummer, with ripening samaras. Note the glossy surface, lack of large teeth or lobes near the base, and drooping sides—these features, not bark color, distinguish it from sugar maple. **Left bottom** Silver maple trunks in typical riverside habitat. **Right bottom** Silver maple leaves showing the namesake underside. The sinuses can be much deeper than seen here.

Left top The leaf of boxelder, unlike that of other maples, is compound. **Right top** Red maple leaves. Note the longer lobe tips and presence of many small teeth. **Left middle** The bigleaf maple really does have a big leaf. **Right middle** Bigleaf maple trunks can be enormous. These are just babies and they are big. (Photo by T. Abe Lloyd). **Left bottom** Boxelder's natural habitat is floodplains, and the growth form is wide and spreading. I love climbing these trees.

There are a few close relatives of sugar maple found outside of the commercial maple region. The canyon maple *A. grandidentatum* of the West, although rather small for tapping, should be of interest to the home syrup maker. In the southeastern United States, southern sugar maple *A. barbatum* and chalk maple *A. leucoderme* (both considered by some to be merely forms of sugar maple) produce good sap, but being found in a region where hard frost is rare, do not generally yield much of it.

The two species collectively called "soft maple" by loggers are red maple *A. rubrum*, and silver maple *A. saccharinum*. Red maples produce a little less sap than a sugar maple, and on average that sap isn't quite as sweet. Nevertheless, a large and vigorous red maple is better than an average sugar maple. Although some syrup makers carefully avoid tapping red maples, others gladly do so; many thousands of them are tapped commercially. The syrup quality is identical. In my region, red maples tend to run later than sugar maples (not earlier, as is often reported), and this may partly account for their bad reputation—since most syrup hobbyists start early and quit when the season is only half over. Silver maple is also a good syrup tree, although it runs substantially less sap than sugar maple. Many people tap silver maples for personal use, but there is very little commercial production from this tree. Large natural stands are in floodplains, where tapping is impractical—otherwise I suspect that silver maple would be tapped more extensively.

Boxelder *Acer negundo* is our only maple with compound leaves, and some people refuse to believe that it really is a maple. If it makes you feel better, call it Manitoba maple, as they do in Canada. There are many people who make boxelder syrup, including a few commercial operations that tap more than a thousand trees in Manitoba. The flavor is distinguishable, but fantastic. Boxelder sap is about as sweet as that of sugar maple, but the trees yield only about half as much of it. Boxelder greatly extends the range over which maple syrup can be made—I have seen excellent boxelder groves, for example, near Silver City, New Mexico, where the climate is quite amenable to sugaring.

Bigleaf maple *A. macrophyllum*, a tree of the West Coast, is the largest North American maple, sometimes reaching six feet or more in diameter. In the Pacific Northwest some people tap these trees for syrup, but due to the milder climate, the sap does not often run very well. Nevertheless, there are a few small commercial operations tapping bigleaf maple, and some hobbyists.

Norway maples, which are feral in many of our eastern urban areas, can be tapped to make good syrup—despite common myths to the contrary. Mountain, striped, Rocky Mountain, and vine maples all yield sap, but are really too small to bother with unless you are desperate for sugar. From this list you can see that the region where maples can be tapped extends well beyond the traditional region for commercial sugar making.

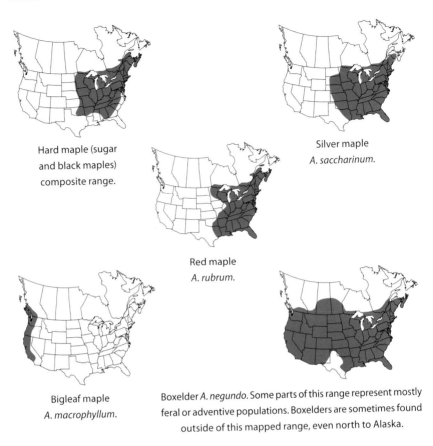

Hard maple (sugar
and black maples)
composite range.

Silver maple
A. saccharinum.

Red maple
A. rubrum.

Bigleaf maple
A. macrophyllum.

Boxelder *A. negundo.* Some parts of this range represent mostly
feral or adventive populations. Boxelders are sometimes found
outside of this mapped range, even north to Alaska.

SYRUP EQUIPMENT

Unlike most wild food endeavors, sugar making requires a significant outlay
of equipment. Most commercial syrup today is made via plastic tubing and
reverse osmosis, but I am writing this section with the home producer or small-
scale syrup seller in mind, and assume that you will be using more traditional
methods. More information about choosing these items will be included later,
in the appropriate sections.

A drill or brace for making holes in the trees
Sap spigots to pound into those holes
A mallet or hammer to drive spigots
Containers for sap to drip into
Buckets for carrying sap
A barrel or other large container for storing sap

A pan in which to boil down the sap
Firewood
Syrup hydrometer and/or thermometer to tell you when it is done
Syrup filters for the finished product
Containers for finished syrup

Choosing or Making Taps

Also variously called spigots or spiles, these are any sort of hollow tube that can be driven into the tree to seal off the hole and direct the sap flow into a container. I suggest that you buy commercial maple taps. There are a number of varieties of these, both metal and plastic. I use the hookless aluminum Soule spouts, but I have used almost every type of metal spigot on the market and they all work. However, if you already have some sap buckets, you want to make sure your spigots are compatible with the holes drilled in them.

Metal sap spouts will last the rest of your life, or until they fall from your pocket in the woods. Occasionally they will break if driven or extracted too forcefully. For over a century the standard size for taps was 7/16 inch. This size is still just fine, but most producers today use 5/16-inch taps, which produce, in the short term, a tiny bit less sap. The smaller holes cause far less damage to the tree, and the wounds heal much faster—and this really matters when you are tapping the same woodlot for many years. The 5/16-inch spigots are smaller and lighter; you can fit three times as many in your pocket. The holes are easier to drill. The only disadvantage is that they are more likely to break when being driven or extracted.

You can also make your own wooden spigots. This is fun, cheap, and not as hard as it may sound. Sumac, elderberry, and highbush cranberry are

Some examples of commercially available metal and plastic spigots.

Wooden spigot made from sumac.

traditionally used for this; they have pithy centers and are commonly found at about the right diameter. (Some people warn against using elderberry because of a toxin in the bark, but I don't think this has any merit. Just don't eat your spigots.) You can also use harder woods, as long as they have a pith large enough for a drill to follow. I've used pin cherry, ash, butternut, and walnut.

To make wooden spigots, cut straight stems that are about 5/8 inch thick into sections about 4 inches long. Do not use last year's shoots—they are too soft; make sure you use growth at least two years old. Scrape off the bark. Then remove the pith with a drill and small bit, working toward the center from both ends. With very pithy woods, you can punch it out with a chainsaw file and hammer. Then whittle one end so that it tapers down to a size slightly smaller than your tap hole. You can cut a small notch in the top of the spigot close to the tapered part to facilitate hanging a bucket—but this may not be strong enough to support 4-gallon pails. Or you can place a bucket on the ground beside the tree and place a piece of wood under one side of the bucket to prop it against the trunk. Drive the spigot so that it is tight but not so much as to crack it. Unfortunately, if you save wooden spigots for the next season, they often dry out and crack.

Sap Receptacles

There are primarily two options here: buckets or plastic bags.

Sap bags are used with a metal bag holder attached to the spigot. The bags are generally discarded at the end of the season, which is at once their greatest advantage and greatest drawback. Many of us are not fond of generating garbage through the use of disposable equipment, but it is incredibly convenient not having to wash buckets at the end of the season. Bags and holders require

Above left If you use a wooden spigot, it is usually better to use a bucket on the ground, propped against the tree. **Above right** A sap bag hanging from a metal holder, with a chunk of ice floating in the sap.

less storage space than buckets. With bags, it is apparent at a glance how full they are, so you can easily tell which ones need to be collected. Bags require a smaller initial investment than new metal buckets, but are not as cheap as some bucket options. A common and serious problem with bags is that flying squirrels like to chew holes in them.

If you are making syrup over the long term, buckets are cheaper and less wasteful, particularly if you purchase used ones. Many people get empty food-grade plastic buckets for free from restaurants and bakeries; these last 12–18 years. The old-fashioned standard sap bucket is 4 gallons, galvanized steel. These buckets are great, but new ones are surprisingly expensive. There are some 2- and 3-gallon buckets available as well. Size matters. The average sap run is 3–5 quarts in 24 hours, but good runs can easily exceed three gallons, especially on large, vigorous trees. Unless they are unemployed and bored superbucketcheckers, people with small containers always lose much sap to overflow. Thus 3- or 4-gallon buckets are best; I discourage using any containers smaller than 2 gallons.

Sap often runs well during rain or snow storms, so your buckets should have lids. These are sold by syrup equipment dealers, or you can devise your own. You can't just boil off the rain—it will run down the trunks and become lichen tea, making your sap bucket look like a urinal and your syrup taste like sweetened firewood.

The Cooker

This is the heart of the syrup operation, and determines how much sap you can cook down. A pot on the kitchen range may allow you to boil off 2–5 gallons in a day. That means tapping 1–8 trees. Most small-scale syrup makers use a flat pan outdoors, supported by concrete blocks or a masonry or metal arch. There are also small evaporators that are designed for those who want to tap 30–140 trees, and the size, complication, and expense goes up from there.

It seems that all people who make syrup spend about the same amount of time cooking. Those who tap 5 trees in the backyard cook it down on the kitchen range and stay up way past midnight a couple times a season, just like people with a 6-by-16-foot flued evaporator who tap 3,000 trees. It is wise to get a cooker with sufficient capacity to make your effort feel worthwhile. If you want to actually make syrup a regular part of your diet, you need something more than the kitchen range. If you are making syrup to sell, you can't even make minimum wage unless you can evaporate 20 gallons of sap per hour.

Basically, there are three kinds of syrup evaporating pans: open flat pans, divided flat pans, and corrugated flue pans. Open flat pans are simple, and make a uniform batch of syrup that is finished simultaneously and can be poured off all at once. The flues or flumes (channels through which sap passes) in a divided flat pan are formed by partitions mounted to the bottom. Sap enters one end of the pan and is drawn off at the opposite end; along this path there

is a gradient of concentration from sap to syrup. Corrugated flue pans have deep, narrow passageways for sap alternating with passageways for hot gas from the fire, greatly increasing the surface area of the pan exposed to heat. These pans

A small evaporator, flat-bottomed with flues formed by dividers. (The "flue pan" that most commerical syrup makers speak of has flues formed by deep corrugations—folds in the metal forming many deep, narrow passages to increase the surface area for heat transfer.) The small tank in the back near the chimney preheats the sap, which drips into the evaporator at the right rear. The boiling sap flows through until it reaches the left front, where finished syrup is drawn off through another spigot. This set-up will cost you about $1500 and can make up to perhaps 35 gallons of syrup per year.

also have dividers creating a gradient of sugar concentration. All divided pans have a draw-off spigot on one end that can be opened to let out finished syrup. Most have a small tank with a spigot to provide a slow but steady inflow of sap.

Many evaporation systems use a combination of these pan types. Modern systems start with a corrugated flue pan, from which the partially concentrated sap moves to a divided flat pan where it is finished. After filtering, the syrup is reheated in a smaller open flat pan. Before divided pans were commonplace, most producers used three open pans or kettles to create a gradient and prevent overcooking the syrup. For about $1,500 you can buy a very nice, new, flued, flat-pan evaporator that will serve about 100 taps, and produce 10–35 gallons of syrup per year. This will make all the syrup a family can consume, using maple as the primary sweetener in the household, with some extra for gifts or cash. It will pay for itself in syrup value in a year or two. If you want to go bigger than that, you'll probably want a modern evaporator with a corrugated flue pan.

Sam's Easy $20 Evaporator: You can make a cheap, simple cooker that will produce 3–10 gallons of syrup in a season, outdoors on a wood fire, and it will outperform many set-ups that cost twenty times as much. At a garage sale or thrift store, buy three old metal casserole pans, the kind with sides about 2½ inches deep, and the surface about 9 by 12 inches. Get eleven or fifteen 16-inch concrete blocks, and line them up in two rows of three, 1 foot apart, on flat ground; then place the last block in back, closing off the space between the rows. Stack the remaining blocks on the closed end to form a chimney. Then lay the three pans across the parallel blocks.

Got all that? OK, your evaporator is done. You'll need small, dry wood to keep this burning intensely, but it will boil off a lot of sap for its size. You periodically dump the second pan's contents into the third, and the first pan's contents into the second, then refill the first pan with fresh sap. Watch that third pan carefully, and when it looks close to finished syrup density, pour it into a pot. Later, you can carefully finish the syrup in your pot indoors on a controlled flame, then filter and bottle it. For a modest increase in price you can scale up this system with larger pans, like chafing dishes.

This set-up actually cost me only $17. It boils off 3-4 gallons of liquid per hour and I have produced up to 10 gallons of syrup per year with it.

The Sugar Shack

You can cook syrup outside without any shelter, but most syrup makers have their evaporator under some kind of roof so that it can be used in bad weather, and so that all the associated equipment can be stored in one place. Some build the sugarhouse right among the maple trees, for the convenience of getting

There are thousands of manifestations of "the sugar shack." This is ours. At 16' x 16' it's a little small for the 3' x 10' evaporator it houses. The arch sits on cement board over a wooden floor—but a concrete slab is preferred. The stainless pipe in front is the steam vent for the syrup pan, the stainless pipe in the rear is the steam vent for the flued pan, and behind that is the chimney. The stainless tank in the foreground holds 1,000 gallons of sap. The black water line is used to pump sap from a collection tank into the bulk tank. The barrel is for storing distilled water, which drips off the preheater, to be used for cleaning at the end of the season. By the time you read this, I'll be using a new evaporator.

the sap there. Others put the evaporator in the garage or machine shed—some convenient pre-existing building with a good roof, concrete floor, and doors, and close to a water and power supply. Whichever path you choose, you will probably kick yourself for not having done the other. In any case, make sure you have enough room for fire clearance around your evaporator, and install your chimney properly.

Firewood

Most syrup today is made by a combination of reverse osmosis and heat evaporation. I'm assuming you will be skipping the reverse osmosis step, and that your fuel for evaporation will be wood. Efficient flued evaporators will produce about 25 gallons of syrup per full cord of typical dry wood; flat pans are not this efficient. Don't worry too much about the wood species, but do make sure that it is dry. Cut your wood a year or more in advance, and stack it under cover. If the chunks are big, split them; you cannot have a good, hot fire with huge pieces of firewood. Make plenty of firewood—many producers are forced to quit when their supply runs out.

Our woodshed holds about a year's supply, and is attached to the back of the shack. The pile that's left here will make about 60 gallons of syrup. Smaller evaporators, however, will use wood much less efficiently.

Tapping

You don't just pound a spigot into a tree—you drill a hole first. A hand brace and bit works fine and is cheap to buy at an antique shop or estate auction. You can drill a hole with this in 20–40 seconds. Today most people tap with a cordless, battery-powered drill. You can make a taphole this way in 1–3 seconds. Whatever kind of drill you choose, the bit should be clean and sharp. A clean-cut hole that starts the season free of dirt and bacteria will run more sap, and run sap for longer. Get a ⁷⁄₁₆ or ⁵⁄₁₆ bit, corresponding to whichever of the standard tap sizes you choose to use. You can buy a special tapping bit from syrup supply dealers, and these perform slightly better, but a regular wood bit also works just fine.

It is preferable to tap trees when the wood is not frozen, as frozen wood is more likely to crack. Drill your hole about 1.5 inches (3.5 cm) into clean, light sapwood. The hole should be angled slightly so that sap drains toward the exterior. Avoid knots, burls, old tapping scars, or cracks from frost or lightning, as these locations yield poorly. The shavings that come out should be nearly white in color; brown or yellow wood will yield discolored and poorly flavored sap, if it produces anything. If you encounter discolored wood, drill a new hole. Be as steady and straight as possible as you push in and pull out the drill—any wiggle causes an oddly shaped hole more likely to leak sap.

Pound in your spigot with a few gentle taps of a hammer or mallet. You want it to be firm enough to hold up a bucket full of sap, and tight enough to seal the hole so that sap doesn't leak down the bark. No tighter. An over-driven spigot tends to split the bark and separate it from the cambium, or split the wood, either of which will heal with a large scar. Tap holes create a zone of discoloration 1–2 inches wide that runs with the grain for 1–2 feet above and below the hole. To avoid drilling into scarred or discolored wood, place your taphole at least four inches to one side and a foot above or below any visible tap scar.

You want to tap before the first good sap run. In regions with cold winters this will be the first serious thaw at the end of winter. The first sunny day at 40° will not make much, if any, sap run. A maple

Drilling a ⁵⁄₁₆" tap hole. The shavings should be creamy-white, with no brown heartwood.

tree has a lot of thermal mass, so it requires a lot of heat before the water in the trunk begins to melt. It takes maple trees several days to break their winter dormancy, so the earliest thaws often produce surprisingly little sap, and the sap produced is weaker in sugar content. Many hobby syrup makers eagerly tap at the first sign of warm weather, but there is little to be gained by tapping unusually early. The fresher your tap hole, the better it will run, so tapping too early will cause you to get less sap later in the season.

But don't wait too long and miss the good runs. Some people have a calendar date at which they tap every year, but most sugar makers just watch the weather. Some people put a couple taps in a convenient location and monitor them to help decide when to put in the rest of them. If you miss the early run, don't despair—maples are usually generous. Most hobby syrup makers quit making syrup well before the season is over.

In warm regions, things are inverted: you aren't waiting for a thaw, you're waiting for a freeze. Any hard freeze from early winter on can produce a run of sap. In the southern quarter of the sugar maple's range, it rarely gets cold enough, or for long enough, for the whole tree to freeze. Warmer regions tend to have poorer sap flows, and they are distributed more unpredictably over a longer time period. In northern Alabama January is likely your best month; in parts of Canada, the sap runs well into May. An average season at my sugarbush (45° north and 1,800 feet elevation) is about March 20–April 15.

WHAT MAKES SAP RUN?

Maple syrup makes one a lover of bad weather: the coming and going of the lion and the lamb. The blustery nights when the tree swallows disappear to God-knows-where and the bluebirds huddle in close to pear trees in the backyards of farmhouses, wondering if riding that south wind on Tuesday was such a good idea; the April dusk when the spring peeper's mouth freezes to silence; the crisp morning when trout lily leaves can shatter like glass—these are the things that call forth sap.

The alternation of freezing and thawing when the trees are dormant is what makes maple sap run. The sap vessels of maples are surrounded by air-filled fibers. As the moist air in these fibers cools and some of its vapor crystallizes, it decreases in volume. This shrinkage creates suction, pulling liquid sap into the wood from the roots. (A long, gradual freeze allows more sap to be pulled into the wood, and creates a better subsequent sap flow.) Upon reheating, the air within the fibers expands, exerting pressure that causes the sap to flow from any wound.

If a maple trunk is very cold, a day or two with above-freezing temperatures may not be enough to thaw any of the liquid inside it. Once it begins to thaw,

Variable forms of sugar maple bark. Note the black on a few of them—this is caused by a lichen, and is a virtual guarantee that the tree is not a black maple.

Red maple trunks begin smooth and gray. With age they develop furrows, then shaggy strips. Although on average hard maples run sap better, it is foolish to ignore large, vigorous red maples in your sugarbush.

Below left Red maple and sugar maple side by side. Can you tell which is which? **Below right** A black maple trunk—the bark is essentially indistinguishable from sugar maple, and, due to drier growing conditions, never gets the black lichen commonly found on sugar maple.

the process may take several days to complete, and sap will flow throughout this period even if the temperature remains above freezing. If the tree trunk is near the freezing point, it takes much less heat or cold to move it either way over that threshold, so smaller temperature swings can cause sap runs. Small trees run sooner than large ones, and they also quit sooner.

Slope strongly affects sap flow on sunny days. South slopes receive more intense sunlight and warm up much faster than level areas; north slopes warm up more slowly. On marginal sunny days the sap may run on south slopes, but not at all on north slopes. Because there is no commensurate difference in cooling between north and south slopes, the south slopes undergo more drastic temperature swings, and thus on average have better sap flow. Barometric pressure is another important factor in sap flow. Excellent sap runs often occur when the temperature is near freezing and a low-pressure front moves in. If there is a storm during syrup season, the sap usually flows before or during it.

The trees move sap to prepare the buds for flowering and leaf-out. This is not so urgent in the middle of winter, so the sap runs tend to be poor at this time, even if the weather seems appropriate. The sap from early runs also has lower

Below left Red maple, just beginning to bloom, but the leaf buds are dormant. **Below right** Silver maple, blooming, but the leaf buds are dormant. **Bottom** Sugar maple twig, dormant. These three photos were taken on the same day, at the same location, and several good sap runs occurred after that day. The flower buds are open on red and silver (soft) maples, but not not on sugar (hard) maple, which blooms simultaneously with leaf-out. For sap flow, only the leaf buds matter!

sugar content. As the trees sense, through daylight and temperature, that the need to prepare buds for growth is more urgent, sap volume and sugar content increase. At some point in spring, when the buds are nearly ready to open, the maples quit flowing sap even if the appropriate freeze/thaw cycle occurs.

Many new syrup makers have heard that sap flow ceases when the trees "bud," but misunderstand the statement; they see the *flower buds* swelling or opening on soft maples, and think this means the syrup season is ending. It doesn't. Red and silver maples flower right during sap season, well before the leaves emerge, and the swelling of their flower buds is of no concern to the sugar maker. The buds you need to pay attention to are the leaf buds, which are far less conspicuous and swell much later. Every year, thousands of amateur syrup makers pull their taps early because of this misunderstanding.

COLLECTING SAP

Most sap today is collected with tubing to each tree, facilitated by vacuum pumps, but this is beyond the scope of our discussion. For the small-time producer, whether using buckets or bags, the sap is usually dumped into 4- or 5-gallon buckets for carrying. It's a good idea to have lids for your collecting pails to avoid sap losses from sloshing. Some people use a shoulder yoke for carrying longer distances, but they are very inconvenient for the actual collection.

The system you choose for sap collection depends on the equipment you have, the number of taps, the terrain and distribution of your trees, your physical

Collecting sap.

capabilities, and preferences. In very small operations sap may be carried in buckets directly to the cooking area. In larger bucket operations, the sap is usually dumped into a tank, barrel, or milk can hauled on a sled or trailer pulled by a horse, tractor, or ATV. I have no such vehicles, so I place 55-gallon barrels at several points in the woods, and when these are full the sap is pumped into my 1,000-gallon bulk tank through potable water lines, using a portable, gas-powered pump. At other locations uphill from the bulk tank, I have a basin set up on a stand, with a hose leading from the bottom of the basin to the bulk tank. When collecting sap in these areas I carry the pails a short distance to the basin and dump them in; gravity does the rest. To take best advantage of gravity, it is a good idea to set up your evaporator in the lowest part of your sugarbush.

Collect sap before your buckets overflow. Some say that it is imperative to collect the sap every day. Actually, the logistics of when to collect, for reasons of freshness and practicality, are not so simple. For example, there is no reason to collect a quart from each pail after a light run if it is going to freeze overnight and run the following day. Don't collect sap if you can't cook it promptly; it stays fresher in the buckets than it will in a tank. But at the end of a run that stops due to warm weather, make sure the buckets are empty. When the sap runs at temperatures barely above freezing, it may freeze quickly in the buckets at night. When this happens you will have a narrow window of time in which to collect sap, and you better take advantage of it, or you will end up with buckets completely filled with ice. Any run in this situation will overflow them, and the freezing of full buckets can damage them.

Many people toss out ice to concentrate their sap. The ice contains less sugar than the liquid sap—how much sugar depends on a complex set of factors. Just yesterday, after pouring the sap from a few frozen-solid buckets that were about 15% thawed, this liquid measured 8.4% sugar; the pure sap that ran later in the day measured 2.1% sugar. The ice I discarded still contained about half the total sugar that the liquid held, but at a much lower concentration. If you have a slow, inefficient evaporator, and more sap than you can use, tossing ice can be a huge time saver. With more efficient evaporators and larger operations its value becomes questionable.

DRINKING SAP

It is a rite of spring to grab a bucket and guzzle fresh, cold, lightly sweet sap during occasional breaks from the hard work of syrup making. However, as the season progresses, a bacteria culture forms in the buckets and becomes more and more prevalent. At some point, you'll want to stop drinking the sap, or it will probably make you sick. As a general rule, if it looks like water, it's safe; but if it has taken on even a hint of color or cloudiness, it should not be consumed raw.

SAP AND SYRUP YIELDS AND RATIOS

A typical tap in a typical sugar maple will yield about a quart of syrup in an average year when used with a gravity system such as buckets or bags. The difference between trees and years, however, is great. Some taps give almost nothing, and some taps will yield a gallon of syrup or more. Careful management of the sugarbush, or careful selection of the trees to tap, can increase the average yield per tap to a half gallon or more. If you have only 10 buckets, don't waste them on spindly, unhealthy-looking trees. The best sap yields are given by large, healthy trees with robust, dense crowns that receive lots of sunlight. Such trees can overflow a four-gallon bucket on a good day.

You have probably heard that 40 gallons of sap makes a gallon of syrup. With hard maple, the average number is closer to 35, but apparently that doesn't make sugaring sound like such a heroic endeavor. It varies from year to year, place to place, species to species, and also over the course of the season. We have had ratios as good as 21:1 and as bad as 46:1. Vacuum pumps will pull out sap with less sugar than that which runs of its own accord, so the industry average is close to the proverbial 40:1. Species other than sugar and black maple will usually yield sap that is less sweet, although the difference is often highly exaggerated.

You can buy a sap hydrometer to test the sugar content of the sap. (Don't confuse this with the syrup hydrometer; the same instrument does not measure both.) The sap hydrometer lets you estimate your syrup yield before cooking. It also allows you to test the sweetness of different trees in your sugarbush, which can inform your decisions about which ones to tap, or which ones to thin for firewood. Here's a nifty trick: Divide 86 by the sugar percentage your hydrometer reads, and that is roughly how many gallons of sap it will take to make a gallon of syrup. For example, if your sap reads 2.4% sugar, then divide 86 by 2.4, to get 36—this is called the "rule of 86."

SAP STORAGE

You can keep small amounts of sap in buckets with lids, but for larger amounts you'll want something more. Many people store sap in stock tanks, but there may be an issue of lead in the galvanization. Some people use garbage cans or plastic totes, which can easily be found in 20-40 gallon capacities, but are not food grade. The best option for a small producer is one or more 55-gallon food-grade plastic barrels. These are inexpensive and durable. I buy mine at an industrial recycling center for $13 each, then saw off the top and clean the inside.

If possible, store your sap in a cool, shaded place. You may find it convenient to heap snow around your storage vessel. You want to cook down the sap as soon as is reasonably possible, because it begins spoiling immediately. How long before it is too spoiled to use depends on the weather—some people hold sap for a week at the beginning of the season, when the weather is cool and the tank is clean. By the end of the season, it can go bad in just a day. The freshest sap is clear and colorless, like water. As sap spoils it turns yellow, then cloudy, then slimy—in this latter state, just dump it out.

SAP FILTERING

Sap collected in buckets often contains bits of bark, moss, lichen, moths, and other debris. It's good to eliminate this crud. It's not a food safety hazard, but most people want pure maple syrup, not moth and moss broth. Bits of leaf can get into your system and block hoses or valves, if you have any. My pump has a filter basket attached to its intake hose. This helps, but I sometimes attach a paint strainer bag to the top of my collection barrels, and pour my sap through it.

COOKING SYRUP AND DRAWING OFF

There are a few rules here:
1. Don't leave for long. Pay attention. Most experienced sugar makers have had to scour a burnt pan, and don't want to do that again.
2. Don't fall asleep. But in case you do, don't be so close to the cooker that your face hits it when you tip over. I have stayed up until sunrise cooking syrup more than once. A burnt pan really sucks.
3. Feed the fire. Don't be lazy. When you think of it again, feed the fire. If you're wondering if you should feed the fire, you should feed the fire. You'll get done sooner that way.
4. Visitors make the time pass quicker, and keep you awake, but don't let them interfere with numbers 1 and 3.

Keep the fire going as hot as you reasonably can without overheating your equipment. Crisscross some of your wood to allow air flow for a quick, hot burn. Periodically pull the coals toward the front of the firebox. Empty the ashes at the beginning of the day. The cooking syrup will periodically foam up and threaten to overflow the pan. Keep a small container of edible oil on hand, and put a few drops into the foam, which will cause it to subside. If you have flues, de-foaming is especially important, as the foam will affect the flow in the evaporator.

Many small producers go by the look and taste to determine when the syrup is done; they tend to make their syrup too thick, but that's no big deal. However, I assume that you want to ascertain that your syrup reaches the appropriate density. Syrup that is too thin takes up more space and is more prone to spoiling once the containers are opened, and people don't like it as much. It

We draw our syrup off into a flat filter that rests in the top of a bottling pan.

turns pancakes to mush. Syrup cooked too dense crystallizes in the jar—although people actually prefer it. The law requires syrup sold to be of the standard density. Most commonly this is determined with a thermometer and/or a hydrometer.

When sugar is dissolved in water, it raises the boiling temperature of that water. The denser the sugar solution becomes, the more the boiling temperature rises. Thus, boiling temperature can be used as a proxy measure for syrup density and sugar concentration. Your starting point for this density monitoring is the boiling point of water (or the boiling point of sap, which contains so little sugar that it is negligibly different from that of water). Don't just assume that the boiling point of water is 100°C or 212°F—take the temperature with the same thermometer you will use to take the boiling syrup's temperature. Thermometers vary in their accuracy, and the boiling point changes perceptibly in different weather due to barometric pressure, and it also varies by elevation. My sugar shack, for example, is at 1,800 feet of elevation, so water boils at 208.7°F (98.1°C), on average. Once you have the boiling point of water, add 7.1°F to get the boiling point of finished syrup.

In a flat pan without flues, you keep adding sap as it boils off, until eventually you decide the pan is full enough that you want to finish the batch. Take the temperature in a few places around the pan. When the syrup reaches about a degree F below syrup density, stop feeding the fire so things can settle down before you dump the pan into your finished syrup container.

If you have flues, with a spigot and valve at the end of the pan, pour your sap into the end opposite the spigot. This creates a gradient within the pan, with the densest syrup at the spigot end of the flues. In this case, take the temperature near the draw-off spigot. Commercial evaporators have a thermometer that screws into the pan near the draw-off valve, making it easy to monitor temperature. Theoretically, you can draw off continuously at a certain rate, but rarely does anyone find that ideal rate. (And when you start a new batch, you won't have that gradient; it will take a few hours of cooking to establish it.) If the temperature spikes to, say, 9 or 10° above boiling, open the valve more to pass that dense syrup out faster before it burns, but there is no need to let it gush out. Remember that, with each degree increase in temperature, the next degree of increase happens faster, and this speed increase is exponential. It may take your batch three hours to go from 1–2° above boiling. But at 55° above boiling (God forbid you ever get there), it may take less than a second to get to 56° degrees, and before you can do anything about it, you're at 220° above boiling and have a pan of burnt sugar. For this reason, many people keep a pail of sap on hand at all times, to douse the pan in case of an emergency. When you fear the syrup is going to burn—say, at 12–20° above boiling—add sap immediately. If you open the spigot to draw off this dense syrup, the syrup in the pan will get suddenly shallower, making it all the more prone to burning.

USING A SYRUP HYDROMETER

A hydrometer is a more accurate way to measure syrup density. Most commonly, sugar makers use a thermometer to determine when to draw off or dump a batch, *before filtering*, and a hydrometer to determine when they have achieved the exact density for bottling—*after filtering*.

A hydrometer measures the density of a liquid, and it consists of a weighted glass tube with a piece of paper inside, showing markings corresponding to different densities. The hydrometer has a metal cup to go with it; this holds the hot syrup of which you are measuring the density. The denser the syrup, the higher the hydrometer floats. While this instrument is much more accurate than a thermometer, it is easy to screw up the measurement. If you follow the protocol below, you'll get a reasonably accurate reading.

1. **Make sure the hydrometer is clean and dry**, with no water or sugar sticking to it. Rinse the hydrometer and cup with warm water after every measurement, then dry it with a clean cloth, or put it in a hot place to air-dry. If there is any liquid adhering to that portion of the hydrometer which is above the syrup level, it will add weight and cause the hydrometer to sink and read too low. (Syrup causes greater inaccuracy than water, because syrup is heavier, and sticks in a thicker layer.) Dried sugar stuck to the portion of the hydrometer under the syrup level will also weigh down the instrument and cause it to read too thin.

2. **Never drop your hydrometer into your syrup**, even if you enjoy watching it bob up and down until it settles. This will cause it to go deeper than the actual

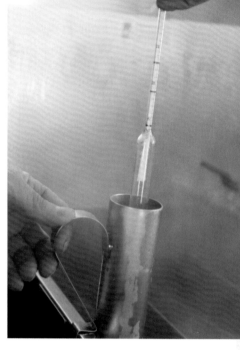

Using a hydrometer to measure syrup density.

measurement level, and will result in syrup adhering to the hydrometer shaft above the syrup level. Instead, slowly lower it to the syrup density marker on the shaft, then gently let go.

3. **Syrup density is temperature-dependent.** The upper red line on most syrup hydrometers represents the proper density when the liquid is at 211°F. At any other temperature, the reading is not accurate. By the time you fill your hydrometer cup and take a reading, the syrup cools down about this much from its finished boiling temperature of about 218°. If you dally, the syrup will cool down more and measure too dense. (However, there are charts that tell how to compensate for temperature variation.)

There is another tool called a refractometer that can be used to measure syrup density at any temperature. A refractometer is problematic when used with hot syrup, because only a drop is needed, and evaporation will very quickly affect the density of such a small amount. A refractometer is the tool of choice for syrup bottlers who need to measure room-temperature syrup from a barrel, but it is not a good choice for the small syrup maker.

FILTERING AND BOTTLING

Maple sap has large amounts of minerals dissolved in it. As the sap is concentrated, these minerals precipitate out of solution, forming granules or sludge in the syrup, commonly known as "sugar sand" or "niter." These particles are primarily composed of calcium malate. You can bottle your syrup with this sludge in it, and it will settle to the bottom of the jar, and you can just pour off the good syrup on top. But when you get to the bottom, your syrup will be cruddy, and after that, you'll have syrupy crud—and if you are the Chicken Feathers Guy, you'll be obligated to consume it. So it's better to just filter it out before bottling.

Large producers achieve extreme clarity using a pressurized filter, but most small producers filter by gravity. A white cotton cloth gets out the larger particles, but not the fine stuff. I use a thin nylon pre-filter and a thick Orlon filter; when used in combination they get the syrup almost completely free of particulate. The prefilter costs $2–4, and the thick filter costs about $6–15, depending on size. You can order these from any maple syrup supply dealer. Some are cone-shaped and designed to fit inside a milk can or metal pot; others are designed to fit into a flat tray. Each filter can be used 10–20 times. If you are making tiny batches of syrup, like a quart or two, you probably won't want the thick filter—it will absorb too much syrup. In this case, use the prefilter by itself.

Soak and rinse a new filter in hot water before use, to get out the new-filter flavor, and to make the liquid pass through better. Filter your syrup when it is hot; it will flow through much better.

"Finishing the syrup" refers to getting it to the exact concentration of syrup, which is legally 66.0–68.9° Brix (when hot), before bottling. The standard for Vermont and New Hampshire is 66.9° Brix, which is what I aim for—syrup any denser will undergo some crystallization. When you draw or pour off from your pan, you should be close to finished density, but rarely will you be spot-on. Some additional liquid will evaporate during filtering. Use the hydrometer to recheck the density before bottling. If it is too dense, add small increments of distilled water and retest until the correct density is reached. You don't want your syrup thin at filtering, because boiling it down further, after filtering, will cause additional sugar sand to precipitate. If you are selling syrup, clarity matters; otherwise, the tiny bit of stuff in there shouldn't bother you.

When your syrup reaches the appropriate density, turn off the heat and bottle it. You can use glass mason jars or syrup bottles. Pour the syrup into the jar, screw on the lid, and flip the jar upside down or onto its side for a minute or two so the hot syrup sterilizes the inside of the lid. After you flip the jar right-side up, you're done. Make sure the temperature of the syrup stays above

Finished syrup.

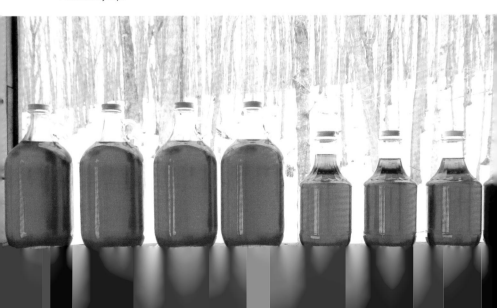

185°F as you bottle (for half gallons or larger), or above 195°F (for smaller glass containers). There is no need to water-bath the jars. In the uncommon event of a broken seal, the syrup may get moldy on top. If you notice this, filter out the mold through a thin cloth, then reboil and rebottle or refrigerate the syrup.

MAPLE SYRUP COLOR AND GRADES

The grade of maple syrup refers to the color. For many years, the lighter-colored syrup was highly valued, but in recent years the price difference between the color grades has decreased. This has been one of the most unexpected changes in the syrup industry over the last 20 years, driven largely by a liquid crash diet known as "The Master Cleanse."

This cleanse was the brainchild of a man named Stanley Burroughs in the 1940s. It was explained in his 1976 book *The Master Cleanser*, and was repopularized in recent decades. The regimen consists solely of lemonade with cayenne pepper, sweetened with maple syrup. Burroughs advised using only grade B maple syrup, which he mistakenly believed to be less refined and more nutritious. Some unscrupulous people realized they could capitalize on this misinformation, buying cheap grade B syrup and selling it at inflated prices. A few even put up websites with the express purpose of lying to consumers about the meaning of syrup grades. Now, every honest syrup producer is forced to explain and re-explain the truth to customers.

Grade A syrup is not more refined than grade B; neither grade is refined at all. They are made by identical processes. Grade B syrup is not more nutritious (Chabot 2007), and there is no good reason to suspect that it would be. It doesn't have more vitamins or minerals. It is not more natural. The difference is that grade B is darker, and it tastes stronger. Why?

The primary reason that syrup gets dark is sap spoilage. The more the sap spoils before being cooked, the darker the finished syrup. The natural flavor of maple is primarily derived from vanillin and malic acid; this is what you taste in light syrup. The strong "mapley flavor" that lovers of grade B syrup crave is the by-product of bacteria in sap, along with some caramelization. Since spoilage is especially prominent in warm weather toward the end of sap season, many producers use euphemisms like "late-season sap" (a term that means "spoiling sap"), but all of them know exactly what is happening.

The second reason for dark syrup is long cooking: The longer the syrup is boiled, the darker it becomes. This doesn't mean grade B is more concentrated—all syrup is required by law to be of uniform density. But some smaller, less efficient evaporation systems require the syrup to boil for longer before becoming sufficiently concentrated. Syrup darkens as it caramelizes in this situation, accentuating the flavor. This is a lesser factor in darkening syrup (especially in the larger operations that supply most of the commercially available syrup).

There is nothing wrong with dark syrup. Any bacteria are killed by cooking. Dark syrup tastes good and is perfectly healthy. Just like light syrup. Choose whichever one tastes better to you. In response to the widespread misinformation about syrup grades, the International Maple Syrup Institute has recommended a new grading system that abandons "grade B" as a syrup designation. Most states have adopted this new system, which hopefully will help sanity return to the discussion of syrup grades and color.

BEYOND SYRUP: MAKING SUGAR AND OTHER CONFECTIONS

To make granulated maple sugar, you need to cook well beyond the syrup density. Before doing this, transfer your syrup to a smaller pot that you can lift from the flame at a moment's notice. Monitor the temperature carefully with a candy thermometer. You want to cook it to 45–50°F (25–28°C) above your boiling point of water, then remove it from the heat and let it cool to around 200°F (93°C), then begin stirring. At a certain moment, you'll notice a white streak in the cooling syrup. When you see this, you're almost there—give it all you've got! Within a short time, your whole pan will magically turn from liquid to powder. Keep working it for a couple of minutes as it cools further.

To make blocks of sugar, pull your syrup off just a bit sooner, at 34–38°F (19–21°C) above boiling, and stir right away. When it starts becoming opaque and stiffening, quickly pour it into molds before it hardens in the pan. For smaller molds, like those nifty maple-leaf shaped candies, pull it off about 2°F cooler. The exact timing of

When stirring maple sugar, it first becomes clumpy; keep stirring vigorously and it will soon become powder.

pouring into molds is a skill learned through experience, but you can eat all your mistakes. We make a delicious candy by stirring in finely ground black walnuts 50/50 with the maple syrup, and then spooning and pressing it immediately into molds.

One of my favorite maple confections is called maple cream in the United States, or maple butter in Canada—both misleading names that suggest dairy products when in fact this spread is made from nothing but maple syrup. To make cream, use a lighter grade of syrup and cook it to 22–24°F (12–13°C) above the boiling point. Then rapidly cool it down by placing the pot in a sink or basin filled with cold water. Do not stir or disturb the syrup as it cools, or crystals will form. When it reaches close to room temperature and becomes slightly solid, stir it slowly until it becomes a smooth paste that is totally opaque. This is hard work and may take half an hour; brief pauses (a minute or less) are fine (in fact, they hasten the process), but long pauses are dangerous (the stuff can harden). A partner is advised, to give you breaks and to hold down the pan.

USING MAPLE SYRUP

Maple syrup is good for so much more than pancakes. In fact, I was hoping to write this whole chapter without using that word. For many generations, maple was the common household sweetener of the northeastern United States and adjacent Canada. It was used in everything that was sweetened: coffee, tea, apple pie, cranberry sauce, cake, oatmeal, cobblers. Maple syrup is still good in all of those ways. We use it to sweeten our hot breakfast cereal, whether that is wild rice, lotus, chia, wapato, or Malt-O-Meal. Maple sugar has the same sweetness as table sugar. As a substitute in baking, 1 cup of syrup replaces ¾ cup of sugar. For each cup of syrup you use, try to reduce the liquid elsewhere in the recipe by ¼ cup, or add the amount of flour that would absorb that additional quarter cup of liquid.

A VERY BRIEF HISTORY OF MAPLE SUGARING

Native Americans throughout much of the sugaring region were making maple sugar when Europeans arrived on this continent, and taught the practice to the newcomers. Sap was gathered by chopping a V-shaped wound into a maple, and placing a sliver of wood at the bottom to direct the sap flow into a bark vessel. This works very well, but damages the trees more than modern methods. The exact methods used to concentrate the sap with primitive technology were not well recorded, but David Zeisberger, a Dutch missionary in the eastern Great Lakes during the late 1700s, reported that the Mingoes made kettles from elm bark for "sugar boiling" (Zeisberger 1910). White historians, generally ignorant

A natural, old-growth stand of sugar maple with an herbaceous layer dominated by wild leek. There are millions of acres of this habitat.

of bark technology, have preferred speculations that feed our sense of cultural superiority—such as the often-repeated contention that sap was boiled by dropping hot rocks into a dugout log trough. People I know who have tried this method contend that not only is it totally impractical, but it gets so much lye and ash in the sugar as to render it inedible. We do know that enterprising native people quickly adopted metal vessels for cooking, and employed a three-kettle system to produce huge quantities of sugar, which was an important item of both subsistence and trade.

There is a reason they call it a *sugar*bush, *sugar* camp, a *sugar* shack, and a *sugar* maple. The normal product made from maples, for hundreds of years, was not a liquid syrup—it was granulated or molded sugar. Even after canning was invented in the early 1800s, glass or metal containers were extremely expensive. Syrup was an ephemeral product, not suitable as a storable or tradable commodity. Sugar, on the other hand, is non-perishable and lighter, and can be easily stored in containers of wood, bark, cloth, or hide. Not until the late 1800s did the production of maple syrup equal that of granulated sugar. Old-fashioned sugar was made from unfiltered syrup and contained all of the sugar sand we now discard, thus it was an incredibly rich source of mineral nutrients, especially calcium.

Although today we esteem maple sugar as a delicacy, colonists originally considered it the cheap, frontier alternative to honey or white sugar. But back in 1750, when maple sugar was the everyday sweetener of poor folks, it was *not* cheaper then than it is today—it was several times more expensive, just like every other commodity. In the mid 1800s, flat-pan evaporators became common, followed by corrugated flue pans in a few decades. These greatly increased the efficiency of production. Syrup production in the United States peaked in the beginning of the Civil War, when Northerners patriotically refused to buy "slave sugar." Even today, with many times the 1860 population, we produce much less syrup than we did then.

Although the real price of maple syrup has been dropping for hundreds of years, other food prices have dropped even more precipitously, making maple products seem expensive by comparison. US consumption and production plummeted for many decades, reaching a low point in the 1980s. In the 1940s, Canadian production surpassed that of the United States and has risen dramatically, to account for about 80% of total production today—despite a much smaller base of tappable maples. US production has increased steadily for the last 30 years, as tubing, vacuum pumps, and reverse osmosis have brought down prices, and a segment of the population seeks healthier and more environmentally sustainable food sources. Still, we have the reasonable potential to increase our production 50-fold or more.

The developing seeds of silver maple in spring. I think they taste best when just formed.

MAPLE SEEDS

Maple sugaring is such a robust wild food tradition that it is easy to forget that these trees produce another edible product: the seeds. Maple seeds are produced in spring or early summer, in pairs, and tumble to the earth on winged samaras called keys or helicopters. Some people claim that all maple seeds are edible, but I can't vouch for that. The only ones I eat are those of silver maple. As a child, my older sisters taught me to carefully peel the seed from its fruit when they reach almost full size, but are still soft and liquidy inside. At this fleeting stage they are delicious. Older seeds are bitter when raw, but can be roasted and eaten, or better yet, boiled and drained.

The sugar woods is a marvelous thing. The forest is left intact, little changed from a natural stand of trees. Remove the buckets or sap lines, and very few untrained eyes would see anything but a magnificent hardwood forest. The red-eyed vireos still nest in summer, the red-backed salamanders still creep across the leaf litter by the thousands. The deer still browse, the bears forage, the wood frogs wait for spiders to amble by. There are no chemical sprays, no fertilizer inputs, no tilling or planting, no heavy machinery—yet there is a crop. The yield per acre may be low—85 pounds of sugar—but it is probably the most sustainable yield of any North American crop commercially grown today. A crop that builds rather than destroys the soil. And this system produces a surplus of the world's most economical biofuel: firewood. Between the trunks of these rugged sugar trees, a lush carpet of vegetables and wildflowers displays itself every spring; in late summer, a bonanza of mushrooms.

The sugar woods isn't just a place to pass the glorious days when spring wins its battle with winter; it's also a template for what I want to do with my life: Eat Nature, and have it, too.

Miner's Lettuce

Montia perfoliata

M iner's lettuce is a wild edible as convenient as one could ask for. No tricky identification here—this plant is so distinct in form that even a novice will have no trouble recognizing it. No arduous preparation, either: This vegetable is so pleasant fresh and raw that even the laziest forager will have no complaint. It calls for no acquired taste; it is so tame that even my brother might eat it. Although miner's lettuce grows here and there in the far backcountry, it doesn't impose that journey upon us to make its acquaintance: it comes to our doorstep (or at least pretty close). There is no need to figure out which part is tasty or tender; the whole thing is fair game. And miner's lettuce has this convenient habit of growing in thick, pure patches that clothe the ground in lush greenery.

What more could a forager ask for? That's easy: miner's lettuce all year. But nothing this good can last.

A lush clump of miner's lettuce in bloom.

DESCRIPTION

Miner's lettuce is one of our easiest plants to recognize. It is an annual, growing from a slender taproot and bearing two very different kinds of leaves. Each root produces a rosette of several basal leaves on petioles 2–3 times as long as the blade. The basal leaves are highly variable in shape. At first they may be linear, almost grass-like—but they are fleshy and soft, and never keeled or folded. Later basal leaves are wide, and may be elliptic, spoon shaped, triangular, or heart-shaped. They are .75–4 inches (2–10 cm) long, devoid of hairs and teeth, and blunt at the tip. Miner's lettuce is a close relative of the spring beauties, and these basal leaves show the affinity—but not to any one species. Interestingly, the variable basal leaves of miner's lettuce can show the form of almost every species of spring beauty.

The basal rosette of miner's lettuce. The basal leaves can be linear and grass-like, elliptic, ovate, triangular, or heart-shaped—you can see it all on one plant here.

Miner's lettuce in bloom (mixed with a bunch of chickweed). Note how the first flowers open when the cluster is compact, on a very short pedicel, but eventually this elongates into a raceme.

The plant also produces multiple erect stems reaching 2–14 inches (5–35 cm) in height depending on growing conditions. The stems are smooth, rounded, and hairless. They are always unbranched and bear a large pair of conjoined leaves, and usually a single smaller leaf above that. The unique pair of stem leaves are what makes the plant so easily recognized: They are fused together, making a roughly circular dish-like structure around the upper stem, with no prominent veins, and an occasional point on the disc's perimeter.

Out of the middle of this disc rises a small cluster of tiny, 5-petaled, white or faintly pinkish flowers. When these flowers begin blooming, the cluster's stem is very short and nestled at the bottom of the funnel formed by the leaves. With time, however, the flower stem elongates several inches into a raceme. The stem is rather limp, often falling to one side or drooping; it bears a single ovate leaf beneath the lowest flower.

All parts of miner's lettuce are bluish-green, succulent, and tender, without hairs, bumps, or glands to annoy your mouth—even at maturity, the plant is only scarcely fibrous.

HABITAT

Miner's lettuce is an annual and thus needs bare soil upon which to germinate. It finds this typically where the land is sloped or shady—and especially where it is both. This plant benefits from erosion, natural or human-caused. It thrives under a combination of rich soil, ample moisture, moderate shade, and gentle

Composite range of miner's lettuces (genus *Montia*). The range in Alaska and most of Canada represents Siberian miner's lettuce *Montia sibirica*.

yearly erosion from winter rains. A native, miner's lettuce can be found in back-yards, parks, roadsides, weedy lots, wild or urban woodlots, sloped pastures, ravines, and around the bases of bluffs and steep hillsides, especially where the soil is loose or sandy. It is primarily a plant of low to middle elevations.

HARVEST AND PREPARATION

Miner's lettuce is an ephemeral whose seasonality is based more on soil moisture than on temperature. It takes advantage of the wet winter conditions prevalent near the West Coast, and the briefer moist conditions of spring further inland. Near the coast in California it may often be collected for 4–5 months, from December through March or April. Inland the season may be only a month or two. The plant has better flavor and texture earlier in its growth, before flower-ing. It can be eaten after blooming, but it gets faintly tough and slightly bitter. I must emphasize that this quality reduction is relative; even older miner's let-tuce is much milder than the youngest leaves of dandelion, chicory, or prickly lettuce. In fact, the only complaint that seems to be levied against miner's let-tuce *is* its mildness. But mildness is great, for one can eat more of a mild thing. Here, then, is a plant asking to be eaten.

A large miner's lettuce plant with dozens of thick, juicy stems. Let some of them go to seed. Also, note that there are poison hemlock leaves in my handful—this is a frequent companion of miner's lettuce.

Siberian miner's
lettuce in bloom.

This green is most
commonly just eaten
raw as a snack, 1.4 sec-
onds after it has been
picked. And not just
by miners, who seem
to have no particular
disposition toward
the plant. The leaves
can be used almost
anywhere in place of
lettuce, only they're
better. Being so mild,
it is a good green for a
smoothie. It is also an excellent ingredient in soups, whole or pureed. You can
cook the greens in any way you like, and the flavor is good, but they are so tender
and laden with water that they quickly cook down to a soft, mushy mess. Thus,
most people prefer them raw, or in some dish where they are quickly cooked.
Not only are the leaves good—the stems and especially the thick petioles are
deliciously crunchy, juicy, and slightly sweet.

When collecting miner's lettuce, be sure not to mow down the entire area,
and don't yank out whole plants by the root. If the plants are isolated, pinch
or cut off a few stems or leaves. If the patch is large and dense, thin out scattered plants.

Siberian miner's lettuce is a relative, also native, with similar flavor. It is an
annual or biennial and tends to be somewhat larger, 5–15 inches (13–38 cm) tall,
and the stems fork in the inflorescence. The raceme of flowers is much longer
and more spread out than with common miner's lettuce. The leaves of Siberian
miner's lettuce are *not* fused into a disc—they are paired, sessile, and broadly
ovate or elliptic. A few smaller leaves are also associated with the inflorescence.
Siberian miner's lettuce grows on streamsides and ravines at low to middle
elevations further north than common miner's lettuce. The flavor is similar, and
best before flowering, although not quite as delicate. This plant should be eaten
not only by Siberian miners, but also by those of any occupation and ethnicity.

There are a few other species of miner's lettuce, each similar enough to be
recognized as such, and each also edible. Try them if you find them.

The gold they came for is mostly gone, but the miner's lettuce is not.

Mint

Genus *Mentha*

There is something magical about mint, something that momentarily defies our reasonable expectations about the experience of life. That familiar crisp scent, that cooling flavor we all know from chewing gum and toothpaste, unconsciously linked to the most neatly packaged and artificial-looking things we put in our bodies, somehow tricks us into thinking that it must be

Lush, young peppermint growing along a spring. If you want to use mint as a culinary herb, this is the best time to get it.

the result of some laboratory accident in a secret room way down the back hall of a sterile factory.

And then we step on one. As we peer into the clear, cold springwater of a hidden trout brook on some dewy summer dawn, far up the remote hollow we wish we had time to visit more than once a year, far in space and thought from any drugstore, the world is turned a little upside-down. That piercing, unmistakable scent actually comes from *here*; only here it is cleaner and sharper and more magnificent than any mouthwash or hard candy. This is when our hearts whelm us to take a deep breath and we remember feelings that we have never put to words: the feelings that pulled us out of bed this morning, and tugged at our heart all week.

For a silly instant we thought that mint was Nature imitating man, and then we laughed. We came here to remember.

DESCRIPTION

Mints are perennials that grow from thin rhizomes and have erect, squared stems that branch sparingly, if at all. The leaves are paired and either sessile, or growing on very short petioles. Leaf shape ranges from lanceolate to broadly elliptic to ovate, and texture from hairless to quite hairy, but the margins are always toothed. The flowers are white or pink, tiny, and packed into dense clusters, either in the leaf axils or in terminal spikes. All true mints of the genus *Mentha* have a strong, pleasant, minty scent; as long as your nose works, you won't confuse them with any dangerous plant.

There are actually several genera within the mint family with a pleasant, minty scent. All of them are safe edibles. Mints of the genus *Mentha* are distinguished by having all of the following characteristics: The calyx is symmetrical, the corolla is nearly symmetrical, and the flowers have 4 stamens protruding well beyond the petals.

A mature plant of *Mentha canadensis* (*arvensis*), our only native *Mentha*. At this stage the leaves are good for tea.

The only native mint found growing wild in North America is *M. canadensis*, called simply wild mint or field mint. This species is found throughout most of North America and much of Asia. It has often been lumped with its close European relative, *M. arvensis*, but differs in chromosome number as well as its scent. Wild mint has lanceolate to ovate leaves that may be hairy or hairless, but its lavender to pink flowers are always borne in the axils of normal-sized leaves.

There are several introduced mints that occur erratically near human habitation in North America. The most common introduced wild mint is probably peppermint, a hybrid between spearmint and water mint. Peppermint has broader leaves that are sometimes curled downward on the edges. It is hairless, or nearly so, and often purplish, especially on the stem. This species has its flowers in short, dense terminal spikes at the top of the plant, or occasionally from branches that come from the upper leaf axils. Other introduced mints that grow wild include spearmint, apple mint, and water mint.

HABITAT

Mints thrive in moist soil in full to partial sunlight; they don't survive heavy shade. *M. canadensis* is found in wet meadows, low pastures, moist spots in semi-open woods, shrub swamps, and roadside ditches, and along the edges of marshes, ponds, streams, and lakes. It prefers localities with high levels of organic matter in the soil. Plants associated with wild mint include stinging nettle, reed canary grass, bugleweeds, blue vervain, and various sedges.

Peppermint is even more specific in its habitat requests. It grows in wet ground along the edges of springs and

Dark blue: native range of *Mentha arvensis*. Light blue: area inhabited only by introduced mints. In arid regions, mints are sparsely distributed.

spring-fed streams, although occasionally it is found in other moist sites. Peppermint often stands right in the shallow water as an emergent aquatic. While very widespread, peppermint is introduced, and therefore its occurrence is spotty and hard to predict; it is locally abundant, but overall not as common as wild mint. Peppermint tends to grow near watercress, American willow-herb *Epilobium ciliatum*, and brooklime *Veronica americana/beccabunga*. The other introduced mints occur erratically in moist habitats, usually where there is a history of human disturbance.

HARVEST AND PREPARATION

Mint is probably the most well known and widely used of all temperate seasonings. Mints are used in chewing gum, alcoholic drinks, cigarettes, toothpaste, and an enormous variety of candies. Peppermint, spearmint, and wild mint are all cultivated commercially for use as a flavoring, although menthol, one of the important essential oils, is now manufactured artificially. Mints also have an extensive list of traditional medicinal uses, especially as an antispasmodic to alleviate stomach pains and cramps. Menthol stimulates cold-sensitive receptors (the opposite of capsaicin in hot peppers) to create the pleasant, cool feeling in the mouth. It is also a local painkiller and has antibacterial properties.

The most common use of mint in our house is to make tea. All of the species are good, either alone or in mixtures with other herbs. I prefer peppermint and spearmint over field mint, but the latter is the one that grows in my yard, so I use that more often. The leaves can be used fresh or dried, and can be steeped in hot or cold water. Boiling will volatize the essential oils and weaken the flavor. I like it mixed with several other wild teas, notably stinging nettle, New Jersey tea, and leadplant.

Mint retains the best flavor when dried quickly but out of direct sunlight or extreme heat. I dry mine by one of two methods: I hang the whole plants in loose bundles from a beam in my living room; or I loosely place them in a paper grocery bag, and then put the bag in a warm, dry place, such as my dining room windowsill or in the car with the windows cracked on a sunny day. The bag, especially with the top open, allows for air and moisture flow but keeps the mint shaded. It also allows for easy mixing of the material—just pick up the bag and shake it gently.

Mint is well known as a flavoring for candies, ice cream, and other sweets, but it is an excellent herb with a great variety of other uses. When mint plants are young and tender, from spring through early summer, I enjoy nibbling a sprig or two raw. They make a great garnish to nibble after a heavy meal. If used sparingly, young mint greens can be used in salads, stir-fries, meatballs, and many other savory dishes. In Persian cuisine, mint and cucumbers are added to yogurt as a side dish. I often add a touch of mint to chicken soup. And of course, mint jelly is a traditional condiment for lamb.

MINTY RELATIVES

Several native plants that are not in the genus *Mentha* still have that classic minty scent and flavor, and can be used like the true mints.

The **mountain mints** (genus *Pycnanthemum*) includes several species (a few of which lean toward bergamot in flavor). Most mountain mints have entire leaves, and on some species they are extremely narrow. Their tiny, irregular flowers are in small, tightly-packed clusters at the tips of branches that fork three ways. Mountain mints are usually found in open woodlands, fields, or prairies.

Blephilia hirsuta, which I call "tall woodmint," is widespread in rich, moist hardwood forests of the eastern United States. It usually branches and grows 2–6 feet tall, making it our tallest minty plant. It has a potent flavor very similar to field mint. Most people who encounter this plant assume it to be a true mint. (A close relative, *B. ciliata* is a shorter, usually unbranched plant of thin, rocky soil in sunny woodlands. It has almost no minty essence.)

Another noteworthy species is **calamint**. Its classification is in dispute: Some say *Calamintha arkansana*, but others say *Clinopodium arkansanum* or *Satureja arkansana*; some split it into two species, in which case one of them has the species name *glabella*. No matter. Calamint is a tiny mint with an odd distribution, being found exclusively on limestone outcrops or gravel beaches with thin soil, where it is sunny but usually moist. When flowering, calamint stands 6–14 inches tall and has tiny, thin leaves, delicate stems, and small purplish flowers borne singly or in small clusters. In the cool season it creeps along the ground, with ovate leaves packed closely together. The two forms look like completely different plants—but both have an incredibly potent and pleasant scent.

Below left Young shoot of the mountain mint *Pycnanthemum virginianum*. **Below right** Mountain mints have the flowers in tight clusters at the ends of tri-forked branches.

Above left Tall woodmint *Blephilia hirsuta* in bloom. Note the stacked whorls at the top. **Above right** The dainty calamint has showy purple flowers, just one per axil. The flavor is intense. **Below** The evergreen, winter growth form of calamint—also good for tea. It's hard to believe this is the same species—but in fact, it's the very same individual.

American pennyroyal *Hedeoma pulegioides*, another small, delicate native mint with a powerful flavor.

Hedeoma pulegioides, usually called **American pennyroyal**, is named for its flavor's likeness to the real pennyroyal, *Mentha pulegium*, a European mint. American pennyroyal stands erect, rarely reaches a foot in height, and produces few to no branches. It has tiny pairs of lanceolate, sessile, nearly entire leaves, and 1–3 tiny bluish flowers borne in each leaf axil. Its flavor is very potent. American pennyroyal, unlike the other species discussed here, is an annual. Look for it in mid to late summer in dry, steep, rocky woods with a sparse canopy, especially under oaks and hickories. It does very well alongside gravel forest roads, logging trails, ravines, and in lightly used wooded pastures. If you find it, scatter seeds in autumn to ideal-looking uncolonized sites.

There is some discussion in the literature, and especially online, about American pennyroyal being dangerous due to its content of an aromatic oil called pulegone (which is also found in several other mints). Like most essential oils (and other mint oils), pulegone is toxic. In large enough doses it will cause liver damage or multiple organ failure. There have been severe poisonings, some fatal, caused by people taking large doses of pennyroyal oil in an attempt to induce abortion (Sullivan 1979). However, this oil is a concentrated extract—the actual plant, or a tea made from it, has no history of such poisoning. You won't get anything close to a dangerous dose through normal use of mint in food and drink. The warnings about pulegone are irrelevant to foraging.

Mint is one of the best "gateway" edibles, a plant for the timid beginning forager. Perhaps more importantly, it is for the doubtful relative who thinks that wild food is scary stuff eaten by unusual people with a deficient sense of either conformity or caution. Shut them up with a glass of maple-sweetened mint tea. There is nothing more normal and everyday than mint, a miracle directly from Nature that has never been, and never will be, improved upon.

Mulberry

Morus alba, M. rubra, M. nigra, M. microphylla

Right around the Fourth of July when I was 7 years old, I was trying to find a praying mantis along one of the brushy fencerows at my grandparents' farm when I made a miraculous discovery: a blackberry tree. Now, I had picked many blackberries before, and I knew that they grew on thorny canes, not trees—so this was clearly odd. And clearly good. I wanted to run into the house and tell my sisters of my incredible discovery, but it was in fact so odd that I doubted myself. If I were wrong, would they laugh at me? There was only one way to tell. I picked one of the blackberries and tasted it. It was so good I picked a few more handfuls before running into the house to share the great news.

"Grandma! Grandma! Did you know you have a blackberry tree?" I shouted as I came into the kitchen.

"Blackberries don't grow on trees," she stated in a puzzled tone, although she figured the whole thing out so quickly that she added with hardly a pause, "Those are mulberries behind the chicken coop."

White (Asian) mulberry *Morus alba* in fruit, with white (unripe) fruit in the background, red-purple (half-ripe) fruit, and black (ripe) fruit. These leaves are not lobed. This is the kind of white mulberry often mistaken for red mulberry. Note the latex where I removed a leaf.

"*Mul*-berries?" I asked, with special emphasis on this unfamiliar prefix to the b-word, adding "Can you eat 'em?"—a little too late if the answer was no.

"Well yes, if you want to, but they're kind of stemmy," she said.

My sister and I went immediately back outside and feasted, not minding the stemminess one bit. And so began a lifelong relationship with one of the best trees on Earth.

DESCRIPTION

North America is home to two native species of mulberry: the red mulberry *Morus rubra* and the Texas mulberry *Morus microphylla*. However, an introduced species, *Morus alba*, is more common and widespread than either native kind and is the one familiar to the greatest number of people. A second introduced species, *M. nigra*, is rare, scattered mostly in the southern states.

Mulberries can be easily recognized by their berry, which is technically a tight, elongated cluster of tiny fruits called a "syncarp." It looks like a blackberry that dangles from a short stem. There is no other North American tree with fruit like this, making mulberries unmistakable when in fruit.

Mulberries are small to medium-sized trees with spreading crowns. The leaves are simple, toothed, and alternate, and grow on short petioles. They may be ovate, heart-shaped, or variously lobed—all forms sometimes found on a single branch. Young trees and stump sprouts, especially those under intense

Form of an open-grown Asian mulberry *M. alba*, a common sight on fence lines like this.

Deeply and erratically lobed leaves of an Asian mulberry *M. alba* sapling. Although the leaf tips are occasionally acuminate on such specimens, the lobes are not. These leaves are about four inches long.

sunlight or in dry soil, are likely to have larger and more deeply lobed leaves. All of the mulberries have milky sap, although it is not produced as profusely as in plants like milkweed or lettuce.

Identifying mulberries, as a group, is quite easy; it is in determining the particular species that trouble comes up—because people wrongly assume from the names that fruit color is a distinguishing feature.

Our most abundant species, the introduced **Morus alba**, is most commonly called white mulberry, but this name causes immense confusion; I call it Asian mulberry. The bark of *Morus alba* has thin, yellow-gray ridges between yellowish-orange valleys. The crown is dense and spreading. The leaves are typically 2–5 inches (5–13 cm) long on mature trees, with occasional lobes; when present, these are blunt-tipped. Saplings and stump sprouts can have larger leaves, which may be slightly rough on top (otherwise, the leaves of Asian mulberry are glossy and smooth above). Young trees typically have prominently lobed leaves. Asian mulberry leaves always have scattered clumps of hair along the main veins underneath, and nowhere else. *The fruit normally ripens to purple-black*, although occasional specimens have fruit that is white or pink when ripe.

The widespread native mulberry is **Morus rubra**. This is most often called red mulberry, although I prefer American mulberry. American mulberry has reddish-brown bark in rough, narrow vertical strips, looking much like that of slippery elm. The crown is sparse, and the twigs often thick. This species is easy to tell from the Asian mulberry by its much larger leaves, typically 4–12 inches (10–30 cm) long, that are broader and never glossy. The leaves feel sandpapery above from a uniform coating of stiff hairs—somewhat like those of slippery elm, although of a finer grit. Beneath, they show a nearly uniform covering of erect, soft hairs on all major and minor veins. The leaves of mature American mulberries almost never have lobes, but those of saplings and seedlings do; most lobes have long, tapered, points. The fruit ripens to purple-black, and can grow much longer than the fruit of Asian mulberry.

The black mulberry, **Morus nigra**, is rarely found growing wild. (Most reports are misidentified *M. alba*.) It has a plump, dark fruit and broad, usually unlobed leaves. The fruit ripens in late summer, long after the white and red mulberries have dropped.

Morus microphylla, variously called little-leaf mulberry, Texas mulberry, little mulberry, canyon mulberry, or western mulberry, is a small tree of the Southwest, with small, rough leaves with large teeth; these leaves are typically lobed. The berries ripen to purple-black and are very small, like the occasional stunted mini-fruits seen on the other mulberries.

THE POWER OF A NAME TO MAKE A TREE INVISIBLE

The Asian mulberry *Morus alba* has been domesticated in China for thousands of years (Kole, 2011), where it is grown for fruit and, more importantly, as

An Asian mulberry *M. alba* with ripe, white fruit. This trait is an abberation that has been selected for in cultivation, but is not characteristic of wild populations. Less than 6% of "white" mulberries growing wild have white fruit when ripe. Note the glossy leaves and blunt lobes and leaf tips.

food for silkworms. In the wild in its native China, the tree's ripe fruit is black (Hu 2005). As with other domesticated plants, untold generations of cultivation have resulted in the development and selection of varieties with new and unusual characteristics. All mulberries go through a white phase just before developing the dark pigments of ripeness, but in certain cultivars of *M. alba*, color development is arrested right there, and the fruit never darkens. Eventually, Asian mulberry cultivars with white fruit found their way to Europe. A well-known taxonomist named *Carl von Linné* observed these cultivars, unaware of their anomalous color, and gave the tree the scientific name *Morus alba*, which means "white mulberry."

White fruit is seen in only a tiny fraction of wild *M. alba* in North America. (In my sampling of hundreds of feral *M. alba* from Wisconsin, Minnesota, South Dakota, and Missouri, less than 6% had fruit that was white when ripe.) Nevertheless, many people insist that fruit color is the way to identify mulberries—and this unfortunately includes some field guide authors. Many invert the truth, pretending that dark fruit is the occasional aberration, calling it form *tatarica*.

If you collect mulberries from urban habitats within any city in the northern half of the United States or in Canada, they are *Morus alba*, regardless of fruit color. However, if you believe that there are two common mulberry species in your area, which look very similar in all respects besides fruit color (this is exactly what many books incorrectly say), you will split *Morus alba* into two species, giving the predominant dark-fruited form the name *Morus rubra*, and the less common white ones *M. alba*. This is a logical deduction from false information, which results in an incorrect conclusion. By this process, both names get used up on the Asian mulberry, and none remain for the American mulberry. No name, no thing. *Voilà!* The tree simply disappears.

Don't believe me? In 2009, a group of university professors (Galla et al.) published a paper called "A New Species of Mulberry from Eastern North America." These folks, victims of the above confusion, became flummoxed when they encountered the real *M. rubra* and decided that it must be a brand-new species. They gave their "new" species the name *Morus murrayana*, but their photos and description of it exactly match the characteristics of typical *M. rubra*. Molecular data confirms that this "new" species was a case of misidentification (Nepal et al. 2012).

Asian and American mulberries are so exceedingly different that it is nearly impossible to confuse them (except as seedlings, when they do look similar). This remarkable dissimilarity actually makes the American mulberry harder for most Northerners, and some urban Southerners, to see. Except in the unlikely case that you notice the fruit, you will probably see American mulberry as basswood (linden). *Morus rubra* looks so much like basswood that almost every person who has studied the tree has felt compelled to warn others of the potential for

Above Typical leaves of red (American) mulberry are unlobed, broadly ovate to heart-shaped, and 3-10 inches long. Note the arrangement in a canopy-like layer, and the highly divergent size, with smaller leaves growing proximally. These are typical characteristics. Looks a heck of a lot like basswood, doesn't it? **Below** Young leaves of American mulberry *M. rubra* in late spring. Notice the drooping form, the depressed secondary veins, and the light green color—all good features for spotting this tree when the leaves are meristematic. Also, notice the "extended tooth" on the rightmost leaf. This occasional but diagnostic feature of American mulberry is shared with catalpa, but not with Asian mulberry or any other tree in its region.

Above American mulberry *M. rubra* leaves on a two-year-old roadside stump sprout about nine feet tall. Such leaves may be wildly lobed. Notice the "sinus-step," a step-like tooth in the rounded interior of a major leaf sinus. This is another diagnostic feature of American mulberry that is not seen in the Asian species. The largest leaf here is fourteen inches long. These could possibly be confused with the invasive paper mulberry, but definitely not with Asian mulberry.

Right These are American mulberry *M. rubra* leaves on a three-year-old seedling, in a sunny, dry, rocky, hilltop clearcut. The leaves are about 3 inches long. Only as seedlings is there any chance of this tree being confused with Asian mulberry. But notice here (as elsewhere) that all major lobes of *M. rubra* leaves have acuminate tips.

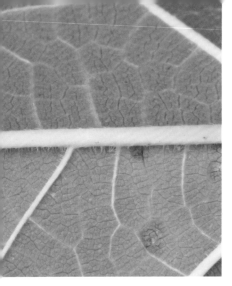

The keyable feature used to positively separate these two mulberries is the hair distribution on the underside of the leaf. The Asian mulberry *M. alba* (left) has scattered, mostly straight hairs along the major veins only, concentrated in the axils. I chose here an unusually hairy Asian mulberry leaf, to show you that even in the most extreme cases these species can be easily separated. Normally, there is less hair than this, and often only in a few axils. Although some keys say that the leaves are glabrous beneath, my examination of well over a thousand specimens in the field and in herbaria did not turn up a single *M. alba* leaf that was hairless below. The American mulberry *M. rubra* (right) has the leaves densely hairy below, on all surfaces of all major and minor veins, and the hairs are often curvy.

confusion. No pair of unrelated trees on our continent is more easily confused; the resemblance can hardly be exaggerated. When I rediscovered this tree in the state of Minnesota (Thayer, 2017), the Department of Natural Resources believed it to be probably extirpated in the state; it had not been documented in 94 years. But it was growing beside a major highway where dozens of botanists, foresters, and naturalists had seen it—and thought it was basswood.

This unparalleled crisis of misidentification has led to a crisis of conservation. Nurseries are selling the invasive Asian mulberry, mislabeled as *M. rubra*—thwarting native reforestation attempts. Botanical collectors are submitting misidentified and mislabeled specimens to herbaria, making it look like *M. rubra* is increasing in distribution even as it disappears. Many botanical gardens and interpretive trails have mislabeled specimen trees. Numerous field guides and major websites have mislabeled photos. An incredibly beautiful native tree with delicious fruit, rich in cultural history, is disappearing from large parts of its range, and virtually nobody is noticing, because most land managers don't know the tree exists. In areas where Asian mulberry outnumbers American mulberry by a huge margin, it is genetically swamping the native species—outcompeting it and absorbing it into its own gene pool (Burgess et al. 2005). Ontario is managing to prevent this, but no US state is doing so. When crews cut out invasive shrubs, they often leave the Asian mulberries, believing them native.

Foragers need to admit, collectively, that we have been guilty of this confusion—then right ourselves and lead the way in preserving this unique and magnificent tree.

HABITAT

Asian mulberry is common, often abundant, in disturbed situations such as roadsides, abandoned farmland, farm woodlots, fence lines, empty city lots, and along railroad tracks. This species likes full sun and well-drained soil, but in other respects is something of a weedy generalist. It is most common in the middle latitudes, and rare in the North and Deep South.

The area in blue is inhabited by both the native *Morus rubra* and the introduced *M. alba*. The area in light blue is inhabited by introduced *M. alba* only. (*M. alba* is most abundant in or near the northern half of *M rubra*'s native range.) The red area is inhabited by the native little-leaf mulberry *M. microphylla*.

American mulberry sapling, graceful and elegant, in typical semi-shade habitat—a clearing in a rich hardwood forest on a steep slope. This looks nothing like Asian mulberry. The terminal eight leaves on each branch are 10-13 inches long. Note, some extended teeth are visible, but no lobes.

American mulberry is almost never encountered in urban settings. Instead, it grows alongside native trees such as Kentucky coffeetree, slippery elm, pawpaw, buckeye, basswood, black walnut, sugar maple, hickories, and oaks in rich-soiled valleys and hillsides. Unlike its exotic relative, the red mulberry is rather shade-tolerant and typically lives as an understory tree in mature hardwood forests, but it also thrives in openings and on edges.

The Texas mulberry inhabits streamside woodlands at middle elevations in Texas and New Mexico.

HARVEST AND PREPARATION

Mulberries are among the first berries to ripen throughout their range, coming into season in early summer just after wild strawberries and slightly before the black caps. Although the crop on one tree may last less than two weeks, some trees always fruit later or earlier than average, extending the season of availability to a month or more. When ripe, the berries will be juicy, sweet, and usually dark. Ripe berries detach easily from their twig. If the crop is heavier than the birds can handle, the fruit will fall to the ground in great quantity.

It is generally agreed that American mulberry has a better flavor than the Asian mulberry, but both are excellent. Among Asian mulberries, the white

The delicious fruit of American mulberry goes from white to pink to purple-black. On average, it is longer and more cylindrical than that of Asian mulberry. Heavily fruiting branches in full sun have much smaller leaves than those in shade, and they are thicker and more folded—such trees, when not in fruit, are often mistaken for slippery elm, but not with Asian mulberry. (Photo by Todd Elliott)

The flowers and emerging spring leaves of American mulberry make a nice addition to salads.

ones are blander than the dark ones. Although the fruit of American mulberry is substantially larger, the tree often crops lightly in the shade of the forest understory. It can fruit very well in full sun. Hybrids of the two are often heavily loaded with large fruit (the Illinois Everbearing cultivar is such a hybrid).

Walking quiet country roads at night during early summer, you can locate the best mulberry trees by listening to the raccoons scurrying around and rustling in the branches; in the daytime, squirrels provide this service. Robins, blackbirds, opossums, woodchucks, and bears also relish the berries. For the most part, people let them go to waste. I was told as a child that they were not fit for "decent" people to eat, which left a good supply for me and my non-white friends.

Smaller mulberry trees or bushes often have many branches within reach of a ground dweller. It is quite easy to get several gallons from a good tree, and the picking goes pretty fast—sometimes 2 gallons or more per hour. Use a blickey. It can be very effective to put a tarp or sheet under a loaded tree and then shake the branches, although you'll have to spend some time picking out twigs, unripe berries, and other uncouth objects.

Mulberry preserves using the whole fruit are good, but the stems, which are hard to separate, are annoying. Straining the fruit through a food mill will leave you with a runny pulp or pulpy juice, depending on how you look at it. This will make a more gourmet jam, ice cream, pie filling, taffy, or any other preparation you choose to grace with mulberry flavor. You can pour it into hot cereal, such as lotus nut mush. Mixed with applesauce and spread to dry, it makes awesome fruit leather. Whole dried mulberries are good, too. For confections, including some slightly under-ripe berries will add tartness that improves the final product.

Mulberry juice is also delicious. You can make it in a steam juicer, or you can simmer them for 15–30 minutes and then strain through a cloth. I prefer

Throughout the summer you can get good greens from the sprouts of American mulberries that have been mowed or cut. Them woodchucks ain't stupid, goin' after these.

totally ripe fruit for juice that I intend to drink—slightly reddish fruit for jelly. The juice or pulp can be easily stored frozen or canned in a water bath.

During one wild food weekend, our group of eight was determined to make a batch of jam. Due to drought, none of the berries had cropped very well. It was mid July—mulberries were almost done, black raspberries at their peak, and gooseberries just starting; we had to scrounged up all three to make a batch. The mulberries and gooseberries went through a strainer to get out their stems, skins, and seeds, while the black raspberries went in whole. It was one of the best jams I've ever tasted, and I counted us lucky to have been forced into making it.

Greens: There is a second edible product of the mulberry, less well known than the fruit: the greens. Although these are edible on all species, they are particularly good on American mulberry. The new leaves of American mulberry can be picked in spring, right around the time the tree flowers. Vigorous, fast-growing shoots, and all attached leaves, can be collected later. If trees are cut during the summer, the stumps will send out excellent new sprouts. Pick the whole tender portion and eat it raw or cooked. They are filling, mild, totally lacking in bitterness; they remind me of nettles without the sting. American mulberry greens are so good that they'd be worth writing about even if the tree didn't have delicious fruit. I think they're the best green from any woody plant in North America. Their only rival is, oddly enough, basswood.

The leaves of Asian mulberry have been traditionally dried and used for tea in China (Hu 2005). This is popular enough that the tea is sold commercially. Tender young leaves of *M. alba* and *M. nigra* have also been dried and added to wheat flour as a nutritional amendment (Couplan 2009).

Mulberries have held the attention of hungry people for thousands of years. There's no reason to forget about them now. Any of them—whether you are decent or not.

Pawpaw

Asimina triloba

The pawpaw is legendary. It is among the best known of our wild fruits, and it has sunk deeply into American rural folklore. A few generations back, every country person within its range knew this fruit—some despising it, but more loving it. Children searched creek bottoms and thickets for the messy but delicious snack, and brought them home as a treat. For thousands of years the pawpaw provided a seasonal feast for the native people of this continent, and early European settlers gladly emulated them.

Why wouldn't they? No other edible fruit native to North America is as large, or can be collected as easily. Pawpaws grown in full sun may exceed half a pound, and a bushel basket can be filled from a few good trees. The fruit is nutritious and hearty, with an unforgettable flavor relished by many. The tree's penchant for rich soil in river and stream valleys—the preferred habitat of humans as well—means that it was abundant in places of settlement.

A ripe pawpaw. They may be single, like this one, or hang in pairs or small bunches.

There are few wild foods honored by a well-known folk tune. My mother sang me the pawpaw song before I had any idea what a pawpaw was. My grandmother explained that this unforgettable name pertained to a fruit that grew here and there in the woods of southwestern Michigan where she lived. She had eaten them from a grove along the Grand River on the way to and from school in the 1920s. I begged her to show me a pawpaw tree, but she said she had not seen one in years and couldn't help me. More than a decade later, I happened upon a grove of them in West Virginia and recognized them instantly. Along a small river, the pawpaws formed a sparse grove underneath a towering stand of sycamore. It was late September. I ran down the steep bank to the flat river terrace and looked up into the branches of the first pawpaw tree I came to, its enormous drooping leaves sheltering my head. And there they were: two green kidneys, too high to reach. I shook the trunk gently, and one of them dropped instantly. I picked it up, broke it in half, and fell in love with this magical fruit.

DESCRIPTION

Pawpaw is a small tree of the forest understory, occasionally bearing fruit when only shrub-sized. The largest pawpaw trees that I have seen are about 35 feet (11 m) tall and nearly a foot (30 cm) in diameter, but this is exceptional; normal size for a fruiting tree is 12–20 feet (4–6 m) tall and 2–5 inches (5–13 cm) in diameter. The smooth, gray bark does not furrow or peel even on older trees, making it one of the best features by which to spot pawpaw in the undergrowth.

Because of its enormous blue-green leaves, pawpaw stands out in the forest understory.

The branches are sparse and spreading, but the crown remains narrow even on open-grown trees. The twigs are thick, with terminal buds that are flattened and dark brown with a feathery look.

Pawpaw trees are easy to spot on account of their enormous leaves, which may be over a foot (30 cm) long and about one third as broad. When growing in full sun, the leaves tend to be smaller. The leaves are alternate, drooping on proportionately very short petioles, and are concentrated toward the tips of the hefty twigs. The leaf tapers gently from a narrow base and is broader toward the tip; the margins have no teeth or lobes. One distinctive characteristic of pawpaw leaves is their strong, musky, petroleum-like scent—suggesting the presence of toxins making them unpalatable to most insects and mammals. (However, the zebra swallowtail *Protographium marcellus* is a notable exception; it feeds exclusively on pawpaw foliage in the caterpillar stage.) Extracts from pawpaw leaves are currently being studied for use as natural insecticides and cancer drugs.

Pawpaws bloom in mid spring, about when the buds break open. The flowers are about 1.4 inches (3.5 cm) across, with 6 petals in 2 layers. Flowers are green at first and turn to chocolate-purple upon maturity. Pawpaw flowers are attached to the naked twigs by very short stems, often in pairs, or with a few flowers close together. They are often inconspicuous—at least from a distance. Pawpaws are generally considered self-incompatible; that is, they need to be cross-pollinated by a different individual to produce fruit. However, the flowers have both male and female parts. (They mature at different times to reduce self-pollination.)

It is often reported that pawpaw flowers smell like rotting meat, to attract flies for pollination. I have smelled rotting meat. I have smelled pawpaw flowers. And I disagree. Pawpaw flowers just smell like raw meat mixed with the strong musky scent of pawpaw fruit and something yeasty. There's nothing putrid about them. Their scent attracts many insects, including fruit flies. They do not emit the dimethyl oligosulfides that characterize decomposing meat, which are produced by tropical flowers that actually do mimic carrion (Goodrich et al. 2006).

The fruit ripens in early autumn, usually well before the leaves fall, and may be shaped like a mango or slightly curved like a kidney. It ranges from 2–7 inches (5–18 cm) long, and the larger fruits may weigh 10 ounces (280 grams), making this the largest edible fruit on any native North American tree. Pawpaws hang singly or in clusters, and due to their green color are notoriously hard to spot among the leaves and branches. The skin is dull green to green-yellow, often washed with darker areas—and after falling, the entire skin will darken. The flesh is yellowish and pulpy, not very juicy, with numerous slightly curved, somewhat flattened, elongated, dark-brown seeds about an inch (2.5 cm) long.

Pawpaw leaves in early autumn. Note the drooping tendency. These are in a sunny area, thus the leaves are much smaller—just as with American mulberry, it's usual consort.

There are actually 8 species of pawpaw native to North America. The foregoing description and this account in general pertain to *Asimina triloba*, the only pawpaw with large fruit and widespread distribution. There is another species, *Asimina parviflora*, that replaces common pawpaw in Florida and the southern parts of the gulf states, and occurs along with it in much of the southern tier of states. This species, in every way, is like a miniature version of common pawpaw. I have never eaten it, and have yet to speak to anyone who has, but it is widely reported as edible. The other 6 species of pawpaw are all shrubs confined to Florida and the southern parts of Alabama and Georgia.

The name "pawpaw" (sometimes spelled "papaw") is most likely a corruption of "papaya," an unrelated but vaguely similar fruit that was formerly associated with it. The scientific name for the genus, *Asimina*, is derived from the fruit's name in the Algonquin languages, as is the Canadian French *asimine*.

FINDING PAWPAWS

There is a mystique about the pawpaw that is hard to explain. People speak as if it is crafty and elusive. Many old-timers talk as if all the pawpaw trees disappeared long ago, like hoopers, coopers, cobblers, and haystacks. But don't believe them; it's a ruse. They lament the disappearance of this fruit so they won't have to admit how many years have passed since they quit spending free time in the woods. The pawpaws are out there, waiting for you.

Pawpaw *Asimina triloba*. The red area to the south is inhabited exclusively by small pawpaw *A. parviflora* (range overlap between these two is not shown).

Pawpaws are common, even abundant, through most of their range. The eastern United States has seen surprising levels of reforestation in the last century: For example, the percentage of forest cover in Ohio, in the heart of pawpaw range, has increased from 10% in 1900 to 31% today (Ohio DNR 2016). Even with the fierce competition from invasive shrubs, I'd wager that pawpaws are more common today than they were when your great-grandparents were born. And with the die-off of ash trees, they are poised to have a heyday in the next few decades.

Shortly after I learned to recognize pawpaws in West Virginia, I went to a park where my grandparents had often brought me to swim and play as a child. I noticed several pawpaws growing at the edge of the woods along the road, so I followed a small creek into the forest. There, under a canopy of green ash and yellowbud hickory, I found a stand of two dozen enormous pawpaw trees. I brought my grandmother her first Michigan pawpaws in half a century.

Pawpaws like rich, deep, well-drained but moist soil in hardwood forests. They are most common in wooded valleys and streamsides, as well as the higher parts of river floodplains. They may appear in any rich hardwood forest, and also occasionally thrive along roadsides and field edges along such forests. If there is a seed source nearby, pawpaws are good at recolonizing abandoned fields, often mingling in such sites with aggressive native and invasive shrubs. Common associates include sycamore, green ash, American elm, buckeye, pecan, yellowbud and shellbark hickory, boxelder, and spicebush. Pawpaw is highly associated with another native understory tree with enormous, attractive leaves and delicious fruit: the American mulberry *Morus rubra*. These species usually grow together, and you can often find them intermingling at the base of bluffs in hilly country.

An average pawpaw trunk, about 3 inches thick. The bark is smooth and gray, often with lighter gray splotches.

Pawpaw flowers in spring. The two layers of petals are visible. These will open up wider.

In all areas, pawpaws fruit best when they have fertile soil and ample sunlight. One robust tree in a pasture is likely to outproduce a quarter-acre clump of crowded, spindly stems in heavy shade. And the fruit of a sunlit tree will be larger and sweeter. If you have a colony of wild pawpaws on your property, you can manage them with little effort and greatly increase their fruit production. If they are in deep woods, you can thin the canopy above them to get some sunlight down to the pawpaws below. Then thin the pawpaw stems in the colony to allow them to develop thick, healthy crowns. If you have pawpaws at a forest edge or in the open, thin them out and remove competing shrubs.

HARVEST AND PREPARATION

A tree-ripened pawpaw provides the most luscious moment in the autumn woods. Tear it in half to reveal the aromatic, pulpy inside, then suck out the contents with a slurp and spit out the shiny seeds as you go. Not just a summer's sun and rain, but also a legion of September memories are encapsulated in that musky bite of rich fruit. The pawpaw reminds me of a juicy banana with a hint of mango, and something else that makes me crave it. A pawpaw is never better than when savored after some hours in the woods—but do make sure the thing is ripe. A perfect pawpaw is still mostly green, sometimes blushing yellow, and usually mottled somewhat with black—but it is clearly identified by touch: It should yield to the moderate pressure of a finger, like a ripe avocado. When pawpaws are ripe they fall to the ground readily, and at the peak of picking season you will often see a few lying under a good tree. This is a clear sign that many of the remainder are probably ready to be picked. If they are low enough to reach, a gentle twist, or sometimes only a slight touch, will get the ripe ones loose.

The majority of fruits will hang out of reach, and you'll have to shake them down. You want to shake gently so that the unripe fruits remain on the twigs—but assertively enough to get the ripe ones down. I like to give the trunk a good, hard, backward kick; with smaller trees I just hit them sharply with the palm of my hand. If your first several shaken pawpaws are rock-hard, you need to lighten up a bit. Or, you might just wait a week or so until they fall of their own accord. Go check on the morning after a thunderstorm.

Pawpaws can produce fruit instantaneously out of thin air. I have witnessed this many times, and so can you. Go into a pawpaw patch in early autumn when the leaves are still drab green, find a small tree, and peer up into the sparse branches. Do you spy any fruit? Maybe three, if you're lucky. Now turn around and face away from the tree, lift one leg, and kick backward against the trunk as hard as you can without injuring yourself. In retaliation, the tree will drop not three, but five or maybe even eight 6-ounce projectiles toward you, one probably aimed carefully at your noggin. How did it do that, when there were *only three* to begin with? It's supernatural. If you want more proof, turn around and look up; the three pawpaws you originally saw are *still there*, dangling like . . . like, you know, dangling danglers—and taunting you for wanting them.

One of the problems with shaking pawpaws is that the ripest ones smash when they hit hard ground. If you have a partner willing to take the risk, he or she could wait under the loaded branches with an outstretched sweater or cloth-padded basket to try breaking the fall of any dislodged pawpaws. Or, you can separate them into two batches as you pick: the smashed ones that need to be eaten or processed right away, and the intact ones that you can keep for a few days. You may also get a pile of under-ripe ones, which you will not want to eat until they soften.

A dense clump of pawpaws. Trees that receive full sun like this are more likely to have a good crop of fruit.

Once you get your pawpaws collected, get 'em protected. Once, while camping in Ohio, my wife and I picked a nice box of pawpaws. Not wanting to drown in their scent, we put the box just outside the door to our tent when we retired for the night, knowing that no human nor animal could possibly come that close without waking us. By morning the pawpaws had vanished—their only trace being a few seeds.

Ripe pawpaws have semi-soft, sweet, cream-to-yellowish flesh. After sitting on the ground for several days, pawpaws become extremely soft and their skins turn black. Some people prefer them this way, but I don't. I will begrudgingly eat these over-ripe pawpaws only if they are the last ones I have for the season.

But an under-ripe pawpaw is worse. If you eat them when they are hard, they'll taste terrible, and more than a bite or two can make you sick. You can get the slightly under-ripe fruit to soften by just letting them sit for a day or two, and the flavor will come out passably good—although never quite as nice as the tree-ripened fruit. A truly under-ripe pawpaw will also soften, but it will never taste right. Ripe fruit keeps for 7–10 days but progressively deteriorates in quality.

While I love fresh pawpaws, I do not like them dried or cooked in any way. Don't take my word for it—some people do.

If you make pawpaw pie, ice cream, bread, cake, custard, or cookies, you'll need to separate the pulp from the seeds and skins. Do this carefully, making sure the fruit is properly ripe. Be absolutely sure to remove all the skin, and also

A nice ripe pawpaw.

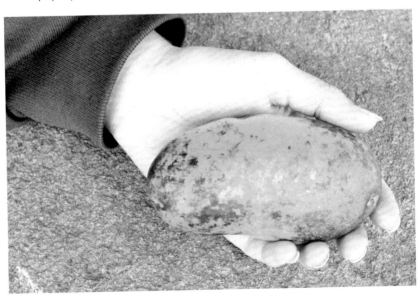

The yellow flesh and large dark seed of a ripe, luscious pawpaw.

the thin layer of off-colored flesh directly beneath it. Then put the remainder through a sieve or colander to get out the seeds. (My friend Mike Krebill uses a french fry basket, which has holes of an ideal size.) If you use under-ripe pawpaws, or don't remove all the skin, the products you make from them will likely be nauseating.

Pawpaw pulp stores well when frozen; this is the only way I recommend keeping it for year-round use. I have never canned pawpaw, nor do I know anyone else who stores it this way. I suspect that it is not acidic enough to safely store by waterbath canning, but I have not tested the pH.

Of all North American fruits, the pawpaw is perhaps the most suitable as sustenance. They were eaten fresh in great quantity during their short season, by Native Americans and early European settlers. Only the advent of modern refrigeration and transportation systems, as well as the drastic general cheapening of food in the last century, has cut into pawpaw's popularity with rural folks. The fresh fruit is about 1% protein, 1% fat, and 19% carbohydrate—meaning that it has nearly the calories of a banana. Three or four nice pawpaws will fill you up and stave off your next meal for hours, if not entirely. On the Lewis and Clark expedition, as the men were nearing St. Louis on their return, they ran low on provisions and subsisted almost entirely on pawpaws for a few days. When the crop is good, one can fill a bushel basket with pawpaws in a pleasant half hour or less.

Pawpaws are particularly high in niacin and mineral nutrients. They have 87% as much potassium as bananas. Amazingly, pawpaws exceed bananas, apples, and oranges in their content of all the other major mineral nutrients: calcium, phosphorus, magnesium, iron, zinc, copper, and manganese. And it's not even close: Pawpaw's content is more than triple in almost every comparison. This wild fruit has 22 times the iron of a banana, 38 times the iron of an apple, and 70 times the iron of an orange. It has about 1½ times the calcium of an orange, and about 10 times the calcium of apples and bananas.[4]

One may wonder why the pawpaw has not become a mainstream fruit of commerce. Beyond the remarkably short shelf life as a fresh fruit, and the fragility of the fruit when ripe, there is the fact that there was no really pleasant way to feast on pawpaws out of season before the invention of freezers. Pawpaws can be made into beverages, preserves, and dried pulp, but these products have never become very popular, and I think we are constrained to admit that this is because they just aren't very good. And pulping is difficult to mechanize because of the intense distaste of the delicate skin.

I am hesitant to misrepresent a fantastic food by pushing the limits of its use to the point where it is likely to be picked too early, stored too long, shipped too far, and poorly processed. That's a recipe for rejection by the consuming public. If pawpaws are to again be common fare, they will have to be grown by diversified small farmers, for whom pawpaws will be just a small part of the yearly income. These growers will have to develop a loyal local following by providing fantastic fruit, gently handled and quickly delivered at the peak of their quality. We can shamelessly promote the widespread gorging on pawpaws during this brief, glorious season.

And we'll be able to eat pawpaws the same way we always have: fresh, as a filling snack on autumn hikes, a dessert to eat on Wednesday evenings, reminiscing on the magnificent woods where we spent the weekend and hope to return the next.

---

4 These values are based on per-weight analysis of edible portions, except that the pawpaw analysis included the skin. The figures are derived from a bulletin of the Kentucky State University Cooperative Extension Program, "Cooking with Pawpaws" by Snake Jones and Desmond Layne (2009). This bulletin relied on analysis from the USDA Nutrient Database for apples, oranges, and bananas, and from Peterson et al. (1982) for pawpaws.

Persimmon

Diospyros virginiana

Visions of sugarplums dance in my head. All year, but especially in autumn. We don't have persimmons where I live, but every fall, when the layers of acorns and oak leaves give off their tea-like scent and shuffle underfoot, when the bare wild grape vines reveal the clusters of plump globes their leaves had been shielding, when my hands smell of sticky butternut hulls, I dream of heading south to the land of persimmons. I have friends who make trips to Colorado for elk hunting, but I take my vacation for a different quarry. It is orange and shaped like a pumpkin—but squishy. It doesn't hide, nor does it run. It doesn't require hundreds of dollars for a nonresident tag. It just dangles there, waiting for my fingers or a possum's mouth. Or it falls with a dull thud and breaks open just enough for the ants to get at its sweet pulp—but not so far that its contents are lost to me. And best of all, there are more than I could ever collect.

Persimmons in late fall.

DESCRIPTION

The persimmon is unmistakable. It is large, as far as wild fruits go—ranging from .75–2 inches in diameter (2–5 cm). The persimmon is roughly spherical, normally a little wider than long and flattened or slightly depressed on the stem end. Sometimes, however, the fruit is longer than wide, with a slightly pointed tip. Persimmons have a large, tough, 4-lobed calyx that is warped and leathery by the time the fruit ripens. The skin is thin and smooth with a bloom, often becoming wrinkly when ripe. At first the fruit is hard and green, but it ripens to a dull orange, occasionally with a dark-bluish cast. Persimmons contain up

A typical fence-line clump of persimmon trees, about 20 feet tall with a moderate crop of fruit.

to 6 elongated, flattened, reddish-brown seeds about 0.6 inch (1.5 cm) long; a few trees produce seedless fruit. The persimmon is virtually stemless, borne on a straight twig that has numerous, closely spaced alternate buds, giving it a zigzag or bumpy appearance. These twigs are clustered near the branch tips in an odd, asymmetrical pattern, often with several growing on one side. Fruiting twigs detach readily from the branches, and several (often with slightly underripe persimmons still attached) can usually be seen on the ground beneath the tree.

Even when not in fruit, the persimmon tree is quite distinct. It is small to medium-sized, typically 6–10 inches (15–25 cm) in diameter and 20–55 feet (6–17 m) tall, although there are some larger trees up to 2 feet (60 cm) thick and 60–100 feet (20–30 m) tall. Persimmons can reach maturity while still nearly shrub-like, sometimes fruiting at 6–8 feet (1.8–2.5 m) tall. The bark is nearly black and composed of thick, raised blocks. The tree is lanky, with a narrow crown and dominant trunk even in wide open spaces. The trunk is irregularly crooked, like that of sassafras. Taller persimmons, especially where they are growing with some competition from other trees, are typically branchless in the lower half.

The leaves are simple, 2–6 inches (5–15 cm) long, borne alternately on petioles about a quarter of the length of the blade. They are about as plain and featureless as a leaf can be: ovate to elliptic in form, with a pointed tip and no teeth, hairless and smooth except for faint pubescence sometimes found on the underside. They are somewhat thick and leathery. In late summer, persimmon trees sometimes suffer severe defoliation from a webworm—this rarely kills them, but it makes the fruit quality poor.

A large persimmon tree in a park, showing dark, blocky bark.

Persimmon trees are usually either male or female, blooming in late spring after the leaves are out. The female flowers grow singly on an extremely short pedicel at the base of a leaf. They are bell-like, with 4 whitish lobes, behind which are 4 spreading green lobes that will persist into fruiting. Male flowers are tubular and grow in small clusters. Both genders have fragrant blossoms.

There is another species of persimmon native to North America, the Texas or black persimmon *Diospyros texana*. This small, scrubby tree is found in central and Trans-Pecos Texas. The leaves are tiny, leathery, oblanceolate with a rounded tip, and hairy beneath. They are often clustered near the twig tips. I had really hoped that I could find this tree and eat the fruit before writing this book, but it didn't work out that way. My friend and foraging expert Mark "Merriwether" Vordebruggen tells me that they are equally delicious, perhaps even better. They ripen a bit earlier than common persimmons and are more forgiving in terms of the astringency if picked a tad under-ripe.

HABITAT

Although persimmons are potentially long-lived, they are pioneer trees that thrive upon disturbance. Few trees are more sun-loving, or more intolerant of shade. In a wilderness setting they are infrequent, mostly confined to the higher parts of floodplains and also ridge tops and steep slopes, where natural disturbances and sunny pockets occur with some regularity. However, scattered persimmon trees may occur in almost any well-drained forest that has been disturbed

American persimmon = light blue. Black persimmon = red. Area of overlap = dark blue.

by logging, fire, or windstorms. Persimmons have benefitted greatly from human activity, thriving where the land has been cleared and then abandoned. When the crop is good, numerous loaded trees can be spotted along backroads, highways, railroads, fencerows, and forest edges, as well as standing alone in old fields and pastures. Young woods, brushy areas, parks, and clearings are also likely places to find them.

DETERMINING RIPENESS

Do not be fooled by an almost-ripe persimmon.

As easy as persimmons are to identify, their ripeness is notoriously confusing to determine, and this is perhaps the biggest reason that wild persimmons are not more popular. An almost-ripe persimmon looks nicer than one that is actually ready to be eaten, and almost-ripe persimmons have the habit of

Persimmons on the tree in early autumn, in varying stages of ripeness. The one in the center is perfect, but the rest are underripe.

tasting pleasant for 7 seconds before commencing to pucker the whole inside of the mouth with an astringency so overwhelming, so unexpected, and so unlike that caused by any familiar food that some people will never get to a second persimmon. Other people, beguiled by the look of the under-ripe fruit, keep eating them that way; many have lived their entire lives in persimmon country without realizing that this puckering astringency is not the *real* flavor of a persimmon.

Persimmons turn orange when ripe, but orange does not mean ripe. They soften when ripe; but soft does not guarantee ripeness. The leaves often drop before the fruit ripens, but the fact that a tree is bare does not make its persimmons ripe. The best place to find a ripe persimmon is on the ground, but every persimmon on the ground is not ripe, either.

Ripe persimmons can be identified thus: They are orange, sometimes with a bluish-black cast, and very soft. The skin is thin and often wrinkly, breaking at all but the gentlest touch. The fruit has no firm parts inside. Persimmons often fall along with the twig they grew on, as if the twig were a disposable appendage to the fruit. Ripe persimmons detach from the branch easily; those that fall to the ground with a twig attached are not ripe—although they may ripen after falling, in which case they will readily detach from that twig. With a ripe persimmon, the calyx will easily detach from the base—if it is hard to pull off, or comes off with an attached chunk of the fruit's core, it is unripe. By the time the persimmon is at its best, it is so soft that it is hard to handle without smushing, seeming eager to get your fingers sticky. Placed in a bag and carried a few miles home, a gallon of good persimmons will form one solid mass of custard-like fruit; its pulp has the consistency of a quick-bread batter mixed with the yucky guts around the seeds of a pumpkin. If a fully ripe persimmon falls to the ground, it is likely to smash upon impact like an over-ripe wind-fallen apple that's been stepped on. Prime persimmons are a few days shy of fermenting or spoiling, and many that are too far gone often litter the ground beside them, to be left for opossums and deer.

Some nice persimmons I picked up off the ground. Even the one with the attached twig was good.

I hope you are beginning to understand. The only ripe is over-ripe. Thomas Hariot, in 1588, called this peculiar fruit from the "New Founde Land of Virginia" "luscious sweet," but warned that "it is only good when rotten." If you can't come to terms with this, persimmons will not be food. Once you get it, they become a delicacy. When in doubt, eat one. Some berry pickers pride themselves on not eating while they pick; shelve this sentiment when it comes to persimmons. Eating your fill will help you identify the best and worst, the ripe and the unripe.

Folklore says that persimmons need frost to ripen, but this is untrue. Ripe ones may be found months before any frost, especially in the South, and many unripe ones can be found even after dozens of hard frosts, especially in the North. It just so happens that persimmons ripen in the autumn, which is when the first frosts occur—the relationship is no stronger than that.

In fact, the ripening period of the persimmon is the longest of any tree fruit we have; the earliest of them fall in late August, while the latest will not come down until January. The ripening period is not this long on any one tree; some tend to be early or late bearers. The peak of ripening is generally from mid September to early November. The fruit drops gradually from any given tree over 2–10 weeks, a small percentage of the crop coming ripe each day. Thus, if you want them to taste good, you can never just go pick a persimmon tree clean—*you must judge ripeness fruit by fruit.*

Persimmon ripening has another idiosyncrasy: Before the leaves fall, soft persimmons readily lose their astringency. In September, a persimmon that looks and feels soft, even on the tree, will probably taste good. However, persimmons that hang into late fall or winter, long after the leaves drop, are very slow to lose their astringency. This happens most often on overloaded trees. It seems that once the trees go dormant, they quit or slow all of their physiological processes, including the ripening of fruit. Such late season persimmons may soften and wrinkle without developing good flavor.

HARVEST AND PREPARATION

You can pick persimmons from the tree or from the ground. Under a loaded, ripening tree will be an assortment of persimmons ranging from under-ripe to fermenting or rotten, with some portion of them perfect. You may want to have two picking containers: one for dead-ripe fruit ready to be eaten, and one for the nearly ripe ones that need to sit for a few days. The fruit will often fall from the tree just before softening and then ripen fully on the ground. Luckily, persimmons suffer rather little from insect infestation.

You can pick them by hand, or get them down by shaking, striking the trunk with a heavy stick, using a throwing stick, or by climbing. Shake gently

This persimmon tree has been completely defoliated by fall webworm *Hyphantria cunea*. This is a common sight—webworm's favorite victims are persimmon and pecan. When this happens to a persimmon with a good fruit crop, the stressed tree cannot manufacture enough sugar to sweeten or ripen the fruit. They will often stick on the tree long into the winter. Most of them will remain astringent, even after falling.

to dislodge only those that are closest to falling on their own. Don't try to get every last persimmon down; even many that fall will not be ripe. Sort carefully, leaving the firm ones behind. To make collecting easier, you can spread a sheet of cloth or plastic under the tree as you shake it; this is almost a necessity if the ground has loose dirt or sand, which could ruin the fruit. A sheet will also help soften the blow of falling persimmons so the dead-ripe ones do not split open.

The almost-ripe persimmons should be spread shallowly in a box or pan to ripen over several days. They can keep for a week or more at room temperature if undamaged, and several weeks in the refrigerator. Fully ripe ones should be processed within a few days (sooner if they are smashed or broken) before they begin to ferment or spoil. They'll keep for longer in the refrigerator.

After you've stuffed yourself on fresh persimmons, you'll want to separate the pulp from all the nice, gooey ones so that it can be used or stored for later. First, I remove the tough calyx from each persimmon, then drop the fruit into a colander. (I have a special one with extra-large holes, just for persimmons). I mash and move the persimmon pulp by hand, scraping it along the sides to force pulp through the holes. The seeds are too large to allow the use of a Victorio-type strainer, and a Foley mill barely works; a colander or a steamer pan works well and is easier to clean anyway.

Since persimmons are often available by the bushel, it is nice to put up a supply. Canned persimmon hardens into a block of dark-reddish-brown stuff that

When the crop is good, persimmons are easy to get in quantity. Millions of tons rot into the soil every autumn. However, as always, these were carefully selected fruit-by-fruit to ensure that they were ripe.

Sam's Persimmon-Hickory Nut Bread

. . . .

Dry Ingredients:

3 ¼ cups all purpose flour

1 ½ cups hickory nut meats

1 ½ tsp. baking soda

1 ½ tsp. baking powder

¾ tsp. salt

½ Tbsp. cinnamon

½ Tbsp. powdered ginger

Wet Ingredients:

3 med. eggs

1 ½ cups maple syrup

1 ¾ cups persimmon pulp

½ Tbsp. vanilla extract

¾ cup coconut oil

Mix dry ingredients and set aside. Mix maple syrup and eggs, then add coconut oil, breaking it into small pieces with a pastry cutter or fork. Now mix in the other wet ingredients. Add dry ingredients and mix just until all flour is moistened. Spread into an oiled casserole dish and bake at 375°F for about 50 minutes.

is quite unlike the fresh pulp in flavor and texture; most people aren't impressed by it. Frozen pulp, however, thaws out to a soft, gooey mass of sweetness identical to the freshly-strained product—this is how I like to store mine. Persimmon pulp also dries into a sweet but very tough fruit leather.

Persimmon pulp, when cooked, tastes somewhere between cooked pumpkin and dates, but with a rich fruity quality not found in either. It is much sweeter than Asian persimmon, and contains less water. Euell Gibbons raved about his persimmon-hickory nut bread in *Stalking the Wild Asparagus*, so I followed the recipe exactly. Everyone in my house loved it. Then I followed the persimmon-nut bread recipe from *Billy Joe Tatum's Wild Foods Field Guide and Cookbook*, and we liked it even better. I hybridized these and came up with my own recipe, perfected after dozens of attempts, and my children beg for it. We make it for holidays and leisure Sundays all winter long.

Persimmon pie, made after the fashion of pumpkin pie, is another delicious treat. I've also enjoyed persimmon pudding, persimmon cake, and persimmon ice cream. This is not a fruit for making jam, however—it is sweet and spreadable straight off the tree.

Persimmons are occasionally used to brew beer or wine. I have not done either, but my friend John Holzwart gave me a bottle of superb persimmon wine that he had made. It was almost colorless, but full of flavor. Another traditional use of persimmons is to make "molasses" by boiling, straining, and then cooking down the resulting sweet liquid.

Above Young persimmon leaves in late spring. This is the best time to get them for tea.
Below Black persimmon *Diospyros texana* has very small leaves and plump fruit. (Photo by John Slattery)

NUTRITION

Wild American persimmons are highly nutritious. Although the analysis provided by the USDA (NNDSR 2015, s.v. "Persimmons, native, raw") is somewhat incomplete, it shows that raw persimmons are a fantastic source of vitamin C (more than oranges), iron, potassium, and phosphorus. Moreover, the comparison of our wild persimmon to its closest domesticated relative, the Japanese persimmon (*Diospyros kaki*), shows in striking fashion how much more nutrient-dense wild foods tend to be. Compared to Japanese persimmons, wild persimmons contain almost twice the calories, and substantially more of every single micronutrient for which there is data, including 9 times the vitamin C, more than 4 times the calcium, and more than 16 times the iron.

OTHER PERSIMMON PRODUCTS

Although the fruit is by far the most important product of the persimmon tree, the tea made from its leaves is also worth mentioning. Persimmon leaf tea is popular enough in Asia that it is harvested and sold commercially. It can easily be found in Asian markets in North America, or online. People drink it for pleasure and as a health tonic. I think the tea is fairly good; I like it better when made from young spring leaves than old summer leaves.

Persimmon seeds can be roasted to black (they are dark brown to begin with), ground up, and used to make a coffee-like beverage. Persimmon coffee is nothing special, but the seeds do turn water brown, if that's what you need. They do something else as well: break things.

You see, a roasted persimmon seed is *very* hard. An acquaintance at the North Carolina Wild Foods Weekend once brought me a few and asked me

how I thought he should crack them. "These darn things are hard as a rock!" he said. I did the instinctive thing, and stuck it in my mouth to check. "No, you can't bite them, we already tried that," he warned. Too late. I had already split one of my premolars in half. But I didn't want him to feel guilty, so I pretended nothing had happened

Persimmon seeds are brown, flattened, large, and tough.

and handed the seed back to him. "Break a tooth?" he asked. "Yeah," I laughed nonchalantly, trying to retain my honesty, but with a dishonest voice that suggested I was joking. (I'm not joking. I had oral surgery when I got home.)

Five years later, my daughter wanted to try making persimmon coffee. We roasted a batch of seeds and put them in our electric coffee grinder—the grinder that had been passed to my wife from her grandmother, then served her, and later us, for two decades, breaking up real coffee, roasted dandelion roots, chicory, coffeenuts, and cleavers. After one minute of persimmon seeds, the plastic housing was cracked in thirty places, and the steel blade had broken off. I shudder to think of what these things could do in the hands of the military.

Just look at the scientific name of the American persimmon: *Diospyros virginiana*. This translates roughly as "fruit of the gods, from Virginia." You see, we have some pretty good stuff out in these American woodlands.

Not only is this the largest persimmon tree I've ever seen (it's 124 feet tall), but it drops the most delicious persimmons I've ever tasted. Visit it at Big Oak Tree State Park in Missouri.

Poke

Phytolacca americana

Time marches on. That's what Tracy Lawrence said, in a country song that pulled on the *chordae tendinae* of my heart valves one spring morning, and I waxed nostalgic over all the things that had come and passed in my short life. I had no children (yet) and a few days free, so just like that I decided to make the 600-mile trip to visit my grandmother, and was at her doorstep just after dusk.

The following morning I was up early, prowling the dewy grass around the barn before anyone had started breakfast, snapping off pokeweed stems and pulling out a few sassafras roots. I was sitting on the deck with my treasures as the sun came over the trees, pulling off my dew-soaked shoes, when Grandma came out of the house and glanced in my direction on the way to the garage. "Pokeweed and sassafras!" she shouted my way, in playful mockery. On the way back she added, "I bet you didn't think your old grandma knew any of that stuff, now did you?"

She had read me right; I had no idea. She recognized those things instantly, from 40 feet away, with a confidence that revealed details of her past that I had never thought to ask about. But she didn't just represent *her* past; it was also our past, as Americans, revealed in her offhand comment. There was a time, still palpably close, when every country girl from southern Michigan down to Alabama knew pokeweed and sassafras at a glance. Time has marched on.

DESCRIPTION

Pokeweed is a large, long-lived perennial herb growing from a thick, fleshy tap-root. Seedlings have a single stem, but older plants usually have several stems clustered at the root crown. I have seen some plants several decades old with 40 or more stems, each of them an inch (2.5 cm) or so in diameter. Pokeweed is typically 5–7 feet (1.5–2.2 m) tall at maturity, although plants may flower when

Opposite These poke shoots are perfect for harvest. Note the ruffled leaves—a characteristic that disappears when the leaves reach maturity. Also, notice the two thin lines that run down the stem below each leaf—these tiny ridges help distinguish the plant. Poke shoots are sometimes found that are purely green, especially in shade, and especially when taller than this—but very young shoots usually have reddish-purple highlights, especially in full sun. This does not mean they are too old to eat.

Above left Poke leaf, not young or tender. It is not upright, and not at the branch tip. Don't eat it.
Above right A mature, single-stemmed poke plant, blooming and fruiting.

less than 2 feet (60 cm) tall, and I have seen several standing more than 10 feet (3 m) high. The outer stems in a poke clump lean when mature. Pokeweed stems are smooth and hairless, tapering, and up to 2 inches (5 cm) thick at the base. They are purplish-red at maturity, but in the shoot stage they are green, often with a reddish tint. The stem is not branched at the base, but usually branches broadly in the top half. Leaves are alternate, on short, broadly channeled petioles only 5–10% of their length. The blades are entire, hairless, 3–10 inches (8–25 cm) long, and broadly elliptic to lanceolate; the tips are rather blunt.

Pokeweed flowers from late summer into fall. The inflorescence is a raceme 4–16 inches (10–40 cm) long, borne at the tips of branches; these may be drooping or erect. (Some botanists have separated our pokeweed into two species: one with short, erect racemes; the other with longer, drooping racemes. Most botanists today consider this separation unwarranted.) Each raceme contains numerous small, white, 5-part flowers on short pedicels. These ripen into dark purple, juicy berries about 0.2 inch (5 mm) across, each containing several tiny, dark seeds. The berries are flattened somewhat, wider than long, and are composed of numerous sections (mericarps) fused together, like a mallow fruit—but upon ripening and turning juicy, these sections are scarcely evident.

Poke is remarkably easy to identify at maturity, but the time you eat it is in the shoot stage, when the leaves are not fully developed and the telltale clusters of fruits and flowers are absent. You can, and should, find patches when the plants are mature, and return to those spots the following spring. Or, look for dead stalks from last year; if you break one open, you'll see that the old pith separates into a stack of coin-like segments. But you also need to recognize the new shoots by themselves. They are thick at the base, normally clumped, and strongly tapered. The outside is smooth and hairless; they are solid inside with light-green flesh. A telltale characteristic is the two minute ridges, one starting on each side of the petiole, that run down the stalk from each leaf and spread gently outward.

Once you learn pokeweed, you'll start to see it all over the place. The magnificent purple stems of autumn plants will catch your eye from a distance, shining like a forager's beacon. Some snow-crunching dusk in January, nuzzling your face into your coat collar, you'll spot the tawny, dry stalks as you round a corner, broken over by the weight of slush but still identifiable to your knowing eyes, reminding you that your hemisphere of the wobbling planet will soon lean again toward the sun. Once you know pokeweed, you'll have it by your side forever, and it will no longer be poke*weed*. It will be *poke*, a legendary American vegetable.

Dead stems from last year's poke—the way to find this year's sprouts in late spring.

HABITAT

Poke's natural habitat is largely river floodplains, but it is opportunistic and will inhabit almost any disturbed site. It is commonly seen in backyards, vacant lots, parks, barnyards, old fields, brushy areas, young or open woods, clearcuts, and along roadsides, trails, fencelines, and forest edges. Pokeweed likes full sun but will thrive also in moderate shade. It grows in most soil types

Poke *Phytolacca americana*. The range west of Texas is non-native.

as long as the site is well drained, but seems especially fond of sandy ground under pines. Poke has been introduced in the West; and in some urban and agricultural regions of California and Oregon it has become a common weed.

POKE IN HISTORY AND TRADITION

Poke goes by a lot of common names. The name "poke," like "puccoon," comes from an Algonquin word for a dye plant. The scientific name *Phytolacca* means "red dye plant," referring to a traditional use of the berries. Pokeberry juice was once used for ink (hence the name "inkberry,") as well as for food coloring—especially to deepen the color of red wines, for which purpose the plant was formerly cultivated in France. It is sometimes called "pigeonberry," as the fruit was once an important food for passenger pigeons. The origin of the name "scoke" is a mystery to me, as is "garget." In the South, you will often hear it called "poke salad." This is variously spelled poke or polk; salad, sallad, salat, sallat, salet, or sallet. Please note that *this name does not mean that the greens are eaten raw*—despite the fact that some irresponsible sources claim this. The definition of "salad" has changed over the centuries (see page 29); the name "poke salad" retains the older sense of the term. Poke greens are only eaten after cooking. (More details on that are coming up.)

Many people imagine wild vegetables as small, hidden, labor-intensive, and strong-tasting. Poke is the opposite of all of these: ready-made to be a garden vegetable, but so lavishly abundant that it never had to be cultivated. Native Americans relished the vegetable, which thrived in the clearings around their villages, gardens, and crop fields. They taught the early white and black settlers to eat it, who quickly adopted the use of the plant, which volunteered in great quantities wherever they cleared the forests. Poke was long ago brought back to the Old World, where its virtues were quickly recognized, and today it is cultivated in southern Europe and North Africa. A similar Asian species of poke, *Phytolacca acinosa*, has been eaten by the peasants of India, Pakistan, and China for thousands of years, and is widely cultivated.

In fact, hand-harvested wild poke greens have been abundant enough to provide a few factories with a sufficient supply for commercial canning. The last of these was the Allen Canning Company of Siloam Springs, Arkansas, which canned pokeweed until 2000. I spoke with employees to get some inside information on the process. The greens were provided by several dozen collectors—mostly the same people year after year—who brought them to a network of buying stations in Arkansas and Missouri. The season was 2–3 weeks in mid to late May. The plant canned "only" about 25–30 tons—not enough to fill all the machinery, so other greens were run simultaneously. Only the tender leafy tips were used, down to a "dime-sized stem." The greens were washed, blanched for 5–7 minutes, and then drained before being packed into cans with brine and pressure-cooked. You can view the can labels online. One version says, "*The Allens* Cut Leaf Poke Salet Greens," and below that, "No Preservatives" and "Organically Grown." Although management reported that the plant halted production due to insufficient collectors, my informants attributed it to "typical third-generation management that didn't want to deal with a small-run product."

In autumn, the stems of poke turn brilliant purple, and the racemes of dark fruit are conspicuous.

A perfect clump of poke shoots, but less red than the smaller shoots at the chapter's beginning.

When talking of wild foods and American tradition, we are often forced to use the past tense. Not so with poke. In *Stalking the Wild Asparagus* (1962), Euell Gibbons wrote that poke "is probably the best known and most widely used wild vegetable in America." This is still true today. It's not just hippie foragers who know and eat pokeweed—it's also regular rednecks and farmers, who outnumber the former by a wide margin. Gainesboro, Tennessee still has a Poke Sallet Festival, complete with cooking and eating contests. Every rural Southerner has heard of "poke sallet." Elvis Presley had a 1970 hit song called "Polk Salad Annie" (originally recorded in 1968 by Tony Joe White). I doubt that "Cow Parsnip Annie" would have gone over as well. Supporters of President James Polk, in his 1844 election campaign, wore poke sprigs as a symbol of their candidate. No other wild vegetable is equally entwined in American history and culture.

Unfortunately, poke has come to be associated with poverty and is scorned by some who grew up eating it. Its consumption has been declining for decades due to rising wages, cheap food, and the decreasing frequency of home-cooked meals. But this glorious weed still takes the crown as America's most popular wild vegetable—and for good reason.

HARVEST AND PREPARATION

Pokeweed must be prepared properly, or it is dangerous. Read this section carefully, and follow the instructions. The only parts of poke to be eaten are the young shoots and tender stem tips, along with their immature, meristematic leaves. These must be boiled in an ample pot of water and then drained. Eating poke raw can cause serious poisoning.

These edible parts of poke are generally boiled for about 10 minutes before draining. Many people parboil for a few minutes in a second change of water—which I advise for all new poke eaters. After this traditional treatment (which is likewise used for Asian pokeweed), the greens and shoots are safe to prepare as you would other cooked vegetables. And they are superb. Although this vegetable is often called "poke salad," it should never be eaten raw.

Poke shoots are not frost hardy, thus they emerge in mid to late spring. Collect shoots that are *still tender*, bending and snapping off easily. Many write that safe shoots must have skin that is purely green, but in fact, very young shoots of perfect quality, when growing in full sun, typically have a reddish hue. If the shoots are reddish, I either peel the skin, or I make sure to boil them in two waters. As with all shoot vegetables, size is only one factor indicating whether a stem is tender—form and feel are more important. Robust poke plants often have eventual stem heights of 7 to 10 feet; these might have shoots with *tips* that remains meristematic and tender at the height of your waist or belly. This doesn't mean you collect *the whole* waist-high shoot—in all cases, *you only use the tender, newly forming, meristematic part.* Conversely, a small poke stem from a seedling plant might actually start to toughen considerably by the time it reaches a foot in height. What is important with poke is to collect the part that is a vigorously growing, tender meristem.

The earliest poke shoots will be thick and strongly tapered, with a small tuft of forming leaves on top. Cut or break these youngest shoots near the base, and use the whole thing, including the leaves. *Always parboil and drain as described above.* Poke shoots are sometimes compared to asparagus because that is the only shoot vegetable that most Americans are familiar with, but the flavor is distinct and milder than asparagus, and the texture is softer and less fibrous.

A little later in spring, the shoots will be larger and the tops more leafy, but both parts will still be meristematic. The leaves will still be clustered near the top, and will be held erect rather than spreading at a right angle to the stem, as happens with mature poke leaves. This is the time to use the young leaves as a cooked green. You can cook young poke greens by themselves, but usually the tender stem tip is also included. After parboiling and draining, they are great as the only green in a fry pan, but also combine well with pungent greens, such as any of the various mustards (which can be added raw to the

This is what I do with a big, tender poke shoot. I break off the top, with its thinner stem and clustered leaves, and boil this as "poke sallet." I always parboil and drain the leaves. I remove the leaves from the lower portion and discard them, then peel the stem, *keeping only the part that is tender.* (The entire peeled stem shown was tender.) These tender peeled stems I cook in a variety of ways. Never eat them raw.

parboiled poke). Parboiled poke greens can also be steamed, boiled, or used in quiches or casseroles.

Larger poke shoots often have an enormous section of tender stem. There may be 20 inches (50 cm) of tender shoot, more than an inch (2.5 cm) thick at the break-easy point, with a tuft of leaves at the end. (Note, I said **may be**. You don't automatically get to collect some prescribed length of shoot. You always collect *the tender part*, and no more. You don't necessarily cut or break it at the base; you break it *at the point where it is tender*.) With very robust *but still tender* shoots, I often separate the leafy tops from the stems, because they are two very different vegetables. Then I can prepare the greens one way, and the stems another.

When preparing these larger *but still tender* stems, I peel the skin, which is thin and comes off easily. I grab it at the bottom and peel toward the top. Thick, peeled stems can be cut into short chunks or medallions, parboiled, and then served as a vegetable in any number of ways. They are so tender and mild that it is important not to cook or season them into oblivion. Many people fry these peeled shoots without parboiling first, but I still recommend a brief parboiling. The peeling presumably removes an important component of the toxin along with the skin. But cooking also appears to be an important aspect of detoxification, so **never eat them raw.**

There is a delicious, traditional poke recipe that is so simple and superb it bears repeating here. If you follow it, you will probably be hooked on poke sallet for the rest of your life.

Some people ask, if the plant needs to be detoxified, why they should eat it at all? First off, try that recipe. It's a delicious vegetable. It is abundant and easy to collect. And it is highly nutritious. The USDA (NNDSR 2015) does not analyze many wild vegetables, but it has long listed poke shoots in its database, because they are so commonly eaten. The USDA analysis shows that poke shoots, after being boiled and drained, still contain the following nutrients per 100 grams of edible portion: 53 mg calcium, 1.2 mg iron, 14 mg magnesium, 33 mg phosphorus, 184 mg potassium, 82 mg vitamin C, and 8,700 IU of vitamin A. Even with parboiling, this is still quite a nutritious vegetable—the vitamin C content is well above that of oranges, and the vitamin A content is outstanding.

> ### Traditional Poke Sallet with Bacon and Eggs
> · · · · · · · · · · · · · · · · · ·
>
> This meal serves 4. Take a nice bundle (about a pound) of poke shoots and leaves, submerge in 3 quarts of water, cover, and turn on the heat. While this comes to a boil, cut up 12 ounces of bacon and fry it in a wok with one large, diced onion, stirring occasionally. Let the poke boil for 8 minutes, drain, add a quart of water, boil for two more minutes, and drain again. Chop your cooked poke into 2–3 inch sections, then throw it into the wok, where the bacon and onions should be browned nicely. Stir-fry 4–6 minutes until most free moisture is driven off, then crack and stir in 2 eggs. I season mine with cumin and black pepper. When the eggs are done, it's ready to serve: poverty food to make rich people envious.

THE TOXINS IN POKE

Poke contains toxic chemicals. Little is known about these toxins, but there are some triterpene saponins and alkaloids reported, and the toxins have been called "phytolaccatoxin" and "phytolaccin," names which may or may not refer to specific chemicals. The toxins are widely reported to be concentrated in the roots, the mature leaves, and the skin of mature stems, and to be associated with the reddish-purple coloration developed at maturity, although I cannot find any analyses upon which these claims are based. Poke root also contains mitogens (chemicals that promote cell division), which have been studied for therapeutic purposes but also may have toxicological concerns. I have found no evidence that these mitogens are present in the young leaves or shoots. Considering the widespread use of poke as food, it is shocking that I have found no research on the toxins its edible parts contain, their distribution and phenology in the plant, their solubility in water, their response to heat, or their action in the body. However, long-standing tradition practiced by millions of people on three continents makes it clear that the toxins are easily removed or destroyed by proper cooking.

If poke is prepared improperly, a burning sensation in the mouth and throat is the first warning. This means that your parboiling was inadequate or your poke is too old. Turner and Szczawinski (1991) report that other symptoms usually begin 1–2 hours after ingestion and commonly include abdominal cramps, vomiting, and diarrhea. Most severe poke poisonings occur from ingesting the root (which was widely used for medicinal purposes in the past), but there are a small number of documented poisonings attributed to the berries and the improperly prepared greens. In one interesting case, while a woman experienced in poke eating prepared some greens in the traditional fashion, her daughter and son-in-law decided to eat some raw leaves. Mama was fine, but the two who ate raw poke ended up in the hospital with vomiting, cramps, diarrhea, and, for one of them, cardiac troubles (Hamilton et al. 1995). In another case, a man became ill from drinking the water in which mature poke leaves had been boiled (Jaeckle and Freemon 1981).

At a day camp in New Jersey in 1980, 21 out of 46 people who ate what was reported as a pokeweed "salad" were sickened (CDC 1981). In 1980 in New Jersey "salad" was generally understood to mean raw greens. Although the write-up states that these greens were cooked properly, I doubt that. According to plant poisoning experts Frohne and Pfänder (2005), poisoning victims often lie about the details, due to embarrassment. Some greens may have been cooked properly—but the obvious and probable explanation for what happened here is that 21 out of 46 people disregarded instructions not to eat the leaves raw. The poisoning occurred on July 11—well past the normal collecting season—so the leaves being too old may have also been a factor.

If you are the kind of person who likes to push the limits, to play devil's advocate and prove the teacher wrong, save it for another plant. Don't play that game with poke.

POKEBERRIES

There has long been debate over the edibility of pokeberries. Most sources list them as toxic. There are reports of people vomiting or feeling ill after eating them. There are even a few claims in the literature of children being fatally poisoned by them, but I have been unable to substantiate this. In one documented case, a Scout group made pancakes with pokeberries in the batter, and the worst symptom was mild diarrhea (Edwards and Rogers 1982). Some sources claim that the toxin has little effect on adults or older children, but is extremely toxic to infants and toddlers (Frohne and Pfander 2005). This claim, too, I have been

A raceme of poke berries starting to ripen. These are generally not considered edible (see text).

NOT EDIBLE

unable to trace to any meaningful source. It is often stated that the berries are toxic raw but not cooked.

There are people alive today who make and consume pie, jelly, or juice from pokeberries. I personally know some of these people. They emphasize to me that the seeds are the toxic part, and should be removed and not broken in the processing. I know of no studies of this. They also emphasize cooking the berries. However, I am scarcely interested in the edibility of pokeberries, because they taste terrible. I advise against eating them.

POKEWEED PARANOIA

Not so long ago, when eating poke was normal for rural Americans within its range, almost everyone had heard of this vegetable. In those days nobody claimed that eating the plant was rash or exceedingly dangerous. John Kingsbury, a poisonous plant expert whose exaggerated and often unsubstantiated claims of toxicity have been a perennial frustration to foragers, does not even mention toxicity or potential poisonings from poke greens or shoots in his 1964 book *Poisonous Plants of the United States and Canada*. But less than 30 years later, Turner and Szczawinski (1991) tell us, "Even young shoots, considered edible by some, *should not be* used. . . . Because of the potential dangers involved, people should avoid using Pokeweed altogether." At the time this was written, there were still two factories canning pokeweed for sale in American grocery stores.

Humans across all cultures accept toxins in familiar foods, but fear them in unfamiliar foods. It is not just the anti-foraging nobots who are programmed this way: Foragers also apply this double standard to the particular wild foods they have not eaten. This prejudice is unrealistic. There is no dichotomy between toxic and edible. All vegetables, wild or domestic, contain toxins, and every day, you ingest many different chemicals that your body must process and remove. Potatoes contain solanine and many allied toxic alkaloids, and have caused fatal poisonings. Most spices contain strong toxins with enjoyable flavors. Potato chips and french fries develop acrylamide, a carcinogen. Bamboo shoots contain taxiphillin; cassava contains linamarin—both of which break down into hydrogen cyanide, which can be deadly (FSANZ 2004). By the way, a thin film of highly toxic sanitizing chemicals is *mandated by law* to coat the surface of every dish and eating utensil in every manufacturing facility and dining establishment that prepares your food. Toxins are intentionally mixed with municipal drinking water. And country music's primary purpose appears to be glorifying a toxin that most people intentionally consume for pleasure.

To remove all of these toxins, you have an amazing, complicated organ holding about 13% of your blood at any moment: the liver. Ever pick one up? It's the largest internal organ we have because toxins are a fact of life for heterotrophic organisms. Hu (2005, 41) says, "A large number of the 1,156 species of Chinese food plants enumerated here . . . are poisonous by nature." Food contains toxins. Simply identifying a toxic compound in a food does not mean that the food should not be eaten. Otherwise, we would not eat food.

How, then, do we decide if it is safe to consume something? If we want science to weigh in on this complex question, it must address: (1) What toxic chemicals does the plant contain? (2) How do these toxins behave physiologically in the human organism? (3) At what concentration are these toxins present in the parts eaten? (4) What level of consumption of these toxins is safe, and at what intervals? (5) How much of the part in question is likely to be consumed? (6) How do traditional preparation methods affect these chemicals? Without this information, a reasonable scientific assessment of safety cannot be made.

This has probably never been done for any food, wild or domestic. It would require a prohibitive investment of money and time. That's why the FDA doesn't expect or require any such thing. Instead, it recognizes a food as safe if it "has been widely consumed for its nutrient properties in the United States prior to January 1, 1958, without known detrimental effect" (CFR Title 21, sec. 170.30, part d). This is the FDA's fancy way of saying that, in practice, safety is assessed *based on traditional knowledge.* Not science. And that's a good thing, because traditional knowledge is more reliable.

Remember a few decades ago, when "science" informed us that vegetable oil, solidified into trans fats through controlled rotting, then chemically descented, salted, and infused with artificial flavors, was somehow way better for us than the clumps of fat from agitated milk? Chemists couldn't identify a toxin in those trans fats. But human physiology is complex and sometimes counterintuitive. A closer look suggested that trans fats were killing us. And butter? Really not so bad. This is what we get for smugly overvaluing credentials and denigrating our ancestors.

Traditional knowledge of plant uses is the most precious body of knowledge that humans have accumulated, and I suspect that a millennium of hard science would be woefully insufficient to replicate it. Tradition has proven far more reliable than chemistry in determining food safety. This makes perfect sense: Real life is infinitely more complex, more extensive, and more rigorous, than the scientific experiments we design to simulate it. Real life can't exclude variables 2–6. A culture's experience with a particular food involves countless perpetual experiments with countless variables: quantity consumed, age and health of subject, preparation method, accompanying foods—all of this on multiple time scales. Traditions distill these perpetual experiments through the perceptions of a multitude, rather than constrain it through the narrow perspective of one. Science gives us facts. Practice gives us answers. Even the FDA recognizes this.

Yet with wild foods, authorities tend to become terrified idiots bumbling in the dark, forgetting the flashlights in their hands. Some doctors writing on acorn "poisonings," for example, noted that a "70-year-old male chronic ingester reported no symptoms" (Martin et al. 1982). That's what rational people call "edible." Intellectually compromised by their food xenophobia, these authorities address question 1 only, coming to irrational conclusions that ignore considerations 2 through 6. Very likely, such a conclusion will get stamped as "peer-reviewed science" no matter how ill founded, and will be perpetuated by an indifferent media because words like "poisonous" and "deadly" sell copies and bait clicks. Nevertheless, it is presumptuous, ethnocentric, and irresponsible to denounce an ancient food tradition based upon such minimal investigation.

Unfortunately, the fear surrounding this plant has infiltrated the foraging world. Poke has been getting scarier by the generation. In 1920, Saunders told

The root mass of a typical 3-year-old poke plant that I transplanted. **Not edible!** The root is potent, and toxic, and has a long history of medicinal use. Most cases of "pokeweed" poisoning in the literature result from overdosing when roots are taken medicinally.

us to use "young spring shoots," giving no indication of the height. Medsger, in 1939, simply stated that young poke shoots are "cooked after the manner of asparagus or spinach." While he warned us not to eat the root, there was no mention of potential toxicity in the greens or shoots, nor did he specify a height at which they are picked. About thirty years ago, maximum picking heights began to appear, with stern warnings for those who disobey. Lyle (2017) says, "Don't eat poke over 7 inches high because it is poisonous." She is generous—the most common height listed in newer books is six inches.

The maximum heights commonly presented for wild shoot vegetables are rough guidelines—and are almost invariably conservative. Plants don't hold up a ruler to determine when to start developing certain chemicals in their tissues. It is never a matter of absolute height; what matters is that the plant is in its young, tender (meristematic) growth phase. Height guidelines may be nice for the novice, until he or she comes to recognize the tender stage of growth, but if we set a guideline, it should be realistic. Six inches is baloney, and has no relationship to traditional practice. Perhaps such authors are afraid that you won't know what "young and tender" means. I worry about that, too. But I'm not going to lie to you—I'm just going to repeat "young and tender" and "meristematic" until you are slightly annoyed with me.

The people who write these overly cautious guidelines may well be the same jokers who put this on my root beer bottle: "Warning! Contents under pressure. Always point away from face, especially while opening, or serious eye or other injury may result." I'd love to see them try drinking pop from bottles that point *away from their faces.*

Interesting things can happen when fragments of traditional knowledge are severed from their tradition, and then stirred in a pot with paranoia. Tradition says to use young shoots, and to avoid the older plants with red-purple stems. Impose excessive dread of wild foods (and of lawsuits) upon those two ideas, and you get "No red! 6 inches max!" This is a dilemma, because the tiny shoots (less than 6 inches) have more red than older shoots (12–30 inches). Trying to follow these over-wrought "safety" guidelines makes use of pokeweed quite impractical, and it confuses people. No wonder so many modern foragers (the ones who have learned primarily from books and websites rather than their elders) completely avoid the plant.

You can eat tiny poke if you want to, but it doesn't make you any safer, nor does it result in better food. The very young shoots apparently have *more* toxins than the older shoots (if the stronger smell, more bitter flavor, redder color, and burning mouth-feel mean anything). This is to be expected—the embryonic shoots of most plants have greater chemical affinity to the root than older shoots. Interestingly, some of these same overcautious foraging books depict short, tough poke seedlings (not shoots!) that I wouldn't eat.

Poke shoots less than 6 inches tall. These are quite red, and apparently have more toxins than the older shoots. Shoots from these same plants, at 14-30 inches tall a few weeks later, were pure green. At maturity they become purple-red.

Many wild food authors do realistically report on eating poke shoots. Susan Tyler Hitchcock (1980) describes "checking every stalk over about eight inches." Yup, she said *over*. That's more like it. She also mentions leaving behind the leafy tips with tiny flower buds in their leaf axils, which means she is collecting from the tops of belly-high shoots. Euell Gibbons (1962) does not specify a height for the shoots, but he tells us to use "only the young, unfolding leaves at the top of the sprout." Such leaves *by themselves* are often 6 inches long. Jan Phillips (1979) writes of peeling stalks and cutting them into "3 or 4 inch sections." Billy Joe Tatum (1976) says, "Until the flower head forms, the young shoots and the leaves are a fine pot green." This means that she is eating tender poke tops when they are waist-high. The people who gathered poke sallet for Allen Canning Company were not filling pickup trucks with the embryonic leaves of six-inch plants.

Wild food writing should not be a contest to see who can make an edible plant sound the most terrifying and impractical. I refuse to live my life hesitantly, ultra-cautiously, iterating the obvious lest some idiot doesn't realize that the ice is cold and the soup is hot. I recognize the boogeyman we are supposed to bow to, the obese monster called Litigation, his countless smiling faces on billboards and the backs of phone books as witness to his power. But I'm not afraid of monsters. Or poke sallet. And you shouldn't be either—just follow the instructions, and enjoy a good lunch.

Prairie Turnip (Tinpsila, Breadroot)

Pediomelum esculentum (Psoralea esculenta)

Jerome opened the cattle gate over the dusty road; when I followed him through, I stopped, jumped out, and darted back to close it behind us. And instantly, crossing that fenceline, I saw that we had passed from South Dakota farmland to real Lakota prairie: from wheat to little bluestem. I could still see the signs of cattle on this side—but the prairie told the story of light and managed grazing. There was silvery scurf-pea, false gromwell, two species of astragalus and a few grasses I couldn't name, clumps of prairie rose and snowberry—plus

A single-stemmed prairie turnip plant. The dense covering of long, straight hairs is distinctive.

two invasive grasses, crested wheatgrass and Japanese brome, telling some history of cattle and man. It looked like a place for tinpsila, but Jerome drove on for nearly a mile of rugged two-track before stopping on a ridge. Rolling mixed-grass prairie lay on all sides, studded with copses of pine and redcedar, stretching to the Badlands on the north horizon.

I knew this ridge. Eight years earlier I dug and ate my first tinpsila in the Black Hills west of here, and on the way home, I stopped on the Pine Ridge Indian Reservation to buy a few pounds of braided tinpsila. I drove the highway beneath this ridge with prairie turnips on my mind, gazing longingly up to the rolling highlands. I pointed north and commented to my wife, "I bet there's prairie turnips up there." From that day, this ridge, its scattered dark trees and the sea of brown and green grasses between them, have lived in my head, the setting for tinpsila daydreams, which I admit to having more than most white folks. And now, somehow, by the grace of God, and the kindness of a few souls, that grass was sweeping my shins.

Jerome stepped out of his truck, and I was soon at his side. "Watch for rattle-snakes," were his first words. I echoed them to my children. We meandered through the prairie for a minute or two with no luck. "I forgot my tinpsila detector," he joked. Perhaps that's why I found the first one. I waited for his instruction; it was his family's land. Was there a size limit, a special technique, a prayer? Did I need to find a patch, or could I take a loner?

Jerome startled me out of my hesitancy: "You found it, you dig it up!"

And so I did.

About then my five-year-old son Joshua arrived, wanting to see the prize before departing to look for his own. For the next three hours we wandered the prairie under the afternoon sun, an old Lakota man and a white couple with three young children—searching, digging, laughing, looking, digging, talking. Jerome was calmly adept at finding them, and hardly seemed affected by the humid 90° (maybe because it had been 107° two days earlier). I admired the diversity of edible plants in a real prairie: prickly pear, bergamot, purple prairie clover, textile onion, leadplant. My children rejoiced in the periodic discovery of ground plums (*Astragalus crassicarpus*), stuffing their faces and filling their pockets. I questioned Jerome about prairie turnips:

"Do you feel like tinpsila is less common than it used to be?"

After several seconds of reflection he says, "No, it seems about the same."

"Do you feel like grazing has a negative impact on it?"

He doesn't hesitate a moment to reply, "Definitely." Then he pauses, and we contemplate a small group of distant cattle. "But I've never actually seen a cow eat one."

I continue to pester him: "Do you eat them in a particular stage of growth? How many do you leave behind for seed? Do you take only the large ones?" I am nervous. I have been involved with prairie conservation and restoration since I was fourteen, when I first volunteered for the Nature Conservancy. I have been taught that prairie plants should never be harmed or collected. Prairie turnips are rare in Wisconsin, but I have found a number of them back home, usually pretty close to a rattlesnake—and I have never done the slightest harm to either. Here in South Dakota, there are millions of acres of tinpsila habitat—but still, I can't stop worrying about overharvesting.

Jerome senses what's troubling me, and says in reassurance: "They'll come back every year. Mother Nature grows her own."

Jerome's family does this every June—wife, siblings, children, grandchildren—sometimes coming home with hundreds of roots. He touches my shoulder and points my attention south, where down the hill 200 yards are the remains of a log structure—the home that his wife's grandparents built more than 100 years ago. And in those distant years, just as today, that young couple walked this ridge in the tinpsila moon, digging these delicious, life-giving roots, knowing there would be more next summer.

We head back, stopping on a gentler hilltop close to the gate. Here, the picking is better, and we get another 20 roots in a few minutes. Dark clouds are looming in the west, flickering now and again. It is time to go, but the swaying grain across the fence beckons me over. As I stand beside the barbed wire, I can see plainly that Jerome is right. On one side, owned by Lakota, by people who

Prairie turnips only grow on the left side of this fence.

daydream about digging tinpsila, is a prairie, home to rattlesnakes, vesper sparrows, and dozens of resplendent wildflowers, including prairie turnip. Across the line, on land owned by a white farmer who has never felt tinpsila soften on his tongue, is wheat and oats, for acres and acres; and beyond that I can see clean pasture that is rotated with hay. This farmer hopes to never see a prairie plant of any kind detracting from his yield. You could walk all day on that side with little hope of finding a wild turnip, and hardly think twice about rattlesnakes.

The Nature Conservancy is right, too. But preservation is the desperate measure of a lost people who still need to learn the value of wildness and the virtue of constraint. The preserve is how we keep tinpsila in a land where there are no turnip daydreams, where few know the silvery halo of its soft hair or the penetrating scent of its crushed leaf. Those who dream of tinpsila keep the living prairie, where Mother Nature grows her own.

DESCRIPTION

Prairie turnip is a short herb, easy to overlook if you aren't familiar with it, but easy to identify if you pay attention. The plant is typically 6–16 inches (15–40 cm) tall when blooming or fruiting, and spreads almost as wide. It usually has a single erect to leaning stem but occasionally produces 2 or 3. They may be unbranched or branching at broad angles. The stems are thin and rather tough with a small hollow in the center. In cross section they have a few gentle angles. The whole plant has a dense coating of long, straight, erect hairs on most surfaces; these hairs are an important feature distinguishing the real prairie turnip from other members of the same genus with underground parts of less interest to the forager.

Prairie turnip's leaves are alternate and crowded at the branch or stem tip. The petioles are 2–5 inches (5–13 cm) long—usually about as long as, or a little longer than, the longest leaflet. They are curved or gently angled upward, often twisted, and have a shallow, narrow groove running their length. The leaves are palmately compound with leaflets that are sessile or nearly so, typically 5 of

Tinpsila *Pediomelum esculentum* in bloom.

Typical form of prairie turnips before being peeled.

them but occasionally more or less. Each leaflet is oblanceolate or obovate with entire margins, nearly hairless above but soft-hairy below and on the margins. The leaflets are deeply folded, especially in hot, sunny weather. The midvein is notably depressed. If you rub the leaf between your fingers, you'll find that it has a strong and unforgettable scent, a bit reminiscent of turpentine or, for those in the know, a bit similar to pawpaw leaf.

Prairie turnip produces its flowers in short, dense, hairy, spike-like clusters that look almost like soft pine cones. The spikes arise on long, hollow, often up-curved stems from the leaf axils. These spikes are usually slightly longer than wide, and each one bears from a dozen to a few dozen flowers. Each flower has an asymmetrical calyx with 5 sharp-tipped lobes; the bottom of the calyx is sac-like and bulging to one side. The light blue flowers are irregular in shape, with a classic 4-lobed form reminiscent of pea flowers. There is a broad, rounded, banner above, slightly recurved with a crease down the center; a pair of small wings protruding below that, and hidden between these is a small keel. The flowers turn pale after they are spent. The fruit is a small pod enclosing a single bean-like seed about 2 mm long. The pod's surface is smooth, but it has a long, hollow, tapered, hairy, needle-like extension.

The root bulges a few to several inches beneath the surface; this bulge may be nearly spherical, or it may be elongated. Rarely, the root enlargements fork, but they do not have side branches—everything is oriented downward. The larger roots weigh a few ounces, but half an ounce is big enough to be happy with.

The only time I get momentarily mistaken about prairie turnip's identity is when I'm a little higher in elevation than it typically grows, usually at the western margin of its range, and I come across certain species of lupine, such as

Lupinus sericeus, before bloom. These can give you pause. However, the lupines tend to have more leaflets, and these are arranged more radially, and crushed lupine leaves lack the pungent-musk aroma of tinpsila. Although most lupines are poisonous, they do not have enlarged, turnip-like roots.

ECOLOGY

Prairie turnip is marvelously adapted for dry conditions. It has a thin, cord-like extension to its taproot that penetrates very deeply into the Earth to seek moisture. Prairie turnip does not have tough leaves or a waxy coating to conserve moisture—it doesn't fight the drought, but avoids it. It appears in spring and grows quickly while the soil is still moist. About the time the sunny days and hot winds begin to severely desiccate the soil, prairie turnip is finishing up with flowering and going dormant for the year. The thick outer coating of the root helps conserve water as the plant meekly waits out the dog days of summer.

Prairie turnip is also fire-adapted. Its root does not reach the surface of the soil; instead, it sends up a thin, vertical, perennial stem (caudex), from which the herbaceous stem grows. When a fire sweeps the prairie, the root will be undamaged, protected by a few inches of soil. The primary fire season on the prairie is early spring, and after such a burn, our lovely little tinpsila is endowed with a huge reserve of energy, allowing it to quickly spring up and thrive in the charred landscape.

Because it has a single taproot that does not spread vegetatively, prairie turnip is obliged to reproduce by seed. Like some other plants of semi-arid environments, it becomes a tumbleweed once dry: breaking off and being rolled by the wind to drop its seeds around the prairie. This same taproot sought by humans was a favored food of the now-extinct Plains grizzly bear (Hayden 1862). The digging action of these bears may have had significant benefits in maintaining populations of prairie turnip, as the small patches of soil tilled up by the great claws would be ideal germination sites for new plants.

Prairie turnip *Pediomelum esculentum* range shown in blue. The area exclusively inhabited by small prairie turnip *P. hypogaeum* is shown in light blue (overlap not mapped). The small area in red is the range of Nashville breadroot *P. subacaule.*

HABITAT

Prairie turnip is a plant of dry prairies. Within the tallgrass prairie region it is primarily confined to well-drained slopes and ridges, rocky outcroppings, or pockets of coarse, sandy soil. On rich soil that supports mesic (tallgrass) prairies,

Prairie turnips in much of the Black Hills have elongated roots, and less hairy stems than typical prairie turnip. Botanists do not recognize this as a separate taxon, but the Lakota do, calling it *tinpsila haska* (long prairie turnip).

prairie turnip cannot compete with the tall, lush vegetation, much of which exceeds 5 feet in height. As one travels west and the plains get drier, prairie turnip becomes more common, but it is still most abundant on slopes and ridges. It is a sun-loving plant, thriving in open prairies, although it is also sometimes found in the light shade of pine woodlands or oak savannahs.

Prairie turnip has lost most of its habitat through conversion to tilled crop fields and overgrazing. This plant is a legume of low preference to livestock, but they will eat it. Under initial grazing of prairies, it is reported that prairie turnip benefits; but more prolonged heavy grazing will eliminate it (Larson and Johnson 2007). Many of the best sites for this plant have been turned into crop fields or intensely managed pastures. In some parts of its range it has lost ground from fire suppression, which allows trees to fill in savannahs and prairies. To find prairie turnip, look for steep, rocky places where the cattle pressure has been light. Good indicator plants include leadplant, ground-plum astragalus, and silvery scurf-pea.

OTHER SPECIES OF PRAIRIE TURNIP

Pediomelum esculentum is the primary species in this genus that was used for food by Native Americans. There are numerous others, but few have roots with any known history of use as food. While they are probably all safe, most are too small or woody for consideration as vegetables. However, there are some other species worth mentioning as food sources.

Little breadroot, or small prairie turnip, *Pediomelum hypogaeum*, is similar to the prairie turnip but smaller, with little to no stem and all the leaves clustered near the base. It also differs in that its hairs are pressed against the surface. The seeds have irregular ridges on the surface—a detail that, while hard to observe, is diagnostic among this group. Little breadroot grows in the southern part of the Great Plains, west into the Rocky Mountains. Much of its range overlaps that of the prairie turnip, but it inhabits drier sites and higher elevations, such as steep rocky ridges or sandy south slopes. The roots of this species were used similarly to those of the prairie turnip.

Another very similar species, *Pediomelum subacaule*, commonly known as Nashville breadroot, is nearly stemless as well. This plant is confined to cedar glades on dry limestone in a limited area of Middle Tennessee and northern Alabama and Georgia. This species is presumably a great edible, but I have not tried it, nor heard from anyone who has—it is rare, confined to a limited region, and protected in some areas.

One of the most common species in this genus is *Pediomelum argophyllum*, the silvery scurf-pea. This plant is often found alongside prairie turnip, but tends to be much more common. It can be easily identified by the silvery underside of its leaves and its tendency to form dense colonies from spreading roots. Silvery scurf-pea grows much taller than prairie turnip—up to 32 inches—and has many branches. Upper leaves usually have only 3 leaflets. The stems and leaves have fine wool but lack the erect hairs of prairie turnip.

The roots of silvery scurf-pea are tough and woody, and they do not form a thickened section as do those of prairie turnip. They taste fine, but are too

Below left *Pediomelum argophyllum* (silvery scurf-pea) is a taller plant, generally more abundant, that grows in colonies that spread by thin roots. The upper leaves have three leaflets, which are broader and less folded. The leaves are silvery, especially beneath, due to fine, soft hairs laying flat against the surface. **Below right** The flowers of silvery scurf-pea are much darker blue than those of prairie turnip, borne in smaller clusters that are not conspicuously hairy.

fibrous to be real food. Plains tribes did supposedly eat them, but only as a last resort in times of food scarcity (Kaye and Moodie 1978). An analysis by these same authors quantifies the difference in eatability: The thickened part of the prairie turnip root was 5.1% crude fiber, while the root of silvery scurf pea was 36.7% fiber.

HISTORY AND LORE

Prairie turnip was probably the most important wild plant food of the Great Plains—a region more than 4 times the size of California. It was eaten by all peoples in the region and formed the starchy staple food for many of them. Breadroot was gathered in great quantity and stored for year-round use, and was an important item of commerce among the Plains tribes. The plant appears in the mythology of several cultures, and many geographic locations are named for it. The prairie turnip was life-changing: It was a reliable, storable, starchy food source that allowed the hunter-gatherers of the northern plains to remain nomadic, flexible, and later, elusive.

Although Lewis and Clark had already heard of this food from the French who had been trading and living on the Plains, they got to experience it first-hand in their exploration of the Louisiana "Purchase" in 1804–1806. Meriwether Lewis was duly impressed with the vegetable he called "white apple" (from the French *pomme blanche*) and wrote what was, until quite recently, the most detailed description of the plant ever published in the English language:

> The white apple is found in great abundance in this neighbourhood; it is confined to the highlands principally. The *whiteapple*, so called by the French Engages, is a plant which rises to the hight of 6 or 9 inches rarely exceeding a foot; it puts forth from one to four and sometimes more stalks from the same root, but is most generally found with one only, which is branched but not defusely, is cylindric and villose; the *leafstalks*, cylindric, villose and very long compared to the hight of the plant, tho' gradually diminish in length as they ascend, and are irregular in point of position; the leaf, digitate, from three to five in number, oval 1 inch long, absolutely entire. . . . The radix a tuberous bulb; generally ova formed, sometimes longer and more rarely partially divided or branching; always attended with one or more radicles at its lower extremity which sink from 4 to 6 inches deep. The bulb covered with a rough black, tough, thin rind which easily seperates from the bulb which is a fine white substance, somewhat porous, spungy and moist, and rather tough before it is dressed; the center of the bulb is penitrated with a small tough string

or liga-ment, which passing from the bottom of the stem terminates in the extremity of the radicle, which last is also covered by a prolongation of the rind which invellopes the bulb: The bulb is usually found at the debth of 4 inches and frequently much deeper. *

Lewis also recounted how the root was used as a food by the Natives:

This root forms a considerable article of food with the Indians of the Missouri, who for this purpose prepare them in several ways. They are esteemed good at all seasons of the year, but are best from the middle of July to the latter end of Autumn when they are sought and gathered by the provident part of the natives for their winter store. When collected they are stripped of their rhind and strung on small throngs or chords and exposed to the sun or plased in the smoke of their fires to dry; when well dryed they will keep for several years, provided they are not permitted to become moist or damp; in this situation they usually pound them between two stones placed on a piece of parchment, untill they reduce it to a fine powder, thus prepared they thicken their soope with it; sometimes they also boil these dryed roots with their meat without breaking them; when green they are generally boiled with their meat, sometimes mashing them or otherwise as they think proper. They also prepare an agreeable dish with them by boiling and mashing them and adding the marrow grease of the buffaloe and some buries, untill the whole be of the consistency of a haisty pudding. They also eat this root roasted and frequently make hearty meals of it raw without sustaining any inconvenience or injury therefrom. The White or brown bear feed very much on this root, which their tallons assist them to procure very readily. The white apple appears to me to be a tasteless insippid food of itself, tho' I have no doubt but it is a very healthy and moderately nutricious food. I have no doubt but our epicures would admire this root very much, it would serve them in their ragouts and gravies in stead of the truffles morella.[5]

---

5 These excerpts are from Lewis's journal for May 8, 1805, as edited by Thwaites (1904). Note that, despite Lewis's statement, the root was generally not collected in autumn. Although Lewis calls it tasteless and insipid, this should not be taken as derision—anyone would make the same assessment of wheat flour. His comments over the course of the expedition suggest that he found prairie turnip a fine and desirable food. Also, keep in mind that in Lewis's time, "nutricious" primarily referred to the content of calories, not micronutrients, as is the connotation today. And finally, "white bear" was how the expedition normally referred to the Plains grizzly bear.

HARVEST

With many wild foods, we are left guessing at how they were used in the not-so-distant past; once they've fallen into disuse, we often have naught to guide us, save a few scanty writings. Not so with tinpsila: The harvest and use of this gift from the prairie remains a strong and vibrant tradition among the Lakota and some other Native people today, a thread unbroken from long before the moldboard plow and barbed wire waged war upon the prairies. On Pine Ridge alone there are thousands of gatherers who eagerly carry a shovel over the hills and bluffs every June in search of this ancient food.

The time to harvest prairie turnips is from late spring to mid summer, depending on the region. The plant is ephemeral—growing for only 7–10 weeks each year before going dormant. The dead stem is inconspicuous and soon detaches from the root, making the dormant plant nearly impossible to find. (This is why it is not gathered in the late summer or autumn.) Early in its growth tinpsila is hard to find because it is small and hidden by grasses. The plant is sought during and just after blooming, when it is conspicuous. In the southern Plains, the tops of the plants may begin to die back as early as April. On the northern fringe of the range, especially at higher elevations, they may flower into August. The timing can also be greatly influenced by microclimate; steep, open, south-facing bluffs may have plants flowering a full month earlier than those on level ground in light shade a half mile away.

Peeling tinpsila.

The roots are often in hard ground and thus difficult to get out. Don't even try it without a digging implement. They are not near the surface—two inches if you're lucky, but four is more typical and six not uncommon. As they are dug, the turnips go into a container, in which they are carried home, or to the comfortable shade of a cedar, to be prepared for cooking or storage.

I spoke with Linda Black Elk, a restoration ecologist, ethnobotanist, and traditional tinpsila harvester, about her family's harvesting practices. Linda only digs plants old enough to have flowers, leaving the younger ones to grow. She advises digging tinpsila only when the plant has finished flowering and the petals are beginning to yellow. Linda tries to get the turnips out of her shovel hole while the stem remains intact in the soil, attached to its caudex. Then she replaces the clod of dirt to fill the hole. If the stem breaks off, she places it upright in the hole, so that it appears as if it were still growing there. Plants thus treated will continue ripening their seeds, she has observed. Some other harvesters place the plant upside down in the hole as the dirt is replaced. Leaving an empty divot in the ground, however, with the dirt clod laying nearby, is frowned upon by all tinpsila gatherers.

THE TINPSILA BRAID

Prairie turnips are traditionally stored in the form of a braid, something like a garlic or onion braid, in which the cord-like taproots are woven together. The tinpsila braid is an emblem of Lakota culture, a confluence of art and practical economy. They hang in prominence inside thousands of kitchens across the reservations and beyond—a message to the visitors, and a reminder to the inhabitants. Yes, the thing is beautiful, a proud display of craftsmanship and symmetry. But it is also an incredibly convenient way to dry, transport, and store the turnips.

Clean the root only if there are big clods of dirt; in this case, wipe or brush them off with something dry. Washing in water is an unnecessary step, since the dirt comes off with peeling. If you insist on washing them, you may want to let the surface dry before peeling, since water on the peeled roots will turn them brown. (Browning won't hurt them, but people who are accustomed to seeing braids of white roots will eye them suspiciously.)

The outer rind of a prairie turnip is tough and almost waxy-feeling, brown to black, and smooth (young ones) or rough and pitted (older plants) on the outside. It is thick and forms a discrete unit, kind of like the rind of a jicama, that easily separates from the starchy inside. To peel, slice off the top of the root where it begins to enlarge—just enough to cut fully through the rind and expose a little bit of the inside. Then grab part of the rind and pull toward the bottom end. The first bit of rind is sometimes hard to grab; you may want to have a

Joshua Price proudly showing off the tinpsila braid that he helped gather and peel.

butter knife or other hard, semi-sharp object on hand to press into the end to loosen it, especially if you have short fingernails. You won't get it off in one piece, but once you peel the first strip, the rest will be easy to grab. Keep a cloth handy to wipe dirt off your fingers so you don't soil the tinpsila. Once you get the hang of it, peeling a root takes only a few seconds, and when done in pleasant company, listening to the prairie birds, it's hard to call it a chore.

At the bottom end of the turnip is a thin, cord-like taproot that runs deep into the soil, usually breaking off at about 8–14 inches (20–35 cm). As you peel the turnip, keep pulling the strip of rind as long as you can, so that hopefully the cord also gets peeled. These cords are what you braid together, in such a way that the turnips hang close to the braid and close to each other. (Don't ask me how to braid—I have short hair. My wife does that part while I peel them.) The few roots that have their cords cut short by the spade will go into a pile for more immediate consumption. Once braided, the turnips can be placed anywhere with good air flow, and they will dry over several days. Once dried, they will keep in good condition for years.

There are a few shops in the Dakotas where you can buy a tinpsila braid. It won't be cheap, as the price speaks for all the labor that has gone into the gathering, peeling, and braiding of the turnips. Once you make your own, it won't seem expensive. If you want to buy one, stop on the reservation and ask around—and be sure to mention that you plan to eat them. Many non-Indians buy these braids as mere decorations, with no intent to ever consume the turnips. Let the harvester know that you understand the real value of food, and will consummate their sacred labor by partaking of its nourishment.

I encountered a decorative, lonely, and unloved braid at the Lewis and Clark Interpretive Center's reconstructed Fort Mandan at Washburn, North Dakota. It was hanging in the captain's quarters, where Sacajawea and her husband Charbonneau would have slept. The tour guide said of it, "These 'vegetables' [read with derisive sarcasm] are wild turnips. They're absolutely disgusting, and nobody eats them anymore [brief pause where perhaps he is considering whether or not Lakota actually count as 'anybody'] . . . except a few Indians. They're extremely bitter, something you'd only eat if you were forced to by hunger."

I asked if he had ever tried one.

"No, and I don't intend to," he replied emphatically.

"You might change your opinion if you did," I told him. "The whole reason we came to the Dakotas was to dig those turnips. They're delicious. My children were eating some in the car on the way here."

After we returned to the museum, one man who had gone on the tour asked if he could try a prairie turnip, so I went to the car and twisted off a small but nice tinpsila from one of our braids. "It's mostly dry and hard, so let it rehydrate slowly in your mouth," I told him as I handed it over. I ate one with him, and gave a turnip to each of my children—in view of the tour guide, who was standing nearby, still searching for explanations as to why he couldn't eat one.

EATING TINPSILA

The first requisite for a staple food is that it must be storable. The majority of tinpsila is eaten outside of the harvest season, after it has been dried. Besides the braids mentioned above, many tribes sliced and dried the roots. In either form, they store exceptionally well.

But that doesn't mean the root isn't edible when fresh. You can dig one out of the dry soil, say a prayer of gratitude, peel its skin, and devour it on the spot. It is one of the best of all wild starches to consume raw, and among the few root vegetables that I really enjoy that way. Apparently, raw prairie turnips digest more easily than most roots, for, in my experience, they do not cause bloating or gas. When Sacajawea had recovered from a long and serious illness in 1805, she apparently craved raw prairie turnips. Meriwether Lewis recorded on June 19 that "the Indian woman was much better this morning she walked out and gathered a considerable quantity of the white apples of which she eat so heartily in their raw state." (Thwaites 1904).

Most tinpsila is eaten cooked, however. While the rehydrated roots are excellent, I like them even better when cooked fresh. If boiled, they impart a bean- or pea-like sweetness to the pot liquor, such that I am apt to drink it down before eating the turnips whole or mashed. The flavor they add to a stew or pot roast is mild and agreeable. The texture is firmer than potato, but not unpleasantly so—except that there is a little bit of stringy core at the bottom end where the root cord is attached. This you may want to pull out before cooking, or while eating. You should try them fried like hash browns, or stick a few whole turnips in the campfire coals to roast, then peel and eat them steaming hot.

If you dry the tinpsila whole, they will be hard as wood, so you should twist some off the braid to rehydrate well in advance of mealtime. Most commonly, they are soaked overnight in a pot of water, which becomes the basis for a stew made the next day. Other vegetables are added—cabbage, onions, carrots—along with beef, deer meat, or bison meat. Tinpsila is often saved for holidays or festive events, but the love and work that goes into it turns any tinpsila meal into a special occasion. Hang that braid where you see it, so you can be reminded to feast; don't you dare let meal moths eat it before you do.

To make flour or meal, I put the dry roots on my nutcracking stone and hit them carefully with a hammer. This breaks them into chunks small enough for a flour mill or dry blender. You can also cut the fresh roots into thin slices across the grain and dry them, which makes them easier to break up. Try the precious flour in something special.

Mandelbaum (1940) related that the Plains Cree made a "very palatable and a favorite dish" from prairie turnip flour and serviceberries. We made such a dish twice one summer, once with raw mashed serviceberries, the second time by mixing the prairie turnip flour into berries that had been heated up to a simmer. Both batches were eagerly finished off.

In truth, this is such a mild, pleasant, and agreeable vegetable that any reasonably competent cook should have little trouble finding more than enough ways to use his or her stock.

THE PRAIRIE TURNIP'S FUTURE

This plant has been declining in abundance for well over a century due to massive loss of habitat. Overgrazing, clearing of prairie for cropland, and fire suppression have been the causes of this decline. Note that "harvesting of roots" is not on that list. I am aware of no case where collecting prairie turnip has caused even a local extermination of the species. (Curtis [1959] suggested that this might have been the case in some locations, but provided no further explanation, nor any evidence.) It was gathered by the bushel by many thousands of people for thousands of years, yet remained widespread and common. It was also eaten regularly by the Plains grizzly bear until a little more than a century ago.

Obviously, the plant can withstand substantial harvest—but I am inclined to say more: It may be adapted to harvest. The symbiotic relationships between flowers and pollinators, and between fruits and the animals that disperse them, have been well studied and long accepted. However, it has hardly even been suggested that underground storage organs could be symbiotic gifts to animals in exchange for tillage of the soil. This is a strange omission in our understanding of plant ecology. Most seeds germinate and grow far better in disturbed seedbeds. (This is one of the basic principles upon which agriculture is founded.) This includes native prairie plants (Daryl Smith et al. 2010). Digging up a root creates a small but ideal seedbed, and loosening the soil is often beneficial to plants that are already established. Thus, digging roots can have a positive effect on the reproductive success of remaining individuals. In some circumstances, this positive effect may outweigh the negative effect of removing an individual plant.

My own experiments with jerusalem-artichoke and parsnip have demonstrated convincingly that this principle can apply in actual practice: both are more abundant and grow larger where I dig up a portion of the tubers or roots yearly. In fact, in my jerusalem-artichoke experiment, where I established two plots 50 meters apart on identical clay soil, the un-harvested plot completely disappeared after 6 years, while the harvested plot thrived and expanded during that time. When the harvested plot was abandoned, it too completely disappeared within 8 years.

A robust tinpsila plant, just after blooming, with straw-colored shriveled remnants of the flowers. Note the variably folded leaves. This is what a harvester's eyes are trained to spot.

The parsnip example, however, may be more instructive—because in this case the plant has a single underground storage organ, and the entire plant is killed when this organ is harvested. And yet clearly I can observe that the act of digging up parsnips makes them more abundant in my meadow, not less. The evolutionary principle of *kin selection*, which states that it can increase fitness to die if by doing so an organism can increase the survival rate of its offspring or relatives, provides a theoretical framework for understanding how a symbiotic relationship of this type can work. There are many examples of plants under heavy competition in ideal growing conditions that die after fruiting to give their progeny a place to grow: many bamboos, and the neotropical tree *Tachigali versicolor*, for example.

Ecologists have mostly laughed off the notion that traditional harvest can have positive effects on the populations of edible root-bearing plants. Linda Black Elk, however, is confident that moderate, responsible harvest of prairie turnip in the traditional manner within healthy colonies promotes the plant's propagation and increases its abundance. In this case, it is the scientists whose opinions are based on a quaint and untested cultural notion. The Lakota, on the other hand, have a wealth of observations in support of their belief. I have every reason to believe they are right.

I'm not saying that you need not worry about the effects of harvesting on prairie turnip. Much the opposite: You *should* worry. Most people, coincidentally, don't. Prairie turnip isn't the talk of the taverns, nor even the coffee shops. Go dig a few up and put them in your next pot roast, and you will start to worry about them—I guarantee it. You'll look at a redcedar-covered bluff top and wonder how many whiteapples used to grow up there, and wonder if any are left, and then *worry* that there are a few dozen, barely hanging on under too much shade, about to wither away once and for all.

Slice up a few breadroots, stick them in a blender, pour into a pot, add some ham, onions, and celery, and then guess what happens? You'll start to *wonder*. Why, in a million-acre national grassland, can't we have a few spots where prairie plants are allowed to grow? Maybe you'll turn an acre of your sunny lawn into your own edible prairie garden. Maybe you'll join the Prairie Enthusiasts (a real organization). Maybe you'll start the first chapter of Prairie Turnips Unlimited (not yet a real organization). Maybe *you'll* talk about prairie turnip at the coffee shop. Maybe, even, someone will listen.

Prairie turnip should be collected only where it grows in ample populations, by people who are actively engaged in conservation of the prairie. It needs more of those people, some bison, and maybe a few grizzlies.

I have a prairie turnip fantasy. It's about a girl who grows up on a ranch somewhere in North Dakota. Somehow, when she's 13, she gets a taste of prairie turnip. Perhaps at an educational event at a local historical site, where she was compelled to go by her history teacher. And as she rolls the crumbled bit of starch around in her mouth, her eyes widen a bit, because she once had a fantasy of her own, in which she came to these prairies a long, long time ago in a covered wagon, pulled by a team of oxen; and then she cracks a smile, her eyes with the telltale emptiness of dreamland, because she has just taken communion with that fantasy. Driven by curiosity, she checks out a book on prairie plants from the closest library, 56 miles away.

One cool dawn, some weeks later, when she wakes up early and can't sleep, she pockets that book and marches through the moist grass toward a spot in the pasture, a high ridge that she often gazes at from her bedroom window. Her eyes search the ground around her tennis shoes for any of those magical flowers with goofy names—hoary puccoon, bastard toadflax, Lambert's crazyweed— and her heart slowly sinks, for half a mile produces nothing but short-cropped grasses and weeds. But she trudges on, flushes a few partridge, avoids a few cow pies, making her way to that ridge to watch the sunrise. She sits down, crosses her legs, and . . . wait, what's that? Hand in her pocket, she fishes out the field guide that already has a bookmark on the prairie turnip page, looks it over, and returns her eyes to the hairy clump of light blue blossoms on the plant next to her. And suddenly, that ox-drawn wagon doesn't seem so long ago.

Ten years later, when she comes home from college, after she stacks all her plant books on the shelf and spends 3 weeks fixing machinery and moving cows so he knows the years in town haven't ruined her, she says, "Dad, I have a crazy proposition. Can I fence off 20 acres around that ridge?" And in ten more years she's shipping tinpsila and leadplant from her restored prairie to 224 customers around the country, and a hip café in Bismarck.

My fantasy is that white folks will learn what the Lakota have long been telling us. Is that too much to dream?

You just wait.

Purple Poppy Mallow

Callirhoe involucrata

wiggled a tuft of poppy mallow leaves and yanked its plump root from the sand, as easily as plucking a carrot from the garden. Peering along the hillside, where thousands of tufts like this one basked their greenery in the October sun, I wondered through the adrenaline why it had taken me so long to discover them. That taproot was a talisman in my hand, and from it flowed a vision, which settled into my breast and fused there with the hopes and memories that feed my dreams. And Kansas looks different to me now.

I first learned of this plant through an excellent write-up by Kelly Kindscher in *Edible Wild Plants of the Prairie* (1987). Otherwise, poppy mallow is rarely discussed in the foraging literature. A brief acquaintance with this robust root vegetable makes one wonder how it is *not* one of our best-known native foods. Indeed, poppy mallow is popular as a native ornamental, grown for its striking purplish blooms, even widely outside of its native range. It is tough, persistent, adaptable—thriving on poor soil in droughty conditions. How, then, have we been able to ignore it for all these decades?

DESCRIPTION

Purple poppy mallow is a showy beauty of the prairie that is hard to overlook and easy to recognize—at least when blooming. If you are familiar with common weedy mallows, you will recognize the many similarities in form here. A

Typical roots of purple poppy mallow dug in autumn.

In fall, after the flowering stems have died, poppy mallow sends up another flush of leaves. These tend to be less deeply lobed than the spring and summer leaves.

low-growing herb, purple poppy mallow has basal leaves year-round (although they are tiny in winter). It is a perennial herb with a thickened root that produces multiple radiating stems, but never spreads by rhizome. The stems are decumbent—at first they hug the ground, but the tips sweep upward to hold their flowers off the earth. The stems are typically unbranched below the inflorescence. They are solid, round in cross section, rarely exceeding an eighth inch (3 mm) in thickness, and grow 18–30 inches (45–75 cm) long. The stems are covered by clustered hairs that radiate, star-like, in all directions. These are tipped with glands, making them a bit sticky and therefore unfortunately good at holding small particles.

The leaves are basal or alternate, borne on long, thin, hairy petioles that are D-shaped in cross section (not channeled). The blades are only 1–3 inches (2.5–8 cm) long, hairy beneath, and less hairy and often nearly glossy above. They are dark green, roundish in outline but palmately lobed. The lobes are often lobed again toward the tip, but there are no small teeth on the margins. Stem leaves have thinner lobes with deeper sinuses between them; otherwise they are similar to the basal leaves. There are two ovate stipules attached to the stem at the base of each petiole.

Purple poppy mallow blooms from late spring to mid summer; it may have a second flush of flowers in early autumn. The flowers are borne singly from upper leaf axils, on long, thin, erect pedicels. As is typical of the mallow family, they are symmetrical, with 5 petals and a 5-lobed calyx. The flowers are fragrant and showy, a bit over an inch (2.5 cm) across, and rose-purple (rarely lighter in color), the petals overlapping and broad at the tip. Other names used for this plant, inspired by the striking flowers, include "prairie winecups," and "buffalo rose." The center of the flower has a column of numerous stamens pressed together, and this bears anthers not only at the tip but at the sides as well. To positively tell this species from all other poppy mallows, look behind the flower or fruit. There is an involucre of 3 bracts directly behind the calyx, which the other species lack. The fruit is a flattened wheel divided into several wedge-like sections, much like that of common mallow.

The root of this plant is the size of a small parsnip, but it is shorter and stouter. They typically weigh 1–5 ounces (25–140 grams). Purple poppy mallow roots bulge to their widest 2–4 inches (5–10 cm) below the root crown, and then taper rather quickly to a thin tip, which extends sometimes a foot (30 cm) or more into the soil as a tough taproot. Occasionally they bulge more abruptly and have a turnip-like shape. The surface is corrugated by many fine rings, especially in the top third. While the roots sometimes fork, both forks will grow downward; they do not have side branches. The root tapers to the top, and the crown is actually quite small—a feature that probably helps protect the bulk of the root from prairie fires.

There are a few palmate-leaved buttercups that might be confused with purple poppy mallow. However, the leaves of these buttercups have 3 main divisions (rather than poppy mallow's 5–7 lobes), and far fewer leaves per rosette. Buttercup petioles are thicker and often hollow. The hairs are not in spreading clumps. Buttercups do not have a taproot similar to that of poppy mallow, and their sap is not slimy.

This is a buttercup, *Ranunculus* (species uncertain). It somewaht resembles a more deeply lobed poppy mallow leaf, but the leaves are fewer per rosette, divided more fully to the base, not glossy, and their hairs are not in spreading clumps. Plus, the buttercups don't have a parsnip-like taproot.

NOT EDIBLE

The flower of purple poppy mallow is striking. To the left can be seen a wheel-like fruit, much like that of common mallow. The upper leaves of flowering stems are the most deeply lobed.

OTHER POPPY MALLOWS

There are several species of poppy mallow in North America, generally found in the Great Plains. Although all species are edible, their qualities are not identical. The purple poppy mallow *Callirhoe involucrata* is one of the best to eat, and is by far the most common and widespread among them. Some of the other poppy mallows are rare and should not be gathered, such as *Callirhoe scabriuscula*, an endangered species found only in sand dunes along the upper Colorado River in western Texas.

Several other species have small ranges and specific habitat needs, and should not be collected except (where legal) by those who propagate and care for them. The gorgeous *C. bushii* is rare in the wild, but popular in native wildflower gardens. Clustered or triangle-leaf poppy mallow *C. triangulata* is the one species whose range lies primarily outside of the Great Plains; its odd distribution is broken into two widely separated regions: sandy soils of the lower Great Lakes region and the Deep South.

Fringed or finger poppy mallow *C. digitata* is found in a rather limited region around the Ozark and Ouachita Mountains, in tallgrass prairies and glades. The leaves of this plant have extremely long, thin lobes. The erect to leaning stems are hairless or nearly so, separating it from most other poppy mallows (the group in general is characterized by very hairy stems). Havard (1895, p. 111) reports that *C. digitata* "has a fusiform root, in shape and size between a small turnip and a parsnip, said to be even more pleasant tasted than that of *Psoralea* [prairie turnip] and highly prized by the natives."

HABITAT

Purple poppy mallow likes dry, sunny sites, with loose, sandy soil. It is prolific and weedy and does well in disturbed situations. Its beautiful blossoms are a common sight of roadsides, barnyards, and weedy places in sandy parts of the southern Plains. Because the stems hug the ground, the plant can thrive in lawns (as long as herbicides are not used); it benefits from mowing.

Purple poppy mallow has spread sporadically as a weed hundreds of miles east of its natural range—taking advantage of human-caused clearing and

Here is a robust purple poppy mallow rosette in a mowed footpath in spring. It thrives in such locations. At this stage, tender young stems and leaves can be eaten, as with most other mallows.

disturbance. These plants may have been intentionally spread, or they may have been moved in hay, animal fur, manure, or stuck to some guy's pant cuffs. Such weedy populations are known from sandy parts of Michigan, Wisconsin, Indiana, Illinois, Pennsylvania, New York, and Virginia, and are surely found elsewhere.

Purple poppy mallow *Callirhoe involucrata*. The easternmost part of the mapped range is adventive. This plant is widely scattered as an escape on sandy soils outside the mapped range, with known populations in Oregon, Florida, Kentucky, Pennsylvania, and Virginia.

HARVEST AND PREPARATION

The primary edible part of purple poppy mallow is the taproot. These should be dug when the tops are dormant, or at least when the flowering stems have died back. The collecting season begins in late summer, goes through the autumn and winter, and continues into spring until the flowering stems have begun to form. Like many roots, they get sweeter through the winter. Let the bold blossoms of mid summer lead you to the colonies of this plant; then learn to recognize the leaves, so they can show you exactly where to find the roots in autumn.

Purple poppy mallow roots look like something you'd dig out of the garden. Indeed, collecting them in a healthy patch is as simple and easy as digging a

Occasionally, purple poppy mallow roots are shaped like this, as if they want to pretend they are prairie turnips.

row of carrots. Step on the spade, wiggle it to loosen the sandy soil, grab the tuft of leaves or the top of the root, and pull it out. If the soil is a little too firm for this to work, unearth a scoop of dirt and break it apart; replant any small roots.

Purple poppy mallow roots are a semi-starchy vegetable. In texture they are like an extra-soft parsnip, except they are not as dense and are mucilaginous like other members of the mallow family. The flesh is nearly white, soft and flexible rather than crisp; it ranges from faintly to slightly fibrous in the center. There may be scattered dark flecks inside older roots. The top inch or so is tougher and rougher than the rest of the root. I like to peel the corrugated parts after I clean them with a vegetable brush.

The flavor is slightly sweet and rather bland—not aromatic or spicy in any way. In other words, it is a hearty and wholesome base to which you can add the flavors of your choosing. I suppose you could eat them raw, if you have a reason to insist on such a thing, but they are definitely better cooked. I think they are excellent in soups, and act as a thickener. Sliced thin, they are a nice addition to stir-fry. For a delicious dish, prepare them like scalloped potatoes (although I recommend pre-cooking the slices, as they are a bit firmer than potatoes). Sliced into medallions, season them and fry with onions for a simple but excellent dish.

Because poppy mallows are adapted to dry conditions, the roots don't handle moisture well. Do not soak them, or they will split open lengthwise and get dirt inside their flesh. Don't even rinse or wash them until just before you use them. Slightly moist sand or

Large roots of purple poppy mallow. This is a vegetable to be taken seriously.

sawdust should be the storing medium. In fact, wild roots in low spots where they might get flash-flooded are often seen with the healed scars from previous moisture splits—they look like lightning scars on tree trunks.

Poppy mallow roots are easily stored in a refrigerator or root cellar, just as one would store other roots; they will keep for months. Like most wild root vegetables of temperate regions, they are resistant to freezing but will be killed by temperatures lower than 15–20°F. A great way to store them is to peel, cut into thin medallions, and dry. Then they can be conveniently dropped into soup or rehydrated for use in casseroles or other dishes.

The roots are not the only edible part of poppy mallow. As with the related mallows of the genus *Malva*, the tender leaves, stems, flowers, and young fruits can all be eaten. These parts are mild in flavor and mucilaginous. The leaves and stems make decent greens raw or cooked, and can be used to thicken soups. You can find a few tender leaves throughout the growing season, but the best time to pick these greens is in spring and early summer, when the plant is growing most rapidly, and sometimes again in fall. The hairs are sometimes stiff enough to detract from the experience of eating the greens raw, especially if the leaves are a tad too old.

The immature fruits are very similar to the "cheeses" of common mallow, and can be used similarly as a snack or a vegetable. They are a fun and delicious wild vegetable, although admittedly a bit small and thus laborious to collect in quantity.

CONSERVATION AND CARE

Prairie plants have been hit very hard by the agricultural invasion of the Plains, and many are seriously imperiled. The purple poppy mallow has fared better than most—it is an adaptable, even weedy species that does well on disturbed soils, so long as they are not too heavily grazed, too regularly plowed, or sprayed with herbicide. However, digging out the root kills the plant, and must therefore be done thoughtfully.

Because purple poppy mallow is adapted to disturbance, it is easy to harvest it sustainably. Collect it where the plants are thriving, preferably where they are packed together and need thinning. Within such a colony, any place you dig will be promptly occupied by new plants. Regular but judicious harvest within a colony, as long as a large portion of the plants are left for seeding, will actually increase the abundance of poppy mallow. In fact, without some combination of soil disturbance, light grazing, or mowing, it will be mostly outcompeted by taller species.

If you find an isolated few plants, build the population up over a few years before harvesting. At blooming time, take a shovel and turn over a few scoops of soil beside established plants, and seedlings will appear on the disturbed soil in autumn—often in huge numbers. Poppy mallows spread only by seed, and are quite effective at doing so, as long as there is disturbed soil upon which to germinate. Spread these seeds not only to your excavation, but also to other sites of likely habitat nearby. And most importantly, find ways to protect little pockets of sandy prairie. The ornate box turtles and racerunner lizards will thank you.

The poppy mallows are excellent candidates for edible landscaping on any scale. As native prairie wildflowers, poppy mallows of several species are recommended by the nursery trade for their beauty and fragrance alone. Poppy mallows are easy to transplant or plant by seed, and once established, they will persist indefinitely if the conditions are satisfactory. When you add the excellent roots they produce, it becomes hard to think of a single good reason not to plant some in your yard, if you've got the sand and space to do it.

Robert Frost's poem "The Gift Outright," read at John F. Kennedy's presidential inauguration, begins with the perceptive line "The land was ours before we were the land's." The challenge of the immigrants who overran this country is now to grow up and settle down, reflect, and naturalize—to become part of the land we have built our homes upon. We can't do that unless we learn to see the treasures who live here with us.

The American settlers who tamed the Plains looked with disdain upon the prairies they destroyed. They came from a land of trees, and saw nothing of value in the diverse community they plowed and grazed into oblivion. All they wanted was the thing that this community had spent thousands of years building: the rich soil beneath it. But the settlers were missing something. They had never tasted prairie turnip, prairie parsley, prairie clover tea, or poppy mallow root. Let us taste them now, close our eyes and dream, and admit our oversight. Listen hard enough, and you can still hear the hooves of bison, pawing in the dirt of soybean fields.

Purslane

Portulaca oleracea

Purslane looks and feels so different from any other weed that all of us who tended garden as children remember it distinctly. Other weeds may have faded into dim memories of nondescript greenery, but purslane stands out, like a tiny spineless cactus, seeming to belong in a fancy ceramic pot on the window sill, not out here between the bean rows. I remember visiting my uncle in the summers, eight blocks away across the train yard, hoping he would ask me to help weed the garden, just so that I could feel purslane's succulent leaves between my fingers, the prize weed in some kind of real-life video game. I wish I had known back then what I was pulling out.

A healthy purslane branch.

DESCRIPTION

Common purslane is a low annual plant, typically laying right on the surface of the ground when growing in full sun. Where the competition is stiff or there is shade, and the moisture is high, the young stems or branch tips will grow upright. This plant branches profusely, and can spread in all directions to form a thick mat over the soil. The stems are round, solid, smooth, and quite thick in proportion to the plant's length. The stems are succulent, and only the oldest ones become tough.

The leaves are small, 0.3–0.8 inches (8–20 mm) long, sessile or on very short petioles, and spoon- or spatula-shaped, with rounded to flattened tips. The leaves have no teeth or hair. They are usually described as alternate, which does nothing to convey the uniqueness of their arrangement on the plant. Most of the leaves are found in whorl-like clumps at the ends of branches; adjacent clumps often have leaves of greatly different sizes. The leaves that are found along the stem often occur in offset pairs. The leaves are succulent, thick, and often tinted with red. The midvein is not depressed and scarcely evident; secondary veins are obscure.

Purslane's flowers open only in sunshine. They are tiny and yellow, sessile, borne singly or in small clusters at branch tips in the midst of a cluster of leaves. The corolla is usually asymmetrical, broader in one dimension, with 5 petals of unequal size (but occasionally with 4 or 6 petals), each petal deeply cleft

Purslane in bloom.

into 2 triangular lobes. The fruit is a green capsule. Upon ripening, the distal half of the capsule neatly severs and falls off, revealing a bunch of tiny, black, comma-shaped seeds.

There are 9 other species of purslane found growing wild in North America, some of them native and some introduced (Matthews, 2003). Most of the other species are confined to the southern states and have leaves that are rounded in cross section rather than flattened like those of common purslane. I have not tried any of the other species and cannot comment on their flavor or edibility.

HABITAT

This is one of the world's most abundant weeds and it grows in almost all of North America, save the coolest regions. Purslane needs disturbed soil and ample sunlight, and it thrives around human activity. You can find it in sidewalk cracks, flower beds, empty lots, dirt piles, construction sites, gardens, roadsides, farm fields, parks, poorly kept lawns, beaches, and other disturbed ground. It can do well in poor, dry soil, but does better with ample moisture on rich ground. Purslane avoids waterlogged sites and is less common in soils that are heavy with clay.

Purslane *Portulaca oleracea*. Highly associated with anthropogenic disturbance.

Common purslane is native to the Old World and North America. Several early European explorers found purslane to be well established upon their arrival and assumed it native, and the seeds and pollen have been verified from at least one pre-Columbian archaeological site (Byrne and McAndrews 1975). Although it is often claimed to be non-native here, this assumption is without basis.

HARVEST AND PREPARATION

Most edible greens have a short window during which the leaves and stems are ideal, but those of purslane are good throughout the growing season—even when the plants are flowering and fruiting. It is true that these parts are best when purslane is vigorously growing from late spring to mid summer, but the leaves and stem tips never become tough and fibrous. That's because they are designed to store water and nutrients, and so are inflated with varying amounts of fluid depending on the time of day and the weather. In order to change size like that, a structure must remain flexible, hence tender. Lucky for us.

Purslane is a traditional vegetable in many cultures, and it has long been used in Mexican, Mediterranean, and Indian cooking. The leaves are good raw, so eat a bunch until you feel you have a good handle on which ones are as nice and tender as you like. Then harvest as much as you want to use. I like to pinch the stems off between my thumbnail and first finger, because this keeps me in tune with their toughness, but you can use a pair of scissors for this part.

Since it grows close to the ground, purslane has a tendency to be dirty. But, being hairless, it is easier to clean than most greens. To avoid dirt, I look for purslane growing over mulch, a board, or bare rock, or purslane in thick vegetation or moist soil, where it stands upright. In these locations the plants will often be larger and better anyway.

The leaves and stems of purslane are a favorite ingredient in salads, and are good just to snack on raw—which is most often how I eat them. I also like them in tacos or burritos. Almost any place where a raw vegetable is appreciated, these excel. But you can also cook them. Purslane has a mucilaginous quality that seems to be countered by the crispness of the raw leaves, but which becomes more pronounced when it is cooked. I don't mind it, but some people dislike any slimy food. Cooked purslane is nice because it doesn't disappear or shrink the way many vegetables do. Try it in a stir-fry with onions, peppers, and dried tomato, then served over rice, couscous, or polenta.

In the foraging community, another popular use of purslane is pickling the stems, in which case the firm, crisp texture is pleasant. The plant is also sometimes chopped fine and used with other vegetables in kimchi.

Purslane does not always hug the ground. When growing in competition it will stand weakly erect, as here.

Young, erect, very tender purslane in a garden.

Purslane, like many plants, uses the C4 photosynthetic pathway, an adaptation to dry, sunny environments that economizes water use while increasing the efficiency of sunlight use. However, purslane also has a nifty trick up its sleeve: It can switch to a process called crassulacean acid metabolism (CAM) when moisture stress is very high. Plants using CAM photosynthesis (such as cacti and several other groups of succulents) respire at night, when temperatures are low, and store the carbon needed for photosynthesis in the form of malic acid. During the heat of the day, the stomata (respiration holes) close to prevent water loss, and the stored carbon is released for use in photosynthesis by breaking down the malic acid. Purslanes are the only C4 plants known to switch to CAM photosynthesis (Koch and Kennedy 1980; Kraybill and Martin 1996). In or just after a period of dry weather, the malic acid stored in the plant's tissues reaches its highest level at mid morning, then decreases over the course of the day. (In moist conditions there is usually little difference.) This helps explain the highly variable flavor of purslane. If you like it tangy, go grab it just before breakfast in a dry spell.

Considering the attributes of this plant, it is surprising that it is not more popular. Not only is it delicious, growing almost everywhere in abundance for free, it is also incredibly nutritious. According to analysis by the USDA (NNDSR 2015), the plant is an excellent source of potassium and iron. A group of researchers (Simopoulos et al. 1992) found purslane to be higher in omega-3 fatty acids than any other leafy vegetable that had ever been analyzed.

Purslane, as an annual, is a heavy producer of tiny black seeds. These seeds are edible, but their use as food has been limited—probably due to the difficulty of harvesting them in quantity, and of separating them from sand. However,

Purslane with a mature pod opened to show the ripe seeds.

research has shown some promising health benefits to the seeds. In one study (Sabzghabaee et al. 2014), they were shown to improve blood cholesterol ratios and reduce triglycerides. Another study (El-Sayed 2011) showed that consuming the seeds reduced blood sugar, triglycerides, and total cholesterol, while improving cholesterol ratios. That might even make up for eating a little sand.

Few plants in the garden provide so much good food, for such a long season, as purslane. Few of them rival it in nutritional density. None of them beats its delicious tang and succulent crunch. And nearly all of them take a lot more work to grow. Purslane, in fact, proves very hard not to grow. If you can't beat 'em, eat 'em.

Quickweed

Galinsoga parviflora, G. quadriradiata

My wife grew up pulling purslane from her family garden, summer after summer. Then, one year, she noticed a new weed—a little hairy thing with dainty white flowers—that must have come in with some manure or compost or however else weeds find new homes. It wasn't long before the pretty new weed was growing thickly over every unattended corner and unused row,

Quickweed, just beginning to bloom.

smothering that poor purslane to death. Within a few years it had accomplished the seemingly impossible, and the purslane was eradicated.

This little plant would be easy to overlook were it not for the fact that it takes over entire gardens in a matter of months. When you pull one up by the root, it feels fragile and delicate, yet it is tough enough to outcompete and kill off the most tenacious weeds. Quickweed, they call it—and for good reason, as many gardeners have found out. And it might not look like food, but quickweed is full of surprises.

DESCRIPTION

Quickweed is a short annual herb, typically reaching only 6–14 inches (15–35 cm) and branching widely close to the ground if it is growing in full sun with plenty of space. In the shade, or where it is crowded (and especially where it is crowded *and* in the shade), quickweed grows erect and lanky with few to no branches, and gets quite a bit taller, perhaps 28 inches (70 cm). All parts are hairy—more on the upper parts, and more densely when growing in full sun. The leaves are paired; the lower ones are on petioles about half their length, but the uppermost are sessile. Each leaf is 1–3 inches (2.5–8 cm) long and sparsely toothed, with a narrow, pointed tip. The upper leaves in the blooming tops are narrowly elliptic or lanceolate, but these are not present at the best time for collecting. Lower leaves, or all the leaves on young plants, are broadly ovate. The veins are notably depressed above, and there are 3 major veins from the base, the outer 2 of these reconverging at the tip. This produces the unique appearance of a narrow leaf outlined within a broader one.

Quickweed tops, just before blooming, when the greens are nice and tender.

When quickweed begins blooming, it is compact and leafy, with the flowers often single and nestled close to the broad leaves. By the end of summer, the stems elongate so the leaves are widely separated, and the flowers are borne in loose, open, forking clusters at the tips of branches. Quickweed blooms over a very long period, and the flowers are a dead giveaway. Each flowerhead is tiny: about 0.2 inches (5 mm) across. *Galinsoga* is a composite—what looks like a single flower is actually a head, or cluster of several mini-flowers, called florets (as with sunflowers and dandelions). Quickweed has yellow disk florets in the center of its head, and on the periphery it has white ray florets, which look like petals. With quickweed, there are 5 of these rays, and I think they are antisocial, because they are always spaced carefully to avoid touching one another. And the rays are distinctly shaped: narrow at the base, broad at the tip, and with 3 (occasionally 2) blunt triangular lobes at the end. The fruit is a triangular achene with a bristly pappus at the end.

There are 2 widespread species of quickweed, both used in the same ways as food. The more common is *Galinsoga quadriradiata*, (also called *ciliata*). This species is hairier, and the hairs are more erect and have more and larger glands; the leaves have larger teeth. Because it is shorter and easier to spell, most people use the flagship name of the less common species, *G. parviflora*, to represent both species.

Speaking of names, *Galinsoga* was given in honor of Ignacio Mariano Martinez de Galinsoga, a Spanish physician and botanist who lived in the late 18th century. Some people have corrupted Galinsoga's name into the obnoxious common name "gallant soldiers." Please don't do that when I'm around.

HABITAT

Quickweed is found almost everywhere in North America where humans inhabit. It is an opportunist that thrives wherever moist, rich soil is disturbed by human activity. Unlike many weeds, it is quite shade tolerant. The most common places to find quickweed include gardens, shaded backyards without lawn cover, construction sites, agricultural fields, and roadsides.

Composite range of both species of quickweed.

HARVEST AND PREPARATION

Quickweed is as simple to use as it is to identify. The greens can be eaten raw or cooked, and they are good either way, although I prefer them cooked. Some people object to their hairiness, especially when raw, but few find fault in the

Quickweed's distinctive flowerheads, with antisocial rays.

flavor. As always, you want to make sure you collect only the tender parts that are actively growing. Eventually you'll learn the look of a tender top: The leaves are robust and crowded, there are few to no open flowers, and the stems break easily. Conversely, a lot of flowers or spent heads, small leaves, and long internodes all point to the stems being tough. Because *Galinsoga* is hairy, it holds dirt more readily than most plants. For this reason you probably want to avoid those growing in the open on bare soil; instead, look for tall quickweed in dense stands of vegetation.

I must admit here that I had gone most of my life having never made nor eaten a smoothie of any kind. But Sergei Boutenko, an avid forager and author of *Wild Edibles*, is way into smoothies, and he convinced me to try them. I'm glad he did. A smoothie is a nice way to have a blender do the work your mouth would otherwise have to do, obliterating the food into tiny particles that make it highly digestible without cooking. Of all the greens I've tried in smoothies thus far, quickweed has been my favorite. Its mild, slightly sweet flavor nicely accompanies that of fruits, and the blending renders its hairiness completely irrelevant.

Quickweed is a warm-weather annual that doesn't make much of an appearance until early to mid summer. This makes sense; it is native to the American tropics and is said to have come north in recent centuries as an invader of agricultural lands. One of the plant's names in Spanish is *guascas*, and it is much appreciated as a vegetable in parts of Latin America. *Guascas* is combined with chicken, potato, and corn in a popular Colombian soup known as *ajiaco*.

If you find a little hairy weed with broad, paired leaves and flowers like this, you've got a *Galinsoga* problem to eat. That's not such a bad problem to have.

Rose

Genus *Rosa*

Where I live there is a foraging lull around the summer solstice. The spring ephemeral greens are a wilted memory, oozing into the leaf litter with each warm rain. The shoots of spring have toughened into blooming stems. Root vegetables have sent their energy skyward. The mosquitoes are fearsome, the days are too long for a good night's sleep; we grab our amaranth quickly and dash inside, waiting for serviceberries.

And then, one dewy morning, I notice the first rose blooming in a brushy ditch, a pink beacon that I see from far off down the hill. The next morning, there are dozens; and then, hundreds. A week later the ditches and brushy hillsides and forest borders glow with glorious pink. I tell my daughter, "The roses are out." She screams in excitement, "Oooh! Let's go, let's go!" That evening, the daylight is just long enough. We pull off at the gravel pit and walk up the road through the county forest, our special rose thicket. The mosquitoes

Rosa acicularis in bloom. A typical wild rose with large, showy flowers, and good petals for culinary purposes.

are terrible but somehow perfectly tolerable. We have two bowls: one for wild strawberries, and one for rose petals. By dusk, we've got a few ounces of each, and the mosquitoes have called in reinforcements, so we pile back into the car. Before starting the engine, I give Myrica a high-five, then sniff that bowl of bold petals and thank them for reminding me.

DESCRIPTION

Roses are a large group, easy to recognize, with dozens of species. Some are tall and erect, some spread below your knees, some are chest-high bushes, while others are lanky and leaning, almost vine-like. But all of them are woody shrubs. Most roses form colonies by stolons or suckers, but on some species these colonies are widespread and loose, and in other cases they form nearly impenetrable thickets. The stems of roses are almost always less than an inch (2.5 cm) thick, and are armed with thorns or bristles.

The leaves of all roses are alternate and pinnately compound, each leaf having 5–11 leaflets. The most distinctive feature of these leaves is the pair of conspicuous wing-like stipules found on each side of the rachis at the base, each with a

Rosa multiflora is one of the most common invasive shrubs of the eastern US. The flowers are tiny, white, and borne in clusters.

pointed tip hanging free. The side leaflets are sessile or on very short petioles, but the terminal leaflet has a longer petiole. The leaflets are lanceolate, ovate, or elliptic. The margins are toothed, and the tips may be pointed or rounded. The midvein and major side veins are distinctly depressed.

Occasionally, a rose has a mutation causing it to produce a preponderance of petals, and people have cherished, bred, and propagated roses with such mutations. These many-petaled cultivars notwithstanding, the normal pattern is for a rose to be radially symmetrical with 5 pointed green sepals and 5 broad petals; the center of the flower shows numerous stamens and several pistils enclosed by a cup-like receptacle. Most roses are rather large (more than an inch [2.5 cm] across) and pink—but one common species, the multiflora rose, has small white flowers.

The fruit of the rose is known as a "hip." While most fruits are formed by the enlargement of the ovary, with roses, the receptacle that holds the ovaries expands and surrounds them. The rose hip has a dry center cavity filled with several seeds (achenes) and some stiff hairs. Outside of this is a thin layer of dry to pulpy flesh with a smooth, waxy outer skin. The end of the rose hip is constricted and nipple-like, often retaining the 5-lobed calyx. Rose flowers and hips may be borne singly or in clusters.

There are about 20 species of rose native to North America, plus a dozen or so more that have been introduced. While all of them can be used as food, their edible qualities are definitely not the same. It is beyond the scope of this book to discuss or identify all of the many species, but several will be mentioned in the text.

HABITAT

Roses are found wherever there is sunlight and moisture. This means they're pretty widespread. In fact, nearly everywhere. From the Rocky Mountains and the Pacific Coast, across the Great Plains to the woodlands of the East; from the Gulf of Mexico north to the tundra. There is even a desert rose. In all these places, you'll find wild roses in ravines, woodland openings, roadsides, meadows, dunes, pine and oak barrens, stream banks, beaches, brushy areas, and woodlots.

Composite range of the genus *Rosa*.

Roses, in general, like disturbance, and therefore are more common on steep ground or in naturally exposed situations, such as rocky outcroppings and seashores. They benefit from human-caused disturbances as well. Most species like well-drained soil, but a few are adapted to swamps. Roses are among the most ubiquitous wild edibles in North America.

HARVEST AND PREPARATION

There are three main parts of the rose used for human consumption: the petals, the hips, and the leaves.

Petals: Roses bloom in early summer, and at this time the petals may be available in enormous quantities. The petals can be added to salads or used as garnish with poultry or fish, imparting their beauty and unique flavor and fragrance. We don't often think of roses as a culinary herb, but they are widely used this way in many cultures, and the flavor actually blends well with many savory foods. Euell Gibbons (1962) even recommends blending a small amount of petals with eggs for omelets. Another traditional use of roses is to make rose water. This liquid is used to flavor drinks, baked goods, or syrups, or in glazes for meats. Rose water is made by boiling the petals in a drip still. I've never done this, but excellent instructions for this can be found in Gibbons's *Stalking the Wild Asparagus*.

Not all rose petals are equal; some are more bitter than others. I have found my local favorite to be *Rosa blanda*, a common species that grows in dense thickets that are often loaded with flowers. You'll have to try out your own local roses and see which you prefer. It is not vital to identify the species—you just need to recognize the ones you like.

Gibbons (1962) talks about cutting off the bases of the petals, which are whitish and have more bitterness than the rest of the petal. However, his account describes the use of cultivated roses, which have numerous petals layered in the flower. Wild roses have only 5 thin petals, and it is already hard enough to collect a quart of them. Having to clip each petal's base would more than double the work involved. I devote most of my life to foraging, but not *that* most. Luckily, some wild roses have petals good enough to not need such treatment.

If you want to make rose petal jam, don't skimp. I try for a loose 3 quarts in the collecting bowl, which will pack down to nearly a quart. You'll need a large patch of wild roses to get this many petals. I have no special trick to picking wild rose petals. Just relax and give yourself plenty of time to enjoy the outing. Some people cheat and use domestic roses, which have way more petals per flower and can be collected much more easily. Cheaters are not as likely to have a pleasant encounter with a fawn, a cuckoo, or a wild turkey, but otherwise they do alright.

The flavor of rose petals is easily lost by cooking, but you need to cook the pectin and sugar mixture to get it to jell. There is a way around this dilemma:

First, put about 1½ cups of hot apple juice concentrate into a blender with 2½ cups of sugar and blend for a minute, until the sugar is dissolved. Then fill the blender halfway with rose petals. Turn the blender on and use a soft spatula to push the rose petals into the liquid until they are all incorporated. Keep adding rose petals until you run out, or until you can't get the liquid to absorb any more of them. Pack as many in there as you possibly can, more than seems reasonably possible. Add little bits of liquid if you need to get all of your petals mixed in. Then take a saucepan and add 1½ cups of water, a quarter cup of lemon juice, and 3 cups of sugar, and whisk in a package of powdered pectin while bringing the mixture to a vigorous boil. Turn off the heat, dump your rose petal mixture into the hot pectin and sugar mixture all at once, and stir it vigorously. Pour it quickly into jars before it begins to set and apply the lids. This jam should not be considered sterile—keep it in the refrigerator for up to 9 weeks, or in the freezer for longer.

Hips: All rose hips are not the same, either. The flavor of most is bland and unexciting. I keep eating them, though, because they are famously high in vitamin C, and my mother taught me that overdosing on vitamin C is the secret to a happy life. The vitamin C (ascorbic acid) content varies dramatically from

The ripe hips of *R. blanda* in fall. Like most rose hips, these are bland.

one species to another, and also within species. In 153 samples from 14 rose species found in Britain, Pyke and Melville (1942) found ascorbic acid content ranging from 10–1,870 mg per 100 grams, with the poorest species averaging 80 mg—still 1½ times the vitamin C of oranges. Most species averaged over 400 mg per 100 grams, which is over 7 times the content of oranges. Two reported analyses of foreign rose hips showed 3,880 mg (about 70 times that of oranges) and 4,800 mg (about 90 times that of oranges). (The ascorbic acid value for oranges was taken from NNDSR 2015.)

I have been unable to find such comprehensive analyses for North American roses, but some of the Eurasian species are also native here, and several others are escaped and naturalized. There is no reason to think our roses wouldn't measure up. The USDA (NNDSR 2015) has one analysis for wild rose hips (from the northern Plains, species not specified) that shows 426 mg per 100 grams—again, remarkably high.

I used to think I was doing myself a world of good with rose hip tea, but analysis of tea made from dried hips (in Romania) showed that it only contained an insignificant 0.22–0.72 mg of ascorbic acid per 100 grams (Leahu et al. 2014). The ascorbic acid content of rose hip syrup was almost as low. The vitamin C content of jam was respectably high, but still less than 10% of what was found in the fresh hips. So, if you want to get a vitamin C boost from rose hips, it is best to eat them fresh and raw—although cooked pulp is still a pretty good source.

Many years ago, as a child, I found a rose bush with hips that were incredibly delicious, with a tang a bit like a dried tomato crossed with a raspberry, but with its own floral element. The bush grew in a park about four miles from home, and I'd sometimes trek there in autumn to nab a few of these heavenly fruits. Then, one day, the bush was mowed down, the victim of park "improvement." It took me almost 20 years to find another like it, growing in a ravine in northern Utah. It was dog rose, *Rosa canina*, a non-native species that occasionally becomes feral almost anywhere in North America. This is the rose hip widely used for jam, jelly, syrup, fruit leather, tea, and a host of other products, in Europe and Asia. In Sweden it is used to make the popular dessert soup *nyponsoppa*, in which the hips are boiled, strained, and then thickened with potato starch and sweetened. This is the species to which rose hips owe much of their culinary reputation.

Rosa rugosa is an ornamental rose that occasionally escapes, especially in sandy areas such as beaches. It has huge hips (sometimes an inch long) that have good flavor and thick flesh, making them easy to process. To my knowledge, we have no native roses to compare with either of these species. None of them taste

Opposite A fruiting branch of dog rose *R. canina*. This introduced rose has hips that are intensely and immensely delicious.

bad—they are just bland. Flour is bland, and so are potatoes. Bland is a canvas upon which you paint your flavors through the application of culinary skill. My friend Arthur Haines collects hips from swamp rose *Rosa palustris* and then dries them whole, grinds them into flour (the seeds included), and adds this to baked goods as a mildly flavored and nutritious amendment.

In using rose hips, you face a straining dilemma. This fruit has several parts you will want to get rid of: a stem at one end and calyx remains at the other, several hard seeds inside, and some stiff hairs around the seeds. With larger rose hips, you can cut off both ends, then cut them in half and scoop out the insides with a tiny measuring spoon. But this is just not practical with the small rose hips of many wild species. If they are reasonably pulpy, they can be boiled and mashed and then run through a strainer. This latter process may or may not take care of the irritating hairs in the hips, which vary by species. Some people

Rosa rugosa hips from an ornamental planting outside a hospital. I picked these in February. Separating the pulp from the seeds was laborious, but the result was a delicious fruit spread.

complain of rose hip hairs irritating the output end of the alimentary canal. (I'm paraphrasing the actual complaint.) I have had them irritate my mouth, but never the other end. Arthur Haines experiences no such problems when he grinds up the whole fruit.

Once you have the rose hip pulp, however you achieve this, you can use it in a variety of ways. If you want to make fruit spread, you don't have to add a bunch of sugar or pectin—the pulp is already thick and spreadable. If you don't have enough to make a batch, or if it is bland, you can always add it to another spread, or apple butter, right at the end of cooking, so you don't lose much of the vitamin C. You can add rose hips to baked goods or even fruit salad. And of course, you can eat them on autumn hikes, carefully nibbling the pulp off the outside and discarding the hairy interior—doing your duty as seed disseminator that way.

Leaves: Rose leaves can be used to infuse a tea, either dried, fermented, or fresh. The young leaves have a milder, more pleasant flavor. This tea has some of the bitterness of rose petals, and a green essence from the leaves. It is not among my favorite infusions, based on flavor; people drink it more for its medicinal virtues than for the pure pleasure of imbibing it. But I'll gladly down a glass if you give it to me.

A wild rose thicket is a delight to have, so spare the mower in some unused corner of the yard, if you can. Of course, the spectacular blooms of early summer will brighten your days. But don't forget the yellowthroats who will nest there, singing you awake before visiting your cherry tree to pluck off leaf rollers and aphids. Don't forget the cottontails who dash that way for cover at the passing shadow of every hawk. Don't forget the bumblebees and jumping mice. You won't be able to forget the rose petal jam, and neither will the queen when she stops over for tea.

Sassafras

Sassafras albidum

On Thanksgiving morning, my uncle Andy took me deer hunting along the Muskegon River in western Michigan, posting me in an oak woods at the edge of a cedar swamp with a scoped 20-gauge pump. As I waited for deer, I was pondering the warm fall and the fact that the ground hadn't frozen yet, recalling the stunning lemony scent of the sassafras twigs my uncle John had taught me to chew, wondering what the roots smelled like. I had noticed a bunch of sassafras saplings in the clearing near Andy's shack, and they were calling me. After a few hours I got bored, went up the hill, laid down the gun, and started grubbing up roots. Andy found me there a while later—covered in sandy mud and snow, my hands numb from scratching in the near-frozen soil, crouched over a small pile of dirty root sections—and laughed with bewilderment. But I left with a trophy.

I got hauled to the home of some other relative that evening, and I toted my bundle of precious roots with me. A sink, a stove, and a saucepan was all I could

The leaves of sassafras can be ovate and unlobed, or deeply lobed on one side, or both. In any case they have toothless margins.

think of. Today, when I inhale the steam from a bubbling pot of sassafras, I can still see the water turning ruddy in that first batch of sassafras root I boiled all those years ago at some aunt's house on Thanksgiving. I don't remember what year it was, whose house it was, what we had for dinner, or who was there. I just remember that there was dull-red pot liquor swirling around a few boiling sticks, and how pleasantly surprised I was that it smelled like root beer.

DESCRIPTION

Sassafras is a small to medium-sized tree, crooked and rugged in appearance, that often grows in clones. It may reach 50–80 feet (15–25 m) in height with trunks more than 2 feet (60 cm) in diameter, but typical trees are 20–45 feet (6–14 m) tall and 4–10 inches (10–25 cm) thick. The bark of mature trunks is brown, thick, corky, and deeply furrowed. The bark of new twigs and saplings is one of the best identifying features; it is smooth and distinctly bright green, with scattered small corky lenticels. The terminal buds are large and egg-shaped, green, with usually 4 overlapping scales, each with a dark margin; lateral buds are much smaller.

Sassafras leaves are alternate, rather thin, typically 2.5–4.5 inches (6–11 cm) long, with margins lacking teeth, and come in a few common forms. They may be ovate, or they may have one lobe on either side (mitten-shaped), or a lobe on both sides (3-lobed). All three shapes are typically found on each tree—often even on the same twig. However, lobes are more common and deeper on saplings and stump sprouts, and in full sun; mature trees often lack lobes. In fall, sassafras leaves turn to a deep orange-red. The combination of variously mitten-lobed leaves and toothless margins distinguishes this tree from any other in North America.

The trunk of a mature sassafras tends to be crooked. The bark has thick gray ridges.

Sassafras flowers in spring, in a cluster of clusters.

Flowers appear in early spring, just before the leaves emerge. They are found in multiple racemes from the branch tips. The flowers are very small and dull yellow, and have 6 spreading sepals. Fruits are about 0.3 inches (8 mm) long, oblong, dark blue, and mealy, with one proportionately large seed in the center; they ripen in late summer. They sit at the ends of bright red pedicels about an inch (2.5 cm) long that widen dramatically at the end where they attach to the fruit.

HABITAT

Sassafras is a rather short-lived pioneer tree that does best in full sun and after disturbances such as logging, fires, and windstorms. It is found along fence lines and roadsides, forest edges, in young woods, and in old fields. In the woods, sassafras does best under thin canopies that let some light through, and is often prevalent in the understory of sparse forests of oak or pine. This

Sassafras *Sassafras albidum*.

tree is most common on well-drained, poor soils, especially sand. It abounds in sandy regions such as the New Jersey Pine Barrens and western Michigan, but foragers throughout its range should have little trouble finding this common tree.

SASSAFRAS ROOT

The most commonly used part of sassafras is the bark of the root, which was the primary flavoring of traditional root beer. The scent is unmistakable and wonderful. You can use roots of any size, but big trees are hard to dig up. I look for small saplings up to 1.5 inches (4 cm) in diameter. At a construction site or along a new logging road, you might be able to score a bunch of roots easily, or perhaps peel the bark from larger roots that have been exposed by heavy machinery.

Sassafras roots can be collected at any time of year. Some claim that they are most potent when the trees are dormant, but the flavor is always present. Wash the roots thoroughly, then dry them out of the sun. Once dried, they

Sassafras roots of various sizes, washed and cut into sections for drying.

can be stored in an airtight container for a very long time with minimal loss of quality. I prefer to work with sassafras roots from pencil to thumb thickness, which can be easily cut or broken—these I use whole. With larger roots I shave off the bark, which reduces the volume and makes handling easier.

Making sassafras "tea" is utter simplicity: Put chunks of the root or root bark into a pot of water and boil until you get the flavor you want. This can be done with either fresh root or dried, but fresh roots impart flavor more quickly. I boil my sassafras when I want a drink and leave the roots in the covered pot to soak between boilings. One set of roots will give you several batches of tea; I generally boil them in four separate waters. The first water will have a stronger, somewhat bitter flavor. In my opinion, the second boiling tastes the best. Sassafras tea can be sweetened and fermented into root beer, with or without additional flavorings.

IS SASSAFRAS SAFE?

This question has been haunting foragers for more than half a century. About 85% of the essential oil extracted from sassafras root is an oil known as safrole (Kamdem and Gage, 1995). On December 3, 1960, the FDA declared this compound a "weak hepatic carcinogen" and prohibited

> food containing any added safrole, oil of sassafras, isosafrole, or dihydrosafrole, as such, or food containing any safrole, oil of sassafras, isosafrole, or dihydrosafrole, e.g., sassafras bark, which is intended solely or primarily as a vehicle for imparting such substances to another food, e.g., sassafras tea. (21 CFR, Sect 189.180)

Seasonings containing smaller amounts of safrole were not banned; these include black pepper, cocoa, mace, cinnamon, nutmeg, tarragon, basil, ginger, star anise, fennel, parsley, bay laurel, dill, allspice, and clove (Cummings 2012). Safrole is also present in most commercially available sodas (Choong and Lin 2001) and many alcoholic beverages. Many foragers have heard of the carcinogenic properties of safrole and are apprehensive about consuming sassafras tea. It doesn't help that the danger has been exaggerated to ridiculous proportions on many websites. I get it. Cancer is a terrifying, hideous disease. That's why, as a long-time consumer of sassafras, I felt compelled to investigate its carcinogenic risk before writing about the plant.

The decision to ban safrole was made based upon weak findings and very limited data from an FDA study (Long et al. 1961) in which groups of rats were fed safrole at different doses for two years. Only at the highest dose, 5,000 ppm of diet (the equivalent of me drinking about 25 cups of sassafras tea per day[6]), did rats show a significantly elevated frequency of malignant liver tumors. Two other studies were reported about the same time: Homburger et al. (1961) found benign liver tumors in protein-malnourished rats fed safrole as 1% of the diet for 200 days. (To get that dose I would have to consume 50 eight-ounce cups of sassafras tea per day.) Abbott et al. (1961) found that when rats were continuously fed safrole as 1170 ppm of diet, some of them developed cancers after 22 months.

The studies demonstrating the carcinogenic properties of safrole and its derivatives in rats and mice used pure safrole—not traditionally prepared sassafras tea. Despite the widespread use of sassafras as a beverage, there have been no studies demonstrating a link between sassafras consumption and cancer in humans, nor have there been any individual cases of human cancer attributed to sassafras tea. The studies that induced cancer in rodents used extraordinarily high doses of safrole—doses that could not be realistically consumed through sassafras tea.

Long et al. (1963) fed safrole to rats as 0.5% of the diet for 2 years, after which liver cancers developed in 14 of 47 animals. (This dose is 350 times my estimated consumption.) Another study feeding safrole to rats at this same dose for 8–10 months (Borchert, Wislocki, et al. 1973) found a low incidence of liver carcinomas. But at 10% of this dose (still 35 times my estimated consumption), the incidence of liver cancer was actually lower among the rats fed safrole than

---

6   Here and elsewhere I use the safrole content of traditional sassafras tea from Cummings 2012: 188 mg per 300 ml. As explained later, I suspect that the actual safrole content is lower, but this is the only figure available. The estimated equivalents for my own diet are based on consumption of .75 kg of food, dry weight, per day (roughly 3200 calories). My estimated consumption of sassafras tea is one 8-ounce glass every 10–14 days.

among controls that ingested none (Long et al. 1963). Liu et al. (1999) showed minor oxidative liver DNA damage that was repaired after 15 days in rats given a single dose of 500 or 1,000 mg of safrole per kg of body weight. For me to get an equivalent dose, I would have to drink 270 or 540 eight-ounce cups of sassafras tea *at one time.* Dogs given doses roughly comparable to a human drinking a glass of sassafras tea 6 days a week for 6 years showed minor liver damage, but not cancer (Hagan et al. 1965). *That's what happens from drinking alcohol.* In another study, dogs fed safrole continuously for 7 years showed initial signs of liver damage that eventually disappeared while they remained on the safrole regimen (Weinberg and Sternberg 1966), suggesting that they adapted to the toxin. There are also studies demonstrating that safrole and its derivatives bind with DNA and other molecules in rodents in ways that suggest carcinogenicity (Daimon et al. 1998). One of these even uses low doses that might be comparable to what you'd get from drinking sassafras tea (Gupta et al. 1993). What this means in terms of human risk is entirely unclear.

Safrole itself is not believed to be carcinogenic (Borchert et al. 1973A,B). In the body, safrole is metabolized into several related compounds. One of these metabolites is 1'-hydroxysafrole (Borchert et al. 1973A), which is associated with cancer induction (Borchert et al. 1973B). 1'-hydroxysafrole can be metabolized further into 1'-sulfoöxysafrole—believed to be the major ultimate carcinogen (Boberg et al. 1983). After safrole was administered to both rats and mice, the level of 1'-hydroxysafrole in the mice was dramatically higher than that in rats (Borchert 1972).

With all the hype about safrole, there has surprisingly been only one study investigating its metabolism in humans (Benedetti et al. 1977). These researchers found that 1'-hydroxysafrole was found in the urine of rats given safrole, but not in the urine of humans. Although more research needs to be done, *thus far, the metabolite responsible for the carcinogenic properties of safrole has not been found in humans.* Humans quickly processed and eliminated the safrole they ingested, but the rats given large doses did not; safrole accumulated in their livers and kidneys. This suggests a detoxification pathway that becomes saturated at high doses. Although the doses of safrole given to humans were much lower than those given to rats, the researchers were confident that their methods should have detected 1'-hydroxysafrole in human urine if it was produced at a ratio comparable to that in rats. This suggests that linear extrapolations from high rodent doses are probably not applicable to low-dose exposures in humans.

What does cancer in rats and mice given massive doses of purified safrole mean for humans who drink sassafras tea? Hirono (1987) says, "The probability that safrole and related carcinogens are possible causes of human cancer does not appear high since they are relatively weak carcinogens in animals." American paranoia about wild foods seems to play a role in our overreaction to safrole's toxicity, and it is probably not coincidence that the above conclusion was reached by a Japanese expert—or that it made American safrole researchers uncomfortable (see Hirono 1987).

Carcinogen researchers Ames and Gold (2000) warn us that giving rodents massive doses of chemicals to test for carcinogenicity might be counterproductive and misleading. They point out that approximately half of all natural chemicals tested in this fashion prove to be rodent carcinogens. Such chemicals are found in every person's diet—in apples, bananas, oranges, cherries, chocolate, coffee, grapefruit, grapes, peaches, pears, potatoes, raspberries, tomatoes, garlic, and carrots, to name a few. The HERP (human equivalent of rodent potency) index is a document designed by biochemist Bruce Ames, and made available online by the National Institutes of Health (NIH, n.d.), to address the relative dangers posed by known carcinogens to which we are commonly exposed. The authors state, "There is an enormous background of naturally-occurring rodent carcinogens in average consumption of common foods," and conclude with this summary:

> The HERP analysis demonstrates the ubiquitous exposures to rodent carcinogens in everyday life. . . . A high percentage of both natural and synthetic chemicals are rodent carcinogens. . . . Tumor incidence data from rodent bioassays are not adequate to assess low-dose risk. . . . Caution is necessary in drawing conclusions from the occurrence in the diet of natural chemicals that are rodent carcinogens. It is not argued here that these dietary exposures are necessarily of much relevance to human cancer.

If the risk of drinking an 8-ounce cup of sassafras once per week is calculated according to the HERP index, using 148 mg safrole (per Cummings 2012), the "possible hazard %" is 0.6. This is admittedly a little higher than the carcinogenic hazard of breathing the air in a conventional home (0.4), but less than half the hazard of breathing the air in a mobile home (1.4); it is only one-sixth the carcinogenic hazard of average per-capita consumption of alcoholic beverages (3.6), and one-twentieth the hazard of taking a daily sleeping pill (12). And the HERP value for safrole assumes that the carcinogenic effect on humans is the same as that for mice—yet research suggests that mice are actually far more susceptible.

Sassafras tea is not safrole. Since the federal regulation of safrole targets sassafras, it is remarkable that no research on the safrole content of sassafras tea was done before this law was enacted. Thirty-two years later, FDA research (Heikes, 1994) finally looked at the percentage of safrole in dried root bark: 8 samples were found to contain .03% to 1.76% safrole. Kamdem and Gage

(1995) found the fresh root bark to contain about 3% oil, which was about 85% safrole. (The smaller amount in Heikes' samples probably indicates loss through volatilization.) Traditionally brewed sassafras tea was not tested for safrole content until more than 50 years after the ban was enacted. Cummings (2012) found that 300 ml (about 10 ounces) of boiled sassafras tea contained an average of 188 mg of safrole, or 3.14 mg per kg of body weight for a person weighing 60 kg. Foragers owe Cummings a debt of gratitude for her insightful research. However, the light-yellowish tea that she prepared and tested differed from the prevailing tradition among sassafras users, who almost uniformly report boiling to a deep red-brown, and often mention boiling the same roots in multiple waters.

In Cummings's study, the tea produced by a non-traditional method of stirring ground sassafras bark in cold water contained much more safrole than traditionally boiled tea—yet it lacked the sassafras odor. This indicates that safrole *per se* is actually not the key flavoring compound in sassafras tea. Sassafras roots contain at least 35 volatile constituents, many of which are highly flavored essential oils (Sethi et al. 1976; Kamdem and Gage, 1995). Sassafras tea also contains water-soluble flavoring compounds. And it has byproducts from the breakdown of safrole (Reynertson et al. 2005).

Safrole is reduced or eliminated through boiling, due to a combination of volatilization (evaporation) and breakdown. Unfortunately, the details of these processes in traditional sassafras tea preparation have not been studied. Although Cummings's results suggest a substantial loss of safrole through boiling, our best information comes from the study of a tropical relative, *Cinnamomum carolinense*, the bark of which is also traditionally boiled to make a beverage. Reynertson et al. (2005) tested tea traditionally made by boiling the finely shaved bark of this tree for 20 minutes, finding that it contained *no detectable safrole*. Alcohol extracts of the same bark had high levels of safrole. They tested the bark after it had been boiled, and only a trace of safrole remained, showing that nearly all of the safrole had boiled out into the water. They boiled bark in water that was spiked with safrole, and there was still no safrole in the finished tea. The obvious conclusion is that boiling eliminated the safrole. To confirm this, they added pure safrole to water and boiled it for 20 minutes, after which no safrole was found, but new compounds were present. The safrole was gone, and some portion of it had broken down.

Cummings's boiled tea, unlike that of Reynertson's group, did contain some safrole. This may be because her samples were covered during boiling, partially preventing loss through volatilization—to which safrole is highly susceptible. Also, Cummings used root pieces larger than the shaved bark in the Reynertson study; these may have retained safrole for longer, preventing it from being broken down or volatilized before release from the bark tissues.

We need more research on this matter, but the evidence implies that once all the safrole has boiled out of the root, longer boiling should dramatically reduce the safrole content of the tea, especially if the pot is uncovered. Sassafras tea from second, third, and fourth boilings of the same roots should also have reduced safrole—and perhaps none at all. As mentioned earlier, the first boiling of sassafras has a strong, somewhat medicinal flavor. I prefer the flavor of the second and third boilings, which clearly have a different chemical profile. If you are concerned about safrole in your sassafras, you may want to discard the first water and then boil subsequent batches for an extended time before drinking.

Safrole was banned based on limited evidence and a flawed model for understanding carcinogenic risk. Research to retroactively justify this action has not been convincing. The scientific evidence regarding sassafras tea is weak and incomplete, but what we know suggests that moderate or occasional consumption entails negligible risk. That makes sense, because millions of people have done this for untold generations.

LEAVES

If you are still worried over safrole, you've still got the top half of the tree to work with. Sassafras leaves are wholly or nearly safrole-free (Carlson and Thompson 1997). They have a lemony flavor entirely distinct from that of the root, and a scent reminiscent of Froot Loops cereal. The tender new leaves in spring are what you want. Next time you are on a date, eat them right off the tree, no hands, like a giraffe; or better yet, tighten your lips, stick out your chin, and show your neck tendons in your best imitation of a tortoise. I guess you can use your hands if you want to. Or you can throw the fresh leaves into salads or cooked dishes. Make sure to do it sparingly, however, as the flavor is strong and can overpower other ingredients. The tender, fast-growing stems of spring shoots can be peeled and eaten raw—they are outrageously good. If you want a second date, ignore my first advice and give your amorous interest one of these shoots. In spring I also like to nibble sassafras flowers. Their flavor is similar to that of the leaves, but even a hint better. They make an unforgettable garnish.

Sassafras leaves are actually collected commercially and turned into "gumbo filé," a powder used for thickening and flavoring gumbo. Okra is the ingredient most commonly used to give gumbo its characteristic thickness—so pleasant when hot and so slimy when cold. Powdered sassafras leaf has a similar mucilaginous quality, but it imparts an entirely different flavor to the soup, which some cooks prefer over that of okra, or use in addition to it. I love okra, but I wouldn't make a gumbo without the delicious and irreplaceable flavor of sassafras leaf.

Above left Newly emerging sassafras leaves in spring, at a good size to get them for soup or salad. Note the green bark of the twigs. **Above right** A sassafras shoot in midsummer, coming up in a mowed area. All the leaves are tender. I collected these for making gumbo filé. The stems of shoots can also be peeled and eaten raw—a mouthwatering lemony treat.

The sassafras gumbo filé that is available commercially is, in my experience, much inferior to the homemade stuff. It seems to be mass-produced from mature leaves with poor flavor, and it is often gritty. Several brands are mixed with thyme, although pure sassafras is available. To make your own filé, gather tender young leaves in spring, or in early summer from the tips of rapidly growing shoots. If you miss those opportunities, find a place where the plants get mowed down some time in the summer, and there will be nice shoots with tender leaves. Spread them on screens to dry in a hot porch, vehicle, or attic; or put them in a food dehydrator, in an oven on low heat, or near a wood stove. You want to dry them as fast as possible so they don't have time to undergo enzymatic toughening. They darken when dried—especially when dried slowly—and lose much of their lemony aroma, but they retain enough of it to add that special flavor to your gumbo. Once the leaves are dry, you can powder them by rubbing between the palms of your hands and then sifting through a strainer or colander; or to get a finer powder, use a dry blender. Seal this filé tightly in a jar and you'll be able to put the taste of spring sassafras in your soup at any time of year.

You can also make filé with fresh sassafras leaves—just stick them in a blender with water, then add that slimy green liquid to your soup pot. Fresh leaves retain more of the lemony flavor.

Sassafras was one of the early exports from North America to Europe, a valuable commodity that played a key role in European settlement of our continent. For decades, the drink enjoyed a reputation for extensive medicinal virtue. Eventually, its marvelous flavor developed into a legendary soft drink generating billions in sales. I doubt we'll ever find it so useful again, but I'll never stop eating, drinking, or sniffing it.

How much safrole is in this rich, red-brown sassafras brew? I don't know. I'm guessing it contains very little, because it is the second boiling of small root chips. In any case, I'm going to drink it. The safrole content of a glass of sassafras tea is probably highly variable. Safrole evaporates, so dry roots have less safrole than fresh ones. The longer they've been dried, the less safrole they contain—especially if they are kept where air flows freely. Safrole also breaks down with boiling. Due to both evaporation and breakdown, the longer the brew is boiled, the less safrole it contains. Safrole is one of many components of the root, and makes up only a small percentage of even a freshly dug root. The red color does not come from safrole. Much of the scent and flavoring does not come from safrole, either. Considering all the tens of millions of dollars spent on hundreds of studies researching safrole over six decades, isn't it odd that nobody has brewed a simple tea like this and then tested its safrole content? That should have been an early research priority.

Shepherd's Purse

Capsella bursa-pastoris

Some people say that timing is everything. Real estate agents say that location is what matters. Foraging requires one to master both.

Robert Wiedmaier is a well-known chef in Washington, DC, with a high-end downtown restaurant specializing in Belgian cuisine. Robert and I took a walk one early March to collect ingredients for a gourmet meal that he would prepare back in his kitchen. From the front door of the restaurant, we spied

Lush spring leaves in a dense patch of shepherd's purse. This makes the finest salad green, fried green, or potherb among all of our common weeds, in my opinion.

luxuriant growth of chickweed just across the street—which was a good start, but I knew we needed to find something more substantial. Edible weeds were easy to find in sidewalk cracks, lawns, old flower beds, parks, the decomposing paper and windblown leaves accumulated along a fence—but I was holding out for something exceptional.

A few blocks from the restaurant, we hit the jackpot: a clump of perhaps two dozen shepherd's purse stems in exactly the prime stage for picking. They were growing in the little ring of dirt surrounding one of those poor concrete-bound street trees, plus in a few pavement cracks nearby. We filled a plastic bag with the choicest specimens and returned to the restaurant after stopping to grab some young Siberian elm samaras.

Robert took a tiny fry pan with olive oil and a teaspoon of finely chopped licorice fern rhizomes and placed it over a flame nearly large enough to engulf it. When the oil was hot, he tossed in one very large, fresh, wild scallop and browned the outside, moving the shellfish constantly in the sizzling oil. He cut the seared scallop into thin slices and threw these into a warmed bowl, followed by a handful each of chickweed greens and shepherd's purse shoots. (Yes, we washed them!) After grinding in some salt and pepper and adding strips of Parmesan cheese sliced from a block the size of a small boulder, he tossed the ingredients just enough to warm up the greens and coat everything with seasonings, hot oil, and scallop juice. It was perhaps the best "warm sallet" I have ever eaten. Which is no surprise, since it contained the finest assortment of ultra-fresh ingredients—foremost among them a much-hated weed of sidewalk cracks and crop fields.

DESCRIPTION

Shepherd's purse is an annual or winter annual with a dense basal rosette of elongated, deeply lobed, dandelion-like leaves 2–7 inches (5-18 cm) long. The lower of these leaves tend to hug the ground, and dense clumps of shepherd's purse often form a complete covering over the soil. Shepherd's purse leaves can be told from dandelion by their deeper and more regularly spaced lobes, their lack of latex when broken, and by the stretchy "strings" that run the length of the midvein and are visible when the leaves are pulled apart. If you look closely, you'll see that there are tiny needle-like hairs scattered about the surface of the shepherd's purse leaf, especially near the margins. Stem leaves are elongated and unlobed, the uppermost being very wide at their base and clasping the stem.

Opposite A nice patch of shepherd's purse with both greens and shoots ready to be picked. Bend each stalk to find the tender point, and pick only the portion above that. Nothing intentionally grown in your garden is better than this.

Shepherd's purse in bloom, showing
the uniquely shaped seedpods
and the tiny white flowers.

Flower stalks are usually multiple, and in good soil they might reach 30 inches (75 cm) in height. Their alternate leaves get smaller and less lobed going up the stem. Partway up the stalk, it typically splits into several branches, each of which terminates in a raceme of flowers. Shepherd's purse begins blooming when its stem is still meristematic. The flowers are tiny, white, and have 4 petals. After fertilization they produce small pods that have a distinct triangular or heart-like shape. These resemble those flat green triangular purses that you always see shepherds carrying around.

HABITAT

Shepherd's purse is found throughout North America wherever humans inhabit. It grows in moist, disturbed soil, and is one of the more prevalent weeds of yards, gardens, waste places, empty lots, building sites, and agricultural fields. It needs ample sunlight to thrive.

Shepherd's purse *Capsella bursa-pastoris*.

HARVEST AND PREPARATION

My friend, and wild cook extraordinaire, Hank Shaw, once asked me what I thought was the most underrated wild edible. I did not hesitate to answer, "Shepherd's purse." This herb is among the unsung heroes of the foraging world: despised by farmers, destroyed by gardeners, ignored by most gatherers. But I think it is simply the finest of all our ubiquitous weedy greens. This plant, rather than the dandelion, should be touted as the gateway weed to foraging. That's no knock on dandelion—one of my favorite spring greens—but shepherd's purse is not an acquired taste, nor does it have any strong flavor that needs to be "masked" by oil or cheese (Smellf, 1987).

Sure, you can find an old, tough, grit-splattered midsummer leaf of shepherd's purse if you want, then masticate it begrudgingly, the overdeveloped flavor matching the uncouthness of the cud it drips from. But that's not foraging; it's fulfillment of a weed-hater's prophecy. Here's a better idea: Look for only the choicest shepherd's purse greens. They will be in moist soil laden with organic matter—perhaps your own garden or backyard. They will be lush with large, splendid foliage sometime during the cool weather of a southern winter, or early spring in the North; the lower leaves will form an unbroken covering over the soil so that no pummeling raindrop can splatter the mud. Don't pick those lower leaves that hug the ground; carefully cut the ones that stand upright above them. Put these up against any salad green you can find—wild or domestic— and you will understand why the few who really know this plant rave about it.

Most edible greens from the mustard family are pungent and strong, but shepherd's purse is mild enough to form the base of a salad, combining really

well with other cool-season greens such as dandelion, dock, spring beauty, and chickweed. As a potherb, it can be enjoyed by itself after a brief boiling or steaming. Fried, the greens are simply fantastic. But you need to watch out for dirt. Shepherd's purse leaves are faintly hairy and therefore often hold grit, even after rinsing. Shepherd's purse greens are not just delicious, they're good for you. John Kallas (2010) calls them "a nutritional powerhouse." According to figures he compiled, the leaves are exceptionally rich in omega-3 fatty acids, calcium, iron, and zinc, and are a very good source of vitamin C.

These superb greens are only the second best part of shepherd's purse. If you really want to try a gourmet vegetable that isn't for sale, pick some tender shepherd's

A young, tender shepherd's purse shoot.

purse shoots. The nicest shepherd's purse shoots are found in the cool weather of winter or early spring, when most garden plants refuse to grow but many of their hardy wild cousins thrive. As with chickweed, this plant produces luxurious growth during long periods of weather that is above freezing but with short, cool days that do not stimulate flowering. Get the shoots before they toughen, before they flower—before *you* even notice them, if that's possible. Stalks with pods are easy to find, but wiry and worthless.

These shoots are great to snack on raw, or in salads. They can be steamed or boiled like asparagus and served in the simplest way, and their rich flavor will not disappoint. I like them chopped into short sections, stir-fried with peppers and onions, and served over seasoned rice. Or, like Mr. Wiedmaier, you can apply some culinary creativity and reap the rewards of using the world's finest ingredients.

In all my years of foraging and reading about wild food, I have never heard mention of shepherd's purse shoots, much less the kind of raving that I am here engaged in. Sometimes I feel like I am the only one to have noticed that this is among the most delectable vegetables ever discovered. But I'm not. The stems are considered a delicacy in northern and eastern China, and they are cultivated in and around Shanghai (Hu 2005). In the latter region, shepherd's purse (called *qi cai*) is considered to be a premiere vegetable for won ton filling. It is easy to find recipes and discussion of this use online.

Basal rosette of shepherd's purse in early winter, trying desperately to flower. (It didn't accomplish that until early the following spring.)

Shepherd' purse roots.

The Chinese are very observant when it comes to vegetables, and they have another use for the plant which seems entirely unknown in North America, also recorded by Hu (2005): The small roots of overwintering rosettes are gathered in fall and used in meat stuffings of Chinese dumplings. Hu reports that the roots are aromatic and slightly spicy; in my experience, however, they are neither. Their flavor is excellent and very similar to that of the shoots, although they tend to be small and a bit stringy. In certain climates and growing conditions, I imagine they might grow to larger proportions and be a much more practical vegetable.

This reminds me of a curious situation regarding shepherd's purse. Many references state that the roots can be used as a ginger substitute. However, their flavor is not even remotely like ginger—not by the wildest and wiggliest stretch—and nobody who makes this claim does so based upon firsthand experience. John Kallas (2010) sleuthed out the actual explanation for the origin of the claim: it just so happened that the shepherd's purse entry in Nelson Coon's 1958 book *Using Wayside Plants* is juxtaposed to the wild ginger entry, in such a way that another author, H. D. Harrington (1967) got confused and read some information from the wrong page, which actually applied to wild ginger, and reported it for shepherd's purse. Since then, dozens of wild food authors, down to the present day, have copied and perpetuated this honest mistake, without thinking to try the root themselves and see if it really tastes like ginger. Spoiler: It doesn't.

Agricultural institutions classify shepherd's purse as one of the worst weeds on Earth. Billions of dollars are spent annually trying to spray it with poisons, till it under, pull it out, or burn it off. It is so despised by farmers that it has been given the name "pickpocket" in some regions. But just the thought of it makes my mouth water, and somehow, I can never find enough of it.

Sochan (Cut-Leaf Coneflower)

Rudbeckia laciniata

Sochan is an ancient Cherokee secret—and a reminder of the preciousness of cultural knowledge. I say "secret" not in the strictest sense. The Cherokee never tried to hide the use of this plant, and they were not the only Native Americans to whom it was an important food. Yet the course of history and the vagaries of culture made it secret in the sense that the use of sochan eventually became practically unknown outside of Cherokee society and Cherokee country. It was, like most good secrets, kept not by secrecy, but by ignorance.

This is not a rare or obscure plant—quite the opposite. It is among the most widespread and common wildflowers native to North America. Although common in the Cherokee heartland of southern Appalachia, it is equally abundant north to New England, and perhaps more abundant in the rich soils of the Midwest. It is also prolific along streams in foothills and lower slopes in the Rocky Mountains, in wooded stream valleys of the Deep South and the Great Plains, and north into Canada. Most outdoors men and women have trodden it thousands of times.

Sochan is not bashful; in striking fashion its tapered golden rays droop from large heads held high on long, naked stalks, turning heads on country roadsides and beside the path to most every fishing hole. Cultivars of it are sold in perennial nurseries, often under the sensational name of "golden glow," and it features prominently in wildflower gardens from coast to coast. It may be the most ubiquitous American plant that has never earned a widely-accepted common name—it is listed by a boggling array of contrived sobriquets in wildflower books: cut-leaf coneflower, tall coneflower, wild golden glow, green-headed coneflower, green coneflower, or in the South, simply coneflower.

This plant is still among the best-known wild edibles in the southern Appalachians, as normal as fiddleheads in New England, or miner's lettuce in California. To give you some perspective on how basic a wild food this is, consider that in *Cherokee Cooklore* (Ulmer and Beck 1951), *so cha ni* is one of only fifteen wild plant foods mentioned—and since it has no common name in English, it is translated "for palefaces" simply as "vegetables." Hamel and Chiltoskey (1975) list it among the five important leafy vegetables used by the Cherokee, along with ramps, cresses, poke, and lamb's quarters. In Asheville, the greens are sometimes sold at the farmers' market. Yet somehow sochan is absent from

Opposite A flowering colony of sochan in a ditch. This "golden glow" is hard to miss when in bloom.

346

nearly every major reference on wild edibles in North America. It is time to bring it to a wider audience.

DESCRIPTION

Sochan has only a weak resemblance to its well-known cousin, the black-eyed-susan *Rudbeckia hirta*. In bloom, it can be shrugged off as just another of our many tall, sunflower-like plants. Sochan stands out, however, even at a high-speed glance, by its tall clumped stems, drooping petals, and deeply lobed leaves. Learn to look for these three characteristics and you will see it more and more on your late summer excursions.

Sochan is a perennial that forms clumps through spreading rhizomes. Early in spring, it sends up a rosette of basal leaves on long petioles with a channeled upper side. Since the root system is multi-crowned, several rosettes often grow very close together, which can make the clump appear like a jumbled mess of leaves. Large leaves may have a petiole up to 16 inches (40 cm) long and a blade equally long, but smaller leaves predominate. Most leaves are *almost*, but not quite, divided into 3 primary sections near the base—but some are fully divided. The leaf sections are long and narrow, widening gradually and usually further lobed toward the tip. The middle section of the leaf is often nearly divided again into 3 more sections. The deep sinuses in the leaf account for "cut-leaf" in one of the common names; this is also the meaning of the species name *laciniata*. The leaf surface is slightly hairy; when young it feels smooth, but with age it becomes rough.

Flower stalks appear in late spring or early summer, eventually reaching 4–8 feet (1.2–2.5 m) tall and 0.4–0.7 inches (10–18 mm) thick. These are erect and slightly zigzagged between the alternate leaves, and remain unbranched except near the top. Leaves are more prominent on the lower third of the stalk and decrease in size as you ascend. Lower leaves have long petioles while the uppermost are sessile. The petiole surface is nearly smooth and ranges from hairless to quite hairy, often with a faint white bloom. Lower leaves are eventually dropped as the stem grows taller.

Typical stalks produce 4–17 flower heads; these are large and erect, not turning sideways like a sunflower to display the full glory of the bloom. Each head is borne at the top of a long stalk—sometimes as much as 14 inches (35 mm)—that is mostly naked excepting an occasional reduced leaf near the base. Greenish-yellow disk florets in the center of the head are arranged on a protruding receptacle the shape of a blunt cone that points vertically. Around the base of this cone is a ring of petal-like yellow ray florets about 2 inches (5 cm) long, tapered toward the base, hanging at about a 45° angle. Blooming occurs in mid to late summer in the North, but early autumn in the South.

Sochan, when vigorous and healthy in ample sunlight, produces three or four flushes of leaves per year. All of them are edible, if tender. These are the autumn/winter leaves; the dying petioles of the late summer leaves can be seen on the outside of the rosette.

When sochan finishes blooming, the tops die back and the roots send out a new flush of basal leaves. These are wider than the basal leaves produced in spring, and often very large. In shady areas, the autumn leaves may be small, and are often confused with those of waterleaf—which have fine hairs and more pointed lobes. Fortunately, there is no danger in confusing these plants, as waterleaf is similarly edible.

Sochan is easy to identify in bloom, but admittedly a bit tricky when young. Since it is perennial, you can mark the spot and return to it later for harvest. None of the similar-looking plants are particularly dangerous, though. The most important toxic plants that one might confuse with sochan are the buttercups, of which there are many species. Most buttercups have much smaller leaves than sochan, and no buttercups grow flower stalks that are even remotely comparable in size. However, a few buttercups have larger leaves that are similar in shape to those of sochan, and share its habitat. The differences can be subtle (see photos). Buttercup leaves are bitter and distasteful, and not as aromatic as sochan. Accidentally eating a leaf is unlikely to hurt you, but you don't want to make a meal of them.

HABITAT

Sochan likes rich, moist soil in light shade or full sun. It is most typical of streamside forests and meadows, floodplains, shrub swamps, fencerows, and forest edges in rich valleys—where it may be extremely abundant. It seems equally at home in wild landscapes and in the proximity of humans. One is likely to find it in small woodlots in town, city parks, roadside ditches, and even some backyard weed patches. It grows near the shores of most lakes and ponds, and along the banks of almost every river within its broad range. It is highly associated with black elderberry, stinging nettle, wood nettle, honewort, hops, cow parsnip, and waterleaf.

Sochan *Rudbeckia laciniata.*

HARVEST AND PREPARATION

Any tender parts of sochan above ground can be eaten. To determine tenderness, rely on the look and feel of the leaf rather than size. Young leaves are smoother and more rubbery, and are a lighter and glossier shade of green. Tender shoots

Below Sochan is a long-lived perennial. Here you see the base of last year's dead stalk, and attached to it are multiple rhizomes, each terminating in a rosette. These rhizomes run farther in shade, where the plant seeks light. Because of it's growth form, sochan is very easy to propagate and transplant. It responds very well to care—weeding and mulching will quickly produce a vigorous colony. **Opposite** Good food isn't the only reason to grow sochan.

Opposite top A new spring leaf of a buttercup, *Ranunculus hispidus*. **Not edible!** (Somewhat poisonous, in fact, but not something you need to get worked up over.) Compare the photos carefully. Buttercups have proportionately narrower petioles that do not taper at the base; they are roundish with a small groove on top, hollow, and are often purple on the bottom and sides. Sochan petioles are much wider and tapering at the base; they are broadly channeled. The channel bottom on young spring sochan leaves is rippled, purplish, and shimmery; the petiole is otherwise green. Also notice how the buttercup leaves are more separated at the first division, and have deeply depressed secondary veins; while sochan leaves are glossier and have secondary veins scarcely depressed and offset by light color. Buttercup petioles usually have a thin-edged sheath at the base; some species have dark "stain marks" at the base of the sinuses; sochan has neither. **Opposite bottom** Buttercup flowers are very differerent from those of sochan. However *Ranunculus hispidus* often grows in floodplain forests beside sochan. The large rosette in the center of this photo is buttercup, and is bearing those yellow flowers. There are sochan leaves on the upper right and lower right. (When growing in competition, sochan rosettes may have only two or three leaves.) Also, near the center are sochan seedlings, the first leaves of which are heart-shaped and entire, but soon become bluntly toothed. Hidden in the top center are leaves of Virginia waterleaf (also edible, often confused with sochan) and Virginia spring beauty; wood nettles are all over the place. Now you see why a good "plant walk" doesn't have to go far. **Below** Early spring leaves of sochan, with the telltale purple of a frost-resistant plant. All of the leaves are nice and tender.

Sochan in late spring, sending up its shoots near the dead remains of last year's stalk. The top half of this shoot is nice and tender. The leaves at the top are also tender, but their flavor at this time is too strong for most palates. The leaves at the base of the flowering stalk are the largest the plant produces, and are the most deeply cut; the lobes are more pointed than other leaves.

Top These are the late summer/early autumn leaves, which have broad lobes and appear on robust plants after the flowering stalks have died, or have been cut. When tender, they are my favorite sochan leaves to eat. **Left** Tender sochan shoots being peeled. **Right** These are the tender, emerging, late-summer leaves, which remind me a little of mini bok choy.

just a few inches tall can be picked along with their leaves. The flavor of sochan leaves is characterized by a faintly aromatic or resinous quality, as is common in the aster family. In tender leaves atop taller shoots, this flavor is intensified to a degree that many find unpleasant. However, tender shoots or shoot tops can be peeled and used as a vegetable. Don't pick all the shoots in the colony—leave a good portion to go to seed and to replenish the roots.

I think the new basal leaves of late summer taste even better than the spring leaves. Sift through the clumps and select the newest and tenderest ones, pinching or cutting them at the base so that you get the petiole as well. They remind me of miniature bok choy.

When the tops are mowed down in mid to late summer, sochan responds by producing a lush clump of large leaves instead of a new flowering stalk. This is a common occurrence along the sides and ditches of rural backroads. If you have a healthy patch on your own property, you can stimulate a new flush of tender leaves by cutting a clump of stems just after peak bloom. Although this may seem harsh, the plant can handle it—many roadside colonies are mowed every summer and still manage to persist and spread.

Sochan greens can be eaten raw but are traditionally cooked, and I prefer them that way. You can steam or boil them and serve as greens, but the classic way is the Southern style: fried in bacon or pork fat and then drizzled with a vinegar-based dressing. This is a favorite way to eat sochan in our house.

The peeled tender stems are both sweet and aromatic, reminding me a little bit of carrot stalks. They can be nibbled raw or sliced crosswise into thin medallions served in salad. The shoots can also be cooked and served as a stand-alone vegetable, or used in soup, stir-fry, or casserole.

Sochan is a lesson in humility. Outside of the southern Appalachians, even the most seasoned foragers are typically unaware of its edibility. How many other weeds and wildflowers have we ignored for decades as they silently and patiently offered us the greatest gifts?

Strawberry Spinach (Strawberry Blite)

Chenopodium capitatum

n June of 2008 there were immense floods in the hilly country of southwestern Wisconsin. Record rainfall broke dams and cut massive gullies, flooded homes above the first-floor windows, washed out roads, and cut stream beds several feet deeper into the hillsides. Riverbank cottonwoods had the ground washed away from under their feet, then tumbled into the torrent, eventually lodging against rock ledges downstream, where their limbs filtered out lumber, bicycles, and bale wrappings caught up in the rushing waters. My friend Lisa awoke the morning after to find her driveway gone. The shrubs and wet meadow forbs beside her little crick had been scoured away, along with the rich soil they grew in—deposited, like her culvert, on the property of a downstream neighbor—leaving behind a barren swath of limestone and mud. And a few seeds.

Around the end of summer she noticed that a most peculiar plant had sprung up among those bare rocks, a low herb drooping under the weight of bright red gobs of stuff attached to the branch tips. A plant person for many years, Lisa had never seen one like this oddball, and none of her friends or neighbors

The luscious but curious-looking fruity things that grow on strawberry spinach.

recalled seeing such a thing, either, before the great downpour. What was it, and where had it come from?

I'm confident that it did not fall to Earth with the rain. If strawberry spinach has a magical power, it is not air travel, but time travel. If this herb could speak of its parents, it might have told us that they had their branches nipped by elk or bison as the first white settlers came to pick these hills for lead ore; or perhaps earlier, in the aftermath of a fire set by hunters who wanted better grass for their game. And patiently in the dark soil, for however many decades or centuries luck would have it, these seeds waited for any kind of disaster that might give them their uncompromising wish: bright, full sun and bare soil.

DESCRIPTION

Strawberry spinach is an annual or sometimes a winter annual. That latter term, winter annual, is a confusing one, so I'll explain what it means. A winter annual completes its life cycle within a year, but this year spans two growing seasons and is interrupted by a winter. In other words, it is like a biennial that doesn't emerge until late in its first growing season, and which usually dies early in its second growing season. These plants might germinate in late August and grow into early November—often in the form of a rosette—before going dormant from the cold. They recommence growing in spring, flowering and fruiting and then dying by early summer. Despite the name, winter annuals are in many ways more like biennials than annuals.

Strawberry spinach keeps most of its greenery near the ground, beginning with a basal rosette of several long-stalked leaves. The petioles are thin, often much longer than the leaf blade, and usually not rigid enough to hold it off the

Basal rosettes of strawberry spinach.

ground. The blades are triangular or arrowhead-shaped, usually 2–4 inches (5–10 cm) long, with a few large teeth or small lobes. All parts are hairless and smooth but not glossy, reminiscent of lamb's quarters or spinach.

Later in the growing season, or during its second season, strawberry spinach will produce stems—usually a few per plant. These are erect or leaning at first, but as the fruit develops, the stems will droop or flop over from the weight unless they are supported by neighboring vegetation. The stems are thin, weak, angled, and rarely over 2 feet (60 cm) tall. Stems bear leaves, but these are largest and most abundant near the base; near the top they become sparse and greatly reduced in size.

The flower clusters are rather inconspicuous green globs attached along the terminal half of the stems, appearing in early summer on winter annual plants, or in late summer or autumn on annual plants. The individual flowers are tiny, and not the sort of flower we write poems about. Many plants have boring flowers like this, but no other boring flower turns out so extraordinary. For after the strawberry spinach is fertilized, it turns into a most remarkable fruity sort of thing—showy indeed, but still not inspiring poetry. Instead, they inspire puzzled stares of wonderment as the uninitiated try to figure out if these amorphous red blobs are a berry or a disease. (This latter supposition brought about the name "strawberry blite.") Well, it's not a disease, but it's not exactly a fruit, either. It is actually the sepals of the flower that become enlarged, red, and juicy; packed between them are the smaller, dark achenes. They have the same purpose as any berry: providing a sweet nutritional package to entice birds and mammals for dispersal.

This plant is usually unmistakable in fruit. In the Rockies the "fruit" is sometimes smaller, less fleshy, and may not turn red. Botanists call this form "variety *parvicapitatum*" (Clemants and Mosyakin, 2003). I have no idea how common this aberration is, because I've never seen it, but even without the red berries the plant is quite distinct.

HABITAT

Strawberry spinach is a forest plant, most prevalent in areas dominated by aspen, birch, spruce, pine, and fir. This plant is found, often abundantly, after soil disturbance caused by stochastic events such as floods, windstorms, or especially, fire. It is also found after human-caused soil disturbance in forests, such as logging,

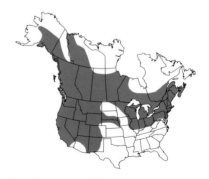

Strawberry spinach *Chenopodium capitatum* is mostly confined to forested habitats within this range, especially where it is mountainous, rocky, or sandy.

Above A lush strawberry spinach plant just beginning to bolt. Opposite A strawberry spinach plant with ripe berries, but not yet enough to pull it to the ground.

road building, and the clearing of building sites. You will usually only find strawberry spinach growing for the first few years after such an event. It sometimes becomes a weed of crop fields and gardens—a situation that would probably be more common if strawberry spinach weren't primarily confined to very poor agricultural regions. But if you want your own patch, it is incredibly easy to propagate: Throw some berries in your garden and let them volunteer.

HARVEST AND PREPARATION

The leaves of strawberry spinach are thin and tender, even on mature, fruiting plants. Pick the larger leaves from the base singly. You can also pick the tender shoots in summer, but they are rather thin and have small, sparse leaves, so I usually let them go to seed. This species is related to lamb's quarters and

spinach; the greens are used raw or cooked in any of the same ways and have a very similar flavor.

Although the leaves alone make this weed worth knowing, the second edible product of the plant is the one for which it is famous: the "strawberry" part. These bright-red, juicy lumps of stuff adorn the plant in late summer and autumn. Many books list the berries as being tasteless or worse, but this is not true. They suffer from a dilemma of expectations; many people suppose that they should taste like strawberries or raspberries. But they are way more unusual and intriguing than that—spinach strawberries taste like a sweeter, juicier version of beets (which are actually rather closely related). Now, I understand that there are five or six people who do not like beets. How they can feel that way beets me. If you are not a beeteater, you still might like spinach strawberries, because they are even better, and they feel totally different in your mouth. Raw, they make a fun snack. They augment the flavor and beauty of a salad wonderfully. We like to dump a handful over fried greens once they are served, or throw them into a dish of wild rice and cooked vegetables. We can never have enough spinach strawberries in our kitchen.

Don't imagine that you need to travel to faraway tropical lands for new culinary adventures. Who needs the exotic when things like strawberry spinach are hiding in the soil under our feet, waiting for some dirt to turn over so they can appear like a conjurer's trick?

Sweetroot (Aniseroot, Sweet Cicely)

Genus *Osmorhiza*

Josh and I made good use of the drizzly May weekends in eighth grade. We convinced people with automobiles to haul us to the woods and let us loose for a few days. The leaves were just opening up on the oaks and the seeds were tumbling from the elms. The mayapple, bloodroot, and waterleaf soaked our socks as we trod lightly across the hillsides and ridges, our legs so driven by the wonders of spring that we forgot our hunger until dusk. We wandered with no map, no plan, no curfew; searching for nothing in particular. And we always found it.

Osmorhiza longistylis in bloom.

We stalked for a glimpse of a turkey we heard gobbling in a distant field. We checked limestone outcroppings for snakes, and hollow basswoods for opossums—hoping all the way that we'd stumble upon a newborn fawn or an ovenbird nest. We checked the dead apple trees and elms for morels, and eventually, by parting the aniseroot and geranium leaves, we would find one, glowing like gold in the gloomy woods. One of us would sacrifice a T-shirt and tie a strip of elm bark around one end for a makeshift gunnysack, and we would hunker down to raccoon level, relaxing our eyes to let the mushrooms show themselves. As we crawled about and leapt to claim our prizes, we'd crush the aniseroot stalks under our knees to release their sweet scent, and occasionally pluck one for a nibble.

Unlike many fantasies, this one I can return to—every year. Today I found only two morels; tonight I dream of tomorrow while listening to the spring peepers outside and the raindrops on the tent. I am fourteen again; foraging is my fountain of youth.

DESCRIPTION

North America is home to at least 7 species in the genus *Osmorhiza*, all of which are edible. The plants in this group are perennials that grow from taproots that usually branch near the top. Sweetroots have a few basal leaves on long, thin petioles that are solid or have a tiny hollow in the center. Sweetroots have a few stem leaves, which grow on shorter petioles or are sessile. The leaves are large and multi-compound, sometimes divided erratically. The leaflets are variably lobed and toothed, packed closely together, and often overlapping. The leaves are fern-like and delicate, but the leaflets have unbroken portions of blade more than a half inch across, which separates them from the many other members of the carrot family with linear or thread-like divisions. In autumn, sweetroots produce a rosette of reduced overwintering leaves.

Sweetroots have erect stems that are straight and unbranched for half of their height; then, they suddenly branch widely in the top half. The naked, lower part of the stem, especially in the shoot phase, often has a single odd bulge. The plants are 1–3.5 feet (30–110 cm) tall at maturity. The stems are rounded and smooth, ranging from nearly hairless to very hairy—but are always much hairier at the nodes or branch junctures and on the petiole sheaths. Stems are solid in the shoot stage, at maturity becoming thick-walled with a small hollow channel in the center that accounts for less than ¼ of the cross section.

The inflorescence is a compound umbel at the end of a long peduncle. The rays are few (usually 2–6). The flowers are tiny, with no sepals and 5 obovate petals. The distinctive fruit is long and narrow, usually with stiff hairs, and splitting in half lengthwise, oftentimes with only the tip remaining fused. These are the annoying, slightly curved, barb-tipped, elongated black seeds that stick into your socks in late summer and fall—the ones that look like a cross between a wild rice grain and a porcupine quill. Find them clinging to the withered stalks and remember the spot for next spring.

Sweetroots are best learned when in flower and fruit, which is not the best time to eat them. But once you become thoroughly familiar with the plant and have located its haunts, you will be able to observe individuals change through the seasons so that you can identify them at any age or size. Distinguishing the individual species can be frustrating, but the entire group is safe. I've tried most of them, and all have been good.

Osmorhiza longistylis, commonly called "aniseroot," is available to the majority of the continent's population, and is one of the best-flavored species; the stems have a strong anise or fennel flavor (but the roots scarcely do). This plant often has reddish stems, which may be hairless or slightly hairy, but it is always hairy on the margins of the leaf sheath. The skin is smooth with a light bloom.

Sweet cicely ***Osmorhiza claytonii*** is also widespread and common in the Eastern Woodlands, but its stems lack the anise flavor. This species is similar to aniseroot in size and form, but its stem lacks bloom and is uniformly much hairier. The leaflets are hairier, lighter green, and have more pointed tips.

The common name "sweet cicely" is incredibly confusing. It is sometimes used to refer to any member of the genus *Ozmorhiza*, but most often it is applied to *O. claytonii*—an eastern species that lacks anise flavor—and to *O. occidentalis*—a

Leaf of *Osmorhiza claytonii*.

western species that has the strongest anise flavor within the genus. The name is also used for *Myrrhis odorata*—another aromatic, edible plant in the carrot family, rarely found in North America outside of maritime Canada.

Another species in this group, **Osmorhiza berteroi** (or *chilensis*), resembles aniseroot but tends to be hairier. It is common in much of the Mountain West, but has far-flung populations in northern New England, the upper Great Lakes, and in South America. Other Western species include **O. purpurea**, a short plant, usually with hairless leaves, with purplish flowers (rarely white) and stiff-hairy fruits. **O. depauperata** is very common in much of the Rockies, has white flowers, and is usually sparsely hairy; it has fruits with wide, rounded tips lacking the beak-like projections found in other species. **O. brachypoda** is a species with yellow-green flowers confined to California and a small section of Arizona.

There is one member of this genus that stands distinct from the others: the western sweet cicely **O. occidentalis**. My experience with this plant is limited to the one specimen generously sent to me from Colorado by Briana Wiles, from which I got to taste roots, buds, and shoots. Western sweet cicely is taller than the other species. Its leaves are divided regularly into discrete leaflets that are toothed but usually not deeply lobed. Instead of a forking taproot with a single crown or a few crowns close together, this species has multiple stems growing from a branching, multi-crowned rootstock. The leaves and stems are hairless or have tiny hairs, and are glossy and light green. The flowers are yellow, and the fruits are hairless and glossy, large, not tapered to a thin base, and at ripening are held vertically and clustered together. All parts of western sweet cicely are extremely aromatic and strong in flavor—something to use sparingly, as a flavoring. The root mass is much larger and tougher than that of the other species, and the flavor is so intense it will numb your tongue. In many ways (especially the fruit) it actually does resemble the Old World sweet cicely, *Myrrhis odorata*.

Sweetroots (the genus as a whole) can be told from poison hemlock and water-hemlock by their smaller size, and the hairs on their stems, leaf sheaths, and leaves, and by their solid or nearly-solid stems and petioles. (Poison and water hemlocks have hollow, thin-walled, hairless stems and petioles.) The baneberries, which grow in similar habitats, are also poisonous. However, baneberry leaflets are not deeply cut, the plant does not have a basal rosette, nor is it aromatic or hairy.

HABITAT

Sweetroots like rich, moist soil in forests or along forest edges, where they grow in moderate to heavy shade. They are especially common on slopes, in ravines, or along watercourses where occasional floods give its seeds a good germination bed.

Above left Close up of the stems of *O. claytonii* (left), which is very hairy, and *O. longistylis* (right), which ranges from hairless to moderately hairy, but in all cases has a hairy margin to the petiole sheath, as seen here. **Above right** I came across this sweetroot near the coast in northern California. I think it is *O. berteroi*, but I can't tell for sure because it isn't mature. The West has more species than the East, and they are easiest to differentiate by flowers and fruit. Luckily, all of them are edible. **Below left** Erect, unripe fruits of *O. occidentalis*. These are larger than the fruits of our other species, and very flavorful. **Below right** Western sweet cicely *O. occidentalis* is unusual in this genus in having yellow flowers. The discrete leaflets somewhat resemble those of water-hemlock (which has white flowers) but the stem of western sweet cicely is thick-walled (water-hemlock's is thin-walled) and the upper parts have some erect hairs (water-hemlock is hairless).

In the East, I see the best stands of *Osmorhiza longistylis* in hardwood forests with rich soil, especially in stream valleys, where it is strongly associated with wood nettle and honewort—two wild edibles whose stalks are ready to pick at the same time. *Osmorhiza claytonii* prefers slightly drier soil and is more typical of oak-hickory forests, but it is a little more of a generalist, and the habitat of these two species overlaps significantly.

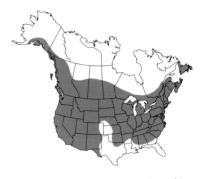

Composite range of the genus *Osmorhiza*.

In the Mountain West, the various sweetroots are found in hardwood, conifer, or mixed forests, particularly on steep ravines near flowing water, and where there are openings in the canopy. They do especially well where deep, rich soil has accumulated, or where there has been a disturbance within the forest.

HARVEST AND PREPARATION

All the tender parts of sweetroot are edible. The leaves, flowers, flower buds, and tender branches can be eaten raw or cooked, and are nice chopped up and used like parsley, although the flavor is milder. Get these in spring or early summer. In the late fall and early winter, the semi-evergreen autumn leaves that lay limp on the dead leaves of the forest floor make a nice nibble or garnish at a time when few greens are available.

However, the best part of sweetroot is the tender shoot in spring. These are a woodland hiker's trail dessert, with a sweet flavor, clean crispness, and aromatic essence that make you wonder, upon the first taste, why you haven't been eating them all your life. They are just right for eating when the stems are tender and supple, before the branches of the flowering top have begun to spread. They are a bit more fibrous than asparagus or fiddleheads, but won't yet qualify as stringy. I love to eat them raw, whole, and unadulterated while I'm out on a hike. My eight-year-old daughter calls aniseroot shoots her favorite wild edible, screaming in delight when we encounter a patch. Occasionally I'll chop the thick part of the shoot into short sections and add them to a salad. Their unique, sweet flavor makes them appropriate for fruit salads as well as green salads. I also use them like fennel in soups.

It is sometimes reported that the fruits make a nice anise-like flavoring. With most species, the flavor of these is weak, although pleasant. These reports may

Opposite The aniseroot shoot in the center is tender and perfect. Pinch at the base and indulge.

Right The fruits (schizocarps) of sweet-roots are elongated, and when they schizz into two seeds, the tips often remain attached. This form is diagnostic of this genus. **Below** The root mass on the left is western sweet cicely *O. occidentalis*, while the one on the right is aniseroot *O. longistylis*. The roots of aniseroot are tender and mild—small, but an excellent carrot-like vegetable. The roots of western sweet cicely will knock your socks off. (Well, depends on how loose your socks are.)

If you want to dig up sweetroots' sweet roots in fall or winter, you'll need to recognize the small rosettes of reduced overwinter leaves, found at the base of old, dead stalks, like this.

be derived from name confusion with *Myrrhis odorata*, which actually does have potently flavored green fruits (as does *O. occidentalis*).

The roots of sweetroot are typically small and slender but tender. Although the name "aniseroot" suggests that the roots of this species are used as a flavoring, they are most often mild and carrot-like, with just a hint of anise, or none at all. Turner (1978) reports that the Thompson and Lower Lillooet of British Columbia gathered the sweet, aromatic roots of *O. berteroi* in spring or fall and steamed them in pits or boiled them. The roots of both western and eastern species were widely used medicinally.

I have long wondered how sweetroot remains such a little-known and rarely used wild vegetable. It is often abundant. Not only are the stalks easy to gather, they have that other quality so highly esteemed by foragers: the convenience of requiring no preparation. And they are readily enjoyed, even by those with the most finicky palates.

Violet

Genus *Viola*

Violets are comfort plants for the traveling forager: easy to identify, reliably edible, and perhaps most importantly, found everywhere. In your lawn. In hayfields. In brushy woodlots and city parks, in swampy swales and dry prairie hilltops. Under ancient groves of beech and yellow birch in the deepest wilds of the Smoky Mountains, in backyards of Cincinnati, under aspens in the remote Colorado high country, in dry sagebrush prairies of Utah, under Douglas fir in the Cascades of Washington. If you look for violets, you will probably find them.

DESCRIPTION

I am generally a proponent of recognizing plants by their vegetative parts rather than their flowers, but violets are a challenge to this policy. Violet leaves come in an incredible array of shapes and sizes, but the form of the flowers is remarkably consistent and distinct. They have a long, thin, erect, unbranched stem (peduncle) with a single flower at the end. The peduncle should be nodding—hooked at the top like an upside-down J. Somewhere along that peduncle

Look, I found some violets.

A rosette of common blue violet. The leaves to eat are the curled up, light green ones hiding in the center. Better yet, find some growing with tall grass where they aren't sandy.

there will be a pair of tiny, reduced leaves—little scale-like things so small you probably overlooked them at first glance. Everything good? If so, it's almost certain that your flower is a violet, but to be sure, proceed to the fun part.

Violet flowers are irregular, with 5 petals arranged in a way that suggests a human form. The petals usually have darker veins within them. Turn your stem upside down and then look at the flower. Imagine a person with outstretched arms. The bottom (now top) petal represents the head. There is a pair of opposing petals for the arms, and two lower petals representing the legs. Turn the flower on its belly and you'll see that the "head" petal has an enlarged sack at the back, which you can think of as the skull. If you see all of the above-named features, your plant is definitely a member of the genus *Viola*. And now, just for giggles, flip the flower back over and tug on the arms a little. Most violets have hairy armpits (but a few of them shave).

The foregoing description refers to the showy violet blossoms that most of us are familiar with. Most *Viola* species also have a second kind: unshowy, self-fertilized, "cleistogamous" flowers. These are often produced beneath the litter or soil. The showy flowers that outcross seek to produce genetically diverse offspring, while the cleistogamous flowers that self-pollinate ensure that some sort of reproduction will take place if the outcrossing doesn't work.

Violet fruits are not commonly noticed; they are small capsules with 3 valves holding multiple seeds. Some species have capsules that open explosively to eject their seeds. The seeds of many violets have elaiosomes attached to the surface—these are fatty food structures supplied for insects (mostly ants) as an incentive to transport the seed to a more suitable site for germination. The elaiosomes are consumed at a safe location, but the body of the seed remains unharmed and viable.

Violets can be divided into two groups by their growth form: stemmed and stemless. Stemless violets have all the petioles and peduncles attached directly to the base of the plant. Stemmed violets may have some basal leaves, but they also have an aerial stem that bears both leaves and flower peduncles. The leaf form of violets is incredibly variable, as you will see with the sampling of species below. In general, the leaves have long petioles, and at the base of the petiole is a pair of stipules. Even basal leaves have stipules, which helps separate them from similar-looking leaves of a few other plants. The basal leaves of larkspur and a few other toxic plants, such as buttercups, can resemble the violets that have palmately cut leaves, so *these* violets are best collected when the flowers are present to verify your identification.

According to Little and McKinney (2015), there are about 70 species of violet growing wild in North America. There is more taxonomic uncertainty and disagreement in this group than with most genera, and some of our best edible species have been divided by certain authors into multiple species in various parts of their broad ranges. However, you don't have to key out your violet to the species—all of them are edible. Just taste it and decide if you like it.

Composite range of violets.

A FEW NOTEWORTHY SPECIES OF VIOLET

Common blue violet *V. sororia* is an incredibly widespread and abundant species of stemless violet inhabiting woodlands, forest edges, parks, fields, lawns, prairies, orchards, roadside ditches, and wetland margins. It is among the larger violets. When growing in moist, rich soil in light shade, under competition with other herbs, it may reach 18 inches (45 cm) in height, the leaves rising on long, thin, erect stems. Blue or purple flowers rise on thin peduncles about as high as the leaves—and when you pluck such a peduncle at its base, it seems incongruously long for the little flower it supports. In dry, sunny conditions the plants may be much shorter. The leaves are unlobed and heart-shaped, sometimes much broader than long, with scalloped or toothed margins, and the edges curled upward. This species is extremely variable in characteristics such as size, pubescence, and flower color; thus a number of species, forms, and

In my opinion, *V. canadensis* has the best tasting leaves of any violet.

subspecies have been described—here I am using the name in its broad sense. Common blue violet's leaves have good flavor, and their larger size makes them easy to collect. The flowers and flower stems are also excellent.

Canada or **tall white violet** *V. canadensis* is a species of rich, moist deciduous or mixed forests, where it is often abundant in association with other spring ephemerals. Three different varieties are recognized, all of which are sometimes classified as separate species—but one rough description will suffice for all of them.

This violet is stemmed, and is typically 5–12 inches (13–30 cm) tall. The basal leaves are heart-shaped with a narrowed tip, borne on petioles as long or longer than the blade; the stem leaves are similar but smaller and narrower, on short petioles. The flowers are mostly white, but the petal bases are yellow, and the three lower petals have purple veins. Canada violet's leaves are my favorite for eating. Their flavor is mild, with a hint of wintergreen that makes it memorable, and they are more tender than most violet greens.

Field pansy *V. bicolor* is a small, native violet of fields and open woods over much of the southeastern United States. It is locally abundant, although easy to overlook. (The

Field pansy: the wintergreen-flavored violet. Check out the stipules that are bigger than the actual leaves.

closely related *V. tricolor/arvensis* is introduced, and similarly edible.) Field pansy has an erect stem and lacks basal leaves. All violet leaves have stipules at the base, which tend to go unnoticed. But the stipules of field pansies are just as large, or even larger, than their leaf, which makes each node effectively have a cluster of 3 leaves: a regular leaf in the middle, and a giant stipule on each side. The true leaf is elongated and elliptic to lanceolate, entire or with a few scattered teeth; the stipules are deeply pinnately lobed, but spoon-shaped in general outline. Pansies have a strong taste of wintergreen, making them delightful in a salad or as a garnish or nibble.

Bird-foot violet *V. pedata* is a stemless species with leaves that are deeply palmately lobed, lacy and almost fern-like. These are rarely more than 4 inches (10 cm) high, and overlap each other in dense clusters. Rising slightly above the leaves are numerous flat-fronted purple flowers, large and showy among our violets. The flowers and peduncles are the best part, and perhaps no other violet produces such an easily collected profusion of blossoms. This species grows in dry, sandy, sunny habitats, such as open oak woods, pine barrens, and sandy prairies.

Downy yellow violet or **yellow wood violet *V. pubescens*** is a common and widespread stemmed species of many forest types in the East, often thriving in heavy shade. This violet may or may not have basal leaves, and it may have

The spectacular birdfoot violet. There is no way you can tell from this photo how unbelieveably bad the mosquitoes were when I took it.

The downy yellow violet *V. pubescens*.

from one to several stems. The leaves are broadly heart-shaped, and the flowers are lemon-yellow, usually with purple lines on the lower petal. This species is characterized by the fine, soft hairs that cover all parts (although the quantity of hairs is quite variable). Although the leaves of downy yellow violet have a faintly bitter aftertaste, they are tender, large, and often abundant. I occasionally nibble them, but most commonly eat them mixed with other greens.

Smooth yellow, yellow wood, or stream violet *V. glabella* is a western counterpart to the previous species, except that it is hairless and tastes better. This species is found in rich, moist, shaded forests with conifers at lower elevations in the Pacific states and provinces, from Alaska to California. The leaves are broad, 1–3 inches (2.5–8 cm) long, and rounded or heart-shaped, glossy, and hairless or nearly so. They are mostly basal, but there are a few smaller leaves near the top. In between, you'll find a succulent stem that remains tender even as the plant commences blooming. The flowers are small and yellow, borne sparsely. This excellent, mild-flavored violet is adapted to the long, mild winters near the Pacific, and is most often available in the cool weather of late winter and early spring.

HARVEST AND PREPARATION

Greens: Although the entire genus is touted as edible, the difference in palatability between species is significant. Some are too bitter. Some are too small to bother with. Some are downright excellent. Assuming you find a species that is to your liking, the greens can be used raw or cooked in the usual variety of ways. Because they are mucilaginous, violet greens are often used in soups; in parts of the South, they are sometimes called "wild okra." Some people complain that large amounts of violet leaves can have a laxative effect. I have never experienced this, probably because there are so many superb greens during violet season that I almost never eat them by themselves.

Some sources warn against eating the greens of yellow- or white-flowered violets. Ignore them. I have eaten such greens for decades, never with ill effect. All of the ethnographically documented food uses of violets by Native Americans listed in Moerman (1998) refer to yellow or white species. I consider all violet leaves, stems, and flowers edible, unless I try them and they taste bad.

Above *V. glabella*, basal leaves and a stem about to flower. All of these parts are tender and good to eat. **Below** The stalk of *V. glabella* is thick, tender, and tasty.

The young leaves of *V. pubescens*.

(The roots or rhizomes are widely reported to be toxic—but you weren't going to eat those anyway.)

For any purpose, it is important to get violet leaves that are tender. Gather them when they are just emerging in spring. Collecting only the top few leaves is a good idea on stemmed violets. With stemless species, you can often see that one or two leaves on each plant are smaller, more curled up, and lighter in color—these are the new ones you want to grab.

However you choose to use violet greens, it is probably a good idea. Euell Gibbons (1966) collected the leaves of common blue violet and had some nutritional analyses performed. Per 100 grams of edible portion, the fresh leaves contained 210 mg of vitamin C (4.5 times that of oranges) and a tremendous 8,258 IU of provitamin A.

Flowers: Violets are beautiful as garnish and have a pleasant flavor—even on some species in which the leaves are rather bitter. However, I have found none of our native violets that are fragrant like the European *Viola odora*. I love to nibble violets while hiking, chewing up the whole stem on my way to the flower, the prize at the end.

Many people candy violet flowers by dipping them in sugar syrup and drying. In this and other violet confections, I must confess, the violets add a lot of color but not much flavor. Picking enough violets to make jam is not as hard as it sounds—they are prolific. To make jam, heat 1 cup of water, ¼ cup of lemon juice, and one box of pectin, whisking until it comes to a boil. Then add 1¾ cups

Violet flowers are beautiful and nutritious, and the coloring dissolves readily in hot water, but the blossoms taste about the same as the stems.

of sugar and stir until it boils again. Now, put 3 packed cups of violets into a blender, pour the hot pectin mixture over them, and add another 1½ cups of sugar. Blend this until it forms a foamy purple paste and pour it into jars. Even if the jars seal, don't consider this jam sterile—keep it refrigerated.

The color of violet blossoms is water-soluble. To make a violet infusion, pack a jar with blossoms, cover them with boiling water, put the lid on, and then let the mixture sit for a day. Strain off the liquid and discard the flowers. You can use this infusion as the base for beautifully colored drinks, or to make violet syrup or jelly. For syrup, add 1¾ cups sugar per cup of infusion, plus a little lemon juice. Then bring the mixture to a boil and seal in little jars or bottles. For jelly, use 2¼ cups of violet infusion, ¼ cup of lemon juice, one package of commercial pectin, and 4 cups of sugar. You can also put violet blossoms into a smoothie, to make it beautiful and nutritious.

With so many uses for these friendly plants, you might wish to have more of them around. Perhaps you will stop seeing violets as a weed in your lawn, and begin to see your lawn as a weed in the violets.

Watercress

Nasturtium officinale, N. microphyllum

There is something miraculous about a spring: the alchemy by which the Earth purifies water, concentrates it, and then issues it back to the surface in a clean, steady stream; the way those cool melted crystals bring life to the ground they flow over; the way millions of these rills wind back and forth around hills and ridges to find each other, forming great rivers that pour them back into the sea they left so long ago. No wonder cultures the world over have held springs in reverence and attributed magical powers to them. I am drawn to springs the way that some are drawn to sunsets and mountains. I like to clean away the stones from the head, wait for the water to clear, and then dip my face for a long drink, a refreshing kiss with the blessing of life. I baptize myself with a double-palm of cold water and sit by the quiet trickle as long as my heart needs rest, hopefully watching a pickerel frog and nibbling a spear of mint. I like to come home from such a place with a gift, a reminder—most likely, a fresh bundle of watercress.

Dense, lush growth of watercress in mid spring, offering lots of tender greens well above the water level. This is just downstream from a magnificent spring that I love to drink from.

DESCRIPTION

Watercress forms thick mats in springs and spring-fed streams. It is a perennial, but has no tough tissues or storage organs to carry it through the winter. Instead, it relies on the springwater's constant temperature to prevent it from freezing, dying back to the underwater portion in the coldest weather. The stems are weak and trailing or decumbent, but thick in proportion to their length and widely branched. They are hollow, hairless, ridged, and buoyant. In summer the stem tips stand erect up to about 18 inches (45 cm). Thin, white roots grow from the underwater nodes.

The leaves are alternate and pinnately compound, about 6 inches (15 cm) long, and hairless, with 3–9 well-spaced leaflets. The leaflets are rounded to lanceolate with blunt tips. Leaflets are toothless, but occasionally have wavy indentations on the margins. The leaflets become much more elongated on the erect, flowering stems. The petioles are shallowly channeled, the edges with narrow, winged ridges.

Watercress just beginning to bloom. Note the leaf form—not irregularly lobed or divided like most mustards, but clearly compound.

Watercress flowers have 4 petals and bloom at the end of a raceme up to 10 inches (25 cm) long at the top of the plant. Flowers are about an eighth inch (3 mm) across and are white. The fruit is a long, thin, claw-like pod, round in cross section and slightly curved upward, on a pedicel about a half inch (13 mm) long.

There are actually two similar and closely related species of watercress, both introduced to North America. *N. officinale* is larger, has 32 chromosomes, and has 2 rows of seeds within the pod. *N. microphyllum* is smaller, more cold hardy (and thus more common in northern regions), has 64 chromosomes, and has a single row of seeds in the pod. At the optimum collection time, the pods aren't there for examination, but no matter—the two are used in the same ways as food. *N. officinale* is the species grown commercially.

A few native mustards, such as *Cardamine pennsylvanica*, are sometimes confused with watercress, although they differ in having prominent basal rosettes. These related plants are also edible, just not as robust or tender.

HABITAT

Being introduced to North America, and needing a specialized habitat, watercress is rather sporadic and unpredictable in occurrence, although it is very widespread. It is found in springwater, especially if the pH is neutral or alkaline. This plant has been spread intentionally by humans, thus it is highly associated with human habitation—although it is also sometimes found in wilderness settings. Watercress is a fully aquatic plant, growing right in the water, sometimes where it is a foot or more deep. It is tolerant of moderate shade but does much better with ample sunlight.

Composite range of both species of watercress. These might be found outside the mapped range in springwater near human habitation.

Watercress is a vigorous competitor that should be seen as an invasive; it should not be spread to areas where it is not already present. It has clearly displaced populations of some native species, such as *Veronica americana*.

HARVEST AND PREPARATION

It *is* OK to harvest and consume wild watercress. A few foraging authors are afraid of eating this plant, and have scared some people away from doing so. For example, Robert Henderson (2000) says, "Sadly, none of it is edible; water pollution and biological contamination have poisoned all the wild watercress in North America." He doesn't elaborate on the reasoning for this extreme claim.

A colony of watercress later in bloom. Even now, the tops are pretty good.

Of course you should avoid watercress growing in water known to be dangerously polluted, but this is true of any plant. In a town near me there is a park full of springs, many of them capped into artesian wells. Thousands of people fill drinking water jugs with this fresh springwater, which is more trusted than the municipal supply. The springs are also a public watercress garden, from which literally hundreds of people share the crop. Nobody is being poisoned by it.

The growing stems and leaves of watercress are so tender that you can pinch or tear them off with ease, although you may want to use a pair of scissors. The eating qualities are best before flowering, but a watercress patch will provide greens throughout the growing season. Even blooming stems are reasonably tender. In milder climates you can collect this plant all year, although the volume available in winter may be limited.

Watercress is hot, with a clean and refreshing pungency like radishes. It can be very good mixed sparingly in a salad or served on sandwiches, where it is a green and a condiment in one. (**Before eating watercress raw, be sure to read the section below on liver flukes.**) When cooked, the hotness of watercress is dramatically reduced, and it becomes a mild green. It is popular in soup, and delicious fried. Watercress is not meant to be stored—it disintegrates through prolonged cooking, and retains nothing of the crisp freshness for which it is adored. Plus, it is stored in Nature, ready for picking, for an incredibly long season.

I have not seen any analysis of wild watercress, but even the USDA's nutrient report for cultivated watercress shows it to be a good source of calcium, potassium, vitamin C, and vitamin A (NNDSR 2015).

LIVER FLUKES AND OTHER BAD STUFF

Liver flukes are parasitic flatworms that live inside the liver and feed on it. Although perhaps a few desperate actresses have intentionally ingested tapeworms to lose weight, and some people give themselves hookworms to reduce allergy symptoms, *nobody wants liver flukes*. Not even for walleye bait. Unlike many foraging fears, this is not a hypothetical danger; it really happens. According to Pantelouris (1962), the majority of liver fluke infections in humans in the UK can be traced to the consumption of raw watercress. In France, the majority of the approximately 300 yearly cases of liver fluke infection are attributed to raw watercress consumption—with some also being caused by eating raw dandelion, lamb's lettuce (cornsalad), and mint (Mailles et al. 2006).

The liver fluke associated with watercress is *Fasciola hepatica*, a common parasite of sheep and cattle, which is also known to infect deer, horses, donkeys, and some other mammals. A snail, *Lymnaea (Galba) truncatula*, is an intermediate host in the transmission of liver fluke. In Europe, approximately 5–6% of these snails in sampled populations were infected (Pantelouris 1962). A few other snails can be carriers but are less hospitable to the fluke larvae, so the infection occurs at much lower rates.

The common liver fluke has a fascinating and incredibly complex life cycle, detailed by Pantelouris (1965). Adult flukes of *Fasciola hepatica*, which can live for at least 8 years, are hermaphroditic and dwell mostly in the bile duct. Their eggs are excreted into the bile and pass out in feces. The eggs hatch into microscopic aquatic larvae called "miracidia" that bore into the tissues of a snail. Inside the snail, the miracidium sheds its locomotive appendages, brain, and other unimportant stuff, and turns into an egg-like thing called a "sporocyst." Multiple cloned larvae called "rediae" develop inside the sporocyst, eventually hatching from it. These little bastards find the snail's liver, feed on it, and divide into more redia. Eventually, some of the redia will transform into another form of aquatic larva called a "cercaria," which looks like a tiny tadpole. The cercaria leaves the snail and swims to find a piece of vegetation, where it attaches to the surface, loses its tail, and morphs to a dormant cyst (metacercaria). A mammal later may eat the cyst along with vegetation. A tiny liver fluke emerges from the cyst, burrows through the intestinal wall, and finds the liver, where it continues doing terribly impolite things. Sometimes, you can't say *YUK!* loud enough.

It is important to put the liver fluke risk in perspective. In England and France there are estimated to be tens of millions of people who consume raw watercress. The infection rate for those consumers is extremely low. Outbreaks are often caused by egregiously unsanitary conditions. For example, a case investigated in France found a commercial watercress bed owned by a cattle dealer, surrounded by high concentrations of livestock, with many *Lymnaea* snails present, and prone to flooding (Mailles et al. 2006). Although an infection from common liver flukes is unpleasant, it is almost never fatal, and often asymptomatic. Liver fluke infections in North America are extremely rare (CDC 2013), probably because the primary intermediate host snail is not native here. Liver fluke infection in livestock is most prevalent near the Gulf Coast and in California.

Remember: Cooked watercress is always safe, in terms of liver flukes or microbial diseases. The liver fluke risk of raw watercress, already very low in most areas, can be eliminated by understanding the parasite's ecology. The

Close-up of watercress leaves in early spring, just beginning to rise above the water level.

cercaria is aquatic—it cannot encyst outside the water. Dry, aerial portions of aquatic plants will not contain cysts, unless they were recently underwater, such as in flooding. How recently is not known for certain, and surely depends on humidity and temperature—studies have shown that the cysts can survive dry air from a few days to a little over 2 weeks (Pantelouris 1965). Although cysts can survive underwater over the winter, the cercariae do not emerge from the snails at temperatures below 48°F (9°C) (Kendall and McCullough 1951). This means that new watercress growth in winter or early spring, when water temperatures are lower than this, is safe to eat because there has been no opportunity for larvae to encyst upon it. Liver flukes are probably absent from water that remains colder than 50°F year-round.

For raw consumption, I follow these rules: (1) Never eat from an area that has livestock. (2) In areas free of livestock, eat only the parts growing above the water. (3) Do not eat from locations that are prone to flooding. When I eat raw watercress, it is normally from clean springs with potable water.

Others advise against eating raw watercress due to a concern with pathogens that may be present in the water. This danger can be avoided with common sense. In an old but famous case where raw watercress consumption was blamed for an outbreak of typhoid fever in London, the plants were literally being grown in diluted raw sewage (*BMJ* 1904). For the ensuing century, the only details that fearmongers could remember about that scenario were "typhoid" and "watercress." Sometimes you can't scream "Double standard!" loud enough.

Simple problems sometimes have simple solutions. Don't grow greens in sewage or manure and then eat them raw. Problem solved. Now enjoy the watercress.

Water Parsnip

Sium suave

n the autumn of 2000, a Cree family was gathering water parsnip roots near Prince Albert National Park in northern Saskatchewan. This root, known as *oskatask*, was highly regarded and regularly eaten by the Cree—so much that, in the Cree language, the domestic carrot was named after it. Among those collecting that day was a 14-year-old boy, who perhaps wasn't paying careful attention. He mistakenly pulled up a water-hemlock plant and ate some of the root. Within minutes he began feeling ill. Seizures, unconsciousness, and cardiac arrest soon followed. The boy was airlifted to the hospital where, despite the best efforts to save him, he died within 20 hours (Heath 2001).

Fatal poisonings from eating wild plants are extremely rare. I have found fewer than a dozen such cases reliably reported in North America in the last 50 years. (This excludes mushrooms and drug overdoses.) These events typically involve non-foragers acting very irresponsibly—they are engaged in some other outdoor activity, see an unknown plant, and spontaneously eat it without making any attempt to identify it. Most victims are young males. The

Below The nice water parsnip *Sium suave* rootlets snapped off of a single robust plant. **Opposite** Water parsnip *Sium suave* plant in early summer before blooming, with typical leaves. Note that this is growing in dry gravel well above the water level. Plants growing in the slough nearby did not even have stalks at this time.

toxic plants, in all cases but one, were water-hemlock or poison hemlock. The incident outlined above is the *only* case I have seen that fits the classic "deadly look-alike" scenario, in which a person intended to collect a specific wild food plant, mistakenly ate the wrong one, and died.

Telling water parsnip from water-hemlocks (the deadliest plants in North America) is widely considered the most demanding and perilous distinction in the world of plant foraging. That's why most foraging guides avoid the topic. But water parsnip's edibility has been published in numerous sources, many of which describe it as delicious. None of these sources contain adequate information on identifying the plant—and some of what is provided is misleading. I do not believe this situation has made anyone safer, so I am tackling the issue head-on, just as I did with wild carrot and poison hemlock in my previous book, *Nature's Garden*. Through two decades of collecting and eating this plant, I have learned many details about its life history and physical form that are not mentioned in the literature. I want to share this information for the sake of any reader who feels confident enough to use it.

I also think water parsnip is a fantastic food plant. Both the roots and the shoots are first-rate vegetables. Water parsnip was widely eaten by Native Americans in the United States and Canada, and most reports suggest that it was highly desired. A similar species of water parsnip, *Sium sisarum*, was domesticated centuries ago in Asia. This vegetable is known as skirret and is available in some seed catalogs today. It is best known for its roots, although Stephen Barstow, in his superb book *Around the World in Eighty Plants*, states that he grows skirret primarily for the shoots. The leaves and roots of wild skirret are still gathered in many places today.

To expunge a superb food from the list of wild edibles because we are afraid that someone will misidentify it would be holding wild plants to an extreme double-standard. After all, we *know* with *certainty* that millions of mistakes will be made by automobile drivers annually, resulting in tens of thousands of deaths and far more injuries. Yet we beg for the speed limits to be raised, and we take countless unnecessary joyrides, vacations, and other trips. *Veer four feet to the left and you're dead.* It happens every day. Literally. We choose our priorities. We ski; we ride horses, motorcycles, and bicycles—extremely dangerous activities that don't terrify us, even though many of the perils are out of our control. But we do control which plants enter our mouths. Our fear of unfamiliar plants is hard-wired, in the form of a protective instinct: *Don't eat a plant if you don't know what it is.* Pay attention, and heed that instinct.

Opposite A mature, blooming water parsnip *Sium suave* plant in late summer, standing in the mud of a dried-up pond that was two feet deep a month earlier. Notice the long, narrow leaflets and the lack of basal leaves.

DESCRIPTION

The identification of water parsnip is uniquely difficult among North American wild edibles. There are multiple related plants that can easily be confused with it, and all of them also grow in wetlands. The water-hemlocks (four species) are exceedingly poisonous and produce enlarged roots that look invitingly like vegetables, and smell pleasantly carrot-like to some noses. I hope you get what I'm saying here: *If you screw this up, you might die.*

This is definitely not a plant for beginners. Because of the high stakes, and because water parsnip is morphologically complex due to its amphibious lifestyle, the description here is more detailed and technical than usual. You should observe water parsnip through at least one full growing season, to become thoroughly familiar with it, before even considering eating it. You should identify water parsnip and water-hemlock *hundreds of times* to build up strong search images of *both* plants, and compare all parts carefully. (I personally did not eat water parsnip until four years after I first identified it.)

Water parsnip is a perennial herb with a basal rosette and one or a small number of erect stalks that reach 3–6 feet (1–2 m) in height. Stems may be produced in the center of a rosette, or beside it. The stalks are ridged with 7–9 angles that become sharper toward the top. The stem also has fine, light green grooves. Stems are hairless with little to no bloom. They are hollow, whitish inside, and jointed at the nodes. Any stem portion that grows underwater will be thick-walled and spongy, with visible air tubes (although this feature is absent on stems that grow in the air and are subsequently flooded). The surface is green except for purple coloration sometimes present at the base. The stems bear ascending branches in the upper half. Underwater stems may have roots growing from the nodes.

Basal leaves can be up to 2 feet (60 cm) long and have round, inflated, hollow petioles. These petioles are about as long as the leafy part of the rachis, and, unlike those of water-hemlocks, are constricted by purple-brown rings—even below the lowest leaflets. Basal leaves come in two very different forms.

The first leaves of spring have leaflets that are deeply cut into thin, lacy, thread-like sections (thus you could call them two or three times compound). The central rachis of lacy leaves is still very prominent and doesn't fork or divide, and the first divisions follow a regular pinnate pattern; but the divisions within the "leaflet" are erratic (see photo). Manuals often describe this lacy-leaflet form as belonging to underwater leaves, but in fact it is typical of the first spring leaves even on dry land.

The typical basal leaves, which come later, are once-compound in a pinnate fashion, with 7–17 leaflets. The leaflets are out of plane with the rachis, forming "ladder leaves" in the same way that parsnip leaves do. The leaflets are lanceolate

The first spring leaves of water parsnip *Sium suave*. These lacy leaves have not been underwater. Although the leaflets are finely divided, they are arranged in a neat pinnate pattern and the central rachis remains large and dominant. Also notice how both leaflets/divisions begin subdividing immediately where they attach to the rachis. Although it is hard to see in the photo, each petiole has one or more purple rings around it below the first attached leafy material. These leaves are in an ideal stage to eat.

to long-lanceolate, with fine, moderately spaced teeth on their margins. The leaflets themselves are rather widely spaced—rarely touching. The midvein and secondary veins of the leaflet are approximately level with the upper leaf surface of the blade. Secondary veins are few and angled less than 45° to the midvein; they divide and normally become indistinct before reaching the margins.

You can find forms intermediate between the lacy spring leaflets and the lanceolate summer leaflets (see photos). These intermediate leaves seem to be a response of later leaves to high water.

Stem leaves are alternate but otherwise similar to the basal ones, except that they are often narrower. They become shorter, with fewer leaflets, toward the top. Stem leaves are sheathing at the base (sometimes to the first leaflets); this sheath has a tiny, crescent-shaped hollow, fine grooves, and papery margins. After the first leaflet, the rachis of stem leaves abruptly narrows and becomes rounded and hollow with a narrow channel on top that soon tapers away. In the fall, when roots are harvested, the stem leaves will usually be the only leaves available for identification.

The inflorescence of water parsnip consists of several symmetrical com-

pound umbels of white flowers, borne at branch tips and upper leaf axils. The umbels are flat-topped, 1.3–2 inches (3.3–5 cm) across, with 13–19 ridged rays, each 0.4–1.4 inches (1–3.5 cm) long (longer in fruit). Beneath the first umbel division, as well as each umbellet, is a whorl of 3–11 linear to lanceolate bracts, entire with thin whitish margins, 0.15–0.5 inches (3–13 mm) long, bent back toward the peduncle or ray. There are minute hairs on and around these bracts. Umbellets only occasionally touch each other, but the flowers within them are often touching. Individual flowers are tiny with 5 white petals that appear about as broad as long—they actually have a long, narrow, claw-like tip folded in toward the center of the flower and nearly touching the base of the petal.

Water parsnip *Sium suave*,
flowers and immature fruit.

The fruit of water parsnip is 2–3 mm long, broadly oval, slightly flattened, hairless, with 3 prominent sharp ridges on each broad side and one on each edge (for a total of 8). This fruit is a schizocarp that splits in half after ripening and drying.

Water parsnip has a radiating cluster of numerous roots (10–30 is typical). These are whitish, with a surface made irregular by numerous smooth depressions or partial constrictions (constrictions do not go all the way around the root). The roots are widest near the middle of their length or toward the tip, and always taper gently. The roots are proportionately long—one as thick as a pencil (about as thick as they grow) may be 6–12 inches (15–30 cm) long. They are flexible and not stiff, but also not tough or stringy. The flesh is white, both inside and out.

Above An intermediate basal leaf form of water parsnip *Sium suave*, in midsummer, stimulated by high water. As always, the rachis is dominant, strongly tapering, and inflated. **Right** Mature stem of water parsnip *Sium suave*, solid green (except at base). Note the angles, which become more prominent toward the top.

CONFUSING SPECIES

Water-hemlocks are exceedingly poisonous—considered the most deadly wild plants in North America. There are four species, three of which have been the cause of fatal poisonings, and at least one is found in every region of North America. The roots of all are highly toxic, although Mulligan (1980) considers those of *C. bulbifera* less poisonous than the other species. The young leaves and stems are also highly toxic, but the older leaves and stems are less so (Kingsbury, 1964).

Important distinctions between the vegetative parts of water-hemlocks and water parsnip are laid out in the charts on pages 398 and 404 for easy comparison. I have not used the features of flowers and fruit in these charts because these parts are generally not available for examination when the edible parts of water parsnip are collected, and they may require additional magnification or technical knowledge to investigate. When using this chart **to identify water parsnip, never use a single characteristic—be sure that every available feature matches**, and that none of them match the features of any of the water-hemlocks.

Common water-hemlock *Cicuta maculata* is remarkably widespread, from Alaska to Labrador, south to Florida, Mexico, and California. It grows along waterways but also in wet meadows and ditches without standing water. **Western water-hemlock *Cicuta douglasii*** is found from California to Montana, through British Columbia north to southern Alaska, in marshes and on the margins of ponds, lakes, and rivers. Although less widespread, this plant is locally common and perhaps resembles water parsnip the most closely. **Northern water-hemlock *Cicuta virosa*** grows in similar habitats in the northern boreal forest region across Alaska and Canada. **Bulblet water-hemlock *Cicuta bulbifera*** is a delicate plant of permanent waterways that grows on shore or on top of floating objects such as logs or mats; it often is not rooted to anything solid. Although widespread from Florida to Alaska, this species is most common in the northeastern United States and adjacent Canada. At maturity, it is easily distinguished from water parsnip and other water-hemlocks by its abundance of tiny bulblets borne in the leaf axils.

Oxypolis rigidior of the East, *O. occidentalis* of California and Oregon, and *O. fendleri* of the southern Rockies, are often presumed poisonous, and are sometimes called "cowbane"—but that name apparently derives from confusion with water-hemlock. Hamel and Chiltoskey (1975) report that the Cherokee called *O. rigidior* "wild potato" and ate the roots after baking. I have seen no evidence that any part of any of these *Oxypolis* species is poisonous. These plants of marshes and streamsides grow in moderate shade to full sun. The leaves are pinnately once compound, but the leaflets are fewer than with water parsnip, and their margins differ. The leaflets of *O. rigidior* are entire or have just a few very large, sharp teeth in the terminal half. The leaflets of *O. occidentalis* have a small number of large, rounded teeth; while those of *O. fendleri* have a few large, blunt teeth or may be entire. The petioles of all species are much thinner than those of water parsnip. The roots of *O. rigidior* are clustered, spaghetti-thick, and white, terminating in a spherical white enlargement; those of *O. occidentalis* form a tuberous knobby mass from which thin, white roots spread. I have not been able to confirm the form of *O. fendleri* roots.

Berula erecta (a species unfortunately also called "water parsnip") is widespread in North America, Europe, and Asia, but rather uncommon because it is confined to spring-fed wetlands. Its toxicity status is unknown. Although the name situation is confusing, this one is pretty easy to tell from *Sium suave*.

It has thinner and weaker stems, and the compound umbels are much smaller—scarcely more than an inch across. *Berula erecta* has a basal rosette that strongly resembles a small parsnip (not water parsnip)—the leaflets are ovate to obovate and blunt. The upper stem leaves, however, have pointed and erratically lobed or deeply toothed leaflets. The petioles of *Berula erecta* are not inflated and have at most a tiny hollow; they are thin, and also lack constrictions below the lowest leaflets. The root system is completely different: *B. erecta* grows from a thin rhizome of nearly uniform thickness, which produces whorls of numerous thread-like roots at its nodes.

NOT WATER PARSNIP
Above right Basal leaves of *Oxypolis rigidior*. The leaflets are either entire, or (like the lowest ones here), have one or two very large teeth per side in the terminal third. Also, the rachis/petiole is much narrower. **Below right** The rootlets of *Oxypolis rigidior* terminate with a smooth, white, marble-like enlargement—totally unlike water parsnip.

Water parsnip versus water hemlock identification chart—features of roots and stems

	Water parsnip *Sium suave*	Bulblet water-hemlock *Cicuta bulbifera*	Common water-hemlock *Cicuta maculata*	Western water-hemlock *Cicuta douglasii*	Northern water-hemlock *Cicuta virosa*
Root arrangement	8–30 long, thin roots attached at stem base and radiating. Up to 1 cm thick and 12 inches (30 cm) long, flexible but brittle "rat tails" widest near center or tip. No enlarged mass at root top	Very short, slightly thickened root, often curved; on large plants develops into a multi-pronged knob. Very small in proportion to plant. From this radiates numerous limp, thread-like roots	Cluster of 3–15 stout, stiff, enlarged roots branches, narrow where attached, tip pointed; up to 3 cm thick and 5 inches (13 cm) long. No enlarged turnip-like mass at top	Somewhat enlarged turnip-like root mass at top, with few to several elongated, flexible root branches up to 1.2 cm thick, not constricted where attached, spreading out beneath this	Enlarged turnip-like mass at root top, with several to numerous thin, elongated root branches up to 3 mm thick spreading from the sides and bottom
Surface of root	White with partial constrictions or dimples	String-like roots light; knob yellowish-brown	Light brown, minutely roughened	Light brownish to yellow-brown, faintly textured	Light brownish to yellow-brown, almost smooth
Root interior	White with NO resin and NO colored veins	Whitish with yellow resin in pockets and veins—resin darkens with air exposure (with bulb-bearing water-hemlock, resin is less prevalent and hard to see except in large knobs)			
Root scent	Faint, parsnip-like	Faint to mild, carrot-like	Strong, carrot-like		
Chambering at stem/ root juncture	Few large chambers in stem base; none in roots	Few large chambers in stem base; smaller ones in root knob (if present)	Chambers in stem base paper-thin and hard to notice	Several flat, coin-slot-like chambers stacked inside turnip-like root top and in stem base	
Stem coloration	Light green, except occasionally purplish near base. Bloom faint to none.	Mostly light green, sometimes purple. Often thin stripes. Bloom faint to moderate.	Light green to purple, usually a mixture of the two. More purple in sun. Often with thin stripes. Bloom moderate to heavy		
Stem cross section	7–9 angles, sharper near top and with age.	Rounded, smooth			

Above Typical water parsnip *Sium suave* root cluster in early autumn. A month later these would be slightly thicker, like the ones in my hand at the chapter's start. **Below** The stem base and root system of bulblet water-hemlock *Cicuta bulbifera*. The J-shape happened because this plant was growing on a log, and the log rolled over in a flood, so the plant grew funny. But note, this stem, from the largest specimen I could find, is an inch thick—but the storage organ (a pronged root knob, shown sliced) is proportionally tiny. On a small plant, this knob is the size of an ant's abdomen, and you won't find it. Most of the root system consists of numerous thin, limp, string-like roots radiating in all directions.

The base of common water-hemlock *Cicuta maculata* sliced in half. Note the yellow resin. Using the "chambered root or stem base" as a distinguishing characteristic (as touted by many sources) is problematic. The large chambers visible at the stem base here are shared by many hollow-stemmed plants, including sometimes water parsnip, and represent the node of a lower stem leaf. The small transverse partitions or chambers in the root top and root/stem interface are supposedly diagnostic of the genus *Cicuta*. The idea that these are a good feature for distinguishing their roots from those of other plants is carried over from Europe, where *Cicuta virosa*, the species with prominent chambers, is found. It is misleading for North America, where we have three additional species of water-hemlock, all with less prominent chambers. In *Cicuta douglasii*, the chambers are smaller but still evident, and are a reasonably good identifier. However, the chambers in *Cicuta maculata*, as seen here, are paper thin and hard to notice—they should not be relied on for telling it from water parsnip. With *Cicuta bulbifera*, the storage organ of the root system is so small that the chambers, while present, are difficult or impossible to notice except on the largest specimens—hardly useful in identification.

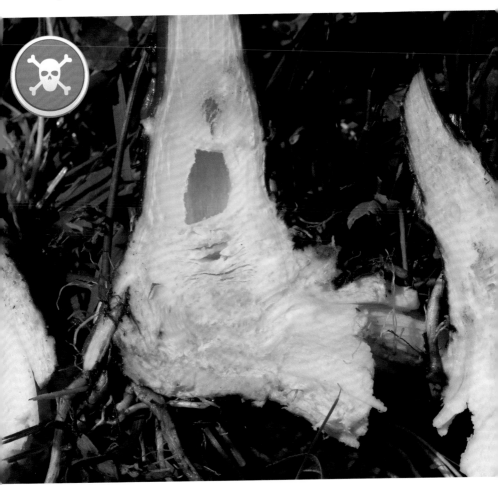

The enlarged, clustered storage rootlets of a robust common water-hemlock *Cicuta maculata* in summer. The largest root branch here is over an inch thick. These "tuberous roots" look and smell like vegetables. No other toxic plant is so insidiously appealing in appearance. This is part of the plant's perfect storm of deadliness: Occasional people foolishly succumb to the temptation to eat this root without identifying it. This brashness—not misidentification—accounts for virtually all water-hemlock poisonings.

Western water-hemlock *Cicuta douglasii*. The root has an enlarged top, with some spreading root branches beneath it. In the sliced part, you can see the thin, stacked partitions (chambers) and also the copious yellowish resin. (Northern water-hemlock *Cicuta virosa* has a more enlarged, turnip-like root top, and the spreading roots are more numerous and smaller. Its root chambers are larger.) Note how this smaller basal leaf is pretty close to being once pinnately compound, like the leaf of water parsnip. Photo by T. Abe Lloyd.

Above A common water-hemlock *Cicuta maculata* storage rootlet, from a robust plant that had 14 of them clustered at the base. It is constricted at both ends. Yellow resin is visible in the broken rootlet. **Below** Basal leaves of common water-hemlock *Cicuta maculata* in spring.

Water parsnip versus water hemlock identification chart—features of typical leaves (reduced upper leaves are simpler)

	Water parsnip *Sium suave*	Bulblet water-hemlock *Cicuta bulbifera*	Common water-hemlock *Cicuta maculata*	Western water-hemlock *Cicuta douglasii*	Northern water-hemlock *Cicuta virosa*
Typical # of leaflets	7–17, distinct	15–30, most indistinct	30–95, mostly distinct	11–45, mostly distinct	25–80, many indistinct
Typical leaflet shape and aspect	Long-lanceolate, tip tapered, flat; out of plane with rachis	Narrow, linear, deeply cut with spreading lobes; in plane	Lanceolate to ovate, pointed, often folded; roughly in plane		Narrow-lanceolate, some deeply cut, often folded; roughly in plane
First spring leaflets	Deeply divided into thread-like divisions	Same as later leaves			
Spear-like leaf shoots	Produced in late spring or early summer	Not produced			
Leaflet mid-vein above	Level with blade or slightly raised, hairless	Slightly depressed, hairless	Very depressed, hairless	Very depressed, hairless or nearly so	Depressed, with tiny stiff hairs
Leaflet secondary veins above	Curvy, not prominent or depressed, 20–40° angle to midvein, branching to obscurity before reaching margin	One visible depressed vein runs to the tip of each division or major lobe, usually ending at a tooth	Several; distinct, deeply depressed, 45–60° to midvein, most running straight and unbroken to the margin (or nearly), usually terminating in the notch between teeth.		Few to several, less prominent, depressed, 25–40° to midvein, running to margin and usually ending at a notch
Form and arrangement of typical large leaf	Dominant central rachis with no branches (Once pinnately compound). Whole leaf elongated. (First spring leaf with subdivided leaflets, each having tiny rachis)	Rachis splits 3 ways once or twice, then leaf divides further (2–4 times compound). Whole leaf broadly triangular or spreading loosely in outline	Rachis first splits 3 ways, the central branch somewhat larger. Each major branch splits again (2–4 times compound). Whole leaf broadly triangular in outline	Rachis dominant but with some compound branches, especially near base. (2 times compound, rarely 1 or 3 times). Whole leaf elongated or narrowly triangular in outline	Rachis dominant but with substantial subdividing branches. (3–4 times compound) Whole leaf triangular in outline
Petiole or rachis rings	Always below first leaflet	Not below first leaflet or division (but observe carefully—stems also have rings, and divisions can get broken or bitten off)			

Above left A water parsnip *Sium suave* leaflet, close up. The midvein is not depressed. The secondary veins are not depressed, not very evident, are at an angle of less than 45°, are curvy, and branch to become indistinct before reaching the margins. Some small veins do terminate in the notch between teeth—despite the fact that many books say this is not so (a few even claim that it is the sole foolproof distinction between water parsnip and water-hemlock). Do not rely on this characteristic, or any other single characteristic, to identify the plant—use all of them. **Above right** A leaflet of common water-hemlock *Cicuta maculata*, close up. The midvein is distinctly depressed. The secondary veins are depressed, and run at an angle of greater than 45°, almost straight to the notches between teeth. Occasionally these veins split before reaching the margins, and in this case one of the prominent branches may terminate in a tooth. **Below right** Basal leaf of common water-hemlock *Cicuta maculata* emerging in spring. These are pure light green. Note that the naked section of the rachis doesn't have any constricted rings around it, and the leaves are not wrapped around the rachis to form a spear-like shoot.

The flowering top of common water-hemlock *Cicuta maculata*. The stems are purple and not angled. At the first juncture in the umbel, bracts range from zero to several, and from compound to entire. At the second juncture (under the umbellets) there are several linear bracts of unequal size, the larger ones sometimes toothed or lobed. These parts are hairless. They eventually fall off after blooming, so cannot be observed on dry tops.

Right Stem leaf of western water-hemlock *Cicuta douglasii*. The general outline is more elongated than with *Cicuta maculata*. The side branches are shorter, and the leaflets more packed. Nevertheless, it is still clearly more than once compound. Photo by T. Abe Lloyd.

Below Common water-hemlock *Cicuta maculata*. The major leaves are two to four times compound and broadly triangular in outline.

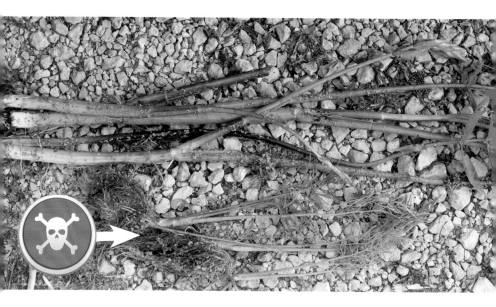

Above Stems of water parsnip *Sium suave* (top) and bulblet water-hemlock *Cicuta bulbifera* (bottom) that were growing in the same pond. Bulblet water-hemlock is more likely to grow beside water parsnip than the other species, but it floats free or grows with its roots in debris at or above the normal water level, whereas water parsnip is almost always rooted in the bottom. You can see that water parsnip is a much more robust plant. The stems, where growing underwater, become thick, spongy, and white inside. The difference in leaf form is evident, as are the pointed shoots of water parsnip, and the rings around its petioles. Note also the numerous thread-like roots of bulblet water-hemlock. **Below** The stem of bulblet water-hemlock *Cicuta bulbifera*. Water-hemlocks do not have rings around the naked petiole—but they DO have rings around the stems at nodes, as seen here. On a young plant like this, if you don't look carefully, you might fool yourself into thinking this stem is a petiole.

Above The stem leaves of bulblet water-hemlock *Cicuta bulbifera*. The leaflets or divisions are linear and erratically toothed or lobed, the divisions or lobes wide-spreading. Notice the major division at the leaf's base, immediately where the sheath ends. Lower leaves are larger with more leaflets, but the form is otherwise similar. Also notice the many bulblets forming along the branch. These get larger by autumn and drop off into the water to reproduce the plant. **Right** The emerging basal leaf of bulblet water-hemlock *Cicuta bulbifera*. It is not wrapped into a spear-like shoot, and the prominent linear divisions are already evident. The naked petiole has no rings around it.

HABITAT

Water parsnip grows in wet, muddy sites such as ditches, warm-water streams, lakeshores, pond margins, and river sloughs. It does best in a soil with lots of dark organic muck, or muck mixed with clay. It is occasionally found in sand or gravel, where it tends to be smaller. Water parsnip is sometimes seen on mudflats or even moist ground some distance from a waterway when water levels are low. More commonly, however, this plant grows right beside or in standing water. Water

Water parsnip *Sium suave*.
Limited to waterways.

parsnip will grow well in full sun, but most commonly it is found in light to moderate shade. It is more prevalent in locations where occasional floods and fluctuating water levels leave bare soil. Probably the best place to find it is in a

Excellent habitat for water parsnip: an intermittent floodwater pond in a sunny opening along the Mississippi River, with silver maple, river bulrush, water plantain, and water smartweed. Some water parsnip can be seen blooming in the depression.

seasonally flooded pond within a river floodplain, especially a pond that is large enough to create an opening in the canopy. However, it doesn't need wet feet; I have seen it on dry gravel roadsides or dikes running through swamps and marshes. It is highly associated with bur reed, river bulrush, water plantain, wild rice, wapato, and bulblet water-hemlock. It is also highly associated with various species of the obnoxious *Bidens* (the flattened, two-pronged sticktights of low ground), so you may want to avoid wearing socks when harvesting it.

Water parsnip's life is ruled by rain, and teaches us the difference between long-term and short-term benefit. High water makes its habitat, by moving mud, scouring banks, piling debris, and drowning vegetation. But high water also makes its life hard. It grows as an aquatic rosette on the pond bottom when flooded, and doesn't produce a stalk until the water level recedes and exposes the leaves to air. If the high water lasts too long, it can drown. Sometimes, plants on dry ground bloom three months before those in deeper water nearby. Like most wetland plants, water parsnip thrives and grows largest in dry years.

HARVEST AND PREPARATION

Water parsnip has two excellent edible parts: the roots and the shoots/greens.

Roots: These are collected in the dormant season, from early autumn through spring. The best time to collect is in late fall; these plants often stay green quite late into autumn. They take advantage of the autumn sun after the trees have dropped their leaves, allowing them to survive in surprisingly shaded swamps. As long as they are still flowering, they will not have invested much energy into the roots. Look for tops that are in fruit—better yet, that have ripened or dropped their seed. If the leaves and stems have begun to brown, after several frosts, the roots will be at their best—but make sure the plants are intact enough to be readily identified.

Monocarpic root crops (those that flower once and then die), such as parsnip and burdock, generally have a single, large taproot and are collected in the rosette stage, before they produce a flowering stalk. Water parsnip is not like this; it is *polycarpic*. Robust and healthy individuals produce a stalk; for collecting efficiency, seek these and ignore those with rosettes only. This is the opposite of what one does with monocarpic root vegetables.

The places where water parsnips grow are seasonally wet. The water is often low in autumn, allowing you to walk in dried-up sloughs or marsh edges with ease. If the slough gets too dry, the roots become harder to dig, and you may need a shovel. I prefer collecting water parsnip when the ground is soft—otherwise the super-tender roots tend to break off in the soil. After heavy fall rains, high water can interfere with gathering. Early spring would be a great time to harvest, but the plants are almost always flooded then.

I dig the whole root mass out of the mud, gently and carefully so as not to break off the tender extremities of the roots. In very soft mud you can do this by hand, but a shovel or garden fork is better. Pick off the larger roots to keep, then replant the crown. I often just pull the root mass partway out of the soil, pivoting it on one side, and pull off a few large roots. Check in the mud underneath the plant: The roots are very tender, and the largest ones often break off and stay in the muck. Grab any detached roots so they don't go to waste. After you've taken your harvest, pivot the root mass back into place and press it down firmly. The plant will survive this treatment, and you can have a perpetual harvest without depleting your patch of water parsnip. In fact, this is exactly how skirret is treated in the

Emerging leaves of water parsnip *Sium suave* in late spring. The early, lacy spring leaves have been flooded and covered with scum. Those standing erect now are the second flush, with intermediate leaflet form. On the left are two leaf shoots, wrapped into spear-like form like asparagus—in the perfect stage to eat. You can see the the rings around the petioles on all the leaves.

garden—you harvest a few nice roots and replant the crown. Water parsnip crowns transplant very well, even after the larger roots are removed, so you can easily thin a crowded colony and start another elsewhere. You can also sprinkle the seeds on a muddy shore where you'd like to see some growing.

During a particularly wet growing season, water parsnips along rivers are flooded most of the summer; these will barely eke by and have virtually no energy to store. In the fall after a year like this, there will be nothing more than a few spaghetti-thin roots attached to the base. In this case, leave the plants alone.

Water parsnip roots are very tender, with a sweet, aromatic flavor reminiscent of a parsnip, but they are less spicy and sweeter. In fact, the name "skirret" is a corruption of the Dutch for "sugar root"; the name in most northern European languages translates similarly. Water parsnip roots are good raw, but before being eaten that way should be thoroughly washed in clean water in case there are some undesirable organisms in their mud of origin. They are delicious by themselves, just fried in butter, baked, steamed, or boiled. You can hardly go wrong cooking them with other vegetables in casserole, stir-fry, or soup. The only problem is that they are small, and you probably won't have as many of them as you want.

The Thompson Indians of British Columbia gathered the roots in fall or spring. They were sometimes eaten raw, but most of the supply was pit-cooked and then dried for storage (Turner et al. 1990). Turner (1978) reports that the roots were eaten by the Okanagan, Shuswap, Thompson, Lower Lillooet, Carrier, and Kootenay of British Columbia. Many of these same peoples also ate the shoots in spring.

Shoots/greens: All of the tender, meristematic leaves and stems of water parsnip are edible, but the shoot in particular is a unique vegetable that I have not seen explained anywhere. The stem of water parsnip grows rather slowly, beginning in summer, well after its leaves have formed—about when regular or "land parsnip" is blooming. It does not form a shoot. The shoot is actually formed by the rapidly growing basal or lower stem *leaf*—but not the first leaf to appear in spring. The first leaves have lacy, multi-compound leaflets and typically do not form shoots. The leaves of the second flush, appearing later in spring, are the ones that produce shoots. Leaf shoots are straight and pointed, and at first they have their leaflets wrapped tightly around the rachis in a bundle at the tip; at a glance you can easily be fooled into thinking this is a stem. The petiole is round, hollow, and tapered, with a few light-colored purple-brown bands around it, corresponding to septa that divide the hollow inside into separate compartments.

Water parsnip shoots have a flavor that is pleasant and aromatic, almost as if you crossed celery and parsley. But they are far more tender than either of those vegetables. They are excellent raw or cooked, alone or mixed with other

Leaf shoots of water parsnip, showing spear-like tip of typical wrapped leaves. Note petiole rings. There is one partially opened leaf tip that shows intermediate (partially cut) leaflets—these cut leaflets can more easily be confused with water-hemlock leaves at this phase. **Observe all features!** In flavor these are something like a celery-cilantro-parsley, but more tender than the best asparagus.

vegetables. Any young, tender leaves and stem tips can be used—even after the shoot tips have opened. However, don't use leaves that have been underwater raw (see liver fluke caution, page 385). You can chop young water parsnip greens into soup for seasoning, just as you would with celery leaf or lovage. They make a nice addition to salads, omelets, or burritos, as you'd use cilantro. Use it as a garnish, or sprinkled into pasta like parsley.

Our ancestors did not fear plants; they respected them. They left us a remarkable body of knowledge about the properties of those plants. It is good to be cautious when using this knowledge. It is good to exercise great care in identifying what we eat. Especially with a plant like water parsnip. And it is good to have the best food on Earth.

Wild Radishes

Raphanus raphanistrum **and** *R. sativus*

planted radishes in the garden because my father had bought the seeds—not because I liked radishes. No indeed; I hated them. But still, I weeded and sometimes watered them, because that's what you do with things in the garden. In early summer my dad would dig up the plants, wash the red roots, and crunch them raw while I looked on and wondered if I would have to punish myself that way when I grew up.

The tender top of feral radish *R. sativus* just beginning to bloom. The upper part of the plant provides great greens at this stage.

And then I grew up. I quit planting radishes, but I noticed that there was a weed called "wild radish" in all the fields and ditches. So I pulled one up: no big red root there. OK, then what? It turns out, the root is the least interesting part of wild radish.

DESCRIPTION

There are two closely related weeds who both get called "wild radish." *Raphanus sativus* is the cultivated radish gone feral, so I call him "feral radish." The other wild radish, *Raphanus raphanistrum*, has never submitted to the hands of gardeners, vexing the same cultivators who took his relation into custody. I call him "wild radish." I use the plural "wild radishes" to refer to these species collectively, as in the chapter heading.

Both wild radishes are knee-to-waist-high annuals or winter annuals, with basal leaves that persist through flowering (not withering away like those of many mustards). The larger rosette leaves are 6–10 inches (15–25 cm) long, ruffled, with depressed veins and several pairs of deep lobes or divisions, pinnately

Wild radish *R. raphanistrum* during a warm spell in late autumn. The greens are fairly good at this stage.

arranged. The first divisions are often very small and widely separated; toward the tip the lobes are much larger and closely packed, often overlapping. The terminal division often accounts for most of the leaf's surface area. The blade is ruffled and the veins are depressed. Toward the top of the plant the leaves become much smaller and less lobed, and the petioles get shorter as well; the uppermost leaves are sessile and unlobed. All parts of wild radishes have long, stiff, tapered, needle-like hairs, formidable enough on mature plants to create some discomfort to bare hands when they are pulled from the garden. The prevalence and size of these hairs helps distinguish wild radishes from most other common mustards.

Of the two, wild radish *R. raphanistrum* averages a bit shorter and tends to produce more stems, which lean in all directions. Its leaves are more concentrated at or near the base. Feral radish *R. sativus* has midveins that are sometimes purplish, and its whole body is glossier in appearance and has fewer stiff hairs.

Like other members of the mustard family, wild radishes produce racemes of 4-petaled flowers, each flower with 6 stamens. The flowers are large for a mustard—up to 0.9 inches (2.3 cm) across. The plants bloom year-round in

Feral radish *R. sativus* rosettes in autumn, with good tender leaves. The differences between the leaves of the two species are subtle.

mild climates, peaking in late winter; in colder climates they flower most prodigiously in early and mid summer. Wild radish *R. raphanistrum* has yellow petals, with slightly darkened veins. (It is sometimes reported to have pink or purple flowers, but I have never seen this and think these reports are the result of name confusion.) Feral radish *R. sativus* has petals that are purple, pink, white, or light yellow—usually with notably darkened veins, which are sometimes of a different color than the main blade of the petal.

The foolproof feature for distinguishing wild radishes—from other mustards and from each other—is the fruit. On both wild radishes these are thick pods bulging around large seeds, and the pods are unusual in that they do not split open to release them. The pods of wild radish *R. raphanistrum* are around 0.2 inches (5 mm) wide and 2–3 inches (5–7 cm) long, curving, with a long, pointed beak. They typically contain 6–8 seeds, and upon drying, the pods develop fine grooves lengthwise and become very constricted between the bulges; they break into short, corky sections, each of which encloses one seed. The pods of feral radish *R. sativus* are much stouter, with only 3–5 seeds; their surface remains smooth upon drying, and they do not become so constricted between the seeds.

I include these distinguishing details in case you want to know which species you are consuming, and so you do not get confused by the befuddled descriptions you may read. (If authors continually admonish our readers to check every detail and make sure they match, we have to uphold our part of the deal and make sure that our descriptions are accurate.)

HABITAT

Being introduced weeds, both of these species are widespread and erratic in their occurrence. They might turn up nearly anywhere in North America inhabited by people. Wild radish is considered the most prevalent weed of small grains and peanuts in the Southeast (Malik 2009). It is also a prevalent crop weed in my region of the Upper Midwest. Part of wild radish's success is due to the fact that it produces allelopathic chemicals inhibiting the growth of other plants. It is so effective at this that it has been researched as a weed-killing cover crop with potential for organic agriculture (Malik 2009).

Wild radish. *R. raphanistrum* is found in varying abundance throughout the mapped range. *R. sativus* is abundant in the darker blue areas near the coast; in the continent's interior it ranges from common to rare, being more common in the South.

Feral radish is extremely common near the West Coast, in both urban and farm settings; it is widespread but less common in the continent's interior. Feral radish abounds in the vicinity of Los Angeles, the San Francisco Bay, Portland, and Seattle, and does well right on the seashore.

Both species need disturbed soil and full sun, and thrive with high levels of soil moisture—although not where it is swampy or waterlogged. The large seeds remain viable for several years, and their size gives the wild radishes a competitive boost among other weeds. The corky pod sections encasing the seeds are both protective and buoyant—ideal for dispersal via floods or ocean waves.

HARVEST AND PREPARATION

Both species of wild radish are used similarly for food. You can eat all the tender parts of the plant: leaves, young stems, flower buds, flowers, and immature pods.

The tuft of rosette leaves that forms before any stalk develops will make excellent leafy greens, and these persist for several weeks. The tender stem tips and

Mature blooming plant of wild radish *R. raphanistrum*. This species is shorter and less erect than feral radish, with thinner stems.

Above Flowers and dry, brown pods of feral radish, *R. sativus.* Note the irregualrity of the constrictions, lack of pod curvature, fewer bulges, and smooth surface (when pods of *R. raphanistrum* dry out, they become grooved). The pods are the easiest way to tell the species apart. **Below left** Here is feral radish *R. sativus* with nearly white flowers, but note the prominent veins in the petals. **Below right** *R. sativus* with yellow petals. Kind of amazing that one species can vary this much.

their half-formed leaves, after a stalk has formed but before flowering, are also ideal. The stem tips will remain tender even into the early stages of flowering.

Being annuals or winter annuals, wild radishes may germinate at any time when it is warm and the soil is moist, but they grow largest where they can germinate in fall, overwinter as a rosette, and then bloom in spring. Plants that germinate in early spring or late winter can grow nearly as robust, but those germinating in summer may grow quickly to a small adult size before setting seed and dying. The greens are at peak abundance at the height of summer in cold temperate climates, although good ones often appear again in autumn as new plants germinate. In milder climates, such as coastal California or the Southeast, they are most prevalent in late winter or early spring. Thus, the wild

Flowers and green pods of wild radish *R. raphanistrum*. Unlike its variable cousin, the flowers of this one are always yellow. At least, that's all I've ever seen. And I've seen billions.

radishes can be found at a particular stage of growth at varying times during the growing season.

The stiff hairs on wild radish can make the greens too prickly for pleasant eating raw; with feral radish, this is less true. I sometimes eat them raw, but much prefer them cooked. They are good steamed or boiled, or used in egg dishes or casseroles, and they make an excellent fried green. Cooking has the additional benefit of toning down their spicy flavor.

Just days before a particular raceme begins to flower, it will have a tender stalk and a cluster of flower buds; this is another excellent part to pick. The flowers, being rather large (for a mustard) and pretty, make a decorative addition to salads. As is generally the case with mustards, the stems and leaves closest to the flowers are the spiciest; it is here that you will definitely note the unmistakable radishy hotness.

The funnest, and perhaps the trickiest, edible part of wild radishes is the pods. Unusually large (for a mustard) seedpods with a long beak are a hallmark of both wild radish species. These pods have a hot radishy flavor similar to that of the stems, only a touch sweeter. They are crisp, juicy, and tender—but only if you get them young enough. Older pods quickly become tough and woody. The racemes of wild and feral radish typically have all stages of development present simultaneously. At the tip will be unopened flower buds, followed by flowers, then tiny pods just beginning to form. At the base, if the raceme is old enough, there will be fully mature, even dry pods. What you are looking for are the largest pods that don't yet have any bulges, as the bulges indicate maturity and toughness. Each raceme has only a few ideal pods, so be choosy. Chew up a few to figure out which ones you like. These radish pods are delicious in Chinese-style quick stir-fry. Foraging authors Kevin Feinstein and Christopher Nyerges both recommend making radish-pod pickles. This is something I have not tried but definitely want to.

The one part of wild radishes that I didn't mention eating is the root. Although some plant books claim that these weeds have enlarged, fleshy roots like radishes, I think this is an assumption more than an observation. The roots of wild and feral radishes (except perhaps recently escaped members of the latter species) are thin, white, and rather tough. There is a thin layer of hot, radishy flesh on the outside of that root, but it is usually not large enough to warrant much attention.

Even without the plump root of its domestic counterpart, wild radish proves to be a surprisingly useful vegetable. Being one of our continent's more widespread and abundant weeds, it is a great plant for the forager to know.

Wintercress (Yellow Rocket, Creasy Greens, Land Cress)

Genus *Barbarea*

When I was in fifth grade, I had a friend named Chris whose extended family owned a large dairy and hog farm encompassing several hundred acres. This family was of Italian descent, and every year, the children would gather bundles of broccoli-like stems from their fields and sell them from a roadside stand, behind a sign that said "mustard greens for sale." Although the greens tasted terrible to me, they made a good pile of cash that way.

A clump of common wintercress *B. vulgaris*. The stems are just beginning to bolt and are now very tender. The leaves are voluminous and tender, but at this stage have a strong flavor that the newcomer may shrink from. Not literally. (That would be weird.) Winter rosettes actually have the mildest leaves—and I've even picked them frozen many times and thawed them for salads.

Some years after the above experience, I learned that the plant that my friend was calling "mustard greens" was called "yellow rocket" by most farmers and "wintercress" in most books, and that supposedly it was popular with Italians. Euell Gibbons reported in *Stalking the Wild Asparagus* that the first sign of spring near Philadelphia was "the Italians, swarming out from town to gather wintercress from fields and ditches." The wild food literature is full of dubious ethnic associations (my former Russian roommate thought it was both hilarious and offensive that one of my books claimed that cattail shoots were popular in his homeland), so I wasn't sure what to think of this claim.

A few years later I was leading a plant walk, and one of the participants was a young woman who had grown up on a small farm in Italy and moved to the United States about two years earlier. I stopped the class to point out a vigorous young wintercress clump with several stalks bearing swelling flower buds, explaining that although this one was in perfect condition, very few people like the greens upon first taste, especially raw. The Italian woman was only marginally interested in the class, having been brought by her husband. She was reading a novel, in fact, as she walked in the woods. An Italian novel. But when I mentioned that this plant was supposedly popular in Italy, she looked

Common winter cress in bloom is quite showy. This is the time to key out your species, if you so wish, but this is not a time to eat it.

up from her book and said, "Oh, that plant. We eat that all the time." She casually leaned over, plucked the largest stem, and started happily eating the top end of it while reading. The other participants looked at each other as if to say, "Well, if the beautiful Italian chick jumped in, it obviously can't be *that* bad," and each of them grabbed his or her own stalk to chomp on. Within seconds, most of them were grimacing or spitting out their mouthfuls. The Italian lady chowed on contentedly.

This is the nature of wintercress: a forager will probably not enjoy its peculiarly strong flavor at first—especially not when raw. But eventually one may come to tolerate, and then appreciate, and finally even crave it. Like beer or hot sauce. It works that way for all ethnicities, not just Italians.

DESCRIPTION

There are three widespread species of wintercress in North America, one of which is native. All of them typically grow as biennials or winter annuals. From late summer through late winter, wintercress is just a basal rosette of leaves that gathers and stores energy for spring flowering. The rosette leaves are up to 9 inches (23 cm) long and have a long rachis bearing a few to several divisions. The leaf divisions are sometimes slightly narrowed near the base, but they remain leafy all the way to the rachis; they sometimes have rudimentary mini-divisions between them. The terminal division is larger than the lateral ones; it is ovate, rounded, or elliptic, with a blunt tip and no teeth, but the edge is often wavy. The rachis is shallowly channeled and edged with a thin, leafy wing in the upper part.

Composite range of all species of wintercress. The far north is exclusively inhabited by the native *B. orthoceras*. The small *B. verna* is most common in the Southeast and along the West Coast.

Leaves are borne alternately on the flowering stem, which may reach 30 inches (75 cm) tall. Both basal and stem leaves have hairless blades and are rather thick with a smooth surface—even when young. This distinguishes them from many other mustards, most of which have hairs on the leaf blades, and leaves that are ruffled by deep depressions or folds along the veins, especially when young. Stems, usually several per plant, are thick, strongly angled, and ridged; they are branchy in the upper part. Wintercress is very showy when in bloom, coloring entire hayfields and meadows in late spring. The top of the plant produces numerous racemes of bright yellow, 4-petaled flowers about 0.4 inch

(1 cm) across. By early summer these mature into long, narrow seedpods, and by mid summer the stems have died, turned brown, and released their seeds.

Barbarea vulgaris, the common wintercress or yellow rocket, is found virtually everywhere in North America that is inhabited by people; it is one of our most ubiquitous weeds. It is most frequent in agricultural regions: abundant at low elevations in the Pacific states, the more fertile sections of the Great Plains, the Midwest, and the Northeast. You can find it in most places in between as well, just not as frequently. Common wintercress loves disturbed, rich, moist soil, and is a common weed of crop fields and gardens. It competes with perennial vegetation much better than annuals and therefore persists for many years after a disturbance—although it is far more common in the first two or three years. (I have seen hayfields that sported stands of wintercress so thick that, when the weed was in flower, they could have easily been confused with fields of blooming canola.) Construction sites are good places to find it, as are pastures, roadsides, and especially ditches. They are also common along trails and logging roads through wooded areas, where their early spring and late fall growth allow them to photosynthesize while the overhead trees are bare. Many of the best areas I've seen for collecting wintercress are along the edges of streams or in gravel bars. In such locations, they thrive due to the periodic soil disturbance caused by floods. Wintercress seems to be a generalist in terms of soil type, as long as there is sufficient moisture—although it grows largest and tastes better in the richest soils.

On the basal leaves of common wintercress, the terminal division is incongruously large—much larger than all the other lobes combined. Normally there are 2 or 4 tiny lateral lobes, and rarely as many as 8. The terminal division is ovate or rounded, lacking teeth but often with a wavy edge; it usually has 2 curled, ear-like lobes at the base. (The terminal division of stem leaves is narrower.) *Barbarea vulgaris* is the largest and most robust of our wintercresses; the young stems on the better specimens may be more than half an inch thick.

Barbarea orthoceras (**American wintercress**) is the native look-alike, differing subtly in that its leaves have narrower terminal lobes. It is a slightly less robust plant. The distinction used in most botanical keys is that the pods of *B. orthoceras* have a shorter beak on the tip (less than 1.5 mm) than those of *B. vulgaris* (more than 2 mm). However, even if this method of distinguishing them were fully reliable (it's not), it is almost useless to a forager, because the plant is tough, bitter, and nearly dead by the time of fruiting. Since they taste similar, telling them apart is certainly not required (except in those few places at the periphery of its range where American wintercress is rare and protected.) This species largely replaces *B. vulgaris* in the boreal forest region of the North, and in the Rocky Mountains. The native species is more prevalent in natural wetland margins such as piles of lakeshore debris, but it also becomes weedy.

Barbarea verna is the third widespread species. The Latin species name means "of spring," but this species is just as wintry and no more springy than the others. It largely replaces *B. vulgaris* in the Southeast, but it is also common in the Pacific states and can be found scattered in most of the United States. My friends in North Carolina call it "creasy greens." It is sometimes grown as a garden vegetable and can be purchased from some seed catalogs; the cultivated varieties have larger leaves, and are usually called "land cress" or "upland cress" to differentiate them from watercress. Creasy greens are less likely to be associated with ditches, swamps, and muddy places than common wintercress, and seem to depend on more frequent disturbance. But there is much overlap in their growing conditions, and they can sometimes be found together.

Creasy greens are easily distinguished by the experienced eye. Common wintercress leaves have only 2–8 lateral division, and these are only 1–10% of the size of the terminal division. Creasy greens have 8–18 lateral divisions, more closely and regularly spaced, and these are about 20% of the size of the

B. verna, the wintercress that is hot like watercress, just about to bolt, when I like the greens best.

B. verna is less robust and showy than common wintercress.

terminal division. While the stem of both species is distinctly angled, that of *B. verna* is more so—to the extent that it is often nearly triangular.

The greens of *B. verna* are strikingly different from their relatives in flavor, and are not culinarily interchangeable. Creasy greens are much more radishy-hot when raw, and they lack the bitter tone of common wintercress. Their flavor is nigh indistinguishable from that of watercress, although the texture is less flimsy. As with watercress, cooking mutes this hotness to no more than a pleasant reminder. Everyone in our household prefers this southern species.

CONFUSING PLANTS

Common wintercress is often confused with watercress because they are two mustards with similar names; this is exacerbated by its tendency to grow along waterways. While wintercress *is* often found on low ground near water, and in doing so occasionally gets flooded, it is also found on dry ground far from any waterway. Watercress, contrarily, is truly aquatic, found only in permanent water. Watercress also differs in lacking a basal rosette, in having hollow stems, and in that its leaves are fully compound, with discrete leaflets.

There is another plant, however, that the novice should be aware of: butterweed. This plant goes by two scientific names: *Packera glabella* and *Senecio glabellus*. Butterweed is very bitter, and probably at least mildly toxic, although I know of no documented poisonings from it. It is a native, found in most of the Eastern Woodlands, and is especially common in a belt across the central

Butterweed, just beginning to bloom. Although it resembles wintercress at a glance, there are many relaible and easy features that distinguish them.

latitudes. Butterweed likes many of the same habitats as wintercress; the two are often found side by side, and at a glance they appear quite similar. Nevertheless, a closer look reveals many ways to distinguish them.

The young stalks of butterweed often have ridge tops with violet highlights, and the leaves have a silvery sheen following the veins on the upper surface. Butterweed stems are hollow and usually single; wintercress typically grows several stems, which are solid. The youngest butterweed rosettes have cobwebby stuff

Older common wintercress shoots and their broccoli-like tops. Still tender. Wintercress lovers can chomp these raw; newcomers want them boiled and drained, or maybe not at all.

on them. The leaf rachis of butterweed is deeply U-channeled near its base, and green or purple, while the same part of wintercress is broad, winged, and very light in color. Butterweed leaves are compound near the base but lobed near the tip. The divisions or lobes have a truncated shape, as if the tip was bitten off; the end has large teeth or small lobes with tiny, sharp points—completely unlike wintercress.

HARVEST AND PREPARATION

The Latin name for the genus, *Barbarea*, is said to refer to the fact that this green was collected and eaten on St. Barbara's Day, the fourth of December. Even where I live in northern Wisconsin, that happens about once a decade. Wintercress grows well in the moist, cool weather of fall, when it is storing energy for the following spring's growth spurt. The leaves at this time are large, tender, and less pungent than midsummer rosette greens. These fall leaves are good to use lightly in a salad, and also make good fried greens. They are quite tolerant of freezing, and can be collected as long as they are not covered with snow. This is immensely appreciated at a time when few other greens are available. In late winter, the plant will produce small, new leaves in the center of the rosette. These are rather slow to collect, but being both tender and mild, they are the best form of wintercress to put in a salad.

Besides the young greens, spring shoots make a good vegetable when their tops are loaded with flower buds that have not yet opened. At this time they look much like a smaller, feral version of broccoli—and they taste like a wilder, stronger version of that vegetable. More robust wintercress shoots usually have a milder taste than thin ones, and these are preferred whenever you can find them. In regions with rich soil, larger shoots are more common. You can eat the young stems of wintercress raw, but this is a vegetable that I much prefer cooked. For a simple dish, try them steamed and then served with cheese melted over the top, like broccoli.

Creasy greens *B. verna* are eaten in basically all the same ways as the other wintercresses, with the understanding that they are much hotter when raw, and much milder when cooked. Fried with bacon, the shoots or greens are great.

I can't help but wonder if Chris still collects mustard greens. Does he have children? Do they have a roadside stand? If so, I'd like to stop and buy a bundle or two. I'd leave a tip.

Ecoculture: Tending to Wildness

odern foragers seek wholesome food, healthy activity, and a daily relationship with thriving Nature. They seek the inner peace of a truly sustainable lifestyle that reflects their values, and the deep security of self-sufficiency. The civilized economy has failed to supply these things. It has given us cheap food in plenty, but impoverished in micronutrients and laced with cancer-causing chemicals. This is better than starvation, but we want to thrive. The civilized paradigm tells us that we must destroy Nature to provide for ourselves, and reduce ourselves to caged livestock for the comforts of modern life. It tells us to be satisfied with luxury cars, air conditioning, and flickering gadgets. It tells us that Nature is boring compared to the distilled content piped to us on little screens. Although our hearts don't want us to believe this, we reluctantly succumb to the message, because we have never heard another. But our hearts are right.

We are ready for another relationship to the Earth: marriage rather than slavery, cooperation rather than war. We seek another economics based on another set of values, another way of producing food, another culture: *ecoculture*.

Ecoculture is the term that I coined to refer to **the management of natural ecosystems to enhance their production of useful products.** It is no surprise that English lacks a word for this ancient concept, since it defies civilization's deeply held beliefs about the human relationship to Nature. Our prevailing understanding of the terms "wild," "cultivate," and "natural ecosystem" leaves no room for ecoculture: it is an oxymoron, an impossibility. Natural ecosystems, we believe, are to be destroyed and replaced—not enhanced. It is time to challenge this dogma of civilization, to replace our agro-centric creation myth that masquerades as history, and expose the lies of our ruthless economy. It is not ecoculture that is impossible; infinite growth is the naïve pipe dream of the unrealistic.

The fundamental difference between ecoculture and agriculture is that ecoculture focuses on plants that maintain themselves in relatively stable communities, while agriculture focuses on disturbance-dependent plants that cannot maintain themselves in a given locality. Ecoculture creates a plant community that produces human food but looks and functions like a native habitat—precisely because it is one. Unlike agriculture, ecoculture considers both ecology and production. Ecoculture acknowledges that the biotic community has multiple roles to play: It has economic value, aesthetic value, environmental value, and inherent value. It is our food, fiber, fuel, and perhaps our income. It builds soil, protects watersheds, absorbs carbon, and is home to wildlife that we cherish. It is our place of refuge and play and prayer, a beautiful and wholesome place. Sacred.

The term "ecoculture" may be new, but the concept is ancient. Gatherers have long engaged in mutually beneficial partnerships with the wild plant communities from which they harvest. In eastern North America, nut groves were thinned to park-like orchards to increase yields. Pine barrens were burned to promote heavy blueberry crops, and to maintain openings for elk and deer. Pond lilies were pulled from wild rice beds. In the Pacific Northwest, coastal wetlands were carefully managed to produce a variety of root vegetables. Canopy trees were thinned to cast light on crabapples, highbush cranberry, and elderberry. Camas meadows were burned, weeded, thinned, and mulched. In California, oak groves were maintained to maximize acorn production. The beauty of these managed landscapes impressed the Europeans who encountered them, but the newcomers misunderstood what they saw, because they believed in a false dichotomy between gathering and cultivation.

The practices of those ancient plant gatherers need to be emulated today. We can choose our role model: the beaver or the bulldozer. Yes, we can harvest sustainably. But we need not "reduce our impact"—that concession is the hopeless fatalism of alienation. It is time to *increase* our impact—our positive impact—on the landscape, and become agents of healing the Earth, even as we gather the Earth's gifts to nourish and heal our selves.

Near my sugarbush is a naturally occurring, nearly pure stand of well-spaced, old-growth sugar maple, its understory dominated by wild leeks: two superb native crops growing naturally together, each enhancing the other's production. I am modeling the management of my own sugarbush—a stand that has been abused and logged off—after stands such as this one. This management and harvest will not compromise the health of my forest in any way; it will improve it. This harmony is the model for ecoculture.

But you don't have to engage in forestry or sell your produce to practice ecoculture. A tiny space will do. Eight feet from my elbow as I write this is a lush, half-shaded corner of the yard that I call my nettle garden. It is about a twentieth of an acre, and provides us with copious greens of several species for seven months of the year. It started with a small clump of stinging nettle that appeared between the house and the nearby woods, and a colony of Virginia waterleaf that had crept into the clearing beside it. These two native plants made me suspect that the soil could be ideal for a floodplain or hardwood forest-edge community, so I set to work planting and transplanting native edibles that would naturally occur together. The centerpiece was a highbush cranberry. Around it are ostrich fern, cut-leaf coneflower, cow parsnip, hairy woodmint, wood nettle, honewort, *Allium canadense*, wild leek, waterleaf, and of course, tons of stinging nettle. The only work required to maintain this diverse and productive garden is a few hours per year weeding out the reed-canary grass, goldenrod, and brambles that want to take over.

Europeans came to this land wanting wheat and cheese, but it wasn't here, so they forced the land to make it. They didn't ask the land what it had to give. I'm not naïve enough to think that we will give up wheat and cheese. But we are mature enough to compromise—we can eat acorns and hickory nuts, too. Native ecosystems will not provide all of the fast-food hamburgers we want, but they might give us something else, like salmon and camas. I'm not arguing impractically for a world of austere absolutes. I am pointing out that, alongside the industrial agriculture that we want, there is another viable option, that we also want. Most of the people who practiced it have been killed, or their economies forcibly modernized, and now we tell ourselves that option is extinct. As long as we cling to the conservative delusion that ecoculture is impossible, we will know nothing of its potential to provide for us. Just like the overweight diabetic who claims that it is impossible to eat real food and be active, we will stubbornly decline and die that way, calling it fate in our final dishonesty.

We live in an age of excess that is destroying our lives. We are obese, bored, addicted, depressed. Our teeth rot out. Our pancreases don't work. Our feet are deformed, and we can hardly walk. Technology's promise to reduce labor has insidiously become a pathological obsession with eliminating physical activity—robbing us of the birthright of human vigor, and inflicting an endless variety of pains, debilities, and diseases upon us. In six generations our homes have octupled in size. We spend half of our incomes overeating and reducing our movement, a quarter of it treating ourselves for the problems this causes, and much of the remainder entertaining and comforting ourselves because this lifestyle sucks. And still, we worry endlessly about The Economy—hypochondriacs in dread of recession—as if that is our problem. Growth Economics is the religion of our era, the dogma we dare not question, the atmosphere from which our thoughts are inhaled. But it is obsolete, and becoming deadly. The age of scarcity is over; we are now governed by the economics of surplus. The inertia of our thoughts has kept us from reckoning what this means, but the time for that reckoning is forcefully here. Our oversuccess has put us in the midst of an unprecedented ecological upheaval that threatens all the earthly things that we hold sacred, imperils the future of our descendants, and is killing us from the inside.

Ecoculture is the answer to the crisis of the civilized economy—the personal one we experience, and the global one we dread. It is the homecoming we long for. But ecoculture is based on principles that challenge some of the most fundamental ideas we have about the world, and our place in it. The greatest barriers to a new culture are not economic, practical, or physical; they are philosophical. We have been indoctrinated with the mythos of civilization since birth; ecoculture will make no sense until this is discarded.

Nature contains good food crops—an almost unimaginable variety of them. It is easy to be ignorant of a food we have never tasted, nor even heard of. It is easier still when we are told by authoritative figures that humans long ago domesticated all of the crops worthy of our attention as food (Diamond 1997). This is perhaps the only frontier of science that has been declared closed. However, this assessment is a reflection of our instinctive culinary xenophobia—a circular logic that ignores everything we actually know about the process of crop domestication.

While cultivation is, by definition, an intentional act, domestication is not. Domestication is the genetic change caused by selective pressure under human cultivation, resulting in a plant that is physically distinct from its wild ancestor. This genetic change requires two things: continuous and systematic selective pressure by humans, and genetic isolation from populations that are not subjected to the same selective pressure. However, many systems of managing perennial crops do not involve systematic selection; and any system that involves the cultivation of a plant within a natural community where it is already abundant cannot produce genetic isolation. It follows logically that most plants that have been managed for food production were never domesticated. We know that hunter-gatherers cultivated plants, because they are the people who initially domesticated our crop plants. But we do not know of a single case where a group of hunter-gatherers domesticated its staple food source. Which makes perfect sense—they relied on plants that were abundant in their landscapes, and thus could not be genetically isolated.

There are profound conclusions to be made from this, which civilized thinkers have been loath to acknowledge. In reality, the suite of domesticated plants upon which the world depends is a narrow assortment of species that just happen to have been simultaneously *useful and uncommon*—they have no special claim to utility or quality. Being uncommon and thus unreliable promotes certain types of management (clearing and planting) that are more likely to produce systematic selection, while also allowing genetic isolation. The disproportionate representation of annuals and early successional species among domestic crops confirms this interpretation of their origin. The abundant, ecologically dominant plants that were appropriate for subsistence were the vast majority of calories once eaten by humans, and they constitute the vast majority of species that have been used for food. But they were never domesticated. Civilization says they are not real, but those who taste them know better. Ecoculture is about using this great majority of food plants that agriculture ignores.

Interestingly, there are a few important crops that are not domesticated, such as cranberry, pecan, and many varieties of coconut. These fruits, as designed by Nature, fit seamlessly into our food production systems. A less well-known example is the apple. There are no morphological features separating the original wild apples of Kazakhstan from those grown in orchards around the world today. Just as most people who eat blackberries and blueberries do not see them as "wild food" because they are "normal" (see p. 58), agronomists rarely acknowledge that these major crops are genetically wild, and for the same reasons. Once we expand our philosophy of food production beyond *destroy and replace*, and embrace ecoculture, we will find that these four marvelous fruits are only the tip of the iceberg in terms of useful, non-domesticated crops.

Nature is productive. Natural plant communities can provide for basic human needs. This principle opposes one of civilization's most deeply held beliefs: that Nature is deficient and mostly worthless, and needs to be replaced with something human-made and productive to be economically useful. This belief is how we rationalize our destruction of Nature. In his Pulitzer Prize–winning book *Guns, Germs, and Steel*, Jared Diamond made the claim that only 0.1% of the plants in a natural community are edible (p. 88). He provides nothing to back this up this utter nonsense, but was never taken to task for it—because his readers almost universally share the delusion. The claim is a religious one, insidiously disguised in a work that pretends to honor science.

It is true that native communities don't produce everything we want, everywhere we want it. It is also true that natural landscapes and communities are extremely variable in their yield of human food. The same things are also true of agriculture. The most productive natural communities often grew upon the soils that made the best farmland, and were removed long ago. Our perception of Nature's productivity is skewed by this, and also by our ignorance of wild foods. But mostly, it is an indoctrinated philosophy.

The potential of ecoculture cannot be reasonably evaluated until it is practiced. I have no delusion that farms will disappear. But I have faith that ecoculture's productivity will impress even the most optimistic among us.

Ecoculture is economically viable. Many of our wood products are still, thankfully, produced sustainably on the ecoculture model. We have fewer examples of ecoculture functioning successfully in today's food economy: wild rice beds, blueberry barrens, Brazil nut groves, and the sugarbush. Yet consider this: A maple sugarbush can sustainably produce more calories and more value of wild leeks, per year, than of maple syrup—and only a few sugarbushes in the country harvest both crops. A family can make a living, producing food, without a tractor, from 40 acres of woods. This is an inkling of the possibility that ecoculture offers.

Many claim that we left the hunting and gathering way of life long ago because it did not produce enough food per acre, and because farming required less work. These beliefs are figments of our agro-centric creation myth that are completely unsupported by evidence. The outcome of a thing does not explain the thoughts that put it in motion. The mastery of Hemingway's novels does not explain why the first Mesopotamian official scrawled debt records onto flattened papyrus. Likewise, the efficiencies created through thousands of years of experience, technological advancement, and crop improvement have no bearing on the original decision to cultivate wild plants thousands of years ago.

However, these same technological advancements can now be applied to wild crops without compromising ecoculture's fundamentally sustainable nature. You can see it with maple syrup: Despite new sap collection methods, different storage vessels, and different evaporating technology, the sugarbush is still a maple forest: building and holding soil, growing a diverse suite of fungi and wildflowers, home to warblers, flying squirrels, wood frogs. It takes far less fuel and labor to produce a gallon of syrup today than it did a hundred years ago—and the price has plummeted accordingly. Mechanized hulling of wild rice has also greatly decreased the labor required to prepare it for consumption. There are dozens of equally promising native crops whose potential has not been tapped. Let's see what we can do with acorns, hickory nuts, and hazel nuts with modern tools and old ideas.

Unlike maple syrup, many of these native crops will not require a huge investment in equipment to be sold at a reasonable price. There are real economic advantages to well-adapted perennial plants that grow themselves and do not have to be sprayed, fertilized, or incessantly weeded. Because native plant communities are adapted to our climate, soil, terrain, and animals, they require less effort to maintain than agricultural systems. This is what allows them to be feasible without the heavy machinery and chemical warfare that characterize agriculture. This is exactly why the maple industry is built upon natural stands of trees, not planted orchards. It is also why pecans from natural stands are often cheaper than those that are orchard-grown outside their native range, and hand-harvested wild black walnuts are often cheaper than pecans. Many wild vegetables take no more labor to harvest than similar cultivated produce—and much less labor to grow. But because ecoculture is small in scale, and the plant communities it comprises are complex, it remains labor- and knowledge-intensive in a way that is difficult to outsource to disinterested humans or machinery. It can be pursued on the hobby scale of the home garden, but there is also the opportunity for hardworking people to make a living this way.

Production is only half of the equation in economic viability. Ecoculture also requires consumers. Here is the upside to the fact that food today costs only a fifth of what it did a few generations ago: For the first time in human history, most of us do not have to choose the cheapest food. We can choose the best food, for ourselves and our world. This trend has been simmering for decades: organic food, slow food, local food. But these are just slightly different categories of the same old stuff; we annihilated the vast wilderness of the American heartland to produce local, organic, and slow food. The shift toward ecoculture will require us to overcome our stubbornly conservative food instincts. This—not economic viability—is the greatest obstacle to a sustainable food economy.

Nature is resilient, not fragile. Plant communities are adaptable. In response to disturbance or abuse, they heal, produce, balance, replace, compensate, and grow perpetually. We stop this growth only through extraordinary measures: the ceaseless application of hard labor, heavy machinery, or chemical warfare. The fetish with virgin wilderness does not serve us in our quest for sustainability; it is selfish, and denies the humanity of the people who long inhabited this land before Europeans arrived.

In the practice of ecoculture, every plant harvested is quickly replaced by neighboring plants, which were already competing for the resources that the removed plant was using. The community will always respond and compensate for the loss. A forager's impact is akin to that of a deer, not a plow. Nature does not disappear because porcupines eat hemlocks, or because rabbits girdle sumacs; and it won't disappear because I eat nettles. We cannot "destroy Nature" by harvesting—we can only modulate the composition of plant communities.

Nature is flexible. It can take many forms. There is not one "correct" or perfect state of being that defines health in an ecosystem.

Some ecologists point to the particular condition of a locality when Europeans first encountered it and claim that this snapshot represents the ideal state of Nature, the only appropriate goal of ecological land management. But

This elderberry was purchased and tended carefully for eight years in my orchard, an old crop field.

Nature doesn't work this way. Plant communities change. Pine barrens grow up into pine forests, shade out their bearberries, and then succumb to fires, which returns them to pine barrens, and the bearberries slowly creep back in from the one rocky slope where they had survived. Pine-oak forests become oak forests, which become maple-oak forests, which become maple-hemlock forests, which burn to a crisp, and become thickets of pine and birch. Who is to say which point in this cycle is the "best" or healthiest one? They are all good, wholesome, vibrant, and beautiful. Each location has an enormous range of potential natural communities. Ecoculture is about choosing, from among this potential, communities that also provide lots of human food, and guiding the process of succession and competition to get there. These managed communities provide equal or better habitat and ecosystem services than currently undeveloped lands, most of which have been degraded and compromised.

Nature includes humans. This is the most important paradigm shift at the foundation of ecoculture. *We belong in Nature.* We belong *to* Nature. She gave birth to us, shaped us, and nourishes us. Our alienation from Nature allows us to destroy her; and perhaps we contrived this attitude to rationalize our

This elderberry was found as three spindly shoots in a clump of alder near my orchard, slightly more than a year before the photo was taken. It has already surpassed the purchased elderberry in size and fruitfulness. This is the benefit of working with Nature.

destruction. It seems like we got mixed up in a downward spiral of pride and selfishness, like a pointless argument that pushes to the brink of divorce, and it left us here, living under the insane proposition that we don't belong in the only home we have ever known, rejecting the greatest gift we have ever received.

Our alienation is not a conclusion that we reason our way to; it is a belief system that we choose. As such, it can be reversed at will. But our separation from wildness is also a physical reality. Our minds are shaped by the world we live in, and our hearts by our minds. Until we know again the smell of hickory husks, the cool of pond water on bare feet, the soft caress of ferns on our shins, the shine of moonlight through naked trees, and the taste of sacred herbs, we will not know our place. We can't just *realize* or *believe* that we belong on Earth—we must viscerally *understand* what it means to belong here. To do that, we need to *be* in Nature, to *partake* of it, in communion; to *participate* in it. When we feel that we belong, we will no longer be able to turn a blind eye to the death of our community. Native peoples all over the world have long seen themselves as belonging this way. It is not coincidence that this understanding comes with entirely different, and healthier, ways of interacting with Nature. Ecoculture is the end we seek, and also the means to get there.

When a deer eats a fern frond, we deem that act a "natural" part of the food chain in an ecosystem. It is good. When a man eats a fern frond, we call that "impact." It is unnatural, bad. Ecoculture rejects this dichotomy.

In ecoculture, plant communities are managed primarily by controlling competition. The fundamental act of plant cultivation is not propagation, as is often supposed—it is the removal of competition. In agriculture, this removal is wholesale, before any propagation takes place, and is renewed annually by mechanical means and now, herbicides. In ecoculture, propagation is minimal. Often, when a forager acquires a piece of property that she wishes to turn into a wild food paradise, her first question is, "What should I plant here?" This is an agricultural question. It is a good question if you have empty space from which the natural community has been removed. But the first question of ecoculture is, "What good things are already growing here, and how can I help them thrive and spread?" The way that you help them is through removing competition.

Planting or transplanting should only be employed to establish or propagate native species *that belong in the community*. Make an educated decision based on thoughtful and careful observation of your land and the plant you hope to establish. Being steeped in the philosophy of agriculture—*destroy and replace*—we are strongly tempted to waste our efforts by pushing the limits of desired species and putting them in marginal habitats where they cannot succeed. Beware of this trap; it derails resources to failing endeavors and negates every advantage of ecoculture. Managing competition among the plants already present will get you better results than planting, much faster, and with far less effort. This point is hard to overemphasize.

Tending the wild landscapes from which we harvest is the natural inclination of the gatherer—an outgrowth of the appreciation that we feel for the gifts that bless us. Don't worry whether or not you are doing enough to justify your harvest, or whether or not you are doing the right thing, or the best thing. Sometimes, the only job to be done is gathering. You belong there, doing that. Gratitude will keep you straight, for it is the opposite of selfishness. Gratitude will keep your heart awake to the next and best opportunity to tend the land you belong to, to return the favors that it has bestowed upon you. When my children and I collected twelve gallons of acorns last October under the big red oak downhill from the chicken coop, there was nothing to repay at that moment but thanks. But the gratitude that I carry every moment for a lifetime of nourishment from nut trees—this is real and powerful. It is the force that planted a grove of nut trees over three acres of hayfield and pasture, and thinned out hundreds of aspen poles to release butternut, hickory, and oak to create a more diverse woodland, better for wildlife.

Some of us believe we are exiled from Nature. It is self-exile. Some of us believe that Nature will not feed us. She will. Turn homeward and pray. Then do your work as a holyday.

Overleaf Sugar maple and wild leek co-dominate tens of millions of acres of northern mesic forest, and both can be harvested sustainably and economically, while maintaining or enhancing the forest's ecological value.

Bibliography

Note: For those entries with unknown authorship that could be listed as "anonymous," I have listed them under the abbreviated name of the institution or periodical associated with the publication, both in the text citations and in the bibliography. The full name of the publication comes in the usual place at the end of the entry. For journal articles, the first number following the name of the journal is the volume number, followed by the issue number (if applicable) in parentheses. Page numbers are listed after the colon.

Abbott, D. D., E. W. Packman, B. M. Wagner, and J. W. E. Harrisson. 1961. "Chronic Oral Toxicity of Sassafras and Safrol." *Pharmacologist* 3:62.

Al-Sherif, E., A. K. Hegazy, N. H. Gomaa, and M. O. Hassan. 2013. "Efeito alelopatico de tecidos de mostarda-preta e exsudatos da raiz de algumas culturas e plantas danhinos" (Allelopathic effect of black mustard tissues and root exudates on some crops and weeds). *Planta Danhina* 31 (1): 11–19

Ames, Bruce N., and L. S. Gold. 2000. "Paracelsus to Parascience: The Environmental Cancer Distraction." *Mutation Research* 447 (1): 3–13.

Ash, Thomas. 1917 [1682]. *Carolina; or, a description of the present state of that country.* Tarrytown, NY: Abbatt.

Avery, Paul. 2012. "Swartswood Resident Gains OK to Tame 'Endangered' Plant." *New Jersey Herald*, Nov. 21, 2012.

Barlow, Connie. 2000. *The Ghosts of Evolution: Nonsensical Fruit, Missing Partners, and Other Ecological Anachronisms.* New York: Basic Books.

Barstow, Stephen. 2014. *Around the World in 80 Plants.* Hampshire, UK: Permanent Publications.

Benedetti, M. Strolin, A. Malnoe, and A. Louis Broillet. 1977. "Absorption, Metabolism and Excretion of Safrole in the Rat and Man." *Toxicology* 7 (1):69–83.

Bertea, M. Cinzia, Chiara M. M. Azzolin, Simone Bossi, Giovanni Doglia, and Massimo E. Maffe. 2005. "Identification of an EcoRI Restriction Site for a Rapid and Precise Determination of β-Asarone-Free *Acorus calamus* Cytotypes." *Phytochemistry* 66 (5): 507–14.

Billingsly, B. B., Jr., and Dale H. Arner. 1970. "The Nutritive Value and Digestibility of Some Winter Foods of the Eastern Wild Turkey." *Journal of Wildlife Management* 34 (1): 176.

Boberg, Eric W., Elizabeth C. Miller, James A Miller, Alan Poland, and Amy Liem. 1983. "Strong Evidence from Studies with Brachymorphic Mice and Pentachlorophenol That 1'-Sulfoöxysafrole Is the Major Ultimate Electrophilic and Carcinogenic Metabolite of 1'-Hydroxysafrole in Mouse Liver." *Cancer Research* 43(11): 5163–73.

Borchert, Peter. 1972. "1'-Hydroxysafrole: A Proximate Carcinogenic Metabolite of Safrole in the Rat and Mouse." PhD diss., University of Wisconsin, Madison.

Borchert, Peter, Peter G. Wislocki, James A. Miller, and Elizabeth C. Miller. 1973A. "The Metabolism of the Naturally Occurring Hepatocarcinogen Safrole to 1'-Hydroxysafrole and the Electrophilic Reactivity of 1'-Acetoxysafrole." *Cancer Research* 33 (3): 575–89.

Borchert, Peter, James A. Miller, Elizabeth C. Miller, and Thomas K. Shires. 1973B. "1'-Hydroxysafrole, a Proximate Carcinogenic Metabolite of Safrole in the Rat and Mouse." *Cancer Research* 33 (3): 590–600.

Boutenko, Sergei. 2013. *Wild Edibles*. Berkeley, CA: North Atlantic.

Bown, Deni. 1988. *Aroids: Plants of the Arum family*. Portland, Oregon: Timber Press.

BMJ. 1904. "Typhoid Fever and Watercress." *British Medical Journal* 1 (2244): 37–38.

Bryant, Charles. 1783. *Flora Diaetetica: or, History of Esculent Plants*. London: B. White.

Bryant, Tim. 2016. "Saint Louis Area Union Painters Strike over Wages." *St. Louis Post-Dispatch*, Sept 1, 2016.

Buell, Murray F. 1935. "Seed and Seedling of *Acorus calamus*." *Botanical Gazette* 96 (4): 758–65.

Burgess, K. S., M. Morgan, L. DeVerno, and B. C. Husband. 2005. "Asymmetrical introgression between two *Morus* species (*M. alba*, *M. rubra*) that differ in abundance." *Molecular Ecology* 14: 3471-3483.

Byrne, Roger, and J. H. McAndrews. 1975. "Pre-Columbian Purslane (*Portulaca oleracea* L) in the New World." *Nature* 253:726–27.

Carlson, Marvin, and Richard D. Thompson. 1997. "Liquid Chromatographic Determination of Safrole in Sassafras-Derived Herbal Products." *Journal of AOAC International* 80 (5): 1023–28.

Chabot, Brian. 2007. *Health Advantages of Grade B Syrup*. Cornell Maple Bulletin 300.

Choong, Youk-Meng and Hsiu-Jung Lin. 2001. "A rapid and simple gas chromatographic determination of safrole in soft drinks." *Journal of Food & Drug Analysis* 9: 27-32

Clemants, Steven E. and Sergei L. Mosyakin. 2003. "Chenopodium." In *Flora of North America*, Vol. 4:75–99. New York: Oxford University Press.

CDC (Centers for Disease Control & Prevention). 1981. "Epidemiologic Notes and Reports: Plant Poisonings—New Jersey." *Morbidity and Mortality Weekly Report* 30 (6; February 20): 65–67.

CDC. 2013. "Parasites—Fascioliasis (Fasciola Infection). https://www.cdc.gov/parasites/fasciola/index.htmlaccessed 1-15-2017.

Couplan, Francois. 2009. *Le régal végétal*. Paris: Sang de la Terre.

Cummings, Kate. 2012. "Sassafras Tea: Using a Traditional Method of Preparation to Reduce the Carcinogenic Compound Safrole." Master's thesis, Clemson University (*All Theses* paper 1345).

Curtis, John T. 1959. *The Vegetation of Wisconsin*. Madison: University of Wisconsin Press.

Daimon, Hirohiko, Shigeki Sawada, Shoji Asakura, and Fumio Sagami. 1998. "*In vivo* Genotoxicity and DNA Adduct Levels in the Liver of Rats Treated with Safrole." *Carcinogenesis* 19 (1): 141–46.

DeFelice, Michael S. 2002. "Yellow Nutsedge *Cyperus esculenta* L.: Snack Food of the Gods." *Weed Technology* 16 (4): 901–07.

Diamond, Jared. 1997. *Guns, Germs, and Steel*. Norton, New York.

Drost, D. C., and J. D. Doll. 1980. "The Allelopathic Effect of Yellow Nutsedge (*Cyperus esculentus*) on Corn (*Zea mays*) and Soybean (*Glycine max*)." *Weed Science* 28:229–33.

Duvall, M. R., G. H. Learn, L. E. Eguiarte, and M. T. Clegg. 1993. "Phylogenetic Analysis of rbcL Sequences Identifies *Acorus calamus* as the Primal Extant Monocotyledon." *Proceedings of the National Academy of Sciences, USA* 90:4641–44.

Edwards, N., and G. C. Rodgers. 1982. "Pokeberry Pancake Breakfast." *Veterinary and Human Toxicology* 24 (4): 293.

El-Sayed, M. I. 2011. "Effects of *Portulaca oleracea* L Seeds in Treatment of Type-2 Diabetes Mellitus Patients as Adjunctive and Alternative Therapy." *Journal of Ethnopharmacology* 137:643–51.

Fernald, Merritt L., and Alfred C. Kinsey. 1943. *Edible Wild Plants of Eastern North America*. New York: Harper & Row.

Fitch, Richard W..N.d. Accessed November 28, 2016. http://carbon.indstate.edu /rfitch/fitch_research.html.

Fitch, Richard W., et al. 2009. "Dioicine, a Novel Prenylated Purine Alkaloid from *Gymnocladus dioicus*." *Heterocycles* 79 (1): 583–98.

Foster, Steven, and J. A. Duke. 2000. *A Field Guide to Medicinal Plants and Herbs of Eastern and Central North America*. 2nd ed. (Peterson Field Guides). Boston: Houghton Mifflin.

Fritz, Gayle J., Virginia Drywater Whitekiller, and James W. McIntosh. 2001. "Ethnobotany of KU-Nu-Che: Cherokee Hickory Nut Soup." *Journal of Ethnobiology* 21 (2): 1–27.

Frohne, Dietrich, and H. J. Pfänder. 2005. *Poisonous Plants: A Handbook for Doctors, Pharmacists, Toxicologists, Biologists and Veterinarians*. 2nd ed. Translated by Inge Alford. London: Manson.

FSANZ (Food Standards Australia New Zealand). 2005. *Cyanogenic Glycosides in Cassava and Bamboo Shoots; A Human Health Risk Assessment*. Technical Report Series no. 28.

Galla, S. J., L. Brittney, P. Viers, E. Gradie, and D. E. Saar. 2009. "*Morus murrayana* (*Moraceae*): A new mulberry from eastern North America." *Phytologica* 91(1): 105–16.

Gibbons, Euell. 1962. *Stalking the Wild Asparagus*. New York: McKay.

Gibbons. 1966. *Stalking the Healthful Herbs*. New York: McKay.

Gilmore, Melvin. 1919. *Uses of Plants by the Indians of the Missouri River Region (33rd Annual Report of the Bureau of American Ethnology)*. Washington, DC: US Government Printing Office.

Goodrich, Katherine R., Michelle L. Zjhra, Courtney A. Ley, and Robert A. Raguso. 2006. "When Flowers Smell Fermented: The Chemistry and Ontogeny of Yeasty Floral Scent in Pawpaw (*Asimina triloba*: Annonaceae)" *International Journal of Plant Sciences* 167 (1): 33–46.

Gretšušnikova, T., M. Koel, and A. Orav. (undated) "Comparison of the essential oil composition of *Acorus calamus* obtained by spercritical carbon dioxide extraction and hydrodistillation methods. Institute of Chemistry, Tallinn University of Technology, Tallinn, Estonia. www.isasf.net/fileadmin/files/docs/archacon/posters/p153-p12%20full%20.pdf. Accessed 6-10-2017.

Grieve, Maude. 1971. *A Modern Herbal*. Vol. 2. New York: Dover.

Gupta, Krishna P., Kenneth L. van Golen, Kim L. Putnam, and Kurt Randerath. 1993. "Formation and Persistence of Safrole-DNA Adducts over a 10,000-Fold Dose Range in Mouse Liver." *Carcinogenesis* 14 (8): 1517–21.

Hagan, E.C., P.M. Jenner, W.I. Jones. O.G. Fitzhugh, E.L. Long, J.G. Brouwer, and W. Welfare. 1965. "Toxic properties of compounds related to safrole." Toxicology and Applied Pharmacology 7(1): 18-24.

Hamel, Paul B., and Mary U. Chiltoskey. 1975. *Cherokee Plants: Their Uses—a 400 Year History*. Cherokee, NC.

Hamilton, Richard J., R. D. Shih, and R. S. Hoffman. 1995. "Mobitz Type 1 Heart Block after Pokeweed Ingestion." *Veterinary and Human Toxicology* 37 (1): 66.

Hariot, Thomas. 1588. *A Briefe and True Report of the New Found Land of Virginia*. London. Electronic Texts in American Studies, paper 20, digitalcommons.unl.edu/etas/20.

Harrington, H. D. 1967. *Edible Native Plants of the Rocky Mountains*. Albuquerque: University of New Mexico Press.

Havard, V. 1895. "Food Plants of the North American Indians." *Bulletin of the Torrey Botanical Club* 22 (3): 98–123.

Hayden, F. V. 1862. *Contributions to the Ethnography and Philology of the Indian Tribes of the Missouri Valley*. Philadelphia: Sherman.

Heath, Barry K. 2001. "A Fatal Case of Apparent Water Hemlock Poisoning." *Veterinary and Human Toxicology* 43(1): 35–36.

Heikes, David L. 1994. "SFE with GC and MS Determination of Safrole and

Related Allylbenzenes in Sassafras Teas." *Journal of Chromatographic Science* 32: 253–58.

Henderson, Robert K. 2000. *The Neighborhood Forager*. White River Junction, VT: Chelsea Green.

Hillman, G. C., E. Medeyska, and J. Hather. 1989. "Wild Plant Foods and Diet at Late Paleolithic Wadi Kubbaniya; The Evidence from Charred Remains." In *Foraging and Farming: The Evolution of Plant Exploitation*, edited by D. R. Harris and G. Hillman. London: Unwin Hyman.

Hirono, Iwao, ed. 1987. *Naturally Occurring Carcinogens of Plant Origin*. Amsterdam: Elsevier.

Hitchcock, Susan Tyler. 1980. *Gather Ye Wild Things: A forager's year*. New York: Harper & Row.

Hoinkernoodle, Wib, J. J. M'helper, Docks E. Cyclist, and Sixide Nërd. 2016. "Incontrovertible and absolutely irrefutable proof from mass spectrometric evidence that fecoloads of feral *Foeniculum vulgare* is actually the coolest thing about California." *Deep Fried Journal* 4(20): 56–83.

Homburger, F., T. Kelley, G. Friedler, and A.B. Russfield. 1961. "Toxic and Possible Carcinogenic Effects of 4-allyl-1,2-methylenedioxybenzene (safrole) in Rats on Deficient Diets." Medicina Experimentalis (4):1-11

Hu, Shiu-ying. 2005. *Food Plants of China*. Hong Kong; Chinese University Press.

Jaeckle, Kurt A., and Frank R. Freemon. 1981. "Pokeweed Poisoning." *Southern Medical Journal* 74 (5): 639–40.

Jones, Snake C., and Desmond R. Layne. 2009. "Cooking With Pawpaw." Frankfort. Bulletin of the Kentucky State University Cooperative Extension Program.

Kallas, John. 2010. *Edible Wild Plants: Wild Foods from Dirt to Plate*. Layton, UT: Gibbs Smith.

Kalm, Pehr. 1945. "Pehr Kalm's Report on the Characteristics and Uses of the American Walnut Tree Which Is Called Hickory." Translated *Agricultural History* 19 (1): 58-64.

Kamdem, Donatien Pascal and Douglas A. Gage. 1995. "Chemical Composition of Essential Oil from the Root Bark of *Sassafras albidum*." *Planta Medica* 61: 574–75.

Kaul, Robert B., David M. Sutherland, and Steven B. Rolfsmeier. 2011. *The Flora of Nebraska*. University of Nebraska, Lincoln, School of Natural Resources.

Kaye, Barry, and D. W. Moodie. 1978. "The *Psoralea* Food Resource of the Northern Plains." *Plains Anthropologist* 23 (82): 329–36.

Kendall, S. B., and F. S. McCullough. 1951. "The Emergence of Cercariae of *Fasciola hepatica* from the Snail *Limnaea truncatula*." *Journal of Helminthology*. 25:77–92.

Kimmerer, Robin W. 2013. *Braiding Sweetgrass: Indigenous Wisdom, Scientific Knowledge, and the Teachings of Plants*. Minneapolis: Milkweed Editions.

Kindscher, Kelly. 1987. *Edible Wild Plants of the Prairie*. Lawrence: University Press of Kansas.

Kingsbury, John M. 1964. *Poisonous Plants of the United States and Canada*. Englewood Cliffs, NJ: Prentice-Hall.

Koch, Karen, and Robert A. Kennedy. 1980. "Characteristics of Crassulacean Acid Metabolism in the Succulent C4 Dicot, *Portulaca oleracea* L." *Plant Physiology* 65 (2): 193–97.

Kole, Chittaranjan (ed.). 2011. *Wild Crop Relatives: Genomic and Breeding Resources; Tropical and Subtropical Fruits*. New York: Springer.

Kraybill, Anthony A. and Craig E. Martin. 1996. "Crassulacean Acid Metabolism in Three Species of the C4 Genus Portulaca." International Journal of Plant Sciences 157 (1): 103-109.

Lander, Vera, and Peter Schreier. 1990. "Acorenone and γ-Asarone: Indicators of the Origin of Calamus Oils (*Acorus calamus*, L)." *Flavour and Fragrance Journal* 5:75–79.

Larson, Gary E. and James R. Johnson. 2007. *Plants of the Black Hills and Bear Lodge Mountains*, 2nd Edition. Brookings, South Dakota: SD State University.

Lawton, H. W., P. J. Wilke, M. DeDecker, and W. M. Mason. 1976. "Agriculture among the Paiute of Owens Valley." *Journal of California Anthropology* 3 (1): 13–50.

Leahu, Ana, Cristina Damian, Mircea Oroian, Sorina Ropciuc, and Ramona Rotaru. 2014. "Influence of Processing on Vitamin C Content of Rosehip Fruits." *Animal Science and Biotechnologies* 47 (1): 116–20.

Little, R. John, and Landon E. McKinney. 2015. "Viola." In *Flora of North America* Vol. 6. New York: Oxford University Press.

Liu, T. Y., C. C. Chen, C. L. Chen, and C. W. Chi. 1999. "Safrole-Induced Oxidative Damage in the Liver of Sprague-Dawley Rats." *Food and Chemical Toxicology* 37:697–702.

Long, Eleanor L., Walter H. Hansen, and Arthur A. Nelson. 1961. "Liver Tumors Produced in Rats by Feeding Safrole." *Federation Proceedings* 20:287.

Long, Eleanor L. et al. 1963. "Tumors Produced in Rats by Feeding Safrole." *Archives of Pathology* 75: 595–604.

Lyle, Katie Letcher. 2017. *The Complete Guide to Edible Wild Plants, Mushrooms, Fruits, and Nuts*. Guilford, CT: Falcon.

Mailles, A., I. Capek, F. Ajana, C. Schepens, D. Ilef, and V. Vaillant. 2006. "Commercial Watercress as an Emerging Source of Fascioliasis in Northern France in 2002: Results from an Outbreak Investigation." *Epidemiology and Infection* 134 (5): 942–45.

Main, Douglas. 2016. "Glyphosate Now the Most-Used Agricultural Chemical Ever." Newsweek.com, February 2. Accessed December 14, 2016. http:

//www.newsweek.com/glyphosate-now-most-used-agricultural-chemical-ever-422419.

Malik, Mayank. 2009. "Biology and Ecology of Wild Radish (*Raphanus raphanistrum*)." PhD diss., Clemson University (All Dissertations paper 386).

Mandelbaum, David G. 1940. "The Plains Cree." *Anthropological Papers of the American Museum of Natural History* 37: 202–203.

Martin, K. D., M. A. Healy, and L. K. Garrettson. 1982. "Seed of the Oak: When Is Treatment Indicated?" *Veterinary and Human Toxicology* 24 (4): 294–95

Matthews, James F. 2003. "*Portulaca*" in *Flora of North America* Vol. 4: 496–501.

Medsger, Oliver Perry. 1939. *Edible Wild Plants*. New York: Collier.

Moerman, Daniel. 1998. *Native American Ethnobotany*. Portland, OR: Timber Press.

Monger, Karen. 2015. *Adventures in Edible Plant Foraging*. New York: Skyhorse.

Motley, Timothy J. 1994. "The Ethnobotany of Sweet Flag, *Acorus calamus* (Araceae)." *Economic Botany* 48(4): 397–412.

Mulligan, Gerald A. 1980. "The Genus *Cicuta* in North America." *Canadian Journal of Botany* 58:1755–67.

Negbi, Moshe. 1992. "A Sweetmeat Plant, A Perfume Plant and Their Weedy Relatives: A Chapter in the History of *Cyperus esculentus* L. and *C. rotundus* L." *Economic Botany* 46 (1): 64–71.

Nepal, Madhav P., M. H. Mayfield, and C. J. Ferguson. 2012. "Identification of Eastern North American *Morus* (Moraceae): Taxonomic Status of *M. murrayana*." *Phytoneuron* 26:1–6.

NIH (National Institutes of Health). N.d. Toxnet (website). Accessed January 12, 2017. https://toxnet.nlm.nih.gov/.

NNDSR (National Nutrient Database for Standard Reference). 2015. Release 28, September 2015, slightly revised May 2016. Accessed December 4, 2016.

Novick, Lisa. 2016. "Forage in the Garden, Not in What's Left of the Wild." *Huffington Post,* 5-31-2016. Accessed 6-7-2016.

Ohio Department of Natural Resources. N.d. "*History of Ohio's State Forests*." http://forestry.ohiodnr.gov/history, accessed 11-9-2016.

Pantelouris, E. M. 1962. "The Hosts of the Common Liver Fluke *Fasciola hepatica* L." *Irish Naturalists' Journal* 14 (4): 69–73 000–00.

Pantelouris. 1965. *The Common Liver Fluke*. Oxford: Pergamon.

Paoletti, Maurizio G., A. L. Dreon, and G. G. Lorenzoni. 1995. "*Pistic*, Traditional Food from Western Friuli, N.E. Italy." *Economic Botany* 49 (1): 26–30.

Peattie, Donald Culross. 1948. *A Natural History of Trees of Eastern and Central North America*. Boston: Houghton Mifflin.

Peterson, Neal R., John P. Cherry, and Joseph G. Simmons. 1982. "Composition of Pawpaw (*Asimina triloba*) Fruit." *Annual Report of the Northern Nut Growers Association* 77:97–106.

Phillips, Jan. 1979. *Wild Edibles of Missouri*. Springfield: Missouri Department of Conservation.

Pieroni, Andrea. 1999. "Gathered Wild Food Plants in the Upper Valley of the Serchio River (Garfagnana), Central Italy." *Economic Botany* 53 (3): 327–41.

Primeau, Liz. 2013. "Creeping Bellflower: Beautiful but Evil, It's the All-about-Eve of the Garden." Liz Primeau: Born to Garden, June 13. Accessed January 20, 2017. http://lizprimeau.com/creeping-bellflower-beautiful-but-evil/.

Pyke, Magnus, and Ronald Melville. 1942. "Vitamin C in Rose Hips." *Biochemical Journal* 36 (3/4): 336–39.

Reid, Laurie A. 2005. "The Effects of Traditional Harvesting Practices on Restored Sweetgrass Populations." Master's thesis, College of Environmental Science and Forestry, State University of New York, Syracuse.

Reynertson, Kurt A., M. Balick, R. Lee, W. Raynor, Y. Pelep, and E. J. Kennelly. 2005. "A Traditional Method of *Cinnamomum carolinense* Preparation Eliminates Safrole from a Therapeutic Pohnpean Tea." *Journal of Ethnopharmacology* 102 (2): 269–74.

Rivera, Diego, Concepción Oblón, Cristiná Inocencio, Michael Heinrich, Alonso Verde, José Fajardo, and José Antonio Palazón. 2007. "Gathered Food Plants in the Mountains of Castilla-La Mancha (Spain): Ethnobotany and Multivariate Analysis." *Economic Botany* 61(3): 269–89.

Röst, L. C. M., and R. Bos. 1979. "Biosystematic Investigations with Acorus L., 3. Communication—Constituents of Essential Oils." *Planta Medica* 27:350–61.

Sabzghabaee, A. M., R. Kelishadi, H. Jelokhanian, S. Asgary, A. Ghannadi, and S. Badri. 2014. "Clinical Effects of *Portulaca oleracea* Seeds on Dyslipidemia in Obese Adolescents: A Triple-Blinded Randomized Controlled Trial." *Medicinski Arhiv* 68 (30): 195–99.

Saunders, Charles Francis. 1920 *Edible and Useful Wild Plants of the United States and Canada*. New York: Dover.

Sethi, Manuhar L., G. Subba Rao, B. K. Chowdhury, J. F. Morton, and G. J. Kapadia. 1976. "Identification of Volatile Components of *Sassafras albidum* Root Oil." *Phytochemistry* 15:1773–75.

Simopoulos, A. P., H. A. Norman, J. E. Gillaspy, and J. A Duke.. 1992. "Common Purslane: A Source of Omega-3 Fatty Acids and Antioxidants." *Journal of the American College of Nutrition* 11:374–82

SLWA (Swartswood Lakes and Watershed Association.) 2010. Public letter to the assistant commissioner, New Jersey Department of Environmental Protection, Nov. 10.

Small, Ernest. 1980. "The relationships of hop cultivars and wild variants of *Humulus lupulus*." *Canadian Journal of Botany* 58:676–686

Smellf, Yelp D. D.. "Older Dog Underdog DefEats IncrEdible Younger Dog." *Journal of RepEat Psychosis* 31(apple π): 623-7,594.

Smith, Daryl, D. Williams, G. Houseal, and K. Henderson. 2010. *The Tallgrass Prairie Center Guide to Prairie Restoration in the Upper Midwest*. Iowa City: University of Iowa Press.

Smith, George, Maureen O'Day, and William Reed. 1995. *Pecan Pest Management: Insects and Diseases*. University of Missouri Extension, Bulletin MP711. http://extension.missouri.edu/p/711.

Smith, Huron. 1928. *Ethnobotany of the Meskwaki Indians*. Bulletin of the Public Museum of Milwaukee 4 (2), 1928.

Spaeth, John P., and John W. Thieret. 2004. "Notes on 'Coffee' from the Kentucky Coffeetree (*Gymnocladus dioicus, Fabaceae*)." *SIDA, Contributions to Botany* 21 (1): 345–56.

Stone, Donald E. 1997. "*Carya*." In *Flora of North America* Vol. 3: 417-25 New York: Oxford University Press.

Strath, R. 1903. "Materia Medica, Pharmacy and Therapeutics of the Cree Indians of the Hudson Bay Territory." *The Saint Paul Medical Journal* 5: 735–746.

Sullivan, John B. 1979. "Pennyroyal Oil Poisoning and Hepatotoxicity." *JAMA: Journal of the American Medical Association* 242 (26): 2873.

Tardio, Javier, Higinio Pascual, and Ramon Morales. 2005. "Wild Food Plants Traditionally Used in the Province of Madrid, Central Spain." *Economic Botany* 59 (2): 122–36.

Tatum, Billy Joe. 1976. *Billy Joe Tatum's Wild Foods Field Guide and Cookbook*. New York: Workman.

Taylor, John P., and Loren M. Smith. 2003. "Chufa Management in the Middle Rio Grande Valley, New Mexico." *Wildlife Society Bulletin* 31 (1): 156–62.

Thayer, Samuel. 2017. "The Rarest Tree." *Minnesota Conservation Volunteer* 80 (472): 56–61.

Thompson, Sue A. 1995. *Systematics and Biology of the Araceae and Acoraceae of Temperate North America*. PhD diss., University of Illinois.

Thwaites, Reuben Gold, ed. 1904. *Original Journals of the Lewis and Clark Expedition 1804-1806, Volume Two, Part 1*. New York: Dodd, Mead.

Turk, M. A., and A. M. Tawaha. 2003. "Allelopathic Effect of Black Mustard (*Brassica nigra* L.) on Germination and Growth of Wild Oat (*Avena fatua* L.)" *Crop Protection* 22 (4): 673–77.

Turner, Nancy. 1978. *Food Plants of British Columbia Indians Part 2: Interior Peoples*. Victoria, BC: British Columbia Provincial Museum.

Turner, Nancy J, Laurence C. Thompson, M. Terry Thompson, and Annie Z. York. 1990. *Thompson Ethnobotany*. Victoria, BC: Royal British Columbia Museum.

Turner, Nancy J., and Adam Szczawinski. 1991. *Common Poisonous Plants and Mushrooms of North America*. Portland, OR: Timber Press.

Ulmer, Mary, and Samuel E. Beck, eds. 1951. *Cherokee Cooklore*. Cherokee, NC: Cherokee Publications.

US Department of Labor. 1934. "History of Wages in the United States from Colonial Times to 1928." Bulletin no. 604.

VanNatta, Andrew R. 2009. *Ecological Importance of Native Americans Culture to the Kentucky Coffee Tree* (Gymnocladus dioicus). University of Wisconsin, Stevens Point, Student Journals. www.uwsp.edu/forestry/stujournals /documents/na/avannatta.pdf.

Van Wyk, Ben-Erik. 2005. Food Plants of the World. Portland, Oregon: Timber Press.

Weinberg, M. S., and S. S. Sternberg. 1966. "Effect of Chronic Safrole Administration on Hepatic Enzymes and Functional Activity in Dogs." *Toxicology and Applied Pharmacology* 8: 2.

Wiles, Briana. 2016. *Mountain States Foraging*. Portland, OR: Timber Press.

Zeisberger, David S. 1910. *History of the Northern American Indians*. Ohio State Archaeological and Historical Society.

Zeven, A.C. and P.M. Zhukovsky. 1975. *Directory of Cultivated Plants and Their Centres of Diversity*. Wageningen, Netherlands: Center for Agricultural Publishing and Documentation.

Zohary, Daniel,TK, and TK Maria Hopf. 1988. *Domestication of Plants in the Old World*. Oxford: Oxford University Press.

Glossary

Abscission: The natural separation of two bonded parts (such as a deciduous leaf from its twig before falling), usually occurring at a predetermined point, the *abscission zone*.

Achene: A dry, single-seeded fruit that does not naturally split open.

Acuminate: Tapering to a long, narrow, needle-like point.

Adventive: A plant native to the continent or region but which has expanded its range, usually by taking advantage of anthropogenic environmental changes.

Aerial: Growing in open air (as opposed to under the ground or water).

Alkaloid: Any of a large group of complex, nitrogen-containing compounds that tend to be alkaline in reactivity and many of which are physiologically potent. Examples include nicotine, caffeine, solanine.

Allelopathic: Releasing chemicals that inhibit the growth of competing plants.

Alliaceous: Pertaining to onions, garlic, or other members of the genus *Allium*.

Alternate: Growing from opposite sides of a stalk at *different* points along its length (rather than at the same point as in opposite leaves). Not paired.

Anther: The pollen-bearing part of the stamen.

Anthropogenic: Caused by humans.

Antinutrient: A chemical that interferes with the body's absorption or utilization of nutrients.

Astringent: Causing the constriction of tissues.

Axil: The upper angle where a leaf or petiole joins a stem.

Barrens: A savannah ecosystem maintained by frequent fire in areas of poor, dry soil, resulting in scattered trees (typically oak or pine) among low shrubs and herbs.

Basal: Growing from the base of the plant, attached near ground level.

Biennial: A plant that normally has a two-year life cycle, spending the first year as a stalkless rosette storing energy, and using that energy to produce a flowering stalk the second year, after which the plant dies. Biennials may spend multiple years as a rosette before flowering, however, if the growing conditions are poor.

Blanch: To briefly boil a vegetable in order to destroy enzymes and kill individual cells; generally done before freezing. Also, to cover growing plants so as to keep light from them, making them grow lighter in color, more tender, and less strong in flavor.

Bletted: A fruit that has been allowed to soften far beyond ripening (but not fermented or spoiled).

Blickey: A berry-picking container that straps onto the waist, leaving both hands free.

Parts of a Regular Flower

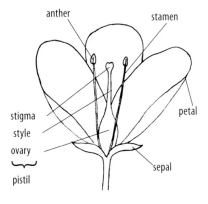

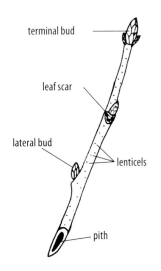

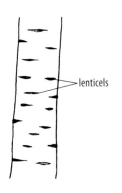

Bloom: A thin waxy or powdery coating that can be rubbed off. Often found on fruit and smooth herb stems, bloom gives the surface a lighter hue.

Boreal forest: The plant community that dominates most of Canada's forested regions, characterized by fir, spruce, aspen, white birch, and other northern plants.

Bract: A small, modified leaf found directly beneath a flower or flower cluster.

Bulb: A modified bud, such as an onion, in which the leaves are enlarged and thickened to store energy.

Calyx: The sepals of a flower, collectively. These sometimes remain attached to fruit after the flower has been fertilized.

Carcinogen: A chemical that induces or causes cancer.

Catkin: A soft, spike-like inflorescence of numerous small, petal-less flowers, often drooping.

Caudex: A tough perennial stem at the top of a root, from which herbaceous stems grow.

Cauline: On or pertaining to the stem; often used in contrast to *basal*.

Chaff: The unwanted, inedible dried flower and fruit parts that are separated from a grain by rubbing and then removed by winnowing.

Chambered: Divided into compartments, often with hollow spaces, by transverse partitions; said of pith.

Channeled: Having a groove or depression running its length; usually said of petioles.

Chromosome: A structure containing a portion of the DNA in a cell's nucleus.

Cleistogamous: A flower that self-pollinates without opening.

Climax community: A plant community that persists indefinitely in the absence of significant environmental changes; the last stage in plant succession on a particular site.

Clone: A colony of genetically identical plants or stems that have propagated themselves through some form of vegetative reproduction; a clone is essentially one large plant with many stems.

Cold storage: Storing food in a cool but not frozen environment.

Colony: A group of many individuals or stems of the same species of plant found growing together.

Composite: A flower cluster that appears as one flower (such as dandelion) in which many tiny florets are clustered on a receptacle. Also, any plant of the Composite family, all of which share this characteristic.

Compound: A leaf that consists of multiple leaflets (see *divided*).

Corm: The base of an upright stem, enlarged to store energy.

Corolla: The petals of a flower (collectively).

Corrugated: Having a rough surface texture formed by valleys, ridges, wrinkles, or folds.

Deciduous: Dying and falling away from the plant at the end of the growing season.

Dermatitis: Rash or irritation of the skin.

Dichotomous key: A tool used for identifying plants by repeatedly deciding which of two technical descriptions applies to it, narrowing down the number of possibilities with each set of descriptions until the species is identified.

Diploid: Having a double-set of chromosomes in each cell. (Similar: triploid, tetraploid)

Divided: A leaf that is indented nearly or fully to the midrib or base, forming separate and distinct contiguous sections of leaf surface. The term *compound* is usually reserved

Flower/Fruit Clusters

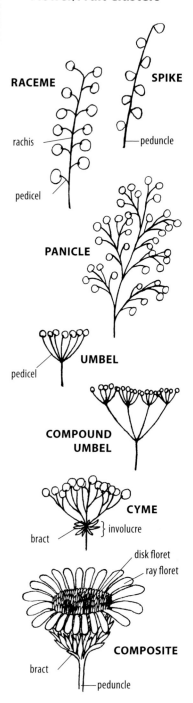

RACEME

SPIKE

rachis

peduncle

pedicel

PANICLE

UMBEL

pedicel

COMPOUND UMBEL

CYME

involucre

bract

disk floret

ray floret

COMPOSITE

bract

peduncle

Simple Leaf Shapes

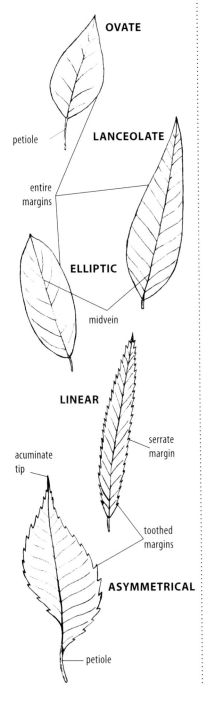

OVATE

petiole

LANCEOLATE

entire
margins

ELLIPTIC

midvein

LINEAR

serrate
margin

acuminate
tip

toothed
margins

ASYMMETRICAL

petiole

for those leaves that are divided all the way to the midrib or base, and whose leaflets are somewhat consistent in form and arranged in a describable pattern.

Drupe: A fruit with pulp surrounding a seed with a tough outer layer.

Ecoculture: The management of natural ecosystems to increase their production of economically useful plants. In distinction to *agriculture* and *horticulture*, which both entail removal of natural ecosystems and their replacement with plant communities that would be impossible without vigorous human maintenance.

Emergent: Extending above the water.

Entire: A leaf or leaflet with no divisions, lobes, or teeth.

Ephemeral: A plant with a very brief growing season. Spring ephemerals begin growth very early in spring and usually die back by late spring or early summer.

Ethnobotany: The study of how people or cultures relate to plants, materially and perceptually.

Ethnography: The description of human cultures; a branch of anthropology.

Flagship name: a name, which normally represents a single species, that is used to represent multiple similar species, often giving the mistaken impression that the group contains only one species.

Float test: Placing nuts in water to see if they float; typically, good nuts will sink and many bad ones will float.

Floret: One of the many tiny flowers in a composite cluster; also, a grass flower.

Flower bud: A flower that is not ready to open; the bud that will later become a flower.

Flower stalk: A stalk that bears a flower or flowers; sometimes used in distinction to the leaf-stalk or petiole.

Fruit leather: Thin sheets of dried fruit pulp.

Genus: A taxonomic group above the species but below the family; a group of closely related species.

Gland: A structure that secretes a liquid, such as oil or resin. These usually protrude and are often shiny and darker than surrounding tissue. Some similar-looking structures that have no secretory function are also called glands.

Greens: The edible leaves or leafy portion of a plant.

Herbaceous: Having no perennial woody tissue above ground.

Hydrolysis: Decomposition of a compound through the action of water or the components of water.

Inflorescence: A flower or cluster of flowers and all that comes with it, such as stems and bracts; the whole flowering portion of the plant.

Invasive plant: A species not naturally occurring in an areas that has been introduced and thrives in native ecosystems, outcompeting and displacing native plants.

Involucre: Collectively, the bracts immediately beneath an inflorescence.

Kernel: An edible seed, or the edible portion of a seed.

Lanceolate: Shaped like a lance head: much longer than wide, broadest near the base, tapering to a pointed tip.

Latex: A white, milky sap that dries as a rubbery substance, used to heal wounds.

Leaflet: One of the smaller leaves or blades within a compound leaf.

Leaf scar: The mark left on a stem or twig where a leaf or petiole was formerly attached.

Lenticel: A small corky spot on the bark of small trees and shrubs.

Leaf Shapes

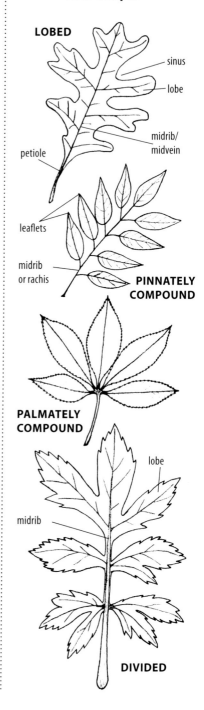

Leaf Patterns

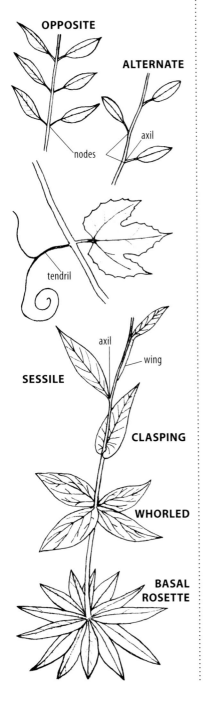

Lobe: An extension of a leaf blade; a division of a leaf that is broadly attached rather than constricted or stalked at the base, as on the leaves of white and red oak.

Margin: The outer edge of a leaf.

Mast: Collectively, the nuts produced and dropped by a tree or stand of trees. Often used in the ambiguous construction *mast year*, which is usually intended to mean a year when the mast is heavy or abundant.

Meristem: The zone of a plant where cell division and growth occurs. The apical meristem is the "young and tender" growing portion.

Mesic: A forest or prairie with a medium level of soil moisture (also, mesophytic); in the East, a *mesic forest* is a rich hardwood forest dominated by long-lived species such as sugar maple, beech, basswood, yellow birch, hemlock, and white ash.

Midrib: The main vein of a leaf, especially one that is enlarged and provides support, as on most divided leaves; sometimes also used to refer to the rachis (main stalk) of a compound leaf.

Midvein: The main vein of a leaf. Same as *midrib*, except in connotation; the main vein is more commonly called a midvein if it is relatively small, as one finds on most simple leaves.

Monocarpic: Fruiting once, then dying.

Monocot: (Short for monocotyledon) One of the two main divisions within the Angiosperms (typical flowering plants). Monocots generally have parallel veins, no main taproot, and a single seed-leaf (cotyledon) when germinating. Examples include grasses, sedges, arums, onions, Solomon's seals, and lilies.

Morphological: Pertaining to physical form.

Mucilage: A sticky or slimy substance,

usually indicating the presence of dissolved starches. *Mucilaginous* refers to plants or plant parts containing mucilage, or which produce mucilage when chewed.

Naturalized: Non-native plants that have become regular and well-established members of the flora.

Nodding: Hanging downward; usually said of flowers.

Node: The point on a stem where one or more leaves are borne.

Nutmeat: The edible portion of a nut.

Obovate: Egg-shaped in outline but broader near the tip rather than near the base.

Opposite: Growing from the same point along a stalk but on opposite sides of it; paired. (Alternate leaves grow on opposite sides at *different* points.)

Ovary: The lower portion of a pistil, usually enlarged, in which the seed or seeds are produced. The ovary ripens into a fruit.

Ovate: Roughly egg-shaped; somewhat longer than broad, with the widest part near the base.

Palmate: Hand-shaped, having several finer-like lobes.

Palmately compound: Having several leaflets radiate from the same point.

Panicle: A flower cluster with a compound branching pattern, the branches growing from an elongated central stalk. Grapes are a well-known example.

Pappus: Bristles or hairs on the achene of a composite, often used to catch the wind for dispersal. (An example is the "parachute" attached to a dandelion seed.)

Pedicel: The stalk of an individual flower or flowerhead in an inflorescence with multiple flowers or flowerheads.

Peduncle: The stalk of an entire inflorescence or a solitary flower.

Underground Parts

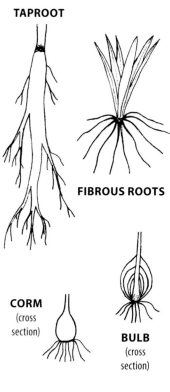

TAPROOT

FIBROUS ROOTS

CORM
(cross section)

BULB
(cross section)

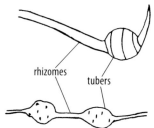

rhizomes

tubers

RHIZOME (ROOTSTOCK)

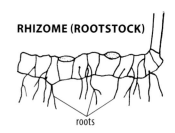

roots

Perennial: Any plant that typically lives for more than two years.

Petal: One of the innermost set of modified leaves of a flower, usually brightly colored.

Petiole: The stem or stalk of a leaf.

Phenology: The timing and sequence of seasonal biological events, and the study of this timing and sequence.

Pinnate: Feather-like; with leaflets, branches, or veins arranged in two rows along opposite sides of a midvein or midrib; the most common form for ferns, also seen in most legume leaves and compound tree leaves such as walnut, hickory, and ash.

Pistil: The central female part of the flower, which receives the pollen. It is usually much larger than the stamens (if both present).

Pith: The soft, spongy material found in the center of many stems.

Polycarpic: Fruiting multiple times in its life.

Potherb: A green eaten after boiling or steaming.

Prostrate: Lying flat on the ground; not erect.

Pubescent: Covered with hairs.

Puree: The pulp of fruit after the seeds, skins, and stems have been removed by straining.

Raceme: A flower cluster in which each flower is borne on a stem emanating from an elongated central stem.

Rachis: The central axis or stem of a compound leaf or inflorescence.

Ray: In an umbel, a ray is one of the multiple stems emanating from the common juncture point. In a composite flower head, a ray is one of the strap-shaped, petal-like structures.

Receptacle: A surface, often spongy in texture, into which flowers or fruits are inserted or attached.

Rhizome: A horizontal stem of a perennial plant, found under or on the ground, usually thick and rooting at the nodes.

Root: The part of a plant which serves to anchor it and absorb water and dissolved nutrients. The root does not have leaves or buds.

Root crown: The transition area from root to stem.

Root season: The time of year when most underground vegetables should be harvested: from late summer to mid spring (being best from late fall to very early spring).

Rootstock: A rhizome that is enlarged to store energy.

Rosette: A circular cluster of leaves radiating from the same point, usually a root crown or the base of a stem.

Samara: A winged fruit, such as maple, ash, and elm seeds.

Sepal: A member of the outer ring of modified leaves in a flower. Sepals may be green or they may be colored like typical petals.

Scape: A leafless stem of an inflorescence (peduncle) arising directly from the base of the plant. Examples include dandelion and wild leek.

Schizz: The act or process of a schizocarp breaking into its component mericarps. Yes, I made this up.

Schizocarp: A fruit that naturally breaks into two or more one-seeded segments (called mericarps) upon maturity.

Serrated: With sharp teeth of somewhat uniform size.

Sessile: Attached directly, without a stalk or petiole.

Shoot: Rapidly growing stem or stalk of a plant, like asparagus. Leaves may be present, but are not fully formed and comprise a small portion of the shoot's volume.

Simple: Not compound; a single-leaf unit.

Sinus: The space between two lobes of a leaf.

SLOTSM: Stands for "small lump of tender starchy material." These are often present at the junction of the root and the stem, and are often more tender than either.

Solid: Not hollow; said of stems or petioles.

Spike: An elongated, unbranched flower cluster in which the flowers are attached directly to a main stem without individual stems.

Stamen: The male, pollen-bearing part of a flower. Usually multiple.

Stigma: The part of the pistil that receives the pollen.

Stipule: A leaf-like appendage that is attached at or near the base of a petiole.

Stochastic: Natural events that are governed by tendencies or probabilities but still occur in a random and unpredictable pattern, such as fires, storms, floods, mudslides, and elephant droppings.

Straining: The process of removing seeds, skins, stems, and other unwanted coarse material from fruit or berry pulp.

Style: The portion of the pistil that connects the ovary and stigma.

Succulent: Thick, fleshy, and juicy.

Tannin: A complex organic acid that precipitates protein. Tannins are common in many plants and cause astringency.

Taproot: A primary, central root that grows downward rather than laterally or horizontally.

Tendril: A modified leaf or branch that grasps or coils around other objects to support a vine.

Terminal: At the tip or end.

Triploid: Having a triple set of chromosomes in each cell.

Tuber: An enlargement of a stem in which energy is stored, primarily in the form of starch.

Umbel: A flower cluster in which all of the flower stalks radiate from the same point.

Vegetative reproduction: Any form of reproduction or propagation that does not involve seeds, such as spreading by tubers, suckers, or rhizomes.

Venation: The pattern and characteristics of the veins in a leaf.

Wing: A thin, flat, usually leafy extension from a stalk, petiole, fruit, or other plant part.

Winnow: To separate kernels or seeds from chaff using wind, air, or the different rates that different materials fall or travel through the air.

Winter annual: Plants that complete their life cycle in less than a year, but this year is interrupted by a winter. Typically, they germinate in fall and mature the following spring or summer.

Woody: Plant parts that survive above ground through the dormant season.

Wool: Long, matted hair, lying on the surface of a plant rather than erect.

Xylem: The tissues of a plant that transport water and minerals from the roots to the other organs; xylem usually has structural functions as well.

Recommended Reading and Resources

Edible Wild Plants and Ethnobotany Books

There are a lot of good books on this topic, but these are the ones I refer to most often, trust the most, or find most helpful for students.

Steve Brill. *Identifying and Harvesting Edible and Medicinal Plants* (1994). Morrow. No photos, but a wealth of first-hand info.

Tom Elpel. *Foraging the Mountain West* (2014). HOPS Press. My favorite for this region. Good ID, good photos, reliable first-hand info.

Euell Gibbons. *Stalking the Wild Asparagus* (1962), *Stalking the Healthful Herbs* (1966), *Stalking the Blue-Eyed Scallop* (1964). Alan Hood Company. Great info on harvest, preparation, and cooking. Not for ID.

Wendy Hodgson. *Food Plants of the Sonoran Desert* (2001). U of AZ. Ethnobotanical, encyclopedic, B & W photos.

Kelly Kindscher. *Edible Wild Plants of the Prairie* (1987). University Press of Kansas. Accurate, thorough, ethnobotanical, good line drawings for ID.

John Kallas. *Edible Wild Plants* (2010). Gibbs Smith. Very thorough info on ID, harvest, preparation, and nutrition. Great photos.

Mike Krebill. *The Scout's Guide to Wild Edibles* (2016). St. Lynn's. A good little introductory book to foraging for people of all ages.

M.L. Fernald and A.C. Kinsey. *Edible Wild Plants of Eastern North America* (1943). Many later books have relied heavily on this. Not good for ID, but extensive and pretty accurate.

Christopher Nyerges. *Foraging California* (2014). Falcon. Color photos.

Janice Schofield. *Discovering Wild Plants: Alaska, Western Canada, the Northwest* (1989). Thorough, good photos—underrated book.

Timber Press regional foraging series (2014-2016) includes *Midwest* (Rose), *Northwest* (Duer), *Northeast* (Meredith), *California* (Lowry), *Southwest* (Slattery), and *Mountain States* (Wiles). Color photos, 1-3 pages per plant. These vary in quality but you'll probably want the one for your region.

Nancy Turner. *Food Plants of Coastal First Peoples* (1995) and *Food Plants of Coastal First Peoples* (1997). Royal BC Museum. Ethnobotanically based, good photos and good info.

Vorderbruggen, Mark. *Idiot's Guides: Foraging* (2015). Penguin. Good photos and info, with many southern plants ignored in most books.

Ellen Zachos. *Backyard Foraging* (2013). Storey. Good photos and info for eating wild and ornamental plants around home and in town.

Plant Identification Books

This is an eclectic mix of the best books I have seen from various parts of the country. There are many others worth getting.

Kansas Wildflowers and Weeds. Multi-author. U. Press of KS. A hardcover cross between a field guide and flora. Good photos and ID info.

Newcomb's Wildflower Guide (1977). Newcomb. Little, Brown. Line drawings and a great ID system for plants in the NE states.

Plants of the Pacific Northwest Coast (1994). Pojar, Mackinnon, others. Lone Pine. Good field guide to all plant types of the region.

Plants of the Black Hills and Bear Lodge Mountains (2007). Larson and Johnson. SDSU. Good photo field guide for the extended region.

Plants of the Rocky Mountains (1998). Multi-author. Lone Pine. Color photos.

Wildflowers of Tennessee, the Ohio Valley, and Southern Appalachians (2005). Cathcart, Horn, others. Lone Pine. Good photo field guide.

Wildflowers of the Pacific Northwest (2006) and *Trees and Shrubs of the Pacific Northwest* (2014). Multi-author. Timber Press. Good photo field guides.

Shrubs of Ontario (1982). Soper and Heimburger. . Great ID info with superb line drawings—good for the northeastern US, too.

Trees and Shrubs of Minnesota (2008). Welby Smith. Minnesota DNR. Encyclopedia with keys, superb photos, and info—the best woody plant book ever written for any region.

Trees and Shrubs of California (2001). Stuart, Sawyer. U of CA Press. Pocket field guide with drawings and some photos.

Trees of Western North America and *Trees of Eastern North America* (2014). Multi-author. Princeton. Thick field guides with maps and color drawings.

Trees of the Northern U.S. and Canada (1995). Farrar. Blackwell. Encyclopedic, good photos, info, and maps.

Floras: Some of my favorites among many. For the more advanced.

The Jepson Manual: Higher Plants of California (1993). Hickman. Key to the astounding diversity of plants in California, with descriptions.

Flora of the Great Plains (1986). Multiple authors. U. Press of KS. Technical key with good descriptions for a broad region.

Manual of Vascular Plants of Northeastern U. S. and Adjacent Canada (1991). Gleason and Cronquist. NYBG Press. Technical key for a broad region, with descriptions, and an accompanying volume with good line drawings.

Flora of Virginia (2012). Weakley and others. BRIT Press. My favorite flora. Very good keys and descriptions.

Flora of Missouri (1999–2013, 3 Volumes). Steyermark, Yatskyevich. MO Botanical Garden. Really detailed descriptions, some additional info, many good drawings, good keys.

Foraging Instructors and Schools

This is not everybody—just some good ones I'm aware of.

Alfs, Matthew. MN. midwestherbalstudies.com
Baudar, Pascal. Southern CA. urbanoutdoorskills.com
Boutenko, Sergei. OR. sergeiboutenko.com
Brill, Steve. NYC area. wildmanstevebrill.com
Calhoun, Kim. Central NC. abundancehealingarts.com
Cohen, Matt. DC area. mattshabitats.com
Conroy, Linda. WI. moonwiseherbs.com
Davis, Erica Marciniec. Central CO. wildfoodgirl.com
Desert Harvesters. Tucson. desertharvesters.org
Elpel, Tom. South-central MT. hollowtop.com
Elliott, Doug. NC. dougelliott.com
Fecteau, Josh. ME. joshfecteau.com
Feinstein, Kevin. SF Bay area. feralkevin.com
Greene Deane. FL. eattheweeds.com
Haines, Arthur. ME. arthurhaines.com
Haritan, Adam. Western PA. wildfoodism.com
Hatter, Ila. Smoky Mts. region. wildcrafting.com
Hueston, Rick. DC area. MAPSgroup.com
Kallas, John. Portland, OR. wildfoodadventures.com
Lloyd, T. Abe. Western WA. cascadianfood.net
Meredith, Leda. NYC (sometimes). ledameredith.com
Muskat, Alan. Western NC. notastelikehome.org
Naha, Debbie. NJ, eastern PA. wildediblesnjpa.com
Nyerges, Christopher. Southern CA. christophernyerges.com
Patton, Darryl. AL. thesouthernherbalist.com
Sherwood, Karen. Western WA. earthwalknorthwest.com
Shufer, Vickie. Coastal VA. ecoimages-us.com
Slattery, John. Southwest. johnjslattery.com
Stephenson, Karen. Toronto area. ediblewildfood.com
Wiles, Briana. CO. rooted-apothecary.com
Vordebruggen, Mark. Houston area. foragingtexas.com
Zachos, Ellen. PA/NM. backyardforager.com

Photo Credits

I would like to express my sincere gratitude to those who generously and enthusiastically allowed the use of their photographs to make this a better book.

Todd Elliott

cross section of *Acorus calamus* leaves on page 82
close up of the surface of *Acorus calamus* leaves on page 83
red mulberry *Morus rubra* in fruit on page 240

T. Abe Lloyd

salmonberry *Rubus spectabilis* fruit and flowers on page 67
bigleaf maple trunks on page 190
western water-hemlock *Cicuta douglasii*, whole plant including roots on page 402
western water-hemlock leaf on page 407
(I'd also like to thank Abe for serving as a hand model for several photos in this book)

Ralph Lloyd

Did not take any photos but he *made me* the squat hickory mortar shown on page 147 that has now served me well for 13 years, and has been the hickory milk crucible for hundreds of people.

Melissa Price

She took many of the photos of syrup making, including those on pages 198, 199, 205, and 212. She also served as a hand model for lots of photos. And she married me.

John J. Slattery

black persimmons on the tree, page 262

Briana Wiles

hops vines on page 167
two photos of western sweet cicely *Osmorhiza occidentalis* on page 367

Index

Pages or page ranges in bold contain photos of the subject matter listed.

LEARN FROM SAM IN PERSON . . .

If you'd like to learn from Sam in person, check out his website, www.foragers harvest.com for information on classes and workshops. Here you can also purchase a variety of nature and homesteading books, maple syrup supplies, foraging tools, and hand-harvested wild food products.

www.foragersharvest.com

IF YOU LIKE THIS BOOK . . .

If you like this book, you'll also like the first two titles in the Sam's foraging series: *The Forager's Harvest* and *Nature's Garden*. Order from the website listed above, or from your favorite bookseller.

There is no overlap in the plants covered by these books.

The Forager's Harvest (2006)
368 pages, with color photos
$22.95

Nature's Garden (2010)
512 pages, with color photos
$24.95

About the Author

Samuel Thayer has been foraging, fishing, hunting, camping, and studying nature since early childhood. At the age of 18 he purchased 60 acres in northern Wisconsin near Lake Superior and built a log cabin to pursue his homesteading dreams. Today, Samuel is an internationally recognized authority on edible wild plants. He has been teaching about wild edibles for more than two decades, and his award-winning books have helped thousands enjoy the wonders of eating wild. Sam earns his living as an author, speaker, teacher, and by selling wild rice, maple syrup, hickory and acorn oil, wildcrafted foods, and products from his organic orchard. Current research projects include mulberry conservation, wild leek ecology, and the relationship between wild and domestic crop plants. Sam lives in northern Wisconsin with his wife, Melissa, and their children: Myrica, Joshua, and Rebekah. All of them eat wild food every day.